How to Complain to the UN Human Rights Treaty System

Anne F. Bayefsky

Foreword by Stephen M. Schwebel
Judge of the International Court of Justice, 1981-2000
President, 1997-2000

Transnational Publishers

Consultative Council of
Jewish Organizations and the
Shoresh Charitable Trust

Published and distributed by Transnational Publishers, Inc.
Ardsley Park
Science and Technology Center
410 Saw Mill River Road
Ardsley, NY 10502

Phone: 914-693-5100
Fax: 914-693-4430
E-mail: info@transnationalpubs.com
Web: www.transnationalpubs.com

Library of Congress Cataloging-in-Publication Data
(on file with the publisher)

ISBN 1-57105-283-6

Manufactured in the United States of America

CONTENTS

Annexes:

FOREWORD

How to Complain to the UN Treaty Rights System, as its first words state, is a "How to . . ." manual. "How to" manuals are high on the best seller lists. This specialized and technical work may not be. That is paradoxical, because its subject matter is, or should be, of great interest to great numbers of human beings, particularly the too many who suffer violations of their human rights. It may be too much to hope that many human rights victims will come to know of and resort to this manual. But it is not too much to hope that the non-governmental organizations that are a driving force for the promotion of human rights, and the human rights lawyers who follow and further developments in the field, will welcome Professor Bayefsky's manual, use it, and find it a valuable tool in their invaluable cause.

Human rights may be as old as inhuman behavior. But their realization - to the extent that human rights are realized - is a relatively modern phenomenon. If primitive life was 'nasty, brutish and short', the life provided by the civilizations of the last five or six thousand years has had minimal regard for human rights. Warfare, the unending human condition in much of the world much of the time, was barbarous. Slavery was ubiquitous. Its prevalence marred leading civilizations such as the Greek and Roman, not to speak of civilizations that followed as late as the 19th Century. The great religions shaped and promoted ethical principles of behavior, but sometimes not in respect to unbelievers. The atrocities and persecutions carried out in the name of religion were many.

The fundamental elements of what today are seen as human rights were given essential and lasting impetus by the growth of the common law and English democratic institutions, the American Revolution and the French Revolution. It was not until the anti-slavery movement of the 19th Century gathered strength, and the beginnings of the law of war were introduced by The Hague Conventions as that century closed, that concern for human rights moved on to the international plane. The introduction of an international law of human rights was a 20th Century innovation.

At the end of the First World War, the minority treaties were concluded and the International Labor Organization was established. The ILO gradually built up a network of treaties promoting human rights in the sphere of its concern, as well as a pioneering system of monitoring international obligations that demonstrated the influence of "the mobilization of shame".

Yet the most profound violations of human rights ever recorded stained the 20th Century: Nazism and the death camps of the Holocaust; Stalinism and the extremities of the Gulag; and even in the latter years of the 20th Century, murder in Cambodia on an appallingly massive scale and genocide in Rwanda.

Partially as a measure of response to the atrocities of the Nazis, it was provided that among the Principles and Purposes of the United Nations is promoting and encouraging respect for human rights and fundamental freedoms for all without distinction as to race, sex, language and religion. The United Nations Charter binds Members to take joint and separate action in co-operation with the Organization to achieve universal respect for, and observance of, human rights. The UN's Economic and Social Council was authorized to make recommendations to these ends, and to establish a Human Rights Commission.

In pursuance of these powers, the UN General Assembly adopted the Convention on the Prevention and Punishment of the Crime of Genocide, and it adopted the Universal Declaration of Human Rights. The Human Rights Commission prepared the International Covenant on Civil and Political Rights and the International Covenant on Economic, Social and Cultural Rights. The General Assembly adopted these Conventions and the Convention on the Elimination of All Forms of Racial Discrimination, and subsequently the Convention on the Elimination of All Forms of Discrimination against Women, the Convention against Torture and other Cruel, Inhuman or Degrading Treatment or Punishment, and the Convention on the Rights of the Child. These Conventions have come into force and are widely ratified.

Professor Bayefsky's book is devoted to the complaint mechanism of the International Covenant on Civil and Political Rights and those of the Conventions on torture, racial discrimination and discrimination against women. The bodies established by these treaties to receive and pass upon complaints falling within the scope of their protective clauses are important. Professor Bayefsky shows why. The most senior of these bodies, the Human Rights Committee constituted by the Parties to the Covenant, has established a record of professionalism and objectivity that favorably contrasts with the proceedings of the UN's Commission on Human Rights, a bloated body which, despite substantial accomplishments, in recent years has suffered from partisan political manipulation.

The individual who seeks to apply for relief to a UN treaty body approaches unfamiliar terrain. Professor Bayefsky takes the potential applicant by the hand and leads him and her across it. She does so in straightforward, lucid style. Yet the subject matter does not lend itself to simplicity. The lay applicant - despite the directions and forms that the book supplies - may find legal advice desirable. Legal counsel certainly will find the book very useful.

The treaties whose complaint mechanisms are the subject of Professor Bayefsky's book, by reason of their wide ratification by States, apply to some 1.5 billion human beings. The complaint systems address a wide range of fundamental rights, including the right to life. These treaties give a measure of standing on the international plane to the individual; they provide a means for the individual victim of national abuse to be heard internationally. As these treaties become more widely known and applied, they should promote human rights standards within, as well as among, States. These treaties are important today; they should become more important tomorrow.

Access to the UN bodies to which this innovative book is devoted presupposes allegations of violation of human rights covered by the four treaties. These treaties are designed to protect the individual against an erring or oppressive government. They do not address the violations of human rights that now transfix the world - the violations of the most fundamental of human rights, that to life, not by governments but by terrorists and suicide bombers (who, however, may benefit from the support or sanctuary of 'rogue' States). There nevertheless remains an excess of governmental violation of human rights which it is the purpose of the UN bodies in question to bring to light and so to moderate if not eliminate. To this noble end, Professor Bayefsky's book makes a material contribution.

Stephen M. Schwebel
Washington, D.C.
June 2002

ACKNOWLEDGMENTS

I am indebted to the Consultative Council of Jewish Organizations, and in particular to its dedicated and indefatigable Chairman, Clemens Nathan, as well as to the Shoresh Charitable Trust, for their invaluable support of this project. Its genesis was also due in large measure to Raphael Walden, International Affairs Advisor of the Consultative Council.

Special thanks to Larry Cox and the Ford Foundation, whose encouragement, concern and interest in the potential of the UN human rights treaty system has been fundamental to my effort to focus on enhancing access to international rights and remedies.

I am extremely grateful to the expert advice in the preparation of the manuscript provided by Alfred de Zayas, Coordinator of the Petitions Teams at the Office of the UN High Commissioner for Human Rights, and Hanna Beate Schöpp-Schilling, Chairperson of the Optional Protocol Working Group of the Committee on the Elimination of Discrimination Against Women.

Much thanks is owed to Claudia Geiringer, Simon de Smet and Chris Gosnell, graduate students at Columbia University Law School, for their excellent research and helpfulness

My thanks also for the research assistance and constant professionalism of Gillian Collins and Goli Yohannes at York University. I appreciated the additional assistance provided by Laura Bisset, Rachel Friedman, Kathryn Garforth, Cara Gibbons, Siobahn McClelland, Maanit Zernel, and Jennifer Zdriluk at York University.

Anne F. Bayefsky

ABBREVIATIONS

CAT	Convention Against Torture
	Committee Against Torture
CEDAW	Convention on the Elimination of All Forms of Discrimination Against Women
	Committee on the Elimination of All Forms of Discrimination Against Women
CERD	Convention on the Elimination of All Forms of Racial Discrimination
	Committee on the Elimination of All Forms of Racial Discrimination
CESCR	Committee on Economic, Social and Cultural Rights
CRC	Convention on the Rights of the Child
	Committee on the Rights of the Child
CSW	Commission on the Status of Women (of the United Nations)
DAW	Division for the Advancement of Women (of the United Nations)
ECOSOC	Economic and Social Council (of the United Nations)
GA	General Assembly
HRC	Human Rights Committee
ICCPR	International Covenant on Civil and Political Rights
ICESCR	International Covenant on Economic, Social and Cultural Rights
NGO	Non-governmental Organization
OHCHR	Office of the United Nations High Commissioner for Human Rights
UN	United Nations

GLOSSARY

Words as they are used in the context of the human rights treaties

accession/accede—"Accession" describes one method by which a state can choose to be bound by the obligations in a treaty. The date the state deposits its instrument of "accession" with the Secretary General of the United Nations will determine the date the state becomes bound by the treaty obligations. See also "ratification."

admissible/admissibility—Admissibility refers to rules concerning the handling of individual cases. The human rights treaties, together with the Rules of Procedure of the relevant treaty bodies, establish certain pre-conditions that must exist before a treaty body is entitled to consider the merits of an individual complaint. If those pre-conditions are met, the complaint is "admissible" and the treaty body can proceed to consider the substance of the complaint. The "admissibility" phase of the decision-making process is the prior phase during which the treaty body considers whether the conditions of admissibility are met.

amendment—The alternation of a treaty by subsequent agreement of the states parties. A treaty may provide for an amendment to come into force upon acceptance by a certain number or percentage of states parties. An amendment may have to be separately agreed upon by a state party in order for it to become bound by the change.

applicant—See "author" or "complainant".

application—See "communication" or "complaint".

author—The term used by the Human Rights Committee, CERD and CEDAW to refer to the person who lodges the individual complaint of a violation of his or her rights. Also known as "complainant," "applicant" or "petitioner." See also "complainant".

communication—The term used by the Human Rights Committee, CERD and CEDAW to refer to an individual complaint brought to the treaty bodies complaining of a violation of the individual's rights under the treaty. Also known as "petition," "complaint" or "application." See also "complaint".

complaint—The term used by CAT to refer to an individual complaint brought to the treaty bodies complaining of a violation of the individual's rights under the treaty. Also known as "petition," "application," or "communication." See also "communication."

complainant—The term used by CAT to refer to the person who lodges the individual complaint of a violation of his or her rights. See also "author," "applicant" or "petitioner."

concluding comments—The final statement issued by a human rights treaty body at the conclusion of its examination of a state party's report, in which the treaty body comments on the state party's record of implementation of the treaty. Also called "concluding observations."

concluding observations—The final statement issued by a human rights treaty body at the conclusion of its examination of a state party's report, in which the treaty body comments on the state party's record of implementation of the treaty. Also called "concluding comments."

convention—A kind of treaty. See "treaty".

covenant—A kind of treaty. See "treaty".

Decision—In the context of CAT the findings on the merits of individual complaints. See also "Opinions" and "Views".

declaration—A statement made by a state when signing or adhering to a treaty in which it claims to define the legal effect of certain provisions of the treaty in their application to that state. Sometimes states make "interpretive declarations" in which they express their understanding of a particular aspect of the interpretation of the treaty. See also "declarations of competence," "reservation."

declaration of competence—A declaration made by a state party (usually upon ratification, but potentially later) in which it recognizes the competence of the relevant treaty body to exercise certain optional functions under the treaty. For example, in the context of the CERD and CAT treaties, states parties have the option to make declarations in which they recognize the competence of the relevant treaty bodies to consider individual communications.

derogate/derogation/derogable—To "derogate" means to suspend. In the context of the human rights treaties, a "derogation" is a suspension of the application of a right, allowable only in certain defined circumstances of public emergency. For example, the ICCPR limits the circumstances in which states parties are entitled to "derogate from" the enjoyment of certain rights contained in the Covenant in times of official public emergency. Rights which are "non-derogable" cannot be suspended under any circumstances.

domestic remedies—National judicial and administrative opportunities for redress that should be engaged before a petitioner applies to a treaty body.

entry into force—A treaty will only become operational, or enter into force, after certain conditions have been satisfied. These conditions, often require a certain minimum number of ratifications by states. A treaty will enter into force for a particular state that ratifies only after the treaty has become operational (or entered into force), normally following a time lapse which has been specified in the treaty.

follow-up—The actions taken (if any) following the finding of a violation in an individual communication, in order to determine whether the state party has complied with the treaty body's recommendations.

general comment—A general statement issued by the treaty body that provides guidance on the interpretation of procedural and substantive requirements of the treaty. The Committee on Economic, Social and Cultural Rights, the Human Rights Committee, the Committee Against Torture, and the Committee on the Rights of the Child, refer to these statements as "General Comments." The Committee on the Elimination of Racial Discrimination and the Committee on the Elimination of Discrimination Against Women refer to these statements as "General Recommendations."

general recommendation—A general statement issued by the treaty body that provides guidance on the interpretation of procedural and substantive requirements of the treaty. The Committee on the Elimination of Racial Discrimination and the Committee on the Elimination of Discrimination Against Women refer to these statements as "General Recommendations." The Committee on Economic, Social and Cultural Rights, the Human Rights Committee, the Committee Against Torture, and the Committee on the Rights of the Child, refer to these statements as "General Comments."

interim measure—A measure that a treaty body asks a state party to take on an interim or temporary basis, in order to avoid irreparable harm to the interests of the complainant, before the treaty body has the opportunity to determine the merits of the complaint.

merits—The substantive correctness, or otherwise, of a complainant's allegation that a right under one of the treaties has been violated. The treaty body's consideration of the merits follows its consideration of the issue of admissibility.

monitoring body—See "treaty body."

multilateral treaty—A treaty that has more than two states parties.

non-governmental organization (NGO)—A privately constituted organization.

Opinions—In the context of CERD, the Committee calls its findings on the merits of individual complaints "Opinions." See also "Views" and "Decisions".

optional protocol—A separate treaty associated with a parent treaty, under which states parties to the parent treaty may choose to undertake additional obligations. Not all states which have ratified the original treaty may have ratified the optional protocol.

petition—See "communication" or "complaint".

petitioner—See "author" or "complainant".

plenary—The treaty body meeting formally as a whole, in accordance with its formal rules of procedure.

protocol—A kind of treaty. See "treaty," and "optional protocol".

rapporteur—One member of the relevant treaty body that has been assigned certain special tasks to undertake on behalf of the treaty body. There are, for instance, special rapporteurs on New Communications (the Human Rights Committee), on Interim Measures (CAT), and on Follow-up (the Human Rights Committee).

ratification/ratify—"Ratification" describes one method by which a state can choose to be bound by the obligations in a treaty. The date the state deposits its instrument of ratification with the Secretary General of the United Nations will determine the date the state becomes bound by the treaty obligations. See also "accession."

reservation—A statement made by a state when ratifying a treaty, in which it claims to exclude or to modify the legal effect of certain provisions of the treaty in their application to that state. See "declaration."

secretariat—United Nations staff that are responsible, amongst many other tasks, for giving administrative support to the treaty bodies. The Secretariat is formally headed by the Secretary-General of the United Nations. The staff of the treaty bodies is made up primarily of lawyers and come from all regions of the world.

signature—By signing a treaty, a state signals its intention to become bound by its provisions. However, a state does not actually become bound until it takes the further step of "ratification" or "accession." Until the state ratifies or accedes to the treaty, it is not a party to it, although it must refrain from acts that would defeat the object and purpose of the treaty. Sometimes a state will sign a treaty but then never take the further step of ratification or accession.

special rapporteur—See "rapporteur".

special procedures—These are human rights mandates which have been created by the Commission on Human Rights and which may be individuals or working groups that study a particular human rights theme or the human rights record of a particular state.

state—A country that is recognized as a separate sovereign entity by other states.

state party—A state that has either ratified or acceded to a particular treaty, thereby becoming bound by its provisions.

state report—A report submitted by a state party to the relevant treaty body on its progress in giving effect to the rights recognized in the treaty. All of the human rights treaties require states parties to submit states reports at regular intervals.

state-to-state complaint—A procedure available under many of the human rights treaties (although usually on an optional basis) under which states parties to the relevant treaty can complain to the treaty body that another state party is not fulfilling its obligations under the treaty.

treaty—An agreement entered into by two or more states, which creates binding rights and obligations in international law. A treaty may go by many different names, such as "convention," "covenant" and "protocol."

treaty body—A committee of independent experts who are responsible for monitoring the implementation by states parties of their obligations under the treaty. Each of the human rights treaties has a treaty body associated with it. Also called a treaty "monitoring body".

Views—In the context of ICCPR and CEDAW, their findings on the merits of individual complaints. See also "Opinions" and "Decisions".

working group—A group of members of a particular treaty body that meet outside of the formal framework of committee meetings to perform certain functions that have been delegated to them by the treaty body.

CHAPTER I

THE PRINCIPAL UN HUMAN RIGHTS TREATIES

1. INTRODUCTION

The human rights treaties are at the core of the international system for the promotion and protection of human rights. Over the last decade participation by states in the treaty system and acceptance of related individual complaints procedures have risen exponentially. What began as an assertion of a few, is now a global proclamation of entitlements of the victims of human rights abuse. This involvement by states has been voluntary. The obligations under the human rights treaties have been freely assumed. It is the legal character of these rights which places them at the core of the international system of human rights protection. These rights generate corresponding legal duties upon state actors to prevent and remedy human rights violations.

The treaty system definitively establishes the legitimacy of international interest in the protection of human rights. It is undisputed that sovereignty is limited with respect to human rights. International supervision is valid, and states are accountable to international authorities for domestic acts affecting human rights. The treaty standards are the benchmark for assessment and concern.

The human rights treaty system has many aims. It seeks to encourage a culture of human rights, and to focus states and governments on standards and obligations. It aims to engage all states. It is intended to encourage a serious national process of review of laws, policies and practices against treaty standards, and to engage in reform through partnerships among members of civil society. It also expects the UN community to assist with implementation of treaty rights and the dissemination of the message of rights and obligations.

This book is about one method of improving the realization of these goals, namely, the empowerment of human rights victims to complain about violations of their rights to an international body, and to have their complaints measured against clear standards. This system of enforcement does not apply universally. It remains open only to individuals whose rights have been violated by states that have voluntarily permitted complaints to be made against them. Even with this limitation, however, the complaints procedures of the UN human rights treaty system apply to one-quarter of the world's population. Today 1.5 billion people have been permitted by their governments to complain of a violation of human rights treaty standards. This book is aimed to translate that potential into practice.

The human rights treaty system encompasses six major treaties:

- the Convention on the Elimination of all forms of Racial Discrimination (in force 4 January 1969)
- the International Covenant on Civil and Political Rights (in force 23 March 1976)
- the International Covenant on Economic, Social and Cultural Rights (in force 23 March 1976)
- the Convention on the Elimination of Discrimination Against Women (in force 3 September 1981)
- the Convention Against Torture (in force 26 June 1987)
- the Convention on the Rights of the Child (in force 2 September 1990).

Each of these treaties are associated with six treaty bodies which have the task of monitoring the implementation of treaty obligations. Five of the six treaty bodies meet primarily in Geneva, and are serviced by the Office of the UN High Commissioner for Human Rights (OHCHR). These are:

- the Committee on the Elimination of Racial Discrimination (CERD);
- the Human Rights Committee (HRC);
- the Committee on Economic, Social and Cultural Rights (CESCR);
- the Committee Against Torture (CAT);
- the Committee on the Rights of the Child (CRC).

One treaty body meets in New York and is serviced by the UN Division for the Advancement of Women:

- the Committee on the Elimination of Discrimination Against Women (CEDAW).

The treaty bodies are composed of members who are elected by the states parties to each treaty, or by the UN Economic and Social Council (ECOSOC) in the case of CESCR. Treaty body members are elected as experts who are to perform their functions in an independent capacity.

Meeting periodically throughout the year, the treaty bodies fulfill their monitoring function through one or more of the following methods.

- **Individual complaints:** In the case of four of the human rights treaties, individuals may complain of violations of their rights under the respective treaty (the International Covenant on Civil and Political Rights (ICCPR), the Convention on the Elimination of All Forms of Racial Discrimination (CERD), the Convention Against Torture (CAT) and the Convention on the Elimination of All Forms of Discrimination Against Women (CEDAW)). These complaints are considered by the treaty body which expresses a view as to the presence or absence of a violation.

- **Inquiries:** In the case of CAT and CEDAW, their functions include an inquiry procedure. The procedure permits investigations or missions to states parties in the context of concerns about systematic or grave violations of treaty rights.
- **State reporting:** States parties are required by the treaties to produce state reports on the compliance of domestic standards and practices with treaty rights. These reports are reviewed at various intervals by the treaty bodies, normally in the presence of state representatives. Concluding observations, commenting on the adequacy of state compliance with treaty obligations, are issued by the treaty bodies following the review.

A fourth mechanism permitting states to complain of violations of the treaties by one another has never been used.

The focus of this book is the first implementation strategy, individual complaints. The successful enforcement of human rights treaty standards, whether at the international or national level, depends on knowledge and empowerment of the victims of human rights abuse. The goal of this manual is, therefore, to empower victims to make use of individual complaints procedures.

It begins by identifying the common features of the four complaints procedures under each of the four treaties. Each treaty is then examined in greater detail. Consideration is finally given to questions of overlap and the choice of a forum. The annexes provide the practical tools for filing a complaint:

- complaint forms;
- addresses of the treaty bodies;
- a checklist for complaints;
- information concerning which states may be the subject of complaints;
- the treaty bodies' rules of procedure;
- an index of the cases which have been brought to date; and
- a guide for the user unfamiliar with the specific treaty rights which permits the identification of the legal provision or right through a thematic or subject index.

Realistically, the human rights treaty system's complaints procedure may be frustrating for individual users. Complaints may not be acknowledged quickly because of backlogs at UN offices. The limited number of languages which complainants may use can delay the submission or registration of complaints. The process is entirely in writing; complainants are not entitled to explain their circumstances in person. Three to five years may pass before a decision is rendered. When the decision is made, states may not be willing to implement a result which indicates a violation of human rights.

On the other hand, the process is not difficult. Decisions are made on the basis of written submissions. Although lawyers can be used, they are not required. Costs can be kept to a minimum. The procedure is open to a very large number of victims. When remedies at the national level have proved inadequate and the individual is stymied by an inability to take action at home, the potential to submit a complaint to an international body and to receive an expert opinion that a violation of rights has occurred, can be a powerful device. The complaints process, and a successful outcome, offer the victim an important advocacy tool for vindication and redress. The isolation and despair felt from the absence of domestic concern or worse, may be alleviated by international interest and attention. This book is, therefore, intended to make the international complaints procedures arising from the UN human rights treaty system available to individuals, lawyers, non-governmental organizations and human rights advocates in many parts of the world. Justice begins with access to justice.

2. THE BASIC INTERNATIONAL RULES

a) What Is a Treaty?

A treaty is an agreement between two or more states which creates binding rights and obligations in international law. The principal international human rights treaties are multilateral, and are open to as many states as want to join. A treaty may go by many different names, such as "convention," "covenant" and "protocol." The obligations contained in a treaty are based on consent. States are bound because they agree to be bound. States who have agreed to be bound by a treaty are known as "states parties" to the treaty.

b) What Is the Effect of a Treaty?

By becoming a party to a treaty, states undertake binding obligations in international law. In the case of international human rights treaties, this means that states parties undertake to ensure that their own national legislation, policies or practices meet the requirements of the treaty and are consistent with its human rights standards.

c) How Does a State Become Bound by a Treaty?

In general, states parties to the international human rights treaties express their consent to be bound by a particular treaty by a two-step process, first, signature and then ratification or accession. A state that *signs* a treaty signals its intention to become bound by its provisions and must refrain from acts which would defeat the object and purpose of the treaty. The state does not actually become bound by the treaty until it *ratifies* it.

For a treaty to enter into force for a particular state, the ratification or accession must be deposited. The depository is an entity which undertakes to receive ratifications, accessions and other related statements, and keeps other states parties informed. For the UN human rights treaties, the depository is the UN Secretary General, specifically the UN Office of Legal Affairs.

d) When Does a State Become Bound by a Treaty?

A state party will become bound by obligations under the treaty on *the later date of:*

i) The date the treaty enters into force. The six major international human rights treaties have all entered into force.

ii) The date the treaty enters into force for the particular state. A state may ratify or accede to a treaty many years after the treaty has entered into force for other states.

e) What Obligations Has a State Undertaken?

In order to determine what obligations a particular state has undertaken by ratifying a treaty, it is necessary to consider the following:

- Look carefully at the text of the treaty. What are the rights and freedoms required to be protected? Are the rights provided for in the treaty limited in any way? Are there circumstances in which states parties are allowed to restrict the rights spelled out?

- Consider how the obligations in the treaty have been interpreted in the past. The treaty monitoring body or treaty body serves as the most authoritative source of interpretation of the treaty. The treaty body's interpretation of the treaty can be found in the following sources:

  - **"Concluding observations" or "concluding comments" made by the treaty body in response to state reports.** Over the past thirty years, more than 1000 state reports have been considered. In the last decade, all treaty bodies have made concluding observations or comments following the examination of a report.

  - **The treaty body's final decisions (also called "Views" or "opinions") on individual cases.** Individual cases are known as "communications," "complaints," or "petitions." Over the past two decades, the treaty bodies have made hundreds of decisions on individual cases, about half of which have been substantive findings on the merits. To date, the vast majority of these cases have been decided by the Human Rights Committee.

- **General Comments/Recommendations made by the treaty body on the interpretation of particular rights in the treaty.** Treaty bodies occasionally issue General Comments or Recommendations on the meaning of treaty obligations. These generally provide a very useful analysis and elaboration of treaty provisions. To date, about one hundred general comments or recommendations have been made.
- Consider the content of any "reservations" made by a state party. A reservation made by a state when ratifying a treaty, is a claim to exclude or to modify the legal effect of certain provisions of the treaty in their application to that state. Many states parties to the human rights treaties have made reservations and they must be examined in order to know the extent of a state party's obligations.

f) Optional Undertakings

Sometimes, treaties contain, or have associated with them, optional obligations. States parties can choose separately to be bound by these additional obligations.

In the human rights treaties, there are two optional mechanisms relating to individual complaints:

- Two of the treaties (CERD and CAT) specify that the state party may make a separate declaration indicating its wish to be bound by a provision permitting individual complaints. Not all the states that have ratified one of the these treaties have made such a declaration.
- Two of the human rights treaties have "optional protocols" associated with them. These are separate treaties under which states undertake additional obligations. The obligations are undertaken by separate ratification of the optional protocol. Not all the states that have ratified the original treaty have ratified the optional protocol.

3. THE FOUR PRINCIPAL UN HUMAN RIGHTS TREATIES CONTAINING COMPLAINT MECHANISMS

a) The International Covenant on Civil and Political Rights

i) *Object*

The International Covenant on Civil and Political Rights (**ICCPR**) seeks to guarantee a broad range of universal human rights across a wide range of human endeavour. The preamble to the ICCPR recognizes that the rights derive from the inherent dignity of the human person. The ICCPR sets out certain "civil and political" rights.

The Human Rights Committee is the treaty body associated with the ICCPR.

ii) Adoption and Entry into Force

The ICCPR was adopted by the UN General Assembly on 16 December 1966, together with an Optional Protocol allowing individuals to submit complaints. Both the ICCPR and the Optional Protocol entered into force on 23 March 1976. For any state ratifying the Covenant or the Optional Protocol after 23 December 1976, the instruments enter into force for that state three months after the date of deposit of its instrument of ratification. The UN Secretary-General, Office of Legal Affairs, acts as depository.

A Second Optional Protocol associated with the ICCPR was subsequently adopted which provided for the abolition of the death penalty. It was adopted on 15 December 1989, and entered into force on 11 July 1991. For any state ratifying the Second Optional Protocol after 11 April 1991, it entered into force for that state three months after the date of deposit of its instrument of ratification.

iii) Obligations Undertaken by States Parties

When a state becomes a party to the ICCPR, it undertakes to immediately guarantee to all individuals in its territory or under its jurisdiction, without any discrimination, all the rights specified in the ICCPR (article 2(1)). These include both collective rights (such as self-determination), and individual rights (such as freedom of expression).

States parties undertake to:

- adopt such legislative or other measures as may be necessary to give effect to the rights recognized in the ICCPR (article 2(2));
- ensure to persons who claim their rights have been violated the opportunity to have the existence of such violation determined by a competent authority and, in cases of violation, an effective and enforceable remedy ordered (article 2 (3)); and
- develop the possibility of judicial remedies (article 2(3)(b)).

States parties also undertake to ensure the equal right of men and women to the enjoyment of the rights guaranteed in the ICCPR (article 3).

iv) Summary of Substantive Rights

The following rights are guaranteed by the ICCPR:

- **Right of self-determination**
  The right of all peoples of self-determination, including a right to determine freely political status and dispose of natural wealth and resources (article 1).

- **Right to life**
  The right to life, including restrictions on the circumstances in which capital punishment may be imposed (article 6).

- **Prohibition of torture**
  The right not to be subjected to torture or cruel, inhuman or degrading treatment or punishment, including the right not to be subjected to non-consensual medical or scientific experimentation (article 7).

- **Prohibition of slavery or servitude**
  The right not to be held in slavery or servitude, or (subject to certain express exceptions) to be required to perform forced or compulsory labour (article 8).

- **Prohibition of arbitrary arrest or detention**
  The right to liberty and security of the person, including a prohibition on arbitrary arrest or detention and on deprivations of liberty other than by law (article 9(1)).

- **Rights upon arrest or detention**
  The rights of persons who are arrested or detained:
  - to be informed of the reason for an arrest and of any charges (article 9(2);
  - to be brought promptly before a judicial officer (article 9(3));
  - to trial within a reasonable time or release (article 9(3));
  - to take proceedings before a court to have the lawfulness of an arrest or detention determined without delay, *habeas corpus* (article 9(4)); and
  - to obtain compensation if unlawful arrest or detention is established (article 9(5)).

- **Rights of prisoners**
  Persons deprived of liberty are to be treated with humanity and with respect for the inherent dignity of the human person (article 10). The essential aim of the prison system should be reform and rehabilitation, and the ICCPR specifies certain special protections that attach to juvenile prisoners and to unconvicted prisoners.

- **Imprisonment for breach of contract**
  The prohibition of imprisonment for inability to fulfill a contractual obligation (article 11).

- **Freedom of movement**
  The right to freedom of movement, including the freedom to choose a place of residence, the right to leave any country, and the right to re-enter one's own country (article 12).

- **Rights to due process in cases of deportation**
  Aliens who are lawfully within a state's territory have a right to due process of law before being expelled from the territory (article 13).

- **Right to fair trial**
  Individuals have the right to equality before courts and tribunals and, in both criminal and civil proceedings, to a fair and public hearing by a competent, independent and impartial tribunal (article 14(1)).

- **Protections for criminal defendants**
  The rights of persons charged with criminal offences include the right:
  - to be presumed innocent until proven guilty (article 14(2));
  - to be informed of the nature and cause of the charge (article 14(3)(a));
  - to have adequate time and facilities to prepare a defence (article 14(3)(b));
  - to be tried without undue delay (article 14(3)(c));
  - to be present at the trial and defend oneself; and to have legal assistance, in certain circumstances, paid for by the State (article 14(3)(d));
  - to examine witnesses against one, and to obtain and examine witnesses on one's behalf (article 14(3)(e));
  - to have the free assistance of an interpreter, if necessary (article 14(3)(f));
  - not to be compelled to incriminate oneself (article 14(3)(g));
  - to have an appropriate procedure for juvenile offenders (article 14(4));
  - to have a review of one's conviction or sentence by a higher tribunal (article 14(5));
  - to compensation for a wrongful conviction in certain circumstances (article 14(6)); and
  - not to be tried twice for the same offence (article 14(7)).

- **Non-retrospectivity**
  The right not to be held guilty for any criminal offence that did not constitute a criminal offence at the time it was committed, nor given a heavier penalty than was applicable at the time an offence was committed (article 15).

- **Recognition as a person before the law**
  The right to recognition everywhere as a person before the law (article 16).

- **Privacy and reputation**
  The right not to be subject to arbitrary or unlawful interference with privacy, family, home or correspondence, nor to unlawful attacks on one's honour or reputation (article 17).

- **Freedom of thought, conscience and religion**
  The right to freedom of thought, conscience and religion (article 18)).

- **Freedom of opinion and expression**
  The right to hold opinions without interference and to freedom of expression, including the freedom to seek, receive and impart information and ideas of all kinds (article 19).

- **Prohibition of hate speech**
  The obligation on states parties to prohibit war propaganda and advocacy of national, racial or religious hatred (article 20).

- **Peaceful assembly**
  The right to peaceful assembly (article 21).

- **Freedom of association**
  The right to freedom of association including the right to form and join trade unions (article 22).

- **Protection of the family**
  The right to protection of the family as the natural and fundamental group unit of society (article 23(1)). The right to marry and to be protected against forced marriage (article 23(2) and (3)). The equality of spouses both during marriage and at its dissolution (article 23(4)).

- **Children's rights**
  The right of children to special protection from the state, including the right to a name and a nationality (article 24).

- **Participation in public life**
  The right to participate in public affairs; to vote and to be elected through genuine, periodic and free elections; and to have access to the public service (article 25).

- **Equality and freedom from discrimination**
  The rights to equality before the law and to equal protection of the law, and freedom from discrimination on grounds such as race, colour, sex, language, religion, political or other opinion, national or social origin, property, birth or other status (article 26).

- **Minority rights**
  The right of persons belonging to ethnic, religious or linguistic minorities, in community with others, to enjoy their culture, profess and practice their religion or use their language (article 27).

Rights not protected

At the same time, there are some significant omissions which are covered in other international instruments directed at similar rights. Examples of rights not specifically protected by the ICCPR include the right to property, to acquire a nationality (except in the context of children), and the right to strike.

v) The Second Optional Protocol

The Second Optional Protocol was adopted on 15 December 1989, and it entered into force on 11 July 1991.

States parties to the Second Optional Protocol undertake:

- not to execute any person within their jurisdiction (article 1(1)); and
- to take all necessary measures to abolish the death penalty within their jurisdiction (article 1(2)).

The Second Optional Protocol is a treaty in its own right, which is open to ratification or accession by all states parties to the ICCPR (article 7).

The rights guaranteed by the Second Optional Protocol apply as if they were additional provisions to the ICCPR (article 6).

The only kind of reservation that is permitted to the Second Optional Protocol is one providing for the application of the death penalty in time of war pursuant to a conviction for a most serious crime of a military nature committed during wartime (article 2).

vi) Limitations on Rights

The rights set forth in the ICCPR can only be limited to the extent specifically provided for in the ICCPR (article 5(1)). The Human Rights Committee, the treaty body associated with the ICCPR, considers whether limitations imposed by a state are justified in the context of its examination of state party reports (article 40) and consideration of communications under the Optional Protocol.

Some of the articles in the ICCPR, which set out the substantive rights, also set out carefully defined circumstances in which states parties are entitled to restrict the exercise of those rights in order to accommodate other societal interests.

The societal interests that are accommodated in this way by the ICCPR are as follows:

- **National security**

  The exact circumstances in which rights can be restricted in the interests of national security differ from right to right. Usually, the restriction must be provided by law, and be necessary in a democratic society in the interests of national security. It is necessary to consult the text of the ICCPR and the particular language of each limitation clause associated with a particular right.

  The following rights can be restricted in the interests of national security:
  - freedom of movement (article 12(3));
  - right of legal aliens to due process before being expelled (article 13);

- publicity of court proceedings, as protected by the ability of the press and the public to attend court hearings (article 14(1));
- freedom of expression (article 19(3));
- freedom of peaceful assembly (article 21);
- freedom of association (article 22(2)).

- **Public safety**

  The exact circumstances in which rights can be restricted in the interests of public safety differ from right to right. Usually, the restriction must be provided by law, and be necessary in a democratic society in the interests of public safety. It is necessary to consult the text of the ICCPR and the particular language of each limitation clause associated with a particular right.

  The following rights can be restricted in the interests of public safety:
  - freedom to manifest religion or belief (article 18(3));
  - freedom of peaceful assembly (article 21);
  - freedom of association (article 22(2)).

- **Public order**

  The exact circumstances in which rights can be restricted in the interests of public order differ from right to right. Usually, the restriction must be provided by law, and be necessary in a democratic society in the interests of public order. It is necessary to consult the text of the ICCPR and the particular language of each limitation clause associated with a particular right.

  The following rights can be restricted in the interests of public order:
  - freedom of movement (article 12(3));
  - publicity of court proceedings, as protected by the ability of the press and the public to attend court hearings (article 14(1));
  - freedom to manifest religion or belief (article 18(3));
  - freedom of expression (article 19(3));
  - freedom of peaceful assembly (article 21);
  - freedom of association (article 22(2)).

- **Public health**

  The exact circumstances in which rights can be restricted in the interests of public health differ from right to right. Usually, the restriction must be provided by law, and be necessary in a democratic society in the interests of the protection of public health. It is necessary to consult the text of the ICCPR and the particular language of each limitation clause associated with a particular right.

The following rights can be restricted in the interests of protection of public health:
- freedom of movement (article 12(3));
- freedom to manifest religion or belief (article 18(3));
- freedom of expression (article 19(3));
- freedom of peaceful assembly (article 21);
- freedom of association (article 22(2)).

- **Morals**
  The exact circumstances in which rights can be restricted in the interests of morals differ from right to right. Usually, the restriction must be provided by law, and be necessary in a democratic society in the interests of the protection of morals. It is necessary to consult the text of the ICCPR and the particular language of each limitation clause associated with a particular right.

  The following rights can be restricted in the interests of protection of morals:
  - freedom of movement (article 12(3));
  - publicity of court proceedings, as protected by the ability of the press and the public to attend court hearings (article 14(1));
  - freedom to manifest religion or belief (article 18(3));
  - freedom of expression (article 19(3));
  - freedom of peaceful assembly (article 21);
  - freedom of association (article 22(2)).

- **Rights and freedoms of others**
  The exact circumstances in which rights can be restricted in the interests of the protection of the rights and freedoms of others differ from right to right. Usually, the restriction must be provided by law, and be necessary in a democratic society in the interests of the protection of the rights and freedoms of others. It is necessary to consult the text of the ICCPR and the particular language of each limitation clause associated with a particular right.

  The following rights can be restricted in the interests of protecting the rights and freedoms of others:
  - freedom of movement (article 12(3));
  - freedom to manifest religion or belief (article 18(3));
  - freedom of expression (article 19(3));
  - freedom of peaceful assembly (article 21);
  - freedom of association (article 22(2)).

- **Privacy**
  The right to a public trial and the ability of the press and the public to attend court hearings (article 14(1)), can be restricted to the extent required by the interests of the private lives of the parties.

- **Interests of justice**
  The right to a public trial and the ability of the press and the public to attend court hearings (article 14(1)), can be restricted to the extent strictly necessary in the opinion of the court in special circumstances where publicity would prejudice the interests of justice.

- **Interests of juveniles**
  The publicity of court proceedings, through publication of all court judgments (article 14(1)), can be restricted in the interests of juvenile persons.

- **Proceedings concerning matrimonial disputes or the guardianship of children**
  The publicity of court proceedings, through publication of all court judgments (article 14(1)), can be restricted where the proceedings concern matrimonial disputes or the guardianship of children.

- **Recognition given to special duties and responsibilities**
  The ICCPR recognizes that the right to freedom of expression (article 19(2)) carries with it special duties and responsibilities.

- **Armed forces and police**
  The right to freedom of association (article 22) can be limited by lawful restrictions placed on members of the armed forces and police.

- **Exceptional circumstances**
  The right of unconvicted prisoners to be segregated from, and treated differently from, convicted persons (article 10(2)) can be restricted in "exceptional circumstances."

- **Limitations derived from the language of the rights themselves**
  Some rights are defined in a way that involves limitations. For example, an arrest under article 9(1) is only prohibited if it is "arbitrary," and delay in bringing a person to trial under article 14(3)(c) is only prohibited if it is "undue." It is therefore important to recognize limitations which might be imposed by the definition of the right itself.

vii) Derogations

In addition to the permissible limitations on certain specific rights, the ICCPR sets out limited circumstances in which states parties are entitled to derogate from—meaning suspend—the enjoyment of the rights contained in the ICCPR in times of official public emergency (article 4).

Before a state party may take measures derogating from its obligations under the ICCPR, the following conditions must be fulfilled:

- There must be a public emergency which threatens the life of the nation;
- The existence of such a public emergency must be officially proclaimed;
- The derogation must only be to the extent strictly required by the exigencies of the situation;
- The derogation must not be inconsistent with the state party's other obligations under international law;
- The derogation must not involve discrimination solely on the ground of race, colour, sex, language, religion or social origin.

In accordance with article 4 of the ICCPR, some rights guaranteed by the ICCPR are non-derogable. They cannot be restricted, even in cases of public emergency. The non-derogable rights are as follows:

- The right to life (article 6);
- Torture and cruel or inhuman punishment (article 7);
- Slavery and involuntary servitude (article 8(1) and (2));
- Imprisonment for breach of contract (article 11);
- The rule against retrospective criminal legislation (article 15);
- Recognition before the law (article 16);
- Freedom of thought, conscience and religion (article 18).

The obligation of states parties to the Second Optional Protocol not to execute any person within their jurisdiction (article 1(1)) is also non-derogable (article 6 to the Second Optional Protocol).

viii) Reservations

When ratifying or acceding to a treaty, a state may formulate conditions which are referred to as reservations, understandings or interpretative declarations, by which it limits the obligations it is prepared to assume. Such statements are deposited with the depository, (the UN Secretary General, Office of Legal Affairs) who forwards them to all other states parties for comment. In considering the extent of the obligations undertaken by any state party to the Covenant, it is therefore necessary to consider whether the state party has made any reservations.

However, not all reservations are valid and succeed in limiting a state's obligations under the treaty. In general, a reservation will not be valid if it is incompatible with the object and purpose of the treaty.

States parties sometimes object to the reservations formulated by new states parties as incompatible with the object and purpose of the treaty. No reservation has yet been rejected by virtue of the objection of other states parties.

Nevertheless, in the course of considering communications and state reports, the Human Rights Committee itself must frequently decide on the application and scope of reservations. In some cases, the Committee has expressed the view that a reservation is invalid as against the object and purpose of the treaty. This occurred, for example, in the Committee's consideration of the reservation of Trinidad and Tobago to the Optional Protocol which purported to exclude persons under sentence of death from availing themselves of the procedure. The Committee has laid down the competence to evaluate, and if necessary reject, reservations in its General Comment No. 24. Hence, if the Committee receives a complaint which might be affected by a reservation, it may still consider the complaint if it believes that the reservation is incompatible with the object and purpose of the ICCPR.

The Committee's concluding observations on a state party's reports should be examined for possible comments on that state party's reservations.

ix) The Monitoring Body/Treaty Body: The Human Rights Committee

The ICCPR provides for the establishment of a Human Rights Committee to monitor the implementation of the Covenant's provisions by states parties.

The Human Rights Committee is composed of 18 independent experts, nominated and elected by state parties to the ICCPR, but intended to serve in their personal capacity.

The Human Rights Committee has the following tasks:

- **Examination of state reports**   States parties are required to submit reports on the measures they have adopted to give effect to the rights recognized in the ICCPR, the progress made in the enjoyment of those rights, and any factors or difficulties that have affected the implementation of the ICCPR (article 40).
- **Consideration of individual cases (communications)**   Individuals may claim a violation of the ICCPR by states parties that have ratified the Optional Protocol (see Chapter 2).
- **General Comments**   The Committee may make general comments based on the examination of state reports and individual communications (article 40(4)).
- **Consideration of state-to-state complaints**   States parties may declare that they recognize the competence of the Committee to receive and consider communications to the effect that a state party claims that another state party is not fulfilling its obligations under the ICCPR (article 41). However, no inter-state complaint has, in fact, ever been received by the Committee.

The Committee meets three times a year, with each session lasting three weeks. These sessions are normally held in March (at the United Nations Office Headquarters in New York), July and October/November (at the United Nations Office in Geneva). Prior to each session, a working group of the Committee meets for one week.

Staff and facilities for the performance of the Committee's functions are provided by the Secretary-General of the United Nations (article 36) through the Secretariat of the Office of the United Nations High Commissioner for Human Rights.

The Committee submits an annual report of its activities to the UN General Assembly (article 45). The report contains the concluding observations which the Committee makes about states parties in the context of reports, the decisions reached on individual cases, and any General Comments.

x) Number of Ratifying States

Over three-quarters of UN member states are now parties to the ICCPR, more than half are parties to the Optional Protocol, and one-quarter are parties to the Second Optional Protocol. This figure changes frequently and can be updated online (see Annex 4).

b) The Convention Against Torture and Other Cruel, Inhuman or Degrading Treatment or Punishment (CAT)

i) Object

The overall objectives of the Convention are to prevent acts of torture and similar acts, and to ensure that effective remedies are available to victims when such acts occur.

The Committee Against Torture is the treaty body associated with the Convention.

ii) Adoption and Entry into Force

The Convention against Torture and other Cruel, Inhuman or Degrading Treatment or Punishment **(CAT)** was adopted by the General Assembly on 10 December 1984 and came into force on 26 June 1987. For any state that ratified CAT after 27 May 1987, the Convention came into force thirty days after the date of deposit of its instrument of ratification (article 27(2)).

iii) Obligations Undertaken by States Parties

States parties undertake a variety of obligations concerning the prevention of torture and cruel, inhuman or degrading treatment or punishment, the investigation of allegations of torture and cruel, inhuman or degrading treatment or punishment, the criminal prosecution and/or extradition of torturers, and the compensation of torture victims.

iv) Summary of Substantive Rights
• **Definition of torture**
Article 1 defines torture as:
". . . any act by which severe pain or suffering, whether physical or mental, is intentionally inflicted on a person for such purposes as obtaining from him or a third person informa-

tion or a confession, punishing him for an act he or a third person has committed or is suspected of having committed, or intimidating or coercing him or a third person, or for any reason based on discrimination of any kind, when such pain or suffering is inflicted by or at the instigation of or with the consent or acquiescence of a public official or other person acting in an official capacity."

The application of the Convention is therefore limited to acts by, or with the consent of, public officials, or persons acting in an official capacity.

• Prevention of torture
States parties undertake to take effective, legislative, administrative or other measures to prevent acts of torture within their jurisdictions (article 2(1)).

• Absolute character of prohibition
The obligation under the Convention to prevent torture is absolute. In particular:
- no exceptional circumstances whatsoever, including public emergency, can be invoked to justify torture (article 2(1)); and
- an order from a superior officer or public authority cannot be invoked as a justification for torture.

• No expulsion
States parties are prohibited from expelling a person to another state (for example, by extradition) if there are substantial grounds for believing there is a danger of that person being subjected to torture (article 3).

• Criminalization of acts of torture
States parties undertake to criminalize and punish acts of torture within their jurisdiction (article 4).

• Jurisdiction to prosecute
States parties undertake to establish wide jurisdiction over the prosecution of acts of torture. This includes jurisdiction over alleged torturers who the state party does not extradite under article 8 (see below) (article 5).

• Criminal process
States parties undertake the following obligations with respect to alleged torturers in their territory:
- Examine the information available (article 6(1));
- If satisfied the circumstances warrant it, take into custody or take other legal measures to enable criminal or extradition proceedings to be instituted (article 6(1);

- Make a preliminary inquiry into the facts (article 6(2));
- Assist the alleged torturer in communicating with his or her state of nationality or residence (article 6(3));
- Notify other states parties (article 6(4)).

• Duty to prosecute

Unless the state extradites an individual to another jurisdiction, states parties undertake to prosecute any alleged torturer found within their jurisdiction, in the same manner and subject to the same guarantees of fair treatment, as any other alleged offender (articles 7).

• Extradition of alleged torturers

States parties undertake to consider the extradition of alleged torturers to states parties, regardless of the existence of an extradition treaty with other state parties or the inclusion of torture in other treaties (article 8).

• Mutual assistance

States parties undertake to afford one another the greatest measure of assistance in connection with the prosecution of alleged torturers (article 9).

• Education of public officials

States parties undertake to educate and inform various categories of public officials and others in contact with those arrested or detained, about the prohibition against torture (article 10).

• Review of interrogation rules

States parties undertake to keep under systematic review interrogation rules, methods and arrangements for the custody and treatment of detained persons (article 11).

• Investigative duties

States parties undertake to ensure the prompt and impartial investigation of possible acts of torture in territory within their jurisdiction (article 12).

• Investigation of complaints

States parties undertake to provide individuals a right to complain of alleged torture, to have the complaint promptly and impartially examined, and to be protected, along with any witnesses, against ill-treatment or intimidation (article 13).

• Remedies

States parties undertake to provide redress to victims of torture or their relatives, including compensation and rehabilitation (article 14).

• Inadmissibility of statements obtained under torture

States parties are prohibited from using statements obtained under torture as confessions or as evidence of other offences in subsequent criminal proceedings. However, if it is established that a statement was given under torture, this fact may be used as evidence against the torturer (article 15).

- ## Cruel, inhuman or degrading treatment or punishment

In addition to the prevention and punishment of torture, states parties undertake duties to prevent and investigate acts of cruel, inhuman or degrading treatment or punishment not amounting to torture as defined in article 1, committed within their jurisdiction and instigated by, committed by or acquiesced in, by a public official (article 16).

v) Limitations on Rights

The Convention emphasizes the absolute nature of the prohibition on torture, and the prohibition on return to a country where there is a personal risk of torture if returned. The Convention stipulates that neither exceptional circumstances such as public emergency, nor an order from a superior officer or public authority may be invoked in justification of an act of torture (article 2, paragraphs (2) and (3)).

Notwithstanding the absolute character of the prohibition against torture, some of the language of CAT incorporates possible limitations.

- ## Definition of torture and of cruel, inhuman or degrading treatment or punishment

The definition of torture, article 1, paragraph 1, does not include "pain or suffering arising only from, inherent in or incidental to" lawful sanctions. The Torture Committee has not yet given guidance as to the meaning of this limitation.

What is considered "cruel," "inhuman" or "degrading" treatment or punishment will depend on a relative assessment of all the background circumstances. This would include consideration of the nature of the offending behaviour justifying the punishment.

- ## Other language used to impose obligations on states parties

The obligation undertaken under article 2(1), to take "effective legislative, administrative, judicial or other measures to prevent acts of torture in any territory under its jurisdiction," may not cover an isolated act of torture where a state party has undertaken extensive measures, in good faith, to prevent torture occurring within its jurisdiction. Other examples of language used in the Convention which define the extent of the obligations include the obligation in article 13 to take "steps" to ensure that complainants and witnesses are protected, and the obligation in article 14 to provide an enforceable right to "fair and adequate" compensation.

vi) Derogations

The Convention explicitly prohibits derogations in times of public emergency (article 2(2)).

vii) Reservations

The Convention expressly entitles states parties to make the following kinds of reservations:

- A reservation declaring that the state party does not recognize the competence of the Committee to conduct inquiries into systematic practices of torture (under article 20), (article 28(1));
- A reservation that the state party does not consider itself bound by a procedure for resolution of inter-state disputes as to the interpretation or application of the Convention (article 30).

The Convention is silent on the possibility of states entering other types of reservations.

viii) The Monitoring Body/Treaty Body: The Committee Against Torture (CAT)

Implementation of the Convention by states parties is monitored by the Committee against Torture (CAT). The Committee is composed of 10 independent experts, nominated and elected by states parties to the Covenant, but intended to serve in their personal capacity.

CAT has the following tasks:

- **Examination of state reports** States parties are required to submit reports on the measures they have adopted to give effect to the provisions of the Convention.
- **Consideration of individual cases (complaints)** Individuals may claim a violation of the Convention by states parties that have specifically accepted the optional complaints procedure (article 22).
- **Inquiries into allegations of systematic practice of torture** The Committee may make inquiries concerning allegations of the systematic practice of torture in relation to states parties that have not exempted themselves from such inquiries by opting out of the inquiry provision (articles 20 and 28)
- **General Comments** The Committee has occasionally made General Recommendations based on its experience concerning the interpretation of the Convention.
- **Consideration of state-to-state complaints** A state party which considers that another state party is not fulfilling its obligations under the Convention may bring the matter to the attention of the Committee (article 21). However, no such inter-state complaint has ever been made.

The Committee meets twice each year in Geneva, in April/May and November, for sessions of two to three weeks.

Staff and facilities for the performance of the Committee's functions are provided by the Office of the United Nations High Commissioner for Human Rights.

The Committee submits an annual report of its activities to the General Assembly of the United Nations (article 24). The report contains the Committee's concluding observations made about states parties in the context of reports, the results of its inquiries into allegations of the systematic practice of torture, decisions reached on individual cases, and any General Comments.

ix) Number of Ratifying States

Over two-thirds of UN member states are now parties to the Convention and one-quarter of UN member states (one-third of states parties) have accepted the individual complaints procedure associated with the Convention (article 22). This figure changes frequently and can be updated online (see Annex 5).

c) The Convention on the Elimination of All Forms of Racial Discrimination (CERD)

i) Object

In the aftermath of World War II and the Holocaust, the phenomenon of racial discrimination was one of the major concerns of the United Nations. In 1965, the International Convention on the Elimination of all Forms of Racial Discrimination (CERD) was adopted by the General Assembly.

The Committee on the Elimination of Racial Discrimination (CERD) is the treaty body associated with the Convention.

ii) Adoption and Entry into Force

CERD was adopted by the General Assembly on 21 December 1965, and entered into force on 4 January 1969. For any state that ratified CERD after 5 December 1968, the Convention entered into force for that state thirty days after the date of deposit of its instrument of ratification (article 19(2)).

iii) Obligations Undertaken by States Parties

States parties undertake to condemn racial discrimination, pursue all appropriate means to eliminate discrimination in all its forms, and promote understanding among all races (article 2(1)).

iv) Summary of Substantive Rights

The Convention addresses the problem of racial discrimination comprehensively:

- **Definition of "racial discrimination"**

Article 1(1) of the Convention defines the term "racial discrimination" as follows:

". . . any distinction, exclusion, restriction or preference based on race, colour, descent, national or ethnic origin with the purpose or effect of nullifying or impairing the recognition, enjoyment or exercise, on an equal footing, of human rights in any field of public life, including political, economic, social or cultural life."

- **The scope of this definition:**
  - It protects against discrimination not only on grounds of "race" but on the related grounds of colour, descent and national or ethnic origin.
  - It does not protect against discrimination on grounds of citizenship, that is, between citizens and non-citizens (article 1(2)).
  - It encompasses both intentional discrimination and also laws, norms and practices that appear neutral but have a discriminatory effect.
  - Temporary affirmative measures aimed at securing the advancement of certain racial or ethnic groups or individuals, and necessary to ensure the equal enjoyment or exercise of human rights and fundamental freedoms, fall outside the definition of discrimination (article 1(4)).

- **Condemnation and elimination of racial discrimination**

States parties undertake to condemn racial discrimination, pursue all appropriate means to eliminate discrimination in all its forms, and promote understanding among all races (article 2(1)). To that end, states parties undertake to:

  - refrain from engaging in racial discrimination and ensure that public authorities and institutions do likewise (article 2(1)(a);
  - refrain from sponsoring, defending or supporting racial discrimination (article 2(1)(b));
  - remove laws, regulations and policies which create or perpetuate racial discrimination (article (2)(1)(c));
  - prohibit and eliminate racial discrimination in the private sphere (article 2(1)(d));
  - encourage integrationist multi-racial organizations and other means of eliminating race barriers (article 2(1)(e); and
  - take special and concrete measures, on a temporary basis, to ensure the development and protection of disadvantaged racial groups (article 2(2)).

- **Racial segregation and apartheid**

States parties particularly condemn racial segregation and apartheid, and undertake to prevent, prohibit and eradicate such practices (article 3).

- **Propagation of racial hatred**

States parties condemn, and undertake to take immediate and positive measures to eradicate (including criminally proscribing), all propaganda or organizations which are based on ideas of racial superiority or which attempt to justify, promote or incite racial hatred and discrimination (article 4).

- **Equality before the law**

States parties undertake to guarantee to everyone, without distinction as to race, colour, or national or ethnic origin:

- equal treatment by the justice system (article 5(a));
- security of the person, including protection from violence or bodily harm (article 5(b));
- political rights, in particular, the right to vote, stand for election and take part in public affairs (article 5(c));
- civil rights, in particular, the freedoms of movement, thought, conscience, religion, opinion, expression, assembly and association; the right to nationality; the right to marriage and choice of spouse; the right to own property; and the right to inherit (article 5(d)); and
- economic, social and cultural rights, in particular, employment rights; rights to housing, health care and social services; rights to education and training; the right to participation in cultural activities; and the right to equal access to public places (article 5(e)).

- **Remedies**

States parties undertake to assure to everyone within their jurisdiction, effective protection and remedies against racial discrimination, including reparation or satisfaction for any damage suffered as a result of discrimination (article 6).

- **Measures to combat discrimination**

States parties undertake to adopt immediate and effective measures, particularly in the fields of teaching, education, culture and information, to combat racial prejudice and promote racial understanding, tolerance and friendship (article 7).

v) *Limitations on Rights*

CERD does not identify societal interests that are considered sufficient to outweigh the substantive rights set forth (in contrast to the ICCPR).

Nevertheless, certain limitations are inherent in the terms of the rights and freedoms.

- **The concept of discrimination itself**

The concept of discrimination contains some inherent limitations. The definition of discrimination does not encompass all distinctions based on race but rather, only those which have the purpose or effect of nullifying or impairing the recognition, enjoyment, or exercise, on an equal footing, of human rights. The CERD Committee has said that differences in treatment, even though they are based on race, will not be considered discrimination if they are "legitimate" or "justifiable."

In addition, under CERD acts of "positive discrimination" as defined in article 1, paragraph 4, are deemed not to be discrimination for the purposes of the Convention.

- **The language used to impose obligations on states parties**

Some of the obligations in the Convention are expressed in terms which incorporate limitations. For example, under article 2, states parties undertake to pursue "by all appropriate means and without delay" a policy of eliminating racial discrimination. It does not necessarily follow that every time an act of discrimination occurs within a state party's territory, the state will have breached this obligation. It will be a matter of interpretation and judgment whether the state party has taken "all appropriate means." In assessing whether the measures taken by the state party are appropriate, sufficient and timely, the Committee may take into account, for example, the extent of the hurdles faced by the state party and the extent of the good faith efforts made by the state party to overcome them.

vi) Derogations

The Convention does not explicitly provide for derogation in times of public emergency.

vii) Reservations

Parties to the Convention are entitled to make reservations as long as they do not conflict with the object and purpose of the Convention (article 20).

In considering the extent of the obligations undertaken by a state party to the Convention it is, therefore, necessary to check for any reservations that may have been made by the state.

viii) The Monitoring Body/Treaty Body: The Committee on the Elimination of Racial Discrimination (CERD)

The Convention establishes a Committee on the Elimination of Racial Discrimination (CERD) to monitor states parties' implementation of the

Convention (article 8). CERD is composed of 18 independent experts, nominated and elected by states parties to the Convention, but intended to serve in their personal capacity.

CERD has the following tasks:

- **Examination of reports** States parties are directed to submit reports at regular intervals on the measures they have adopted to give effect to the provisions of the Convention. The Committee examines reports and adopts "concluding observations" about those reports. CERD has also created an "urgent action and prevention procedure," for examining situations of particular concern to it.
- **Examination of individual cases (communications)** Individuals can make complaints alleging a violation of the Convention by any state party that has accepted the optional complaints procedure under article 14.
- **Elaboration of General Recommendations** The Committee may make general recommendations based on the examination of the reports and information received from the states parties (article 9(2)).
- **Consideration of state-to-state complaints** A state party which considers that another state party is not giving effect to the provisions of the Convention may bring the matter to the attention of the Committee (article 11). However, no such inter-state complaint has ever been made.

The Committee meets in Geneva for two three-week sessions in March and August.

Staff and facilities for the performance of the Committee's functions are provided by the Office of the United Nations High Commissioner for Human Rights.

The Committee submits an annual report of its activities to the UN General Assembly (article 9). The report contains the concluding observations which the Committee makes about states parties in the context of reports, decisions reached in individual cases, and any General Recommendations.

ix) *Number of Ratifying States*

Over 85% of UN member states are now parties to the Convention, and one-fifth of UN member states (one-quarter of states parties) have accepted the individual complaints procedure under article 14 of the Convention. This figure changes frequently and can be updated online. (See Annex 6)

d) The Convention on the Elimination of All Forms of Discrimination Against Women (CEDAW)

i) *Object*

The spirit of the Convention is rooted in the goals of the UN: to reaffirm faith in fundamental human rights, in the dignity and worth of the human person and in the equal rights of men and women. In its preamble, the Convention acknowledges that "extensive discrimination against women continues to exist" and emphasizes that such discrimination "violates the principles of equality of rights and respect for human dignity."

The Committee on the Elimination of Discrimination Against Women (CEDAW) is the treaty body associated with the Convention.

ii) *Adoption and Entry into Force*

The Convention on the Elimination of all Forms of Discrimination Against Women (CEDAW) was adopted by the General Assembly on 18 December 1979, and came into force on 3 September 1981. For any state that ratified CEDAW after 4 August 1981, the Convention came into force thirty days after the date of deposit of that state's instrument of ratification.

iii) *Obligations Undertaken by States Parties*

States parties undertake to adopt all necessary measures at the national level aimed at achieving the full realization of the rights recognized in the Convention (article 24).

iv) *Summary of Substantive Rights*

- **Definition of "discrimination against women"**

  Article 1 of the Convention defines "discrimination against women" as:
  ". . . any distinction, exclusion or restriction made on the basis of sex which has the effect or purpose of impairing or nullifying the recognition, enjoyment or exercise by women, irrespective of their marital status, on a basis of equality of men and women, of human rights and fundamental freedoms in the political, economic, social, cultural, civil or any other field."
  In accordance with this definition, measures that have a discriminatory impact or effect on women will amount to discrimination, even when it is not possible to establish a discriminatory purpose.

- **Condemnation and elimination of discrimination against women**

  States parties condemn discrimination against women and agree to pursue, by all appropriate means and without delay, a policy of eliminating such discrimination. To that end, states parties undertake to:

- embody the principle of gender equality in domestic legislation and constitutions, and ensure the principle's practical realization (article 2(a));
- adopt legislative and other measures to prohibit discrimination against women (article 2(b));
- establish legal protection of the equal rights of women and ensure through public institutions the effective protection of women against discrimination (article 2(c));
- refrain from engaging in racial discrimination and ensure that public authorities and institutions do likewise (article 2(d));
- take measures to eliminate discrimination against women in the private sphere (article 2(e)); and
- remove laws, regulations, practices and penal provisions that constitute discrimination against women (article 2(f) and (g)).

- ### Measures to ensure advancement
States parties undertake to take appropriate measures to ensure the full development and advancement of women, for the purpose of guaranteeing the equal enjoyment of human rights (article 3).

- ### Affirmative action
The Convention stipulates two kinds of affirmative measures that are not considered discriminatory:

- temporary affirmative measures aimed at accelerating *de facto* equality between men and women (article 4(1)); and
- special measures aimed at protecting maternity, even when not of a temporary nature (article 4(2)).

- ### Modification of social and cultural patterns
State parties agree under article 5:

- to modify social and cultural patterns of conduct with a view to achieving the elimination of prejudices and practices that are based on an idea of gender inferiority and superiority or gender stereotyped roles (article 5(a));
- to ensure that family education includes a proper understanding of maternity as a social function, and the recognition of the common responsibilities of men and women in the upbringing and development of children (article 5(b)).

- ### Suppression of trafficking in women
States parties agree to take all appropriate measures to suppress all forms of traffic in women and the exploitation of prostitution of women (article 6).

• Political and public life

States parties undertake to protect women's rights in political and public life. In particular, they agree to ensure to women the equal right to:
- vote and be eligible for elections (article 7(a));
- participate in government as officials and policy makers (article 7(b));
- participate in non-governmental organizations and associations (article 7(c));
- represent their countries internationally (article 8);
- acquire, change or retain their nationality (article 9(1)); and
- exercise rights with respect to their children's nationality (article 9(2)).

• Education

States parties make detailed commitments to take appropriate measures to eliminate discrimination against women in the field of education (article 10). The measures agreed to be undertaken include:
- ensuring women equal access, opportunities and conditions in all educational institutions and at all stages of education and training, including vocational guidance and training (article 10);
- eliminating stereotyped concepts of gender roles in education, for example, by encouraging co-education and by revising textbooks, school programs and teaching methods (article 10(c));
- reducing female drop out rates and organizing programs for females who have left school prematurely (article 10(f)); and
- providing access to specific educational information to help ensure the health and well being of families, including information and advice on family planning (article 10(h)).

• Employment

States parties make detailed commitments to take appropriate measures to eliminate discrimination against women in the field of employment (article 11). In particular, states parties undertake:
- to ensure women equal treatment in relation to a wide range of work-related rights, including the right to work, to equal employment opportunities, to free choice of profession, to promotion, job security and employment related benefits and training, to equal remuneration and to social security (articles 11(1)(a) to (e));
- to ensure to women the right to protection of health and safety, including the safeguarding of the function of reproduction (article 11(1)(f));
- to take appropriate measures to prevent discrimination against women on the grounds of marriage or maternity and to ensure

their effective right to work. Such appropriate measures include:
- prohibiting the imposition of employment sanctions for pregnant women (article 11(2)(a));
- introducing paid maternity leave (article 11(2)(b));
- encouraging the provision of support services to enable parents to combine work and family responsibilities (article 11(2)(c)); and
- providing special protection for pregnant women from dangerous work (article 11(2)(d)).
- to periodically review protective legislation (article 11(3)).

• Health care
States parties undertake:
- to take all appropriate measures to eliminate discrimination against women in the field of health care and ensure equal access to health care services, including those relating to family planning (article 12(1)); and
- to ensure to women appropriate health services in connection with pregnancy, confinement and the post natal period (article 12(2)).

• Other areas of economic and social life
States parties undertake to take all appropriate measures to eliminate discrimination against women and ensure equal rights in other areas of economic and social life, in particular:
- family benefits (article 13(a));
- access to financial credit (article 13(b)); and
- participation in recreational activities, sports and cultural life (article 13(c)).

• Problems faced by rural women
States parties bind themselves to take into account the particular problems faced by rural women, eliminate discrimination against them and ensure that they participate in, and benefit from, rural development on the same basis as men.

• Equality before the law
States parties agree to accord women equality before the law and equal legal capacity with men in civil matters such as contracts and administration of property (article 15).

• Marriage and family relations
States parties agree to take all appropriate measures to eliminate discrimination against women in all matters relating to marriage and family relations (article 16). This includes:
- equal rights to choose whether to enter marriage and to choose a spouse (article 16(1)(a) and (b));

- equal rights during marriage and at its dissolution, including equal rights with respect to children (article 16(1)(c), (d) and (f));
- equal rights over reproduction (article 16(1)(e));
- equal personal rights as husband and wife, including the right to choose a family name, profession and occupation (article 16(1)(g)); and
- equal property rights (article 16(1)(h)).

• **Child marriage**

The Convention provides that child betrothal and marriage shall have no legal effect. States parties are to take all necessary action, including legislation, to specify a minimum age for marriage and to make official registration of marriages compulsory (article 16(2)).

• **Violence against women**

The text of the Convention does not expressly refer to violence against women. However, the Committee that monitors the Convention has interpreted the Convention to mean that gender-based violence is a form of discrimination that seriously inhibits women's ability to enjoy rights and freedoms on a basis of equality with men. Hence, the Committee has said it is accordingly prohibited by the Convention (General Recommendation No 19, UN Doc A/47/38 (1992)).

v) *Limitations on Rights*

CEDAW does not identify specific societal interests that are considered sufficient to outweigh the substantive rights set forth. Nevertheless, certain limitations are inherent in the terms of the rights and freedoms.

• **The concept of discrimination itself**

The definition of discrimination does not encompass all distinctions based on sex but rather, only those which have the effect or purpose of impairing or nullifying the recognition, enjoyment, or exercise by women, on a basis of equality, of their human rights.

An example of distinctions on the basis of sex that fall outside the concept of discrimination under the Convention, are acts of "positive discrimination" which are deemed not to be discrimination by article 4.

• **The language used to impose obligations on states parties**

Some of the obligations in the Convention are expressed in terms which incorporate limitations. For example, under article 2, states parties undertake to pursue "by all appropriate means and without delay" a policy of eliminating discrimination against women. It does not necessarily follow that every time an act of discrimination occurs within a state party's territory, the state will have breached this obligation. It will be a matter of interpretation and judgment whether the state party has taken "all appropriate means." In assessing whether the measures taken by the state party are appropriate, sufficient and timely, the Committee may take into account, for example, the extent of the hurdles faced by the state party and the extent of the good faith efforts made by the state party to overcome them.

vi) Derogations

The Convention does not explicitly provide for derogations in times of public emergency.

vii) Reservations

Parties to the Convention are entitled to make reservations as long as they do not conflict with the object and purpose of the Convention (article 28).

In considering the extent of the obligations undertaken by a state party to the Convention it is, therefore, necessary to check for reservations that may have been made by the state. It is also important to check concluding observations of the Committee on particular states parties, because the Committee has occasionally expressed views about whether a specific reservation is consistent with the object and purpose of the Convention.

viii) The Monitoring Body/Treaty Body: The Committee on the Elimination of Discrimination Against Women (CEDAW)

The Convention provides for the establishment of a Committee on Elimination of Discrimination against Women (CEDAW) to monitor the implementation of the Convention's provisions by states parties. The Committee is comprised of 23 independent experts, nominated and elected by states parties to the Convention, but intended to serve in their personal capacity.

CEDAW has the following tasks:

- **Examination of state reports** States parties are required to submit reports on the measures they have adopted to give effect to the provisions of the Convention, the progress made, and any factors and difficulties affecting fulfilment of their obligations under the Convention.
- **General Recommendations** The Committee may make General Recommendations based on its experience including the examination of state reports (article 21(1)).
- **Consideration of individual cases (communications)** Individuals may claim a violation of the Convention by states parties that have ratified the Optional Protocol.
- **Inquiries into grave or systematic violations** The Committee may make inquiries concerning allegations of grave or systematic

violations of women's rights in relation to states parties that have ratified the Optional Protocol (articles 8 and 9).

Staff and facilities for the performance of the Committee's functions are provided by the United Nations Division for the Advancement of Women in New York.

The Committee submits an annual report of its activities to the UN General Assembly. The report contains the concluding observations which the Committee makes about states parties in the context of reports, any General Recommendations, and in due course any decisions on individual cases.

ix) *Number of Ratifying States*

Almost 90% of UN member states have ratified the Convention, and one quarter are parties to the Optional Protocol. This figure changes frequently and can be updated online. (See Annex 7)

4. BRIEF OVERVIEW OF PRINCIPAL UN HUMAN RIGHTS TREATIES THAT DO NOT CONTAIN COMPLAINT MECHANISMS OR CONTAIN COMPLAINT MECHANISMS NOT YET IN FORCE

a) The International Covenant on Economic, Social and Cultural Rights

The International Covenant on Economic, Social and Cultural Rights (CESCR) was adopted by the General Assembly on 16 December 1966. The CESCR entered into force on 3 January 1976. Over three-quarters of UN member states are parties to the Covenant.

The Covenant guarantees economic, social and cultural rights, including rights relating to work in just and favourable conditions; an adequate standard of living, including clothing, food and housing; the highest attainable standards of physical and mental health; education; and the enjoyment of the benefits of cultural freedom and scientific progress.

The Covenant outlines the legal obligations of states parties under the Covenant. States are required to take positive steps to implement these rights, to the maximum extent of their resources, in order to achieve the progressive realization of the rights recognized, particularly through the adoption of domestic legislation (article 2).

The treaty itself does not provide for the creation of a monitoring body, and during the initial years the states parties merely reported to a working group of the Economic and Social Council (ECOSOC) of the UN. In 1985 however, ECOSOC decided to establish an expert committee. Thus, since 1986 responsibility for monitoring the implementation of the Covenant has been delegated to a committee of independent experts, the Committee on Economic, Social and Cultural Rights (CESCR).

The Covenant does not have an individual complaints mechanism associated with it, although the Committee has recommended the adoption of such a complaints procedure. In 1996, the Committee adopted and submitted to the Commission on Human Rights, for its consideration, a report and proposed text of a draft optional protocol which would provide for such a complaints procedure.

b) The Convention on the Rights of the Child

The grave afflictions suffered by children, such as infant mortality, deficient health care and limited opportunities for basic education, as well as child exploitation, prostitution, child labour and child victims of armed conflict, led the United Nations to codify children's rights in a comprehensive and binding treaty. The Convention entered into force on 2 September 1990, within a year of its adoption by the General Assembly. The Convention is approaching universal ratification, with only two UN member states not having ratified to date.

The Convention sets forth an extensive catalogue of civil, political, economic, social and cultural rights, which states are to guarantee to children within their jurisdiction "without discrimination of any kind and irrespective of the child's or his or her parent's or legal guardian's race, color, sex, language, religion, political or other opinion, national, ethnic or social origin, property, disability, birth or other status."

Some of the enumerated rights seek to protect children against practices of special danger to the welfare of children, such as economic exploitation, illicit use of drugs, all forms of sexual exploitation and abuse, and traffic in children.

One of the guiding principles of the Convention is set out in article 3(1), which declares that in all actions concerning children, whether undertaken by public or private social welfare institutions, courts of law, administrative authorities or legislative bodies, the best interests of the child shall be a primary consideration.

Two substantive Optional Protocols to the Convention have been adopted by the General Assembly. The Optional Protocol on the Sale of Children, Child Prostitution and Child Pornography was adopted on 25 May 2000, and entered into force on 18 January 2002. The Optional Protocol on the Involvement of Children in Armed Conflict was also adopted on 25 May, 2000, and entered into force on 12 February 2002.

There is no individual complaints mechanism associated with the Convention or its Optional Protocols.

c) The International Convention on the Protection of the Rights of All Migrant Workers and Members of Their Families

The International Convention on the Protection of the Rights of All Migrant Workers and Members of Their Families was adopted by the

General Assembly on 18 December 1990. Twenty ratifications are needed for its entry into force. It is not yet in force.

A migrant worker is defined in the Convention as a person who has been engaged, is engaged, or will be engaged in remunerated activity in a state of which he or she is not a national. The Convention draws a distinction between migrant workers who are lawfully working within the host state and migrant workers whose situation has not been regularized.

Under the Convention, states parties undertake to guarantee to all migrant workers, regardless of whether their status has been regularized or not, an extensive array of rights. These include many of the civil and political rights found in the ICCPR, as well as certain special rights not found in other treaties that are particular to the situation of migrant workers. Rights relating particularly to the situation of migrant workers include a right upon arrest or detention to notify the consular or diplomatic authorities of one's state of origin, a right to have humanitarian considerations related to the status of a migrant worker taken into account in the imposition of a sentence, limits on the circumstances in which identity or immigration documents can be destroyed or confiscated, and certain procedural rights attendant on expulsion from the state. The Convention also includes a more limited selection of social, economic and cultural rights. With respect to workers rights, all migrant workers, regardless of whether their status has been regularized or not, have the right to non-discrimination with respect to remuneration and conditions or work, and the right to participate in trade unions.

In addition, migrant workers and members of their families who are documented, or in a regular situation, are assured an array of additional rights, aimed at protecting the human rights of migrant workers and their families throughout the migration process. The process covered includes preparation for migration, departure, transit, stay and work in another country, and return to their state of origin or habitual residence.

The Convention also recognizes certain subcategories of migrant workers, including frontier workers, seasonal workers, itinerant workers, project-tied workers, specified-employment workers and self-employed workers. It establishes certain additional rights specific to the circumstances of these categories of worker.

States parties are obliged to establish a variety of policies and procedures to promote sound, equitable, humane and lawful conditions in connection with the international migration of workers and members of their families. States parties also agree to collaborate to prevent and eliminate the illegal or clandestine movements and employment of migrant workers in an irregular situation.

When the Convention comes into force, it will establish a treaty body, called the Committee on the Protection of the Rights of All Migrant Workers and Members of Their Families, to monitor its implementation.

An individual communication system is also part of this Convention. Article 77 of the Convention establishes an optional communication system which will come into force once ten states parties have made a declaration recognizing the Committee's competence to deal with individual cases. However, to date, no state has made such a declaration of competence and a new migrant workers treaty body will not be enabled to deal with individual cases for some time.

CHAPTER II

INTRODUCTION TO COMPLAINTS PROCEDURES

---

1. INTRODUCTION

a) What Is a Complaints Procedure?

A complaints procedure is a formal process by which an individual or, in some cases, a group of individuals, make a complaint to the treaty body associated with the treaty. The individual would claim that a state party has violated his or her individual rights under the treaty.

Complaints of human rights violations are referred to in the treaties as "communications." One treaty body prefers the word "complaints." A complaint may also be referred to as an "application" or "petition."

b) What Is the Purpose of Making an Individual Complaint?

The purpose of an individual complaint is to address an individual case of violation by a state party of its human rights obligations under the treaty. This can be contrasted with other international procedures that may focus on the general human rights situation in a state, rather than addressing a particular violation. In this sense, an individual complaints procedure functions in a similar manner to domestic legal proceedings.

The advantage of making an individual complaint is that a person who believes his or her rights have been violated has an opportunity to receive a determination from an international expert body that supports his or her claim of a violation and an entitlement to a remedy. Although the decisions of the UN human rights treaty bodies are not legally binding, the treaty bodies have been given the authority by states parties to express their expert views as to whether a violation of rights, and the states' international obligations to protect those rights, has occurred. The expertise of the committees developed over decades of monitoring the implementation of the treaties, combined with the legal requirement that states parties ratify treaties in good faith, means that there is an obligation for states parties to take the decisions of the treaty bodies seriously. The treaty bodies expect states parties to implement their decisions, and call upon states to provide the victim with an appropriate remedy. Even if this call is not enforceable in a domestic court, and there is no international police force to ensure its implementation, a decision of an international expert body that an individual's human rights, and a particular state's obligations to protect those rights, have been violated can be a powerful tool for achieving redress.

c)   Which Treaties Have Complaints Procedures?

Four human rights treaties, the International Covenant on Civil and Political Rights (ICCPR), the Convention on the Elimination of All Forms of Racial Discrimination (CERD), the Convention on the Elimination of All Forms of Discrimination Against Women (CEDAW) and the Convention against Torture and Other Cruel, Inhuman or Degrading Treatment or Punishment (CAT), currently have operating individual complaints procedures associated with them.

d)   Which States Can Be the Subject of an Individual Complaint?

Although the four treaties, ICCPR, CERD, CEDAW and CAT, have individual complaints procedures associated with them, mere ratification of the treaty itself does not empower the treaty body to scrutinize complaints made against a particular state.

In each case, specific acceptance of the complaints procedure is optional for states parties to the treaty. A complaint can only be brought against a particular state if, in addition to ratification of the treaty itself, the state has separately recognized the competence of the treaty body to receive and consider complaints.

2.   THE BASIS FOR THE RIGHT TO LODGE A COMPLAINT

a)   The International Covenant on Civil and Political Rights (ICCPR)

i)   The Optional Protocol to the ICCPR

The International Covenant on Civil and Political Rights does not contain an individual complaints procedure within the text of the actual treaty. A complaints procedure is contained in a separate treaty, the Optional Protocol to the Covenant.

By becoming a state party to the Optional Protocol, a state recognizes the competence of the treaty body, the Human Rights Committee, to receive and consider written complaints (called "communications" or "petitions") from individuals who believe their rights under the Covenant have been violated by the state party concerned (Optional Protocol, articles 1 and 2).

ii)   When Entered into Force

The Optional Protocol was drafted at the same time as the Covenant and came into force on the same day, 23 March 1976. It is a treaty in its own right, and only binds states parties that have separately ratified it. Where a state party ratified the Optional Protocol after 23 December 1975, the Optional Protocol came into force three months after the date of deposit of its instrument of ratification.

iii) Number of Ratifying States

The Optional Protocol is only open for signature and ratification by states parties to the ICCPR. Almost three-quarters of states parties to the Covenant have ratified or acceded to the Protocol. In order to lodge a complaint, it is necessary to first determine whether the state that is the intended object of the complaint is a party to the Optional Protocol.

iv) The Committee's Jurisprudence

The complaints procedure under the Optional Protocol has been used much more extensively than the procedures under the other treaties. Communications have been registered against at least 70 different states, and over 1000 individual communications had been registered by the Committee.

The Human Rights Committee is responsible for receiving and considering communications under the Optional Protocol.

The Human Rights Committee has been able to develop case law that more specifically interprets and develops the principles and rights set out in the ICCPR. Past communications are indicative of how the Human Rights Committee has previously interpreted, defined or addressed a specific right.

The Views and other decisions of the Human Rights Committee regarding complaints are published in the annual reports of the Committee. Most of these decisions are also available online. (See Annexes 17, 18)

b) The Convention Against Torture and other Cruel, Inhuman or Degrading Treatment or Punishment (CAT)

i) The Article 22 Procedure

The Convention Against Torture and other Cruel, Inhuman or Degrading Treatment or Punishment (CAT) contains an individual complaints procedure which enables individuals who believe they have been victims of a violation of the rights set out in the Convention, to complain to the treaty body, the Committee Against Torture (CAT).

Individuals can only submit a complaint to CAT if the state party they believe violated their rights has made a declaration that it recognizes the competence of the Committee to receive and consider such complaints (article 22).

ii) When Entered into Force

The complaints procedure became operative on the same date as the Convention came into force, 26 June 1987. Where a state party made the declaration of competence under article 22 after 26 June 1987, the complaints procedure became operative immediately upon making the declaration.

iii) Number of States Which Have Made the Declaration of Competence under Article 22

Over one-third of states parties have made the declaration under article 22 recognizing the competence of the Committee to receive individual communications.

iv) The Committee's Jurisprudence

The complaints procedure under article 22 of CAT has been used quite frequently by individuals, although not to the same extent as the Optional Protocol to the ICCPR. Communications have been registered against at least 20 different states, and approximately 200 individual communications have been registered.

The Committee Against Torture (CAT) is responsible for receiving and considering communications under article 22.

CAT has developed case law that more specifically interprets and develops the principles and rights set out in the Convention. The majority of cases to date have concerned the provision which prohibits a state party from expelling, returning or extraditing a person to another state where there are substantial grounds for believing that the person would be in danger of being subjected to torture (article 3). It is valuable to examine past communications to help determine how the Committee has previously interpreted, defined or addressed a specific right.

The Decisions of CAT regarding complaints are published in the annual reports of the Committee. Most of these decisions are available online. (See Annexes 19, 20)

c) The Convention on the Elimination of All Forms of Racial Discrimination (CERD)

i) The Article 14 Procedure

The Convention on the Elimination of all Forms of Racial Discrimination contains an individual complaints procedure that enables individuals, or groups of individuals, who believe they have been victims of a violation of the rights set forth in the Convention, to complain to the treaty body, the Committee on the Elimination of Racial Discrimination.

Individuals (or groups of individuals) can only make a complaint to the Committee if the state party that they believe violated their rights has made a declaration that it recognizes the competence of the Committee to receive and consider such complaints (article 14(1)).

ii) When Entered into Force

The complaints procedure entered into force on 3 December 1982. Where a state party to the Convention has made the declaration of competence under article 14 after 3 December 1982, the complaints procedure became operative immediately upon making the declaration.

iii) Number of States Which Have Made the Declaration of Competence under Article 14

Only about one-third of states parties have made the declaration recognizing the competence of the Committee to receive individual communications under article 14. In order to lodge a complaint, it is necessary to determine whether the state that is the intended object of the complaint has made the declaration under article 14.

iv) The Committee's Jurisprudence

The complaints procedure under CERD has been used infrequently to date by individuals. Communications have been registered against less than 10 different states, and only about two dozen communications have been registered in the history of the complaint process.

The Committee on the Elimination of Racial Discrimination is responsible for receiving and considering communications under article 14 of CERD.

CERD has been able to develop some case law that more specifically interprets and develops the principles and rights set out in the Convention. The decisions (Opinions) of CERD are published in the annual reports of the Committee and are available online. (See Annexes 21, 22)

d) The Convention on the Elimination of All Forms of Discrimination Against Women (CEDAW)

i) The Optional Protocol to CEDAW

The Convention on the Elimination of All Forms of Discrimination Against Women does not contain an individual complaints mechanism within the text of the treaty. In 1999 a right of individual communication associated with the treaty was adopted in the form of an Optional Protocol. The Optional Protocol establishes, among other things, an individual complaints procedure.

By becoming a state party to the Optional Protocol, a state recognizes the competence of the treaty body, the Committee on the Elimination of Discrimination Against Women (CEDAW), to receive and consider written communications from individuals or groups of individuals who claim to be victims of a violation by that state party of any of the rights set forth in the Convention (articles 2 and 3).

ii) When Entered into Force

The Optional Protocol was adopted by the General Assembly on 6 October 1999 and entered into force on 22 December 2000. The Optional Protocol is a treaty in its own right, and only binds states parties that have separately ratified it. Where a state party ratified the Optional Protocol after 22 September 2000, the Optional Protocol came into force three months after the date of deposit of its instrument of ratification.

iii) Number of Ratifying States

The Optional Protocol is only open for signature and ratification to states parties to CEDAW. About one-quarter of the states parties to the Convention have ratified the Optional Protocol.

iv) The Committee's Jurisprudence

As the Optional Protocol has only recently come into force, the Committee on the Elimination of Discrimination Against Women does not yet have a body of case law.

3. GENERAL OVERVIEW OF THE PROCESS

Although the complaints procedures associated with each of the four human rights treaties are not identical, the process of making a complaint is similar. This chapter describes the general process of making a complaint and explains the kind of information that needs to be included in a communication to a treaty body. Chapters IV–VII will discuss separately and in more detail the individual complaints process for each treaty.

The diagram opposite indicates the main steps in determination of a complaint.

The main steps to making a complaint:

- The author or complainant prepares the complaint, also called a "communication" or "petition."
- The communication is received by the Secretary-General of the United Nations (Secretariat of the Office of the UN High Commissioner for Human Rights in Geneva or the Division for the Advancement of Women in New York), who brings it to the attention of the relevant treaty body.
- The treaty body registers the communication.
- The treaty body examines the communication and considers:
  - the admissibility of the communication, and if admissible
  - the merits of the communication.
- The treaty body issues its "Views," also called an "Opinion" or "Decision," to the parties.
- The treaty body may engage in some follow-up activities to monitor the states parties' response to its Views.

Overview of the Human Rights Treaty Complaints Procedures

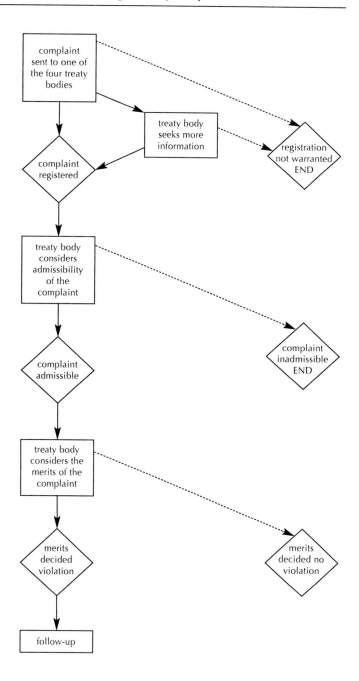

Each of these steps is discussed below.

4. PREPARATION OF THE COMMUNICATION

The first step is for the person who believes his or her rights have been violated ("the author"/"the complainant") to prepare a complaint ("communication").

Important points to note:

- The communication must be in written form.
- For some of the treaty bodies, there is no formal time limit for bringing a claim. CERD, however, requires that the claim be brought within six months after the final national judgment. In any event, delay in bringing the claim should be avoided so as to ensure that the claim is credible and so as to maximize the availability of evidence.
- A victim may seek assistance in drafting the communication (for example, from a lawyer or a non-governmental organization (NGO)).
- In general, a communication must be lodged in the name of the victim. A person submitting a communication on behalf of a victim must show proper authority to do so. Class actions or cases brought by parties not personally affected, are not accepted.
- None of the relevant treaties facilitate the provision of legal aid for the purposes of submitting an individual complaint to the treaty bodies. Accordingly, the treaty bodies are unable to assist in that regard. However, national legal systems may provide legal aid in this context, and domestic provisions for legal aid should therefore be checked.
- Every attempt should be made to include in the communication all the information necessary to enable the treaty body to determine both that the complaint is admissible and that there has been a violation of a treaty provision.
- One or more of the treaty bodies provide model complaint forms to assist prospective complainants (see Annex 1). The model form outlines the information that needs to be included in the communication. Use of this form is optional.

5. SUBMITTING THE COMMUNICATION

Once the communication has been drafted, it should be submitted to the relevant treaty body. In the case of the ICCPR, CERD and CAT, the address is the Office of the High Commissioner for Human Rights in Geneva. In the case of CEDAW, the address is the Division for the Advancement of Women in New York. The addresses are:

ICCPR

Human Rights Committee,
c/o Office of the UN High
   Commissioner for Human
   Rights,
Palais Wilson,
52 Rue des Pacquis,
1211 Geneva, Switzerland

fax: (41 22) 917-9022
e-mail: tb-petitions.hchr@unog.ch

CAT

Committee Against Torture,
c/o Office of the UN High
   Commissioner for Human
   Rights,
Palais Wilson,
52 Rue des Pacquis,
1211 Geneva, Switzerland

fax: (41 22) 917-9022
e-mail: tb-petitions.hchr@unog.ch

CERD

Committee on the Elimination of
   Racial Discrimination,
c/o Office of the UN High
   Commissioner for Human Rights,
Palais Wilson,
52 Rue des Pacquis,
1211 Geneva, Switzerland

fax: (41 22) 917-9022
e-mail: tb-petitions.hchr@unog.ch

CEDAW

Committee on the Elimination of
   Discrimination against Women,
c/o Division for the Advancement
   of Women, Department of
   Economic and Social Affairs,
   United Nations Secretariat,
2 United Nations Plaza,
DC-2/12th Floor,
New York, New York 10017 U.S.A.

fax: (1) (212) 963-3463
[no e-mail address yet]

Important points to note:

- The complaint should clearly specify the treaty body which the author intends should examine the communication.
- Communications sent by fax or email can be received, but not registered unless the Secretariat receives a signed original.
- Communications specifically requesting urgent action should be sent by fax or email, if necessary with documentation to follow.
- If the communication is not sufficiently detailed, before registering the communication, the UN Secretariat may seek more information from the author. This will slow down the process of having the communication reach the intended treaty body for consideration.

6.   RECEIPT OF THE COMMUNICATION BY THE TREATY BODY

The treaty bodies will not receive complaints unless they concern the actions of a state party that has both:
- ratified the relevant treaty; and
- either:

(a) in the case of the ICCPR and CEDAW, ratified the Optional Protocol recognizing a right of individual communication; or

(b) in the case of CERD and CAT, made the declaration recognizing the competence of the treaty body to receive and consider such communications.

Accordingly, prior to submitting the communication, it is important to verify whether the state party has ratified the relevant treaty and made the necessary declarations of competence.

Points to note about verifying ratification:

- States parties' ratifications and declarations can be obtained online. (See Annexes 4–7)

7. RESERVATIONS

When verifying whether the state party has ratified the relevant treaty, the author or complainant should investigate whether the state party has made any reservations that affect the complainant's ability to bring a complaint about a particular matter. Reservations may be substantive or procedural in nature.

a) Substantive Reservations

These are reservations that affect the content of the obligations undertaken by the state party under the treaty. States parties may make reservations that limit or qualify their assent to be bound by a particular right.

A complaint cannot be brought alleging the breach of an obligation under the relevant treaty if the state has indicated, through a reservation, that it does not consent to be bound by that obligation. Such complaints will be declared inadmissible.

Note, however, that certain reservations are deemed to be ***contrary to the object and purpose*** of the treaty. If the treaty body considers that a reservation is contrary to the object and purpose of the treaty, it might disregard the reservation and treat the relevant obligation as binding on the state party. The Human Rights Committee and CEDAW have directly told states parties their conclusions as to whether a reservation is incompatible with the object and purpose of their respective treaties. CERD and CAT have not yet made a statement about the incompatibility of reservations with each of their treaties.

b) Procedural Reservations

The state party may have made procedural reservations when ratifying the Optional Protocol or making the declaration of competence, that limit the circumstances in which the state recognizes the competence of the relevant treaty body to receive and consider individual communications. For example, a state party may specify in a reservation that the relevant treaty body cannot consider complaints against the state if the complainant has already utilized some other international investigative procedure.

8. DATE OF RATIFICATION

Since the four treaties do not have retroactive effect, violations that took place before the date of ratification to the relevant treaty cannot be the subject of complaint.

Exception:

Where a right was breached prior to the relevant treaty being ratified, but the effect of the breach continued after ratification, the breach of that right can be the subject of a complaint. An example would be where a person has been arbitrarily detained by a state prior to ratification of the ICCPR, but remains in prison after the date of ratification.

9. MAKING DECISIONS

The treaty body proceeds to hear and decide the communication. The procedure followed may differ among treaty bodies and from case to case. However, there are some common features:

- The treaty bodies usually deal with communications in the order in which they were received.
- In each case, the relevant treaty body will make two decisions: (a) a decision about the admissibility of the communication; and (b) if the communication is admissible, a further decision about the merits of the complaint.
- If the treaty body considers that the communication is clearly inadmissible, the treaty body may declare the communication inadmissible without inviting the state party against whom the allegation is made to respond to the complaint on the merits, or deal with the substance of the complaint.
- In all other cases, the treaty body will invite the state party against whom the allegations are made to respond to the communication, both on the question of the admissibility of the complaint and on the merits of the complaint. In some cases, a treaty body may ask a state party to respond to the question of admissibility first as a separate and prior issue.
- The author/complainant will be given an opportunity to respond to any submissions received by the treaty body from the state party.
- Regardless of whether the state party has been asked to respond on the questions of admissibility and merits separately or at the same time, the treaty body will not determine the merits of a communication unless it has determined that the communication is admissible.

- If a communication is found to be inadmissible and the complainant subsequently believes that the ground of inadmissibility no longer exists, the complainant may ask the treaty body to reconsider the complaint.
  Example: if the complaint is found to be inadmissible because the complainant has not exhausted all domestic remedies and the complainant subsequently exhausts all such remedies, the complainant is entitled to re-submit the complaint.
- If the communication is found to be admissible, the treaty body will proceed to determine the communication on the merits.
- All deliberations take place in private, on the basis of the written information provided to the treaty body by the parties. Although the Human Rights Committee and CAT theoretically have the power to hear from the complainant and the state party in person, that power has never been exercised. A complainant who believes an oral hearing would be appropriate should make that request known to the treaty body.
- Since this is an individual complaints procedure aimed at solving the problems of a particular person, the name of the person must be communicated to the state party so that the state party may investigate and take appropriate action. However, when necessary, confidentiality is maintained in relation to the broader public during the examination of the complaint and the "Views"/ "Opinions"/" Decisions" may be issued without disclosing the name of the author or victim.

10. INTERIM MEASURES

At any stage prior to the final determination of a communication, a treaty body may request that a state party take interim measures in order to avoid irreparable damage to the alleged victim. The treaty bodies will only do so when the matter is urgent, and delay will result in irreparable damage. Such a request, however, will only be made where the author has provided sufficient information to indicate that his or her case will likely meet admissibility criteria.

A request for interim measures from the treaty bodies to the state party does not imply any result on the merits of the communication, or that the treaty body will ultimately find in the author's favour.

Example: a case in which the death penalty may be applied imminently, or extradition to a state in which the complainant fears torture.

11. ADMISSIBILITY OF COMMUNICATIONS

A number of admissibility requirements are common to all four complaints mechanisms. These are as follows:

- **Standing: the complaint must be made by an individual or, in certain circumstances, a group of individuals.**

The rights guaranteed in the treaties are, for the most part, individual rights. The Optional Protocol to the ICCPR and the complaints procedure under article 22 of CAT only allow for communications to be brought by individuals. In certain circumstances, a right may be held by an individual to engage in a group based activity. Breach of such a right can be complained about by any member of the group. However, it is still the individual who is making the complaint, not the group itself.

Examples: the right to practice one's own religion "in community with others"; or the right of persons belonging to a minority to enjoy their culture "in community with the other members of the group."

Several members of the group may complain at the same time about the same matter. In this situation, the treaty bodies are likely to join the cases.

In contrast, the complaints procedure contained in CERD and the Optional Protocol to CEDAW specifically contemplate that complaints can be brought by "groups of individuals," but not by businesses or corporations. However, one individual is not permitted to bring a case on behalf of many individuals in the same position as him or herself, unless he or she has been given express permission to act on their behalf.

The CAT and CEDAW Committees can also investigate systematic violations by states parties of treaty rights, but this is distinguished from the individual complaint process.

- **Standing: the author of the communication must be personally affected by the violation**

Ordinarily, the victim himself or herself must bring the claim. If, however, the victim is unable to make the claim, another person (a relative or representative) may bring a claim on his or her behalf. In such cases:

  - The person bringing the claim must justify his or her authority to act on behalf of the victim.
  - The person bringing the claim does not necessarily have to be a family member, but there must be a ***personal relationship*** with the victim.

- Unrelated third parties cannot submit a claim on behalf of a victim, unless they can clearly show that the victim authorized them to act on his or her behalf.

In certain circumstances, the consent of the victim may be unable to be obtained. If so, the author must explain why not, and why the individual is authorized to bring the complaint on the victim's behalf.

Examples: the victim is dead or being held incommunicado.

An unrelated person cannot bring a complaint simply because they know a violation has occurred, even if there is abundant evidence to prove the violation. Accordingly, an NGO cannot bring a claim on behalf of a victim on the NGO's own initiative. However, if the victim is unable to make the claim, the family may bring the claim and authorize an NGO or legal counsel to act on behalf of the victim. An NGO can also assist the victim or his or her family or representative in making the claim (for example, by paying for a lawyer or gathering evidence).

- **The complaint must not be anonymous**

The identity of both the victim and the complainant (if different from the victim) must be revealed in the communication.

If the complainant fears reprisals from the state party which has committed the violation, he or she may request that the identity of the victim and/or the complainant not be revealed to the public.

- **Victims must have been subject to the jurisdiction of the alleged violating state party at the time the alleged violation occurred.**

Victims must have been subject to the jurisdiction of the state party at the time the violation occurred. In most cases, this will mean that the victim was present within the territory of the state party at the time of violation. In some cases, however, a person may have been subject to the jurisdiction of a state party even though they were not within the state's territory at the relevant time.

Example:
(a) A person who is refused the right to enter the territory of the state party when his or her spouse is in that territory, can claim that his or her right to family life has been violated by the state, even though he or she was outside the state's territory at the relevant time.
(b) A victim who has fled the state that violated his or her human rights can bring a claim, even though he or she is no longer subject to the jurisdiction of that state. What matters is that the victim was under the jurisdiction at the time of the violation.

Note, however, that even though a victim is outside the territory of a state party at the time he or she makes the complaint, he or she must still exhaust any domestic remedies that are available within the violating state party before bringing a claim.

The victim does not need to be a citizen or resident of the violating state party. Refugees and illegal immigrants can bring claims. Persons who are held in transit zones at airports can complain about violations that occur there, even though the states may try to claim that such persons are not under their jurisdiction.

- **Victims must exhaust all domestic remedies before bringing a communication**

In principle, the victim of a violation must, before bringing a communication, use all procedural means that are at his or her disposal within the legal system of the violating state to obtain relief. This includes exhaustion of all available judicial remedies (including appeal to the highest available court) and, in addition, exhaustion of any non-judicial procedures that might be available.

The requirement of exhaustion of domestic remedies may be satisfied, however, if it is shown that such remedies are ineffective, unavailable, or unreasonably prolonged.

In the following circumstances, the victim will not be required to exhaust all domestic remedies:

- The local remedies are not available:
  - because there is no *legal* process available to protect the rights;
  - because access to the courts or other legal procedures to bring the claim related to the right has been denied; or
  - because in a criminal case there is no legal aid available, or the legal assistance that can be obtained is not effective because of fear in the legal community to argue such claims.
- The local remedies are not effective in bringing relief:
  - because there is no independent adjudicator available;
  - because the prior case law concerning the violation of the right which is the subject of the complaint indicates that there is no real possibility of a remedy;
  - because there is a consistent pattern of violations which makes recourse to legal proceedings meaningless;
  - for any other reason, the available procedures are unlikely to provide effective relief;
  - using the domestic procedures would involve unreasonable delay, or the courts have delayed hearing the complaint for an unreasonable length of time.

The author must go beyond a certain threshold of evidence to substantiate why he or she believes that local remedies are not effective.

To enable the treaty body to establish the admissibility of the complaint, the complainant should set out in detail in the communication both the domestic procedures that the complainant has attempted to utilize and the outcome of such procedures. If domestic remedies have not been fully exhausted, the complainant must explain why in detail.

- **The same complaint must not be pending before another international forum in the case of ICCPR, CAT and CEDAW; in the case of CAT and CEDAW, the same complaint must not have been examined under another procedure of international investigation or settlement**

With respect to all the treaty complaint mechanisms except CERD, at the time the complaint is lodged, the matter must not be under investigation by another procedure of international investigation or settlement.

Exception: some international procedures are not considered to amount to procedures of "international investigation or settlement." For example, the fact that the matter has been brought to the attention of a United Nations Special Rapporteur, or is being considered under the UN Economic and Social Council "1503 procedure" by the Working Groups of the United Nations Sub-Commission on the Promotion and Protection of Human Rights (Working Group on Communications) or the Commission on Human Rights (Working Group on Situations), will not be considered sufficient to render an individual communication inadmissible.

Once a procedure of international investigation or settlement has fully ended, with respect to ICCPR and CERD there is, in theory, nothing to prevent an individual communication being brought about the same matter. However, in practice, many states parties have made reservations to these treaties that preclude recourse to the treaty bodies once another international procedure, whether regional or universal (UN), has been utilized.

- **The victim's claim must be sufficiently substantiated**

If there is not sufficient evidence to make the claim credible, the treaty body may dismiss the claim for lack of substantiation. Although the treaties themselves do not provide for a criterion of "manifestly ill-founded," the rules of procedure of the treaty bodies have created the similar category of non-substantiation.

- **The victim's claim must not be incompatible with the provisions of the relevant treaty**

This means the case will be found to be inadmissible if the right itself is not protected by the treaty. For example, the ICCPR does not protect the right to property, the right to seek asylum, the right to acquire a nationality, or the right to strike. Sometimes, however, committees have declared communications inadmissible as incompatible when they were compatible, but not properly substantiated.

- **The complaint must not constitute an abuse of the right of submission**

The same matter may not be complained about several times. This means that identical claims will not be accepted. However, different victims of the same act of violation can all bring their claim separately.

There may be no insulting language in the complaint. Since this is a quasi-judicial procedure, the parties are required to argue in an appropriate manner.

The treaty bodies will dismiss a complaint if they believe the complaints procedure is being used for other reasons than for a genuine human rights complaint.

Examples:
(a) The complaint constitutes a political attack on the state party.
(b) A racist group complains about limitations on their freedom of expression when they were inciting racial hatred.

- **Time delays in bringing a complaint may result in inadmissibility**

A long delay in submitting a case entails difficulties for the state party and for the Committee to determine the facts. Thus, if the delay is unjustified, the Committee may deem it an abuse of the right of submission. CERD specifies a 6-month rule in bringing a complaint past the exhaustion of domestic remedies.

12. DETERMINATION OF THE MERITS

At the merits stage, the treaty body will determine whether any of the rights guaranteed in the treaty have been violated, bearing in mind any relevant reservations made by the state party.

Important points to note:

- The complainant does not have to prove the facts beyond any doubt but he or she must make an initially sufficient (*prima facie*) case and submit enough evidence to go over the admissibility threshold.
- In order to enable the treaty body to reach a decision on the merits, the author should include in the communication a detailed fact statement, containing all the evidence that is at his or her disposal. The committees attach importance to specific dates. Copies of arrest warrants, court judgments, affidavits and medical reports should be submitted, whenever available.

- If the treaty body considers that it does not have sufficient information to decide the complaint, it may ask the complainant for more information.
- Burden of proof: if all or most of the information is in the hands of the state party, non-cooperation with the Committee will lead to a reversal of the burden of proof.
- Third-party/*amicus curiae* briefs: the Committees do not formally accept third-party submissions. However, the usefulness of submitting supporting, well-argued analysis from third parties cannot be completely discounted and may prove more valuable in the future.

13. ISSUANCE OF VIEWS

Once the treaty body has reached a view on the merits of the communication, it will send its decision ("Views"/"Opinions"/"Decisions") to the complainant and to the state party.

Important points to note:

- In its Views the treaty body expresses its opinion about the complaint, after having considered the position of both the complainant and the state. If the treaty body finds that there has been a violation, it can recommend measures to the state to remedy the violation.
- These Views and recommendations are not legally binding. At the same time, by ratifying the treaty the state party undertook legal obligations not to violate those rights. The treaty body's considered opinion as to whether those legal obligations have been breached should be considered as authoritative.
- There are no sanctions for non-implementation of Committee Views. Although a treaty body cannot "force" a state to remedy a violation, in many cases states have in fact provided remedies to the complainants involved.

14. FOLLOW-UP TO VIEWS

States parties must report to the treaty bodies on the measures they have taken in response to Views. The Human Rights Committee has appointed one of its members to undertake to ensure the treaty body has this information and to recommend further action when unsatisfactory replies are received from states parties. This individual, known as the Special Rapporteur on Follow-up, monitors the compliance with the Committee's decision. The mechanism of a Rapporteur for Follow-up has recently been adopted by CAT, and is also anticipated in relation to the CEDAW Optional Protocol.

15. SUMMARY OF MATTERS THAT SHOULD BE INCLUDED IN THE COMMUNICATION/COMPLAINT

In order to ensure that the treaty body has sufficient information before it to determine both the admissibility and merits of the complaint, the following information should be clearly included:

- The name of the treaty body to which the complaint is directed;
- The name of the victim and, if different, the author of the complaint. If possible, the application must be signed by the victim. (Otherwise, the author must sign the complaint and show the authority on which he or she is acting).
- A contact address (this can be the address of a representative rather than the complainant).
- The nationality of both the victim (and if different the author) of the complaint.
- The state against which the complaint is brought.
- The rights under the relevant treaty that are alleged to have been violated (indicate the relevant articles in the treaty and keep in mind any relevant state reservations).
- The domestic remedies that have been exhausted and the outcome of any such domestic procedures, or evidence as to why domestic remedies are ineffective, unavailable or unreasonably prolonged.
- Any other procedure of international investigation or settlement that has been engaged. (In the case of CAT and CEDAW, a prior or pending decision of another procedure of international investigation or settlement on the same matter will preclude a communication to either treaty body).
- A detailed fact statement, including all available evidence, such as medical reports.
- The remedy requested.

16. PITFALLS TO AVOID

Common grounds for failing to satisfy preliminary criteria for the registration and subsequent examination of the petition:

- the state alleged to violate the rights of the author is not a party to the relevant complaints procedure (the Optional Protocol to the ICCPR, article 14 CERD, article 22 CAT, the Optional Protocol to CEDAW);
- the state party has entered a reservation to the relevant treaty as a result of which the complaint cannot be examined;
- the complaint is being examined (in the case of ICCPR, CAT and CEDAW) by the European Court of Human Rights, the Inter-American Commission or Court of Human Rights, the African Commission on Human and People's Rights;

- the complaint has been examined (in the case of CAT and CEDAW) by the European Court of Human Rights, the Inter-American Commission or Court of Human Rights, the African Commission on Human and People's Rights;
- the object of the complaint, such as the rights violations cited, fall outside the scope of the relevant treaty;
- the events complained of occurred prior to the entry into force of the relevant treaty or treaty provision for the state concerned;
- domestic judicial/administrative remedies do not appear to have been exhausted, and it has not been substantiated that the application of domestic remedies would be unreasonably prolonged or that the remedies would be otherwise unavailable or ineffective;
- the Human Rights Committee will generally not review the evaluation of facts and evidence by the national courts and authorities, nor the interpretation of domestic legislation;
- the Human Rights Committee will generally not review a sentence imposed by national courts, nor the question of innocence or guilt;
- the treaty bodies will not generally examine disputes between private individuals or alleged violations of human rights that have been committed by non-state actors;
- the individual petition has not been presented by the alleged victims themselves or by duly authorized representatives;
- the petition is anonymous;
- the petition does not provide sufficient details as to the facts of the case, and/or how the alleged victim's rights under the relevant treaty have been violated; and
- correspondence has been submitted in a language which is not a working language of the Secretariat (English, French, Spanish and Russian).

CHAPTER III

THE COVENANT ON CIVIL AND POLITICAL RIGHTS

---

1. OVERVIEW OF THE HUMAN RIGHTS COMMITTEE

The Human Rights Committee is responsible for receiving and considering complaints under the Optional Protocol to the International Covenant on Civil and Political Rights (ICCPR). The Committee is composed of 18 experts, nominated and elected by states parties. Members serve in their personal, independent capacity.

A Committee member may sit in judgment of Optional Protocol cases even though his or her state of nationality has not ratified the Optional Protocol.

The Committee follows specific procedures in the consideration of individual communications. The individual communications procedures originate from three sources: the provisions of the Optional Protocol itself, the Rules of Procedure that have been adopted formally by the Human Rights Committee, and the Committee's customary practices.

To help maintain impartiality in the complaint process, the Rules of Procedure of the Human Rights Committee provide that members shall not take part in the deliberation of a case involving the state party in respect of which they were elected, in which they have a personal interest, or in which they have participated in any way in the making of any decision in the case before it reached the Committee (Rules 84 and 85).

The Committee meets three times per year, with each session being three weeks in duration. The meetings are held in Geneva (July and October/November) and in New York (March). Although most meetings are public, when the Committee considers individual communications, the meetings are "closed" to the public (Optional Protocol, article 5). The summary records of closed meetings remain confidential.

Generally, the Human Rights Committee tries to make decisions on communications by consensus, although formal decisions can be made by a majority. In cases where no consensus can be reached, or where a member wishes to explain his or her position in greater detail, the individual members may express their concurring or dissenting Views which are appended to the Committee's decision.

a) Special Rapporteur on New Communications

The Human Rights Committee has appointed, from among its members, a Special Rapporteur on New Communications. This is a position that was created by the Committee in 1989 to assist both the Secretariat and the Committee in dealing with cases at the preliminary stages. The responsibilities of the Special Rapporteur on New Communications are to:

- decide on the registration of cases;
- decide whether additional information is to be requested from the author prior to the Committee's consideration of the case;
- decide whether the examination of admissibility should be separated from that of the merits; and
- request states parties to take interim measures where they are warranted (Rule 86).

b) Case Rapporteur

Case rapporteurs are appointed at every session. They prepare draft recommendations on each case for the Working Group. The case rapporteur gives instructions to the Secretariat on how the decision is to be drafted and presents the draft to the Working Group and to the full Committee.

c) Working Group on Communications

The Committee has established a Working Group on Communications which meets for one week prior to every session and reviews all of the draft decisions prepared by case rapporteurs. The Working Group makes recommendations to the full Committee. The five-member Working Group can declare cases admissible if all five members agree. The Working Group may decide to join the issues of admissibility and the merits, and does so in almost all cases.

d) Special Rapporteur on Follow-up

The function of the Special Rapporteur on Follow-up of Views was established in 1990. The Rapporteur monitors compliance with the Committee's recommendations. The Rapporteur may visit the state party concerned to further the goal of implementation. The latter, however, has occurred only once in twelve years. The Rapporteur also conducts private meetings with state party representatives on an ad-hoc basis to encourage compliance with the Committee's Views.

See Diagram on pp. 60–61.

2. INDIVIDUAL COMPLAINTS PROCEDURE OF THE HUMAN RIGHTS COMMITTEE

The basic process for submitting a communication, outlined in Chapter 3, should be read together with the more specific information provided in relation to the Human Rights Committee.

a) Registration of the Communication and Preliminary Procedures

i) *Submission of the Communication*

A communication should be submitted to the Secretariat of the Office of the High Commissioner for Human Rights, Geneva in writing, by letter, fax or email. Fax or email communications must be confirmed by signed copies received by the Secretariat. Communications cannot be anonymous. The state that is the subject of the communication must be clearly identified. Although there is no mandatory format for communications, the use of model communication forms created by the Committee can streamline the communication process, and is advisable. (See Annex 1)

Of the thousands of general letters of complaint that arrive at the UN each year, only a small fraction are channelled to the Human Rights Committee by the UN secretariat. If the communication is not expressly addressed to the Human Rights Committee, it may not get there, or its receipt may be delayed.

Where the communication does not provide the necessary information in order for it to be registered, the secretariat may send a standardized form to the author and request that the communication be resubmitted providing all the information indicated on the form. Since the Committee relies heavily on the facts in each particular case, it is important to set out all the relevant information at the outset.

At a minimum, the following information should be included:

- the identity and contact information of the victim;
- the state against which the communication is directed;
- the provisions of the Covenant alleged to have been breached;
- all the relevant facts together with any supporting documentation (such as a statement signed by the victim, witness statements, court documents);
- steps taken to exhaust local remedies, or evidence why local remedies are ineffective, unavailable, or unreasonably prolonged;
- information regarding whether this matter is before any other procedure of international investigation or settlement; and
- the remedy requested.

Other important points:

• Languages

The Human Rights Committee's working languages are at present English, French, and Spanish. Although communications theoretically can be registered in any of the official languages of the UN (Arabic, Chinese, English, French, Russian, Spanish), there will likely be significant delays in the processing of the case if the author uses a language other than English, French or Spanish. Cases received in Russian are sent to translation once initially processed, sometimes at a considerable delay. Cases received in Arabic or Chinese are nor-

The Human Rights Committee Complaints Procedures

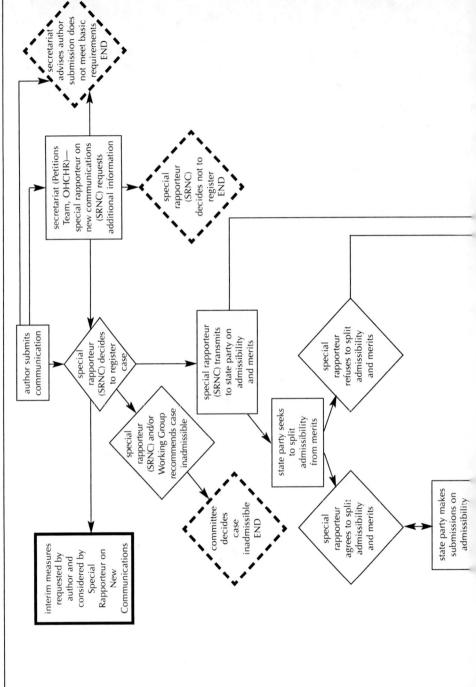

- author submits communication

- secretariat (Petitions Team, OHCHR)—special rapporteur on new communications (SRNC) requests additional information

- secretariat advises author submission does not meet basic requirements END

- special rapporteur (SRNC) decides to register case

- special rapporteur (SRNC) decides not to register END

- interim measures requested by author and considered by Special Rapporteur on New Communications

- special rapporteur (SRNC) and/or Working Group recommends case inadmissible

- special rapporteur (SRNC) transmits to state party on admissibility and merits

- committee decides case inadmissible END

- state party seeks to split admissibility from merits

- special rapporteur refuses to split admissibility and merits

- special rapporteur agrees to split admissibility and merits

- state party makes submissions on admissibility

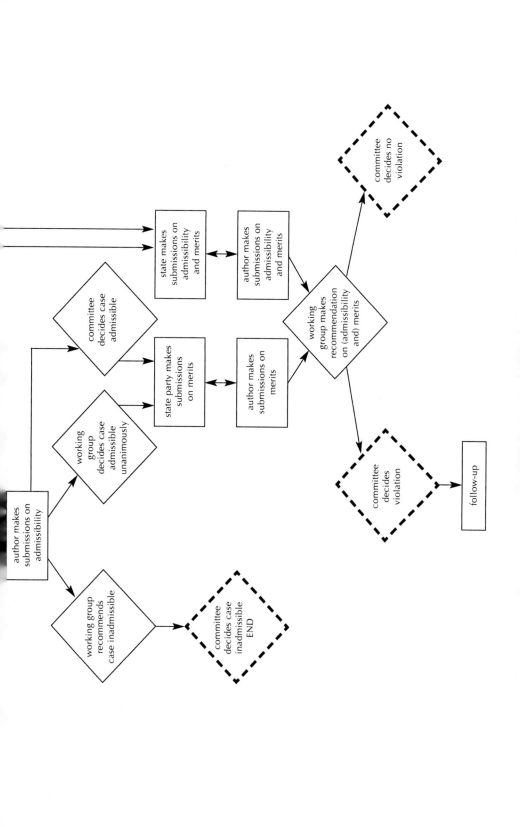

mally returned to the author who is requested to resubmit in English, French or Spanish. If a communication is received in a non-UN official language, the author will normally receive at the outset a letter requesting the re-submission of the communication in English, French or Spanish. If it happens that a communication has been submitted in an additional language which a UN secretariat member servicing the Committee understands, it may be processed initially without translation. Authors are strongly advised to submit communications in English, French or Spanish.

• Time Limitations

There is no time limit within which to bring a claim, but very long delays in bringing the claim may be considered by the Human Rights Committee to be an abuse of the right of submission. The Human Rights Committee requires that a 'convincing' or 'reasonable' explanation be given to justify a significant delay in bringing a communication in order to avoid the finding of an abuse of the right of submission.

• Legal Aid

The UN does not provide legal aid or financial assistance to authors, nor does the Optional Protocol require that states parties provide legal aid where an individual wishes to submit a communication. Authors should determine whether or not their own domestic legal aid system voluntarily provides for the possibility of legal aid.

However, NGOs and other legal professionals are allowed to represent the victims. Victims are encouraged to seek assistance from NGOs or legal professionals, or to appoint them as representatives, so as to focus their claims and facilitate the Committee's examination.

• Withdrawal of the Communication

An author may subsequently withdraw his or her communication.

The Committee normally accepts the withdrawal, but if there is an indication there might have been external pressure to do so, the Committee will try to ascertain whether withdrawal was the result of undue pressure by the state or other threats.

• Confidentiality

All documents relating to a communication are confidential and the Human Rights Committee does not publicize cases, except by the eventual release of a decision. However, the author and the state party may make public 'any submissions or information bearing on the proceedings,' provided that the Committee does not expressly ask them to refrain from doing so. At all times, the Committee may decide that certain elements of the case must remain confidential. This relates especially, but not exclusively, to the identity of the author.

Decisions concerning inadmissibility, discontinuation or merits (Views) will be made public. A discontinuance may be made public by number without divulging the name of the author or victim. Decisions concerning interim measures are also made public. With respect to follow-up information concerning the Committee's Views received from the author or the state party, everything is in principle within the public domain.

ii) Registration of the Communication

All communications are initially reviewed by the UN Secretariat servicing the Committee prior to their registration. The secretariat must bring to the attention of the Committee all communications which are, or appear to be, submitted for the consideration of the Committee. In practice, the Secretariat may wait to do so until further information is requested and obtained from the author.

The secretariat may ask the author for clarification regarding any or all of the following issues (Rule 80):

- Name, address, place and date of birth, and occupation of the author;
- The state against which the communication is directed;
- The object of the communication;
- The precise ICCPR provision which is being invoked;
- Clarification about the facts of the claim;
- Information about which local or domestic remedies have been used;
- Information about other international procedures that have been used;
- Medical or other records where relevant.

The Secretariat will indicate a time limit for replying to such requests (Rule 80), but strict sanctions are not applied when this limit is not met. Failure to provide adequate information necessary to register a case, may result in a communication not being registered. A decision to register a case may be made pending the response to questions for additional information.

Once a communication appears to contain sufficient information required for registration, the Secretariat forwards a summary to the Special Rapporteur on New Communications who will decide whether or not to register the case. If the Special Rapporteur determines that there are genuine issues as to a violation of the ICCPR, the case will be registered and added to the Committee's list of registered cases. The Special Rapporteur will not register cases that manifestly do not meet the admissibility criteria set out in the Optional Protocol and elaborated in the Rules of Procedure of the Committee.

If the Special Rapporteur finds that there are no real issues in the case or that it clearly does not meet admissibility criteria, then the communication is not registered and the author is informed of the decision not to register. Generally, this ends the case. However, a decision of the Special Rapporteur not to register a case is not final in the sense that the author of the communication may insist that the case be registered and the practice is for the Special Rapporteur to comply. In these circumstances, however, the Special Rapporteur will usually send the communication directly to the Committee with a recommendation that the case be declared inadmissible. The recommendation not to address the case on the merits will normally be adopted by the Committee.

In order to expedite the registration process, authors should consider submitting a summary of their case (limited to about 5 pages) along with the full argument and supporting documentation.

iii) *Transmittal to the State Party*

If the Special Rapporteur believes that the communication is likely to be admissible, then he or she will transmit the case to the state party and request submissions on both the issues of admissibility and merits. A state party may object to the two issues being determined simultaneously and may request that the issue of admissibility be dealt with separately and resolved by the Committee, before a consideration of the merits. The Special Rapporteur has authority to separate the two issues. The Special Rapporteur may refuse a request by the state party to separate the admissibility and the merits and insist on a state party response to both. The normal practice of the Committee is to consider the issues simultaneously in order to avoid delay. Most states parties agree to the Committee's request to consider the two issues together.

iv) *Interim Measures*

The Special Rapporteur on New Communications will also review the communication to decide whether or not to make a request for interim measures. Interim measures are measures taken in the interim between the receipt of the case and its final determination. The Special Rapporteur may decide to ask a state to take urgent measures in order to avoid irreparable damage to the author prior to a final decision being taken. These types of requests are made in emergency situations (for example, the claimant is on death row awaiting imminent execution, or faces imminent expulsion or extradition to a state where he may be tortured). The Human Rights Committee expressly states that these requests do not mean that the communication will result in a finding of a violation by the state of Covenant rights. In half of the cases to date the Committee eventually finds no violation. The point of interim measures is to avoid harmful and irreparable outcomes prior to the Committee's ability to reach a final conclusion.

Interim measures may be requested before or after a decision has been made about the admissibility of the case. In some cases, interim measures may be requested from a State even in order to allow a person to complete the filing of a claim before the Committee.

b) Admissibility and Submissions from the Parties

After a communication is registered, the case is handled by the Secretariat until it is ripe for decision. Only when the case has been fully prepared will a Committee member be appointed as a case rapporteur. The Rapporteur's task is to study the case and all supporting documents closely and provide the Working Group, and later the Committee, with a draft decision of the case on both admissibility and merits. The Rapporteur usually sits on the Working Group, but if he or she is absent, another member of the Working Group may present the Rapporteur's draft. The Working Group does not always agree with the Rapporteur's recommendations and may make a different recommendation to the plenary, which in turn, is free to disagree with the Working Group's recommendation. The Working Group on Communications will make an initial evaluation of admissibility. It is possible for the Working Group to recommend to the plenary that a case be dismissed as inadmissible without requesting comments from the state party.

A frequent ground of inadmissibility is article 2 of the Protocol which states that authors must "claim that . . . their rights enumerated in the Covenant have been violated." The Rules of Procedure interpret this to mean that an individual must claim "in a manner sufficiently substantiated, to be a victim of a violation . . . of the rights set forth in the Covenant." In other words, a case must sufficiently substantiate that a right has been violated for the purposes of admissibility. In practice, this criterion serves a similar function to the "manifestly ill-founded" criteria of the European Convention on Human Rights system.

Another important ground of inadmissibility, the requirement that domestic remedies be exhausted, is frequently misunderstood. The exhaustion of domestic remedies condition may be satisfied, not by the existence or use of domestic proceedings, but by the fact that they are ineffective, unavailable, or unreasonably prolonged. According to the jurisprudence of the Human Rights Committee the rule of exhaustion of domestic remedies "applies only to the extent that those remedies are effective and available" and not "unreasonably prolonged."

In the case where admissibility and merits have been separated, and the Working Group unanimously decides that the case is admissible, it will inform the state party of its decision and the state party will then be required to make submissions on the merits. The Working Group is empowered to declare communications admissible if all five of its members unanimously so decide. A recommendation on inadmissibility, however, must be reviewed by the Committee in plenary. A formal written decision will be adopted declaring the communication inadmissible, including the reasons for such a decision. This ends the case.

If the Working Group cannot reach unanimity on the admissibility of the case, it will forward the case to the Committee as a whole, which will then decide the issue. If at this stage the Committee considers the case to be inadmissible, this will be a final decision. A formal written decision will be adopted declaring the communication inadmissible, including the reasons for such a decision. This ends the case.

Once the state party is sent a written request from the Committee on both the admissibility of the communication and on the merits, article 4 of the Optional Protocol requires that the state party respond within six months. The author is subsequently sent the state party's response and given the opportunity to respond to the state's submissions within two months. Subsequently, the author's comments are sent to the state party and further submissions are permitted. The Committee's practice permits the exchange to continue, but it does not encourage a limitless number of rounds. After the first round each party's submission is transmitted to the other party "for information." Of course, the other party may—and often does—react to the submission, thus resulting in a back and forth exchange of submissions. The Committee, however, determines at some point that it has enough information to proceed to a decision on the merits. The Committee will not rely on one party's information unless the other party has received it and has had the opportunity to comment thereon. Time limits for states and for authors are not strictly adhered to, which tends to lengthen significantly the overall process. The Committee may, in the future, change its practice and demand that the parties respect the deadlines or risk that their submission will not be accepted.

If the state party does not submit replies, then it will be perceived to have accepted the admissibility of the case. On the merits, the absence of a state response is viewed very negatively by the Committee, and may result in a finding of a violation of Covenant rights.

c) Determination of the Merits and Follow-up

When all arguments on both the admissibility and merits of the case have been submitted, the submissions are considered by the Working Group on Communications. The Working Group will make recommendations to the Committee as to an appropriate disposition of the case. The Committee as a whole will then take the final decision. A decision that the communication is inadmissible ends the case and the Committee does not go on to consider the merits of the communication. If the Committee decides that the communication is admissible, then it will go on to make a decision on the merits of the communication and will find either that there is, or is not, a violation of a treaty right.

The final decision may set out a specific remedy, but often leaves the determination of the remedy to the state party. The Committee may recommend, for example, compensation, amending legislation, a new trial, commutation of a sentence of death, or release from police custody. Authors of communications should include a request for a specific remedy in the initial complaint, although the Committee may choose to leave the matter open to the state party, and simply recommend that the state party grant an "appropriate remedy."

If the Committee finds that a person's rights have been violated, the Committee will request the state to inform them within 90 days (from the date of the "note verbale" transmitting the decision) of the remedy provided to the victim.

The Committee has appointed one of its members as Special Rapporteur on Follow-up (of Views). The Rapporteur on Follow-up is responsible for monitoring the responses of states parties to the Committee's request for information on the remedy provided. He or she will also meet at each session with representatives of selected states parties that have not responded positively to the Committee's request. The Annual Reports of the Committee contain information from the Rapporteur on state responses and these meetings. On one occasion, the Rapporteur has visited a state party in the course of follow-up activities, although their report on the mission was not made public.

Other important points:

- ### Annual Report
  The Human Rights Committee publishes an Annual Report which contains information on the number of cases pending before it and all the Views and inadmissibility decisions adopted during that annual reporting cycle. The Committee will also indicate the number of cases it has found admissible or has discontinued during its sessions that cycle.

  Before publication of the Annual Report, the final Views on individual communications may already be posted online.

- ### Reservations
  Reservations to the ICCPR or the Optional Protocol may substantially limit the ability of an individual to successfully make a case against a particular state party. It is, therefore, necessary to check the reservations made by the state party.

  At the same time, some reservations may not be legitimate, that is, they may be incompatible with the object and purpose of the treaty. In these cases, it is possible that the treaty body will refuse to apply the reservation in a manner which would limit the application of the ICCPR or the Optional Protocol in the context of a communication. Where reservations would potentially affect the communication, it is also important to check prior comments of the Committee which may have been made on the compatibility of the reservation with the object and purpose of the treaty. The Human Rights Committee has directly told some states parties, in the course of considering state reports, their views as to whether a reservation is incompatible with the object and purpose of the Covenant.

Reservations to the Optional Protocol concerning the prior examination of the complaint by another international procedure of investigation or settlement may or may not preclude the Committee's competence, since the Covenant may provide for rights not justiciable under the other procedure. Moreover, if a case is declared inadmissible by another body on the grounds of late submission, it is not deemed to have been examined and the reservation would not apply.

• **Individual opinions**
Members of the Committee can append their individual concurring or dissenting opinions to the Committee's Views. Sometimes these opinions are more revealing of the Committee's actual rationale than the majority opinion, which may have been reduced to a brief common denominator so as to reach a compromise on the reasoning or the result. Individual opinions are a source of legal reasoning that may point to the direction of the Committee's jurisprudence in future cases.

3. EXAMPLES OF HUMAN RIGHTS COMMITTEE CASES

The Human Rights Committee has developed a body of case law which interprets and applies Covenant rights. The prior decisions of the Committee are a valuable tool in advancing a case, since the Committee will attempt to be consistent in its interpretation of the substantive rights in the ICCPR.

Below is a sample of the types of cases decided by the Human Rights Committee. *This list is not exhaustive*, and the Committee is continually being asked to make decisions in different types of cases. Under the Optional Protocol, the Committee considers violations of the provisions in Part III of the Covenant (articles 6–27), whereas the provisions in Parts I and II are deemed general undertakings by states parties, not directly invocable under the Optional Protocol.

• *Right to self-determination (article 1)*
The Human Rights Committee has decided that the right to self-determination is not "justiciable." In other words, it cannot be the subject of a claim or decision by the Committee, on the ground that this is a group right and that an individual cannot claim to be a victim of a violation of such a right. On the other hand, self-determination issues are often discussed in the context of minority rights (article 27).

• *Right to a remedy (article 2)*
States parties must ensure the rights in the Covenant to all persons under their jurisdiction. This right cannot be invoked autonomously, or on its own, by an individual. Nevertheless, the Committee fre-

quently makes findings of violations of "article 14, in conjunction with article 2," or of "article 26, in conjunction with article 2," when it wants to emphasize that the state has failed to ensure a remedy for a violation of Covenant rights.

• *Equality of men and women (article 3)*
The Committee has made findings of violation of article 3 in conjunction with article 26, but not of article 3 alone.

• *Derogation (article 4)*
States may derogate in times of national emergency, and only for limited periods of time, from certain Covenant rights. The UN Secretary General must be officially notified of a derogation.

• *Most favourable law and practice (article 5)*
A state party must apply the most favourable law to an individual and cannot misuse the Covenant to limit enjoyment of rights under national law.

• *Right to life (article 6)*

• **Killings during police action**—The Human Rights Committee has considered many cases where the killing of individuals by police or other state actors could not be justified as self-defence or for any other legitimate purpose. Even if killings by state actors are considered to be lawful actions under the domestic law of that state, the Human Rights Committee will scrutinize the situation in order to determine whether the killings were proportionate to the requirements of law enforcement. The Committee takes the position that if killings are lawful, where the use of force is disproportionate, the domestic law has not adequately protected the right to life, and the victims' right to life has therefore been violated.

• **Killings while in detention**—Many cases have been brought to the Committee involving deaths while in detention by police or in prisons. When the Human Rights Committee finds that the use of lethal force cannot be justified under the circumstances, a violation of the right to life will be found. States are said to have a duty to protect persons in their custody and take effective measures for that purpose.

• **Duty to investigate killings by state actors**—States not only have a duty to protect the right to life, they also have a duty to investigate who is responsible for the death of an individual, for example, unexplained deaths in police custody or in prisons, and to pay compensation to the family of the victim. A similar duty of investigation exists in cases of 'disappearances,' where there is evidence to suggest state involvement.

States have an obligation to punish the perpetrators of extra-judicial or illegal killings by state actors. If domestic legislation does not provide for adequate penalties, this will be held to be a failure to protect the right to life.

- **Attempted killings**—Attempts on the life of an individual, even if unsuccessful, carried out by state agents also entail a violation of article 6.

- **Killings or attempted killings by non-state actors**—Killings or attempted killings by non-state actors, such as paramilitary forces, whose actions cannot be directly imputed to the state, do not constitute a violation of article 6. They may, however, entail a violation of article 9, paragraph 1, security of the person.

- **Death penalty cases**—The ICCPR does not prohibit the imposition of the death penalty, although this is prohibited by the Second Optional Protocol which must be separately ratified to take effect with respect to a particular state. Nevertheless, the Human Rights Committee has found that the imposition of the death penalty entails a violation of the right to life in certain circumstances, including:
  - The death penalty may only be imposed for the "most serious crimes" (article 6(2)). The Committee has limited the meaning of "most serious crimes" to crimes such as those that involve the infliction (or attempted infliction) of death or serious injury to other human beings. Capital offences, according to the domestic laws of some states parties, such as drug offences, robbery, crimes against property, apostasy or adultery, do not justify the imposition of capital punishment, and the imposition itself would entail a violation of article 6.
  - Mandatory death sentences for certain crimes without consideration of mitigating circumstances.
  - The imposition of the death penalty against minors (under 18) or pregnant women is prohibited by article 6(5) of the ICCPR.
  - Extradition to a country which still has the death penalty is not a violation of the right to life, even if the extraditing country has itself abolished capital punishment. However, the Human Rights Committee has held that if the method of execution may amount to a violation of article 7 (torture, cruel or inhuman punishment), extradition is prohibited.
  - In many cases, the Human Rights Committee has held that where a trial resulting in the imposition of the death penalty does not meet the requirements of a fair trial under article

14, a violation of the right to life also occurs by virtue of the imposition of the sentence regardless of the actual execution. In these cases, it is not sufficient for individuals to allege their innocence; they must establish that they have had an unfair trial.

- **Duty to prevent deaths**—States must adequately train, equip and regulate police forces in order to protect the life of citizens during police action. States are responsible for the lives of those persons they hold in detention. Therefore, they have a positive duty to ensure that detained people do not die while under detention, and to take measures to avoid and prevent suicide.

  Although states are not responsible for killings by non-state actors, a state will be held to violate the right to life if they do not take adequate measures to prevent and punish killings by private actors. This duty also requires criminalizing all forms of killings including the deliberate refusal of help to persons in serious danger.

- **Abortion and euthanasia**—The Human Rights Committee has not examined cases of abortion or euthanasia under the Optional Protocol. In its concluding observations, it has criticized states for laws permitting euthanasia. On the other hand, it has not held abortion to be a violation of the right to life and has criticized certain anti-abortion legislation.

- *Freedom from torture and cruel, inhuman or degrading treatment or punishment (article 7)*

  - **Torture by state agents**—Numerous cases have been successfully brought concerning torture, cruel, inhuman or degrading treatment or punishment. Apart from the actual physical infliction of pain, the infliction of mental distress or fear (for example, mock executions, threats against family), humiliation, and the refusal of medical care in some circumstances can also amount to torture.

  - **Time spent on death row/Death row phenomenon**—The Human Rights Committee does not recognise the time spent on death row in itself as a violation of article 7. A violation of article 7 has been found in rare cases involving very prolonged periods of detention on death row that were attributable to the state, and in which there were harsh living conditions.

  - **Death cell detention**—Distinct from death row detention is the detention of a person in a death cell immediately before execution. If a person is detained in such a cell for an unreasonably long period, this can violate article 7.

- **Method of execution of death penalty**—The Human Rights Committee has accepted that certain methods of execution can amount to torture, cruel, inhuman or degrading treatment and that others do not. For example, death by gas asphyxiation is a violation of article 7, whereas death by lethal injection does not violate article 7. Public executions or lapidation (stoning) may amount to degrading treatment or punishment, but no such cases have yet been decided.

- **Extradition and non-refoulement/return**—States are not allowed to extradite or return persons to another country where they run the risk of being tortured. The issue of non-refoulement arises with respect to asylum seekers whose applications for refugee status have been unsuccessful. Although the Committee cannot decide the asylum question, it has said that the Covenant requires the protection of an individual from the risk of torture. (To date, most of these cases have been brought to the Committee Against Torture.)

- **Medical experimentation**—One author has claimed that he was subjected to medical and pharmacological experiments during detention, and that he was subjected to torture and ill-treatment. A violation of article 7 was found without, however, elaborating on the alleged medical experimentation.

- **Corporal punishment**—Corporal punishment is prohibited under article 7, and criminal penalties involving corporal punishment, such as whipping, have been held to violate article 7.

- **Conditions of detention**—There have been cases where article 7 has been violated because of appalling prison conditions. This may relate directly to the physical conditions (such as very confined spaces, too many persons in one cell) or the way the detainee is treated. A person should be allowed to have sufficient contact with other human beings and be afforded a minimal level of respect by the guards. Note that poor living conditions in themselves do not necessarily amount to a violation of article 7, but rather fall under article 10.

- **Incommunicado detention**—Incommunicado detention of a person or denial of contact with anyone outside of the prison (including family, friends or lawyers) can amount to cruel and degrading treatment if it is for prolonged periods of time. Very long periods of solitary confinement (several years) have also been found to breach article 7.

- **Duty to investigate, prosecute and punish violators of article 7**—There is a duty upon the state to investigate all allegations of torture, cruel, inhuman or degrading treatment and provide for adequate penalties against the perpetrators. A state must also provide remedies and compensation to victims of torture.

- ***Prohibition of slavery, servitude and forced labour (article 8)*** So far, no cases have been successfully brought under the prohibition of slavery. Attempts have been made to subsume the right of conscientious objection under the prohibition of forced labour, but this argument has not been successful.

- ***Liberty and security of the person, including the prohibition of arbitrary arrest or detention (article 9(1))***

  - **Security of the person**—The right to security of the person is independent from the issue of liberty of the person and has to be guaranteed as such. Persons who are in real danger must be protected by the state. For example, a state was found to violate article 9 because it failed to take appropriate measures to ensure the security of a person who had received death threats. Arguably, if the state is aware of serious situations of domestic violence and abstains from interfering, this will also be a violation of article 9.

    States must also protect individuals against threats made by officials. Consequently, a state was held to have violated article 9 by not investigating the shooting from behind of a person during an arrest.

  - **Liberty of the person**—The right to liberty does not only apply to cases of criminal detention. Liberty also includes detention in the context of immigration, psychiatric institutions and military discipline. Other kinds of limitations on the freedom of movement, such as the prohibition to leave a certain geographical area do not amount to a deprivation of liberty in this sense (see article 12).

  - **The legality or arbitrariness of the deprivation of liberty**— There must be a legal basis for any deprivation of liberty, which may not be arbitrary in form or application. The Human Rights Committee has held this requirement to mean that detention must not only be lawful, but also necessary and reasonable. Even if the initial arrest is not arbitrary or unreasonable, the duration of the detention subsequently can be arbitrary. Hence, cases where persons were kept in prison after they had finished their sentence were found to be violations of article 9. If the purpose of the detention is illegal or arbitrary, even very short periods of detention are prohibited.

The detention of undocumented aliens and persons seeking refugee status is not in itself arbitrary, but the detention must be justified and the duration of the detention cannot be unreasonably long.

Detention in a mental institution has also been before the Human Rights Committee as a claim under article 9, although the Committee found no violation of article 9 in the particular case. The detention was justified on the basis of several reports of psychiatrists.

Detention of persons because of the danger they pose to society has not as such been found to be a violation of article 9.

- **Rights upon arrest or detention (articles 9(2), 9(3), 9(4))**

  - **Right to be informed of the reason for the arrest (at the time of arrest) (article 9 (2))**—Providing reasons for arrest is not identical to informing the accused of the precise criminal charges. However, article 9(2) requires that the accused also be "promptly" informed of any charges against him or her. Failure by the state to provide reasons for any deprivation of liberty is a violation of article 9(2). Even if no charges have already been brought, pending the police investigation, people held in remand have the right to know why they are kept in custody. These reasons must be given immediately, although the shortest period which has been found to be a violation was seven days. However, in cases where the author was undoubtedly aware of the reasons (for example, because he or she was present during a house search and drugs were found), it is accepted that he or she is aware of the reasons, even if the charges still have to be specified.

    Cases have also been brought because the arrested person allegedly did not understand the language and no competent interpreter was provided.

  - **Right to be brought promptly before a judicial officer (article 9(3))**—Although there is no specific time limit that is deemed unacceptable, the Committee has found delays of five days or more to be in violation of article 9(3). The independence and impartiality of the "judicial officer" has also been challenged and found to be a breach of article 9(3) where the arrested person was only brought before the public prosecutor, and not an impartial judicial officer.

  - **Trial within a reasonable time or release (article 9(3))**—Article 9(3) refers to the period of detention of an accused before a criminal trial. Article 14(3)(c) refers to the period of time between the laying of the charges and the trial, regardless of whether the person is in detention or not. Violations of article 14(3)(c) will also be violations of article 9(3) where the accused is in pre-trial detention.

Although the reasonable time requirement differs from case to case, (depending, for example, on the seriousness of the crime and the likelihood of escape or danger to society), states must give adequate reasons for long delays. Detention without bail must be justified, for example, when it is feared that the person will tamper with the evidence, intimidate witnesses or escape the jurisdiction. Budgetary restrictions, or administrative arguments, have not been accepted by the Committee as sufficient justification. The behaviour of the accused, or the conduct of the accused's defence, will be taken into consideration to determine the reasonableness of the duration of detention.

- **Right to take proceedings before a court to have the lawfulness of an arrest or detention determined without delay (article 9(4))**—This is a right of the detained person to initiate proceedings (*habeas corpus*). If the detainee fails to seek review of detention or arrest, the state is not responsible to initiate such proceedings.

- **Review of lawfulness of detention to be determined without delay (article 9(4))**—The delay experienced awaiting a judicial decision on the lawfulness of detention will be judged on a case-by-case basis. Periods of delay of as little as three days have been found to violate article 9(4), but in another case, a delay of three months after an appeal was brought was not found to be incompatible in itself. It is the state's responsibility to give reasons for the delay.

  Detainees have the right to have the lawfulness of their detention reviewed on a regular basis.

- **Effective exercise of the right of review**—The Committee has linked the right to review of detention under article 9(4) with the right to have legal representation (article 14). However, it has been held that there is no violation of the ICCPR where a detainee was moved to several different places of detention and was thus forced to seek different legal representatives each time.

  Persons held incommunicado cannot exercise their right to review, so prolonged periods of incommunicado detention amount to a breach of article 9(4). For example, five days of incommunicado detention has been held to be a violation.

- **Review before a "court"**—Situations where a detained person only has access to a real court on appeal violates article 9(4) because this article requires access to a court without delay. A prior appearance before another authority only delays this right.

- **Military discipline**—Disciplinary sanctions against military personnel depriving them of their liberty to an extent that cannot be considered to fall within the normal requirements of military discipline also falls under the requirement of article 9(4). Review of such sanctions by a superior officer does not fulfil the requirement of a court review.

- **A court must exercise real review**—When the review of the court is found to be only formal, with no real possibility for the judge to determine the lawfulness of the detention, the state has not guaranteed the right to review.

- ***Right to compensation for unlawful detention (article 9(5))***

When it is established that the detention was unlawful, the individual has a right to receive compensation. This applies to all aspects of the rights guaranteed under article 9.

- ***Rights of prisoners (article 10)***

  - **Right to adequate food, basic medical care and decent sanitary facilities**—The Committee has held that prisoners have a right to adequate food, basic medical care and decent sanitary facilities, as well as minimal recreational facilities (for example, being allowed out of the cell for a minimum period of time each day). It is unacceptable under article 10(1) for a prisoner to become ill due to the prison conditions and especially the lack of medical care. Prisoners also have a right to have a bed or mattress to sleep on. The Committee has accepted the UN Standard Minimum Rules for the Treatment of Prisoners (adopted by the United Nations Congress on the Prevention of Crime and the Treatment of Offenders, held at Geneva in 1955, and approved by the Economic and Social Council by its resolution 663 C (XXIV) of 31 July 1957 and 2076 (LXII) of 13 May 1977) as the minimum standard, and will consider lower standards of treatment or detention to be in violation of article 10(1). It makes reference to these Rules in decisions under the Optional Protocol.

  - **Incommunicado detention**—Very long periods of incommunicado detention have been found to amount to violations of article 7 (torture). However, shorter periods of incommunicado detention can amount to a violation of article 10(1). Periods of incommunicado detention as short as 15 days have been held by the Committee to violate article 10(1). There is no set minimum or maximum time period which will amount to a violation. The Committee makes its decisions on a case-by-case basis.

Prisoners have a general right to communicate with family and friends under article 10(1), and only justifiable restrictions are allowed.

- **Time spent on death row/Death row phenomenon**—The Committee has not found the time spent on death row in itself to amount to a violation of article 10.

- **Segregation of accused from convicted prisoners**—The requirement to segregate convicted from unconvicted persons is considered to be met when accused persons are kept in a separate part of the building. Occasional contacts with convicted persons does not violate article 10, paragraph 2.

- **Segregation of juvenile prisoners from adults**—A juvenile means a person below the age of 18. A case on this issue has not yet been decided.

- *Freedom of movement (article 12)*

  - **Freedom of movement within the territory of a state**—Restrictions to enter one's home province, district or village are prohibited, unless justified for public order.

  - **Asylum seekers who are lawfully within the territory**—The state can restrict freedom of movement, but only on a case-by-case basis. Blanket restrictions on refugees' freedom of movement are prohibited.

  - **Freedom of choice of residence**—The Committee has held that this right may be restricted to certain ethnic or minority groups. The issue has been discussed mostly in the context of state party reports, but in one case the Committee recognized the right of a member of an indigenous group to live in a particular locality.

  - **Freedom to leave**—In several cases, it has been determined that the state has an obligation to provide its citizens with passports, even if they reside outside of the country. However, exceptions have been found to include situations where the citizen had not performed required military service. The Committee has also indicated that the right of women to leave the country may not be restricted by the requirement of the consent of her husband.

- **Right to enter one's own country**—This right, stipulated in paragraph 4 of article 12, applies not only to nationals of a country, but also to persons who have "special ties" to the country and cannot be considered mere aliens. This right means that a person may not be expelled from a country if he or she has a claim that it is "his own country," even if technically he or she is an alien.

- ***Rights of aliens (article 13)***
The Committee has confined the rights under article 13 mostly to procedural guarantees. Moreover, the Committee has shown great deference for states' invocation of security reasons. There is no right to asylum under the Covenant, but a person has a right to due process in determining whether he or she should be expelled.

- ***Right to a fair and public hearing (article 14)***

  - **Procedural rights**—The right to a fair and public hearing is in essence a procedural one. The Committee examines the procedural fairness of the trial only, not the fairness of the outcome. Complaints about bias of judges, or an incorrect evaluation of the facts, have usually not been accepted by the Committee. In the context of a right to a fair and public hearing, the Committee will not review the facts of a case and decide for itself what occurred (in place of an existing determination of the facts by a domestic court). In exceptional cases, a domestic court's decision has been corrected because it was blatantly irreconcilable with proven facts, but such cases remain exceptional.

    Complaints about procedural fairness generally must have been raised in the original trial court (or court of "first instance"), or on appeal, in order for the Committee to consider the issue of procedural fairness on the merits.

    The right to a public hearing has not been interpreted as always giving a right to an oral hearing.

  - **Civil /non-criminal proceedings (article 14(1))**—The right to a fair and public hearing applies not only to criminal cases, but also to non-criminal proceedings. The concept of a 'suit at law' is based on the nature of the right in question, rather than the status of the parties and includes civil claims between private parties as well as claims against public authorities. But the alleged violation must be imputable to the state party and not to a private adversary in a civil dispute.

- **Competent, independent, and impartial tribunal**—In clear cases of government influence over the judiciary, the Committee has found that an individual was denied access to an independent court. Trials by anonymous or "faceless" judges are also a violation of article 14.

- **Right to be presumed innocent until proven guilty (article 14(2))**—This right does not apply in civil proceedings.

- **Right to be informed of the nature and cause of the charge (article 14(3)(a))**—As soon as the authorities decide to prosecute someone, they must formally inform the individual of the law and the alleged facts.

- **Right to have adequate time and facilities to prepare a defence (article 14(3)(b))**—The Committee examines the facts of each case and the behaviour of the author to determine whether sufficient time was available to prepare a meaningful defence. When the state withholds certain evidence or information, this will violate the right to adequate facilities to prepare a defence. However, there is no right to have all documents translated into the defendant's language when he or she has the assistance of a lawyer who understands the language of the proceedings and the documents.

- **Right to be tried without undue delay (article 14(3)(c))**—The Committee proceeds on a case-by-case basis, and will take into account the nature of the alleged crime and the behaviour of the author as well as the state. There is no set time that is considered either to be reasonable or unreasonable. In some cases, the Committee expected the author to prove that the trial could have been held earlier, whereas in other cases it has asked the state to explain why there was a long delay. Economic and financial difficulties do not excuse long delays, nor does judicial backlog.

- **Right to be present at the trial and defend oneself; and to have legal assistance, in certain circumstances, paid for by the state (article 14(3)(d))**—In absentia trials are permitted if the defendant was duly notified and informed about the trial but failed to show up. In such cases, there may be a right to demand a retrial.

  It is impermissible to force a defendant to take a specific lawyer, or choose among a limited list, when the defendant has indicated that he or she was appointing a specific lawyer of his or her own choice. Individuals also have a right to defend themselves without assistance of a lawyer.

The right to legal aid is not absolute and applies only in criminal cases.

The right to have legal aid extends beyond the trial to the appellate level. Cases have been successfully brought where convicted persons wanted to challenge the validity of their conviction on appeal or before their constitutional court. The Committee has not applied the right to legal aid to appeals that clearly have no merit, although this does not apply to capital punishment cases.

If the state appoints a free lawyer for the accused, that lawyer must be qualified and competent to handle the case.

- **Right to examine hostile witnesses, and obtain and examine own witnesses (article 14(3)(e))**—It is for the author to establish that this right was violated by a refusal of the courts to allow an examination of a certain witness.

- **Right to have the free assistance of an interpreter, if necessary (article 14(3)(f))**—This right has been interpreted narrowly. If the defendant is capable of understanding the language of the trial and can express himself or herself in that language, there is no right to have an interpreter.

- **Right to have a conviction reviewed by a higher tribunal (article 14(5))**—This right applies only to persons convicted of a crime. The Committee has interpreted the right of review to mean a full review. It requires that there be the opportunity for an appellate court to re-evaluate both the evidence and the law, and also include a review of the sentence. The admissibility of new evidence at appeal may be restricted, however, when the evidence was already available during the trial at first instance.

- **Right to compensation in case of miscarriage of justice (article 14(6))**—This applies only when a conviction has been reversed, or a person convicted has been pardoned, on the ground that a newly discovered fact showed there was a miscarriage of justice.

- **Right not to be tried twice for the same offence (article 14(7))**—The prohibition on trying a person twice for the same crime has not been applied to trials that take place in different states.

- **_Non-retrospectivity (article 15)_**

An accused person shall benefit from an amendment to the law providing for a lighter penalty. Article 15 only applies to penalties and not to other measures that may be imposed by a court, such as mandatory supervision. Parole conditions may be considered as penalties.

- *Interference with privacy, family, correspondence and reputation (article 17)*

  - **Privacy**—The Committee has not given an expanded definition of what is meant by "privacy," but it has been held to include aspects of one's identity such as one's name and the right to change it. The right to privacy has been held to protect burial sites of indigenous peoples.

  - **Protection of family and home**—These are concepts that have to be interpreted on the facts of each case and taking into consideration the prevailing concepts of the culture in question. The workplace has been included under the concept "home." The Committee takes a broad interpretation of the concept of family so as to encompass the large meaning prevalent in certain cultures.

  - **Protection of correspondence**—Censorship of correspondence must be prohibited by law and any interference with correspondence must be subject to sufficient legal safeguards. Prisoners have a right to correspond with family and friends, under reasonable supervision.

  - **Protection of honour and reputation**—The state must ensure that its laws provide sufficient means for a person to defend himself or herself against unlawful attacks. This also means that when someone's honour is attacked by a lawful exercise of authority (for example, disclosure of certain information during official proceedings), this will not violate article 17. Libel campaigns by the media at the instigation of the government are prohibited.

  - **Right to privacy—sexual orientation**—The Committee has condemned domestic laws which criminalize homosexuality.

  - **Protection of data**—Although no cases have been decided on this issue, the Committee has indicated that collection and storage of data must be regulated by law, and that individuals must have access to the information that is kept about them and have a right to correct inaccuracies.

- *Freedom of thought, conscience and religion (article 18)*
Although the Committee has interpreted the freedom of thought and religion broadly and has included atheists, it has shown little willingness to allow exceptions from legal obligations on the basis of religious prescriptions. Limitations based upon public health and safety, public order and public morals have been successfully used

to refuse such exceptions. Limitations on the manifestation of religion are possible in certain conditions.

- **Right to conscientious objection**—The right to conscientious objection has not been recognized as such. However, when a state does recognize such a right, the Committee will determine whether there are too many obstacles to effectively exercise it. Moral or religious objections against the use of violence have not been accepted as a ground to refuse paying part of one's taxes (for example, destined for the defence budget).

- **Religious education**—Compulsory religious or moral education does not violate article 18 as long as it is not doctrinal and provides for a pluralistic view.

- *Freedom of opinion and expression (article 19)*

The freedom to hold an opinion is absolute, but the freedom to express that opinion is not. Both verbal and non-verbal expression are protected. The ICCPR itself provides limits, and the Committee has also expressed its views on the limits of expression. For example, demolishing property during a protest is not protected expression. Limitations are permissible in as far as they are prescribed in law to protect the rights and reputation of others, national security, public order, public health or morals, but only if the restrictions are proportionate to the value that is sought to be protected.

In this context, the Committee does not espouse one standard of morals or values, but examines the prevailing opinion in the state in question. Thus, in some countries but not in others, the Committee may accept bans on pornography as acceptable limits to expression.

The Committee has also decided several cases involving the prohibition of languages other than the official language as a violation of the freedom of expression.

- *Prohibition on hate speech (article 20)*

The right of freedom of expression does not extend to persons inciting racial hatred, antisemitism or to Holocaust deniers.

- *Right to peaceful assembly (article 21)*

Article 21 includes the right to assemble for political demonstrations. Peaceful assembly may be subject to reasonable restrictions, but permission to demonstrate may not be denied arbitrarily.

- *Freedom of association (article 22)*

The right to form associations (including political parties, non-governmental organizations, trade unions and sporting clubs) is not absolute. Limitations for reasons of national security, public order or other grounds may be acceptable. The Committee has upheld a state ban on neo-fascist parties as a reasonable limitation.

The Committee has not extended article 22 to include a right to strike. It has not had the opportunity to decide whether forced membership in an association can be compatible with article 22.

• *Protection of the family (article 23)*
The Committee has adopted a broad, culturally sensitive definition of "family."

- **Family unification**—With respect to spouses of different nationalities, a state cannot unreasonably, or on discriminatory grounds, interfere or restrict access of foreign spouses to each other. Deportation which results in the splitting of a family is not in itself contrary to article 23.

- **Equality of spouses during marriage and at its dissolution** —The Committee has been very reluctant to scrutinize the judgments of domestic courts in these matters, on the grounds that they involve very personal matters and factual evaluation of the circumstances in each case.

• *Children's rights (article 24)*
The ICCPR does not contain a definition of "child." The Committee has left it to states to determine the majority age in each country, except in matters of criminal law and the age of criminal liability.

A violation of article 24 was found where a state refused to give legal standing in its domestic courts to a grandmother, in proceedings involving her orphaned and abducted grandchild. A minor seeking asylum may be detained while his or her case is being examined.

• *Political rights and participation in public life (article 25)*
One-party political systems have been found to violate article 25. The rights under article 25 to participate in public life are not absolute, however, and restrictions are allowed as long as they are not discriminatory, or unreasonable and based on objective criteria. Nevertheless, the Committee has held that the right to equal access to public service was violated when public servants were dismissed on the basis of their political activity.

• *Equality and Freedom from discrimination (article 26)*
Article 26 includes several concepts, including equality before the law, equal protection of the law, the prohibition of discrimination, and equal and effective protection against discrimination.

Article 26 obligates states to ensure that legislation applies to all people in a non-discriminatory manner. This obligation applies to all the rights and protections that a state affords in its laws. If an author can establish that a right exists in domestic law, he or she can bring a claim for violation of article 26 if there is any discrimination in the application of that law. Article 26 is an autonomous right to equality and non-discrimination, not limited to the rights enumerated in the Covenant. Hence, article 26 can extend to civil and political rights beyond the Covenant such as the right to property, and to economic, social and cultural rights, including social security. Different treatment has been found to violate article 26, for example, in a case in which some categories of persons received less social security benefits on grounds which the Committee held were arbitrary, and a case in which compensation for confiscated properties was not disbursed in an equitable manner. The latter occurred in the context of post-Communist restitution legislation containing conditions for restitution or compensation which the Committee found to be arbitrary.

Article 26 specifies that race, colour, sex, language, religion, political or other opinion or social origin, property, birth or other status are prohibited grounds for discrimination. The Committee decides on a case-by-case basis what "other grounds" also fall under article 26, or the meaning of "other status." It has found a number of additional grounds.

There have been clear-cut cases where the legislation itself has discriminated, for example, against women, and violations of both articles 3 and 26 have been found. Other cases have been more subtle, in that the law was not discriminatory on its face, but its application was discriminatory.

According to the Committee, the right to equality before the law and to equal protection of the law without any discrimination does not make all differences of treatment discriminatory. A differentiation will amount to prohibited discrimination where it is not based on reasonable and objective criteria.

The Committee is of the opinion that affirmative action is sometimes required, and hence when proportionate, is not a violation of the anti-discrimination provision.

• *Rights of minorities (article 27)*

There is no definition of 'minority' in the ICCPR. The Committee determines itself whether a minority is involved in a certain case and whether a person belongs to that minority. It does not rely on the state's position on these issues. Importantly, the Committee looks at the country as a whole to determine the existence of a minority. It has not regarded persons belonging to the overall majority as minorities in specific regions or provinces which are dominated by the minority on state level.

Indigenous peoples, although considered distinct from minorities generally under international law, also enjoy the protection of article 27.

The right to exercise culture comprises not only traditional practices and religions, but also the broader way of life and specific socio-economic activities which are specific to the group, for example, reindeer husbandry by the Scandinavian Sami.

Interference by large-scale industrial logging or mining activity on the territory of minorities or indigenous peoples, may violate article 27.

These cases are only samples of decisions made by the Human Rights Committee, or suggested from its General Comments, or concluding observations on state reports. This list is not exhaustive, and individuals are entitled to make many more kinds of claims on the basis of the rights in the ICCPR.

CHAPTER IV

THE CONVENTION AGAINST TORTURE

---

1. OVERVIEW OF THE COMMITTEE AGAINST TORTURE (CAT)

The Committee Against Torture (CAT) is responsible for considering all complaints received under article 22 of the Convention. The Committee is composed of 10 experts nominated and elected by states parties. Members serve in their personal, independent capacity.

The Committee follows specific procedures in the consideration of individual complaints. The individual complaints procedures originate from three sources: the provisions of the Convention itself, the Rules of Procedure that have been adopted formally by the Committee, and the Committee's customary practices.

To help maintain impartiality in the complaint process, the Rules of Procedure of CAT provide that members shall not take part in the deliberation of a case in which they have a personal interest, or in which they have participated in any way in the making of any decision in the case before it reached the Committee (Rule 103).

The Committee meets twice annually in Geneva, in April/May and November for a total of five weeks. Although most meetings are public, when the Committee considers individual complaints, the meetings are "closed" to the public.

Registration may be made by the Secretariat. If there is a request for interim measures, then the case usually proceeds to the Rapporteur on New Complaints and Interim Measures. If not, it will proceed directly to the Working Group (who may also deal with requests for interim measures).

a) Rapporteur on New Complaints and Interim Measures

CAT has appointed, from among its members, a Rapporteur on New Complaints and Interim Measures. The responsibility of the Rapporteur include the power to:

- register cases;
- request further information from the complainant; and
- request the state party to take interim measures.

b) Working Group on Complaints

The Committee has established a Working Group which meets prior to each session, reviews the draft decisions prepared by the Secretariat, and makes recommendations to the full Committee. The three to five member Working Group can declare cases admissible by majority vote, or inadmissible by unanimity. The Working Group may also decide to join the issues of admissibility and merits. In about half of the cases these issues have been joined.

c) Case Rapporteur

Rapporteurs may be designated by the Working Group to deal with specific complaints, by preparing draft recommendations on each case for the Working Group, giving instructions to the Secretariat on how the decision is to be drafted, and presenting the draft to the Working Group and to the full Committee.

d) Rapporteur for Follow-up

The Committee has recently adopted Rules of Procedure which provide for a Rapporteur for Follow-up of the Committee's Decisions. The Rapporteur is expected to monitor compliance with the Committee's findings, and to conduct meetings with state party representatives on an ad-hoc basis to encourage compliance. The Rapporteur may visit the state party concerned, with the approval of the Committee, in the course of his or her activities.

See Diagram on pp. 90-91.

2. INDIVIDUAL COMPLAINTS PROCEDURE OF CAT

The basic process for submitting a complaint, outlined in Chapter 3, should be read together with the more specific information provided in relation to CAT.

a) Registration of the Complaint and Preliminary Procedures

i) Submission of the Complaint

A complaint should be submitted to the Secretariat of the Office of the High Commissioner for Human Rights, Geneva in writing, by letter, fax or email. An original signed complaint must be sent following a submission by fax or email. Complaints cannot be anonymous. The state that is the subject of the complaint must be clearly identified. While the Committee has not developed a standardized complaint form, a model form based on the complaint form of the Human Rights Committee can be found in Annex 1, and will likely be helpful in the preparation of a complaint.

Of the thousands of general letters of complaint that arrive at the UN each year, only a small fraction are channelled to the Committee Against

Torture by the UN secretariat. If the complaint is not expressly addressed to the Committee Against Torture, it may not get there, or its receipt may be delayed. It may be directed by UN staff to the Special Rapporteur on Torture rather than to the Committee.

Where the communication does not provide the necessary information in order for it to be registered, the secretariat may request that the communication be resubmitted providing further information. Since the Committee relies heavily on the facts in each particular case, it is especially important to set out all the relevant information at the outset.

A complaint should include all the information necessary for the Committee to determine both the admissibility and the merits of the complaint. At a minimum, the following information should be included:

- the identity and contact information of the victim;
- the state against which the complaint is directed;
- the provisions of the Convention alleged to have been breached;
- all the relevant facts together with any supporting documentation;
- steps taken to exhaust local remedies, or evidence why local remedies are ineffective, unavailable, or unreasonably prolonged;
- information regarding whether this matter is, or has been, before any other procedure of international investigation or settlement; and
- the remedy requested.

Be as specific as possible as to details, such as dates, names and places. A complaint should also include all the supporting evidence available to verify the complaint. Supporting evidence should include:

- a signed statement from the victim, setting out in as much detail as possible the factual basis of the complained violation;
- signed statements from any available witnesses;
- medical reports or certificates, including both physical and psychological assessments that might support the allegation that torture has occurred;
- autopsy reports if applicable;
- photographs; and
- general information about the country situation that might prove a practice of torture in the country.

Other important points:

- **The Relationship between the Special Rapporteur on Torture and the Committee Against Torture**
  The Special Rapporteur is an individual appointed by the UN Commission on Human Rights. The Rapporteur has the task, on a part-time and unpaid basis, to review compliance by all UN members

The CAT Complaints Procedure

author submits complaint

secretariat advises author submission does not meet basic requirements END

secretariat requests additional information

secretariat does not register END

secretariat (Petitions Team, Office of High Commissioner) registers complaint

working group decides unanimously case inadmissible END

interim measures requested by author and considered by rapporteur on new complaints and interim measures (RNC), or working group or committee

secretariat transmits to state party on admissibility and merits

state party seeks to split admissibility from merits

rapporteur (RNC) refuses to split admissibility and merits

rapporteur (RNC) agrees to split admissibility and merits

state party makes submissions on admissibility

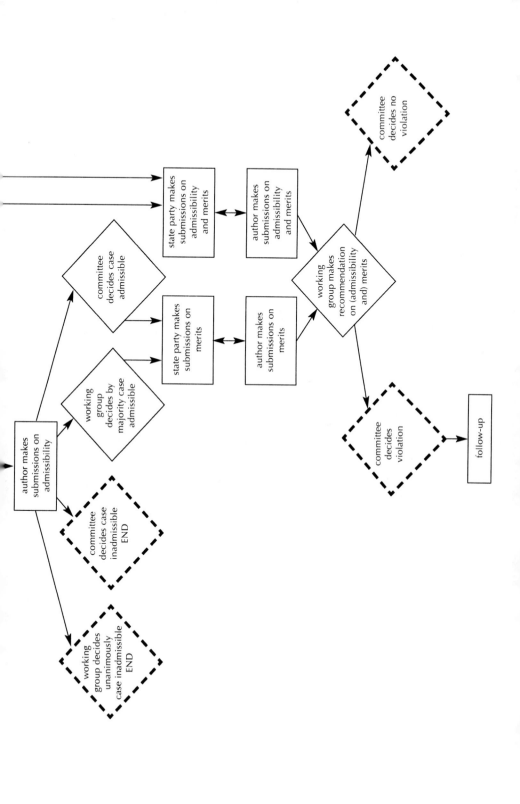

with norms against torture. The Rapporteur considers torture even in the context of states which have not ratified the Convention Against Torture. The role of the Rapporteur in the case of states which have not ratified the Convention is clear, since these states may otherwise avoid scrutiny in this context. But the role of the Rapporteur in the context of those states which have ratified the Convention is more complex. The mandate of the Special Rapporteur has included consideration of individual cases, and hence individual cases on the same subject can go both to the Rapporteur and to the Committee. Any action taken by the Rapporteur to investigate, decide, and to seek a remedy for individual violations is not done under the authority of a treaty obligation. The Rapporteur's interventions are made on the basis of appealing to a state's national and international interests, reputation and moral responsibilities, for example, under the Universal Declaration of Human Rights and other General Assembly resolutions, or legal responsibilities created by international customary law. This is in contrast to the operation of the Committee Against Torture, which investigates and seeks remedies in individual cases on the basis of state legal obligations under the Torture Convention.

There may be some instances in which an individual would prefer consideration of his or her case by the Special Rapporteur. To date, in practice, in many if not most instances, individual complaints concerning torture which do not specify the intended addressee of the Committee Against Torture, will be sent to the Special Rapporteur by UN staff. Hence, it is important to specify the Committee, if this is the intended venue of the complainant's case.

• Languages

The Committee's working languages are at present English, French, Spanish and Russian. Although complaints theoretically can be registered in any of the official languages of the UN (Arabic, Chinese, English, French, Russian, Spanish), there will likely be significant delays in the processing of the case if the complainant uses a language other than English, French or Spanish. Cases received in Russian will be sent to translation once initially processed, sometimes at a considerable delay. Cases received in Arabic or Chinese are normally returned to the complainant who is requested to resubmit in English, French or Spanish. If a complaint is received in a non-UN official language, the complainant will normally receive at the outset a letter requesting the re-submission of the complaint in English, French or Spanish. If it happens that a complaint has been submitted in an additional language which a UN secretariat member servicing the Committee understands, it may be processed initially without translation. Complainants are strongly advised to submit complaints in English, French or Spanish.

- **Time Limitations**

There is no time limit within which to bring the claim, but the Committee's rules indicate that a case will be found to be inadmissable if the time elapsed since the exhaustion of domestic remedies is so unreasonably prolonged as to render consideration of the claim unduly difficult for the Committee or the state party.

- **Legal Aid**

The UN does not provide legal aid or financial assistance to claimants, nor does CAT require that states parties provide legal aid where an individual wishes to submit a complaint. Claimants should determine whether or not their own domestic legal aid system provides for the possibility of legal aid.

However, NGOs and other legal professionals are allowed to represent the victims. There is no prohibition on a victim seeking assistance from NGOs or appointing them as their representative.

- **Withdrawal of the Complaint**

A complainant may subsequently withdraw his or her complaint.

The Committee normally accepts the withdrawal, but if there is an indication there might have been pressure on the complainant, will try to ascertain whether withdrawal was the result of undue pressure by the state or other threats.

- **Confidentiality**

All documents relating to a complaint are confidential. The Committee may decide that certain elements of the case must remain confidential and not be published, including the identity of the complainant.

CAT considers complaints in closed meetings (article 22(6); Rule 101). The Committee has discretion under its rules of procedure to invite the complainant or his or her representatives, and representatives of the state party, to be present at the meetings in order to provide further clarifications or to answer questions on the merits (Rule 111). However, this power has never been exercised by CAT.

ii) *Registration of the Complaint*

Once the complaint has been received, along with information regarding any obvious or manifest deficiencies, the complaint will be registered. The Committee has delegated to the Secretariat the authority to register new cases.

The secretariat or the Rapporteur on New Complaints and Interim Measures may ask the complainant for clarification regarding any or all of the following issues (Rule 99):

- Name, address, age and occupation of the complainant;
- The state against which the complaint is directed;
- The object of the complaint;
- The precise CAT provision which is being invoked;p
- Clarification about the facts of the claim;
- Information about which local or domestic remedies have been used; and
- Information about other international procedures that are being or have been engaged.

The Secretariat will indicate a time limit for replying to such requests, approximately 3 months, (Rule 99), but strict sanctions are not applied when this time limit is not met. Failure to provide adequate information necessary to register a case, may result in a complaint not being registered.

After the complaint is registered, it is transmitted to the Working Group. It is important to attempt to adhere to any deadlines given by the Committee and, if observance is not possible, to write to the Committee and formally request an extension. If deadlines are not respected by either party, the Committee may proceed to determine the question of admissibility in light of the information already available (Rule 109(7)).

iii) Transmittal to the State Party

After the complaint has been registered, it is transmitted to the state party. The state party is requested to submit a written reply on both the issues of admissibility and merits within 6 months.

iv) Interim Measures

At any time after the receipt of the complaint, the Rapporteur for New Complaints and Interim Measures, the Committee, or the Working Group, may request a state party to take interim measures to avoid irreparable damage to the victim of an alleged violation (Rule 108(1)). The Committee has appointed one of its members as Rapporteur for the purpose of being able to act quickly upon receiving such requests. This interim procedure is frequently used by CAT, particularly in extradition or expulsion cases, where there is danger of the victim being tortured on their return to another state. CAT's practice has been to ask the state party to take interim measures if there is even a small danger that the person may be tortured if they are expelled.

In making a successful case for a request for interim measures, the complainant must satisfy the threshold that he or she personally risks being tortured if, for instance, he or she is removed to a particular country. It is not sufficient that there is a general pattern of torture existing in the receiving state. Such a case can be made out, for example, if individuals can establish that they have already been subjected to torture, or their current activities would reasonably put them at risk.

b) Admissibility and Submissions from the Parties

The practice of the Committee is to consider complaints in the order in which they have been readied for consideration, unless interim measures are involved. CAT retains a discretion to consider complaints out of order. Accordingly, if the matter is urgent, the complainant should consider requesting that the matter be expedited.

If the Committee believes the complaint is manifestly inadmissible, the Committee is empowered under its rules of procedure to declare the complaint inadmissible without referring the matter to the state party.

The Committee cannot, however, determine the complaint to be admissible without first sending the text of the complaint to the state party concerned, and giving the state party an opportunity to furnish information and observations relevant to the question of admissibility (Rule 109(8)).

The presumption under the Committee's rules of procedure is that the questions of the admissibility of a claim and the merits of a claim will be considered jointly. The Committee can decide to request submissions on the issue of admissibility alone (Rule 109(2)). The state party may apply for separation of the two issues, although the Committee may not agree to this request. The Committee's practice is to allow states parties 3 months to provide their comments on admissibility. Deadlines are not strictly enforced, and submissions after the deadlines have been accepted in practice.

As soon as the Committee receives any information or observations from the state party, they are sent to the complainant, who in practice is given four weeks to submit a response. Although it is strongly advisable to observe the deadlines, the Committee's practice has been to accept submissions received subsequently. The Committee's rules of procedure direct that, ordinarily, non-receipt of a response within the established time limit should not delay the consideration of the admissibility of the complaint (Rule 109(7)).

The Committee may designate one of its members as a rapporteur to deal with specific complaints, and make recommendations (Rule 106(3) 109(5), 112(1)).

In light of all the information, the Working Group can decide by simple majority that a complaint is admissible, or inadmissible by unanimity.

If the complaint is found inadmissible because of a failure to exhaust domestic remedies, the Committee may subsequently review that decision, on receipt from the complainant of a request for review and documentary evidence that the reasons for inadmissibility no longer apply.

Other important points:

- **The complaint must be made by or on behalf of an individual**
Complaints can only be made by individuals, not groups of individ-

uals. However, the Committee may also, if it deems appropriate, decide to consider jointly two or more complaints (Rule 105(4)). Accordingly, if two persons wish to consider making complaints under the Convention of acts arising out of the same incident, separate complaints could be filed with a request that they be considered together.

- **There must not be a parallel complaint before another international forum, either currently, or in the past**

A complaint is inadmissible if the matter is being, or has ever been, examined under another procedure of international investigation or settlement (article 22(5)(a); Rule 107(d)). This is a more stringent rule than under the ICCPR, because it applies whenever a procedure of international investigation has been invoked, even if that procedure has been concluded. Moreover, complainants must not split their claims and submit some aspects of it to the Inter-American Commission on Human Rights (for example, the fair hearing aspect), and other aspects (such as the prohibition of expulsion if there is a risk of torture) to CAT. If complainants do so, they risk inadmissibility under article 22(5)(a).

- **Procedure if the merits and admissibility have been joined**

The complaint is transmitted to the state party for its comments or explanations on both the admissibility of the complaint and the merits. CAT's practice is to require such comments to be provided within six months. Upon receipt, any explanations or statements from the state party are transmitted to the complainant, who is given an opportunity to submit additional written information or observations, usually within six weeks.

In practice, there is more than one round of submissions between state party and complainant. Sometimes, both parties continue commenting on each other's submissions.

CAT considers all the information before it and adopts its findings on admissibility and the merits.

- **Exhaustion of domestic remedies**

An important ground of inadmissibility, the requirement that domestic remedies be exhausted, is frequently misunderstood. The exhaustion of domestic remedies condition may also be satisfied, not by the existence or use of domestic proceedings, but by showing convincingly that such remedies are ineffective, unavailable, or unreasonably prolonged. According to the rules of procedure of CAT, the requirement of exhaustion of domestic remedies "shall not be the rule where the application of the remedies is unreasonably prolonged or is unlikely to bring effective relief to the person who is the victim of the violation of this Convention."

c) Determination of the Merits and Follow-up

If the issue of admissibility and merits has been considered separately, once a complaint is found to be admissible, the state party is given an opportunity to make submissions on the merits of the claim. CAT's practice is to give the state party six months to submit written explanations or statements to the Committee. The Committee, however, has set shorter deadlines when appropriate.

The submissions of the state party are transmitted to the complainant, who is given an opportunity to submit additional written information or observations, usually within a six week time frame.

Frequently, neither the state party nor the complainant adhere to deadlines. Thus far, the Committee has always accepted late submissions. The Committee has also sent reminders to states parties and complainants informing them that a case will be considered at a given session, whether or not the submission has been received. The Committee, however, dislikes to adopt decisions by default.

The case rapporteur and/or the Working Group may make recommendations on the merits prior to the consideration of the merits by the full Committee (Rule 112(1)).

The Committee will consider all the information before it and adopts its "Decisions" on whether or not there has been a violation of the treaty. After considering the state party's submissions on the merits, the Committee is also entitled to revoke its decision that the complaint is admissible.

CAT considers complaints in closed meetings (article 22(6). The Committee has a discretion under its rules of procedure to invite the complainant or his or her representatives, and representatives of the state party, to be present at the meetings in order to provide further clarifications or to answer questions on the merits (Rule 111(4)). However, this power has never been exercised by CAT.

The Decisions of the Committee will not necessarily be unanimous. Any member of the Committee may request that a summary of his individual opinion be attached to the Decisions of the Committee.

The usual remedies which CAT requests are: (1) non-refoulement in cases under article 3 of the Convention, when the Committee establishes that a real risk of torture exists; (2) investigation of reported cases of torture; (3) punishment of persons responsible for torture and ill-treatment; and (4) compensation to the victim or to his or her family.

The Committee transmits its Decisions to the complainant and the state party.

In its Decisions, CAT asks the state party to inform it of the action taken in response to a finding by the Committee of a violation of the Convention (Rule 112(5)).

The Committee has recently adopted a follow-up mechanism, and will designate one of its members as Rapporteur for Follow-up. The

Rapporteur is expected to monitor the responses of states parties to the Committee's request for information on the remedy provided, and to meet with representatives of selected states parties that have not responded positively to the Committee's request. They are also enabled to make visits to states parties in the course of follow-up activities.

- **Annual Report**

There is no sanction for failure to comply with the Committee's Decisions. Publicity is given to the Decisions through the Committee's annual reports to the General Assembly. In its report, the Committee includes the text of its Decisions and the text of any decision declaring a complaint inadmissible (Rule 115(2)). Information on follow-up will also be part of the Committee's Annual Report (Rule 115(3)).

- **Reservations**

Reservations to CAT may substantially limit the ability of an individual to successfully make a case against a particular state party. It is, therefore, necessary to check the reservations made by the state party. At the same time, some reservations may not be legitimate, that is, they may be incompatible with the object and purpose of the treaty. In these cases, it is possible that the treaty body will refuse to apply the reservation in a manner which would limit the application of the Convention in the context of a complaint. CAT itself has as yet not directly made a statement about the incompatibility of reservations with the Convention.

3. EXAMPLES OF CAT CASES

When determining how the Committee might approach the interpretation of an article in the Convention, consideration should be given to the Committee's final "Decisions" expressed in previous complaints on the same subject matter, the Committee's concluding comments on states parties' reports, and the Committee's General Comments (the Committee having issued to date one comment on article 3).

Torture—The right of complaint under the Convention Against Torture is for victims of a violation by a state party of the Convention's provisions.

A victim is, for example, a person subject to the jurisdiction of the state party who has been tortured. Such a person may potentially be the victim of a violation not only of the state's obligation to prevent the acts of torture happening in the first place, but also of those articles in the Convention that require the state to respond to the fact that acts of torture may have already occurred and provide a remedy. Articles that may be used by victims of torture when bringing a claim include:

- article 2(1) (duty to take effective measures to prevent acts of torture);
- article 4 (failure to criminalize torture);
- article 5 (failure to establish jurisdiction over acts of torture);
- article 6 (failure to take the alleged torturer into custody or take other legal measures to ensure his presence);
- article 7 (failure to prosecute);
- article 12 (failure to investigate);
- article 13 (right to complain);
- article 14 (right to obtain redress); and
- article 15 (duty to exclude statements made as a result of torture).

Cruel, Inhuman or Degrading Treatment or Punishment—A person who has been subjected to acts amounting to cruel, inhuman or degrading treatment or punishment will also be a victim of a violation of the Convention. That person may complain about failure to prevent the acts of cruel, inhuman or degrading treatment or punishment, or about the state's subsequent responsibility to respond to the fact that acts of cruel, inhuman or degrading treatment or punishment have occurred. The articles which can be used are more limited than in the case of torture. The victim can potentially use:

- article 16 (duty to take effective measures to prevent acts of cruel, inhuman or degrading treatment or punishment);
- article 12 (failure to investigate);
- article 13 (right to complain).

Other—There are at least three circumstances in which complainants may legitimately claim that they are victims of a violation of the Convention, even though they have not been subjected to acts of torture or cruel, inhuman or degrading treatment or punishment.

- **Forcible Return to Another State**—A complainant can legitimately claim that they are the victim of a violation of article 3 of the Convention if the state against which the complaint is made has forcibly returned them, or intends to forcibly return them, to another state where there are substantial grounds for believing that they would be in danger of being subjected to torture. The majority of complaints which have been submitted to CAT to date concern a breach of article 3.

- **Investigation of Claim Torture or Cruel, Inhuman and Degrading Treatment or Punishment**—A complainant can legitimately claim a breach of articles 12 and 13 of the Convention if the state party has failed adequately to investigate an allegation of torture (or cruel, inhuman and degrading treatment or punishment) in accordance with certain standards.

If the state fails to conduct an adequate investigation, a breach of the Convention will have occurred, even though it might be subsequently established that the original allegation of torture (or cruel, inhuman and degrading treatment or punishment) was unfounded.

- **Protection of Complainants and Witnesses**—States parties have an obligation to protect complainants and witnesses in inquiries concerning torture, from ill-treatment or intimidation. If a state party fails in this duty of protection, such persons will be victims of a Convention violation, whether or not they have ever been tortured (article 13).

Below are **examples** of the Committee Against Torture's approach to the interpretation of the Convention, as disclosed in the Committee's final Decisions, concluding comments and general comment.

- *The definition of "torture" (article 1)*
  Under article 1, the definition of torture contains three elements:
  1. Torture is an act by which severe pain or suffering, whether physical or mental, is intentionally inflicted on a person;
  2. The pain or suffering must have been inflicted by or at the instigation or with the consent or acquiescence of a public official or other person acting in an official capacity; and
  3. The pain or suffering must have been inflicted for one of the purposes stated in article 1 of the Convention, which include obtaining information or a confession, punishment, intimidation or coercion, or discrimination.

- **Infliction of severe pain or suffering**—Whether a given act constitutes torture will depend on the severity of the pain or suffering inflicted in the particular case. However, the Committee has given some indication to states of the kind of acts the Committee considers are capable of constituting torture. These include:
  - beatings by fists and wooden or metallic clubs, on the head, the kidney area and on the soles of the feet;
  - use of electro-shock;
  - restraint or shackling in painful positions;
  - hooding;
  - sounding of loud music for prolonged periods;
  - sleep deprivation for prolonged periods;
  - threats, including death threats;
  - violent shaking; and
  - using cold air to chill.

- **Infliction by a public official**—The requirement that the acts complained of were inflicted by, at the instigation, or with the consent of a public official or person acting in an official capacity is sufficiently flexible to encompass a regime having effective control or control in fact, even if that regime has not been formally recognized as the legitimate governmental authority. Thus, in the case of an individual from a particular state who reasonably feared torture at the hands of a specific clan if forcibly returned to his country, the Committee considered that the "public official" requirement of the torture definition was met. Although the state was without a lawfully recognized central government, the clan controlled most of the capital city, had established quasi-governmental institutions, and were providing a number of public services.

- *Prevention of torture (article 2(1))*

In order for a complainant to be in a position to argue that they have been the "victim" of a failure by the state to take effective measures to prevent acts of torture, they will usually have been subject to acts of torture. To substantiate a claimed violation of the state's obligation to take effective measures to prevent acts of torture, the complainant will likely point to the fact that the act(s) of torture have occurred. A complainant may reinforce the claim that a failure of prevention has occurred by pointing to the existence of a state of affairs that made the commission of acts of torture (or cruel, inhuman or degrading treatment or punishment) more likely to occur. For example, in its concluding comments on states parties' reports, the Committee has identified at least the following situations that, in the Committee's view, lead to an increased risk of torture or cruel, or inhuman or degrading treatment or punishment occurring:
  - the non-publication of standards of interrogation;
  - prolonged incommunicado detention;
  - certain length and conditions of police custody and administrative detention;
  - lack of access to counsel;
  - lack of detailed provisions on the inadmissibility of unlawfully obtained confessions and other tainted evidence; and
  - the slow pace of trials of persons responsible for acts of torture or ill treatment

- *Absolute character of the prohibition (article 2)*

The Committee has repeatedly emphasized that no circumstances whatsoever, no matter how exceptional, can be invoked to justify torture.

- ***No forcible return of persons to another state if danger of torture (article 3)***

The state's obligation under this article is not to return the person to "another state" where there are "substantial grounds" for believing that he or she would be in danger of being subjected to torture. The Committee has been largely unresponsive to concerns by state parties that implementation of this article might be "abused" by asylum seekers and has applied the article rigorously to protect asylum seekers. The article has been used by the Committee both to take action pending a final decision on the merits of the case in the form of an order for interim measures, and upon reaching final Decisions.

- **"Another state"**—The Committee has stated that the phrase "another state" in article 3 refers both to the state to which the individual concerned is being expelled, returned or extradited, as well as to any state to which the complainant may subsequently be expelled, returned or extradited. Thus, the obligation is to refrain from forcibly returning the complainant:
  - to a country in which there is substantial grounds for believing torture might occur; or
  - to any other country that would not, themselves, torture the complainant, but where there is a real risk of a subsequent forced returned to a country where torture might occur.

- **"Substantial grounds"**—Under article 3, the burden is on the complainant to present an arguable case. The Committee has said that "substantial grounds" means something more than mere theory or suspicion. There must be a factual basis for the complainant's concern. On the other hand, the risk of torture does not have to be "highly probable." The state's obligation to ensure that a complainant's security is not endangered exists even if there are some remaining doubts about the facts adduced by the complainant.

  The Committee gives considerable weight in exercising its jurisdiction to findings of fact that have been made by organs of the state party. At the same time, the Committee does not consider itself bound by such findings but rather will make an assessment of the facts based upon all the relevant circumstances. In determining whether there are "substantial grounds" for concern, the Committee will consider all relevant evidence presented to it, including medical or other evidence that might support a claim of torture, and any available evidence that helps the Committee determine the credibility of the complainant's claim.

  The Committee will take note of any factual inconsistencies in the complainant's account. On the other hand, the Committee has observed that, due to the nature of the human rights violation, complete accuracy may not always be expected by victims of torture, and that the presence of some inconsistencies in a complainant's story does not necessarily raise doubts about the general veracity of a complainant's claim. The Committee is especially understanding of inconsistencies if there is evidence that the complainant is suffering from post-traumatic stress disorder.

Article 3(2) of the Convention specifies that, in determining whether there are "substantial grounds", the state shall take into account "all relevant considerations" including "the existence of a consistent pattern of gross, flagrant or mass violations of human rights."

The Committee has reiterated that the aim is to establish whether the individual concerned would be *personally* at risk of being subjected to torture. The existence of a consistent pattern of gross, flagrant or mass violations of human rights in a country does not generally suffice, on its own, to prove such personal risk.

Conversely, if there is evidence that the complainant is in danger in his or her specific circumstances, the absence of a consistent pattern of gross violations by the state party is not determinative.

Factors the Committee has been prepared to take into account as indicating personal risk include:

- a complainant's ethnic background (for example, membership of a persecuted clan);
- alleged political affiliation and activities;
- any prior history of persecution of the complainant by state authorities (for example, detention, torture, the imposition of internal exile, or threats). Such prior history will be particularly relevant if it occurred in the recent past. It will be less relevant if there has been an intervening change in political circumstances in the country of origin;
- previous targeting of family members;
- any acts of the complainant that might have incurred the disapproval of state authorities. For example, in one case, previous desertion from the army followed by a clandestine flight from the country was considered relevant. In other cases, the Committee has considered it relevant that a complainant's asylum application, including criticisms of the country of origin, had received publicity that might have come to the attention, and incurred the disapproval, of the country of origin;

- evidence of ongoing interest being shown by the authorities in the complainant's whereabouts;
- the fact that the state to which the complainant is in danger of being returned is not a party to the Convention and that, accordingly, the complainant would have no further protection from the Committee once they were returned; and
- reports from international bodies concerning the treatment of persons in a situation like the complainant.

- **The torturer must be a state entity or official**—Because the definition of torture in article 1 of the Convention is limited to acts committed by, at the instigation of or with the consent or acquiescence of a public official or other person acting in an official capacity, the Committee considers that article 3 does not protect persons from being forcibly returned to a country where they may be at risk of pain or suffering inflicted by a non-governmental entity, without the consent or acquiescence of the Government. Thus, in one case, the Committee considered that the deportation of a complainant to a country where she claimed she would be at risk of suffering at the hands of a guerrilla group that did not have governmental backing, did not raise issues under article 3.

  For the same reason, the Committee has reiterated that under article 3, the existence of a consistent pattern of gross, flagrant or mass violations of human rights will only be relevant if the human rights violations are committed by, at the instigation of, or with the consent or acquiescence of, a public official or other person acting in an official capacity.

- **All persons have the benefit of protection, regardless of prior conduct**—The obligation under article 3 not to return a person to a state where they are at risk of being tortured, protects all individuals, irrespective of the individual's own prior conduct. The protection given by article 3 is, in this respect, wider than the protection given by the Convention Relating to the Status of Refugees 1951, under which a person may be excluded from protection if they have engaged in certain forms of past conduct (for example, commission of certain categories of crimes) (Article 1F). Accordingly, persons who have been excluded from refugee status under Article 1F of the Refugee Convention are nevertheless entitled to the protection of article 3 of the Torture Convention.

- **Remedy**—A finding by the Committee under article 3 that a complainant cannot be forcibly returned to a given state does not require any particular determination by the competent national authorities concerning, for example, the granting of asylum. The state party is entitled to meet its obligation under article 3 by any means available to it. This might include solutions of a legal nature (such as, by temporarily admitting the applicant to its territory) or solutions of a political nature (such as by finding a third state that is willing to admit the applicant to its territory and to undertake not to return or expel the applicant).

- ***Criminalization of acts of torture (article 4); jurisdiction to prosecute (article 5)***

States parties need to provide for a definition of torture in their penal legislation that fully incorporates all the elements of the definition of torture contained in article 1 of the Convention.

- ***Duty to prosecute (article 7)***

In order to meet this obligation, criminal proceedings must be systematically initiated against persons accused of acts of torture, and should be conducted independently of any disciplinary measures taken.

- ***Investigative duties (article 12)***

  - **Triggering event**—A state party's obligation to proceed to a prompt and impartial investigation under article 12 is triggered whenever there is a "reasonable ground to believe" that an act of torture or ill treatment has been committed under its jurisdiction. An allegation from the victim is not needed to trigger the state party's obligation under article 12. The authorities have an obligation to proceed to an official investigation whenever there are reasonable grounds to believe that acts of torture or ill-treatment have been committed. The state party's reasonable belief may be the result of information received from a source other than the complainant.

  - **Delay**—The investigation should be prompt. The Committee has observed that such promptness is essential both to ensure that the victim does not continue to be subjected to acts of torture or ill treatment, and because the physical traces of torture and, even more so, cruel, inhuman or degrading treatment or punishment, are often transient.

    In past cases, delays of 15 months, 10 months and, in one case, slightly more than three weeks, have been held by the Committee to be unreasonably long delays between the initial reporting of facts and the initiation of an investigation.

  - **Findings of breach, even where no torture**—The Committee will consider whether the state has complied with its duty to proceed to a prompt and impartial investigation of an allegation of torture, even if the Committee has already decided that an allegation of torture is unsubstantiated. Accordingly, a person might be a victim of a violation of article 12 of the Convention, even though their initial allegation of torture, cruel, inhuman or degrading treatment or punishment, has proved to be unfounded.

- **Investigation of complaints (article 13)**

  - **Triggering event**—In principle, article 13 does not require the formal submission of a complaint of torture. It is enough that the victim brings the acts constituting torture to the attention of an authority of the state.

  - **Delay**—The Committee has held that a delay of almost 11 months, during which time the complaint was under examination but was not completed, did not satisfy the requirement for promptness in examining complaints. This defect was not excused by a lack of protest from the victim about the delay.

  - **Impartiality**—The obligation of impartiality is an obligation to give equal weight to both accusation and defence during the investigation. The Committee has considered this obligation to have been breached:
    - where the judicial authority refused to allow other evidence (such as examination of alleged perpetrators and witnesses) to supplement forensic evidence;
    - where the investigator relied on a medical evaluation and denials by persons the complainant had identified as witnesses, but did not pursue other avenues such as checking records of detention centres, did not identify and examine the accused officials and arrange a confrontation between them and the witnesses, and did not order the exhumation of the body despite major disparities in the findings of the forensic official; or
    - where the public prosecutor failed to appeal a decision.

- **Redress/compensation (article 14)**
In accordance with the Convention, the state should be held civilly responsible for the acts of its servants. Given the distinction between civil and criminal liability, a state might be liable to compensate victims of torture even in the absence of a criminal conviction.

- **Inadmissibility of statements obtained under torture (article 15)**
Evidence obtained in violation of article 1 of the Convention should never be taken into account by judicial decision-makers in any legal procedure, except against a person accused of torture as evidence that the statement was made.

- *Cruel, inhuman or degrading treatment or punishment (article 16)*

  - **Acts that may amount to cruel, inhuman or degrading treatment or punishment, or prevention of cruel, inhuman or degrading treatment or punishment**—Acts that constitute torture will also constitute cruel, inhuman or degrading treatment or punishment. In addition, the following are examples of acts that may amount to cruel, inhuman or degrading treatment or punishment:
    - maltreatment by police;
    - prison conditions, such as overcrowding, lack of facilities, lack of segregation and mixing of pre-trial and convicted prisoners, deprivation of food or medical treatment, and violence in jails;
    - the warehousing of asylum-seekers in large detention centres;
    - some methods of execution of prisoners sentenced to death;
    - internal exile;
    - corporal punishment;
    - solitary confinement of prisoners for long periods particularly as a preventative measure during pre-trial detention, and in the absence of careful regulation and judicial supervision.

    These acts may also create the conditions leading to an increased risk of cruel, inhuman or degrading treatment or punishment.

  - **Acts that do not amount to cruel, inhuman or degrading treatment or punishment**—The Committee has held in at least one case that the mere fact that deportation to another country might exacerbate a complainant's poor state of mental health does not amount to cruel, inhuman or degrading treatment.

These cases are only samples of decisions made by CAT, or suggested from its General Comment, or concluding observations on state reports. This list is not exhaustive, and individuals are entitled to make many more kinds of claims on the basis of the rights in the Torture Convention.

CHAPTER V

THE CONVENTION ON THE ELIMINATION OF RACIAL DISCRIMINATION

1. OVERVIEW OF THE COMMITTEE ON THE ELIMINATION OF RACIAL DISCRIMINATION (CERD)

The Committee on the Elimination of Racial Discrimination (CERD) is responsible for considering all communications submitted under Article 14 of the Convention. CERD is composed of 18 experts, nominated and elected by states parties to the Convention. Members serve in their personal capacity.

The Committee follows certain and specific procedures in the consideration of individual communications. The individual communications procedures originate from three sources: the provisions of the Convention itself, the Rules of Procedure that have been adopted formally by the Committee, and the Committee's customary practices.

To help maintain impartiality in the complaint process, the Rules of Procedure of CERD provide that members shall not take part in the deliberation of a case in which they have a personal interest, or in which they have participated in the making of any decision in the case before it reached the Committee (Rule 89).

The Committee meets annually in Geneva for two three-week long sessions in March and August. Although most meetings are public, when the Committee considers individual communications, the meetings are "closed" to the public (Rule 88).

Generally, the Committee tries to make decisions on communications by consensus, although formal decisions can be made by a majority. In cases where no consensus can be reached, the individual members may express individual Opinions which are attached to the Committee's decision.

CERD does not have a formal pre-sessional working group which handles communications. Registration is determined by the Secretariat. An informal open-ended working group on communications meets during the CERD sessions on an as-needed basis. All decisions concerning communications are taken by the committee as a whole.

The CERD Complaints Procedure

- author submits communication

- secretariat requests additional information

- secretariat advisies author submission does not meet basic requirements END

- secretariat does not register END

- Secretariat (Petitions, Team, Office of High Commissioner) registers communication

- secretariat transmits to state party on admissibility and merits

- state party seeks to split admissibility from merits

- committee decides case inadmissible END

- secretariat transmits to state party on admissibility separately

- interim measures requested by author and considered by committee

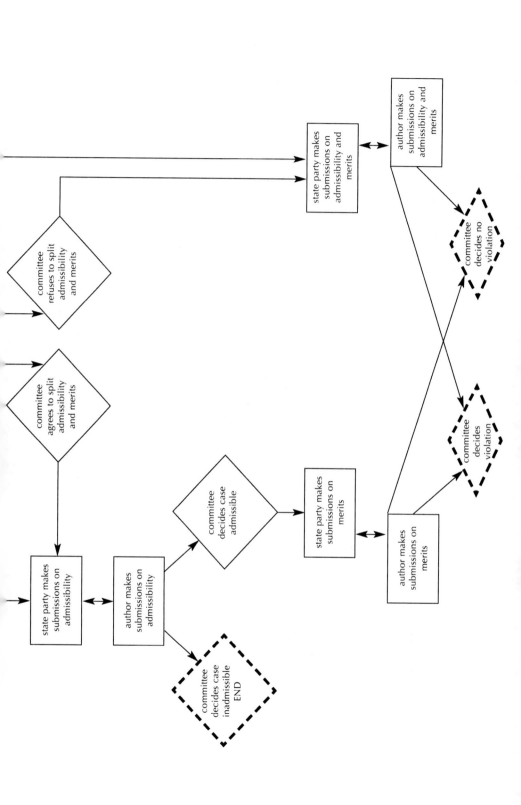

2. INDIVIDUAL COMPLAINTS PROCEDURE OF CERD

a) Registration of the Communication and Preliminary Procedure

The basic process for submitting a complaint has been outlined in Chapter 3, and should be read together with the more specific information provided in relation to CERD.

i) *Submission of the Communication*

A communication should be submitted to the Secretariat of the Office of the High Commissioner for Human Rights, Geneva, in writing, by letter, fax or email. Faxed or electronic communications must be confirmed by signed copies received by the Secretariat. Communications cannot be anonymous. The state that is the subject of the communication must be clearly identified. While the Committee has not developed a standardized complaint form, a model form based on the complaint form of the Human Rights Committee can be found in Annex 1, and will likely be helpful in the preparation of a complaint.

Where the communication does not provide the necessary information in order for it to be registered, the secretariat may request that the communication be resubmitted providing further information. Since the Committee relies heavily on the facts in each particular case, it is especially important to set out all the relevant information at the outset.

It is important to include, at a minimum, the following information:
- the identity and contact information of the victim;
- the state against which the communication is directed;
- the rights and articles of the Convention alleged to have been breached;
- steps taken to exhaust local remedies, or evidence why local remedies are ineffective, unavailable or unreasonably prolonged;
- all the relevant facts together with any supporting documentation (such as a factual account signed by the victim, witness statements, court documents); and
- the remedy requested.

Other important points:

• Languages

The Committee's working languages are at present English, French, Spanish and Russian. Although communications theoretically can be registered in any of the official languages of the UN (Arabic, Chinese, English, French, Russian, Spanish), there will likely be significant delays in the processing of the case if the author uses a language other than English, French or Spanish. Cases received in Russian are sent to translation once initially processed, sometimes at a considerable delay. Cases received in Arabic or Chinese are normally returned to the author who is requested to resubmit in English, French or Spanish. If a communication is received in a non-UN official language, the author will normally receive at the outset a letter requesting the re-submission of the communication in English, French or Spanish. If it happens that a communication has been submitted in an additional language which a UN secretariat member servicing the Committee understands, it may be processed initially without translation. Authors are strongly advised to submit communications in English, French or Spanish.

- **Time Limitations**

A claim must be brought within 6 months after the exhaustion of domestic remedies (article 14, paragraph 5). Cases have been declared inadmissible on this ground.

- **Legal Aid**

The UN does not provide legal aid or financial assistance to authors, nor does CERD require that states parties provide legal aid where an individual wishes to submit a communication. Authors should determine whether or not their own domestic legal aid system provides for the possibility of legal aid.

However, NGOs and other legal professionals are allowed to represent the victims. There is no prohibition on a victim seeking the assistance of NGOs or appointing them as their representative.

- **Withdrawal of the Communication**

An author may subsequently withdraw his or her communication.

- **Confidentiality**

All documents relating to a communication are confidential and CERD does not publicize cases, except by the eventual release of a decision. Decisions concerning inadmissibility, discontinuation or merits (Opinions) will be made public. The Committee may decide that the identity of the author remain confidential from the public.

However, the communication must not be anonymous. The identity of both the victim and the author (if different from the victim) must be revealed to the Committee and state party.

If the author fears reprisals from the state party which has committed the violation, he or she may request that the identity of the victim and/or the author not be revealed to the public.

ii) *Registration of the Communication*

Communications are initially reviewed by the UN Secretariat servicing the Committee prior to their registration. The secretariat brings to the attention of the Committee all communications which are, or appear to be, submitted for consideration by the Committee. The Committee has delegated to the Secretariat the authority to register new cases. The Secretariat may defer registration until further information is requested and obtained from the author.

The secretariat may ask the author for clarification regarding any or all of the following issues (Rule 84):

- Name, address, age and occupation of the author;
- The state against which the communication is directed;
- The object of the communication;
- The precise CERD provision which is being invoked;
- Information about which local or domestic remedies have been used; and
- Clarification about the facts of the claim.

The Secretariat will indicate a time limit for replying to such requests (Rule 84), but strict sanctions are not applied when this time limit is not met. Failure to provide adequate information necessary to register a case, may result in a communication not being registered. A decision to register a case may be made pending the response to questions for additional information.

iii) Transmittal to the State Party

Once the secretariat is satisfied the communication contains sufficient information, the communication is transmitted by the Committee to the state party for a response.

iv) Interim Measures

At any time after the Committee has determined that a claim is admissible, the Committee may request the state party to take interim measures to avoid possible irreparable damage to the claimant. Any such requests are not prejudicial to the Committee's final Opinion (Rule 94), nor are they an indication that the Committee has made any final decision as to the merits of the claim. Until now, CERD has not requested interim measures from states parties.

b) Admissibility and Submissions from the Parties

Once the communication has been transmitted to the state party, the state has three months in which to respond to the communication (CERD article 14(6)). The practice of the Committee is to seek a response from the state party on the issue of admissibility separately from the merits.

Neither the Convention, nor the Rules of Procedure, provide for specific requirements or deadlines for the author to respond to the state's submissions. However, in practice, the author is normally given three months to respond.

The Committee may decide a communication is inadmissible before transmitting it to the state party for submissions.

CERD will review all the information submitted by the parties, and adopt a decision on whether or not the communication is admissible. If the Committee decides that the communication is inadmissible, the case is finished. If the Committee decides that the communication is admissible, then it moves on to the merits stage. All decisions of CERD concerning individual communications are taken by the full Committee.

c) Determination of the Merits

Once the Committee has decided that the communication is admissible, the admissibility decision is transmitted to the state party and the claimant is advised of the decision. The state then has three months to submit its arguments or explanations as to the merits of the claim (Rule 94).

The Committee will then send the state's submissions to the author for reply (Rule 94). The author is usually given three months to respond.

The Committee will consider all the information before it and adopt its Opinion on whether or not there has been a violation of the treaty. After considering the state party's submissions on the merits, the Committee is also entitled to revoke its decision that the communication is admissible (Rule 94(6)).

CERD considers communications in closed meetings. The Committee has discretion under its rules of procedure to invite the author of the communication or his or her representatives, and representatives of the state party, to be present at the meetings in order to provide further clarifications or to answer questions on the merits (Rule 94(5)). However, this power has never been exercised.

The final decision on the merits by CERD is termed an "Opinion" not "Views" as it is in the case of the Human Rights Committee. CERD invites the state party to inform it "in due course" of the action it takes pursuant to the Committee's Opinion (Rule 95(3)).

The Opinions of the Committee will not necessarily be unanimous. Any member of the Committee may request that his or her individual opinion be attached to the Opinions of the Committee.

Remedies which have been requested by CERD from the state party are compensation to victims, a call to the state party to investigate a particular situation, amend legislation, or to ensure that similar violations do not occur in the future.

Unlike the Human Rights Committee, CERD does not have a formal procedure to follow up after Opinions have been adopted to determine if the victim has been provided with a remedy for the violation of his or her rights.

Important points:

- **Annual Report**

  There is no sanction for failure to comply with the Committee's Opinions. The Committee's Annual Reports to the General Assembly include the text of its Opinions and the text of any decision declaring a communication inadmissible.

- **Reservations**

  Reservations to CERD may substantially limit the ability of an individual to successfully make a case against a particular state party. It is, therefore, necessary to check any reservations made by the state party. At the same time, some reservations may not be legitimate, that is, they may be incompatible with the object and purpose of the treaty. In these cases, it is possible that the treaty body will refuse to apply the reservation in a manner which would limit the application of CERD in the context of a communication. CERD has as yet not directly made a statement about the incompatibility of reservations with the Convention.

3. EXAMPLES OF CASES RELATING TO CERD

Since the Committee has issued very few Opinions, guidance as to the meaning and application of treaty rights may also be drawn from the Committee's General Recommendations and concluding observations on state reports. The following examples of the Committee's approach to the interpretation of Convention rights and freedoms are based on CERD cases, general recommendations and concluding observations.

- ***The definition of "racial discrimination" (article 1)***

  - **Which groups are protected**

    - **Meaning of "based on"**—The definition of "discrimination" in article 1(1) of the Convention protects against distinctions, exclusions, restrictions or preferences "based on" race, color, descent, or national or ethnic origin. The words "based on" have the same meaning as the words "on the grounds of," which are found in paragraph 7 of the preamble to the Convention.

    - **How to identify group membership**—The question arises as to how it is to be decided whether a person belongs to a particular racial or ethnic group for the purposes of the Convention. The Committee has said that, unless there are good reasons to the contrary, the primary method should be self-identification by the individual concerned.

    - **Meaning of "descent"**—The term "descent" does not solely refer to race, and also covers the situation of certain castes and tribes (for example, under the traditional Indian caste system).

- **Meaning of "nationality"**—A preference for persons trained in a particular country is not considered by the Committee to amount to discrimination on grounds of "nationality." Thus, in a case involving an Australian examination and quota system for overseas trained doctors that favoured doctors trained in Australia and New Zealand, the Committee considered that the system did not discriminate on the basis of race or national origin since medical students in Australia did not share a single national origin, and all overseas trained doctors were subject to the same system, irrespective of race or national origin. Accordingly, the system did not work to the benefit or detriment of persons of any particular race or national origin.

- **Guidance with respect to particular vulnerable groups—** There are certain, particularly vulnerable, groups that have come to the Committee's attention with sufficient frequency that the Committee has issued special guidance to states parties concerning their situations.

  - **Indigenous peoples**—The Committee has stressed that indigenous peoples fall under the scope of the Convention and that all appropriate means must be taken to combat and eliminate discrimination against them.

  - **Roma**—The Committee has expressed particular concern about the treatment of Roma and has issued a lengthy General Recommendation setting out specific "recommendations" to states parties on their treatment.

  - **Refugees**—The Committee has also expressed concern about the vulnerability of refugees and displaced people, and has issued a General Recommendation on their treatment, particularly once they return to their homes of origin. This entails rights to:
    - have property restored;
    - be compensated for property that cannot be restored;
    - participate fully and equally in public affairs at all levels;
    - have equal access to public services; and
    - receive rehabilitation assistance.

  - **Women**—The Committee is conscious of the fact that because of the different life experiences of women and men, in areas of both public and private life, there are circumstances in which racial discrimination only or primarily affects women, or affects women differently than men. Examples of forms of racial discrimination which may be directed towards women specifically because of their gender are:

- sexual violence committed against women members of particular racial or ethnic groups in detention or during armed conflict;
- the coerced sterilization of indigenous women;
- abuse of women workers in the informal sector or of domestic workers employed abroad by their employers.

In addition, racial discrimination may have consequences that affect primarily or only women. For example, in some societies, in the case of pregnancy resulting from racially motivated rape, women victims of such rape may be ostracized. Women may also be further hindered by a lack of access to remedies and complaint mechanisms for racial discrimination because of gender-related impediments, such as gender bias in the legal system and discrimination against women in private spheres of life.

Recognizing that some forms of racial discrimination have a unique and specific impact on women, the Committee endeavours to take into account gender factors or issues that may be interlinked with racial discrimination.

- **Relationship with article 5**—The definition of discrimination in article 1 refers to distinctions that nullify or impair the recognition, enjoyment or exercise of human rights, on an equal footing "in any field of public life, including political, economic, social or cultural life." Article 5 lists a number of "notable" examples of human rights that must be protected in the fields of political, economic, social or cultural life.

- **Permissible distinctions**—The definition of "discrimination" in article 1 refers to distinctions, exclusions, restrictions or preferences that nullify or impair the recognition, enjoyment or exercise of human rights on an equal footing. However, there are a number of situations in which such distinctions, exclusions, restrictions or preferences are not considered to amount to discrimination under the Convention:

  - **Distinctions between citizens and non-citizens**—The Convention does not protect against distinctions between citizens and non-citizens. (This does not mean that it is permissible to differentiate between different kinds of non-citizens.) Where a private (non-state) party seeks to justify a distinction on the grounds of citizenship, states parties must be vigilant to ensure that citizenship is, in reality, the basis for the distinction that is being drawn. Thus, in a Danish case where a bank denied a permanent resident a loan on the basis that he was not a Danish citizen, claiming that it was motivated by the need to ensure that the loan was repaid, the Committee expressed skepticism as to whether a person's nationality was relevant to his or her capacity to repay. The Committee concluded that the state should have initiated a proper investigation into the "real reasons" behind the bank's loan policy with respect to foreign residents in order to ascertain whether or not criteria involving racial discrimination within the meaning of article 1 were being applied.

- **Positive discrimination**—Differentiation of treatment is legitimate if it falls within the scope of article 1(4) of the Convention, which allows for positive but temporary measures aimed at securing the advancement of certain racial or ethnic groups or individuals that have been disadvantaged, and are necessary to ensure such groups or individuals equal enjoyment or exercise of human rights and fundamental freedoms.

- **Justifiable differentiation**—The Committee has said that differentiation of treatment will not constitute discrimination if the criteria for such differentiation, judged against the objectives and purposes of the Convention, are "legitimate." Similarly, in seeking to determine whether an action has an effect contrary to the Convention, the Committee will ascertain whether that action has an unjustifiable impact upon a group distinguished by race, colour, descent, or national or ethnic origin.

- *Condemnation and elimination of racial discrimination (article 2)*

  - **The Committee's role when reviewing the decisions of domestic tribunals as to whether discrimination has occurred**—Where a claim of discrimination brought before the Committee has already been examined by a domestic tribunal, the Committee faces a question as to how much respect to accord the domestic tribunal's factual assessment of the case.

    The Committee considers that, as a general rule, it is for the domestic courts of state parties to the Convention to review and evaluate the facts and evidence in a particular case. The Committee will consider whether the author was treated by the domestic tribunal that examined the allegation of discrimination, in a non-discriminatory fashion. Where, however, such a domestic tribunal has examined the case in a thorough and equitable manner, in the absence of an obvious defect in the decision the Committee will not substitute its own judgment for that of the domestic tribunal.

- **Obligation to bring to an end racial discrimination by private (non-state) parties (article 2(d))**—The Committee requires that states parties prohibit private acts of discrimination in their laws, and that they enforce such laws in good faith. Accordingly, findings by the Committee of a breach of article 2(d) are accompanied by findings of a breach of article 6 (the obligation to provide effective protection and remedies).

- *Racial segregation and apartheid (article 3)*

Although the reference to apartheid may have been initially directed exclusively to the situation in South Africa, article 3 as adopted prohibits all forms of racial segregation, whether institutional or non-institutional, in all states. The obligation to eradicate all practices of this nature includes the obligation to eradicate the consequences of such practices undertaken or tolerated by previous governments in the state, or imposed by forces outside the state. The Committee has also expressed concern with "racial segregation" arising without any initiative or direct involvement by the public authorities, as an unintended by-product of the actions of private persons.

- *Propagation of race hatred (article 4)*

  - **Scope of article 4(a)**—Article 4(a) requires states parties—to penalize four categories of misconduct:
    - dissemination of ideas based upon racial superiority or hatred;
    - incitement to racial hatred;
    - acts of violence against any race or group of persons of another colour or ethnic origin; and
    - incitement to such acts.

    By way of example of what constitutes "incitement," the Committee has found that acts amounting to incitement to racial discrimination and to acts of violence had taken place in a case involving the antagonistic reaction of members of a local community to a prospective lessee. The behaviour that the Committee considered amounted to such incitement included shouting the slogan "no more foreigners" when the author came to look at the house, intimating that if the author were to accept the house they would set fire to it and damage his car, telling officials that they could not accept the author as their neighbour, and drafting a petition rejecting the author's right to live in the neighbourhood.

Article 4(a) also penalizes the provision of assistance, including financing, for "racist activities." The term "racist activities" includes activities deriving from ethnic as well as racial differences.

- **Scope of article 4(b)**—Article 4(b) requires states parties to prohibit all organizations and activities that promote and incite racial discrimination, and to prohibit participation in such organizations or activities.

  Penal legislation must be drafted in sufficiently wide terms to catch all such organizations. Thus, an offence provision limited solely to organizations adhering to "fascist" ideology does not fully comply with article 4, since the protection provided by law does not cover the wide variety of racist organizations that may exist or develop.

- **Scope of article 4(c)**—Article 4(c) outlines the obligations of public authorities and public institutions not to promote or incite racial discrimination. Public authorities at all administrative levels, including municipalities, are bound by this provision.

- **Requirement both to enact penal laws and to enforce them**—The enactment of appropriate penal legislation does not, on its own, represent full compliance by states parties with their obligations under article 4. States parties must, in addition, ensure that such legislation is effectively enforced.

  This does not mean that states parties are obliged to prosecute every case of behaviour prohibited by article 4. The Committee recognizes that prosecuting authorities have a degree of discretion in deciding whether to institute a prosecution, which is governed by considerations of public policy. The Committee refers to this as the "expediency principle." Nevertheless, any prosecutorial discretion must be applied in light of the guarantees laid down in the Convention. When threats of racial violence are made, and especially when they are made in public and by a group, it is at least incumbent upon the state to investigate with due diligence.

- **Obligations under article 4 are mandatory and immediate**—The provisions of article 4 are of a mandatory character. Further, the Committee has said that because threats and acts of racial violence easily lead to other such acts and generate an atmosphere of hostility, only immediate intervention can meet the obligations of effective response.

- **Relationship with freedom of expression**—The Committee considers that article 4 is consistent with the obligations undertaken by states parties in other international human rights treaties to protect freedom of expression. In particular, the requirement in article 4 that states parties act with "due regard" to the principles embodied in the Universal Declaration of Human Rights, requires balancing the right to protection from racial discrimination with the right to freedom of expression.

  Not all states parties, however, consider that the relationship between article 4 and the right to freedom of expression is clear, and accordingly, there are a high number of reservations and interpretive declarations to this article.

- *Equality before the law (article 5)*

  - **General**—Article 5 reiterates the state's obligation laid down in article 2 to prohibit and to eliminate racial discrimination in all its forms, and to guarantee the right of everyone, without distinction as to race, colour, or national or ethnic origin, to equality before the law. Article 5 then lists in detail a number of "notable" human rights that the state must guarantee to everyone without discrimination. This list is not exhaustive. It contains examples of contexts in the social, political, economic and cultural spheres in which the principle of freedom from racial discrimination must apply.

    The rights and freedoms listed in article 5 are principally derived from the Universal Declaration of Human Rights, as recalled in the preamble to CERD. Most of these rights have been elaborated in the International Covenant on Civil and Political Rights, and/or the International Covenant on Economic, Social and Cultural Rights. Under CERD, however, these rights are not guaranteed in themselves, rather, states parties are required to prohibit and eliminate racial discrimination in the enjoyment of such rights. Whenever a state imposes a restriction upon one of the rights listed in article 5 of the Convention, it must ensure that, neither in purpose nor effect, is the restriction incompatible with article 1 of the Convention.

    The protection of the rights listed in article 5 may be guaranteed either by the use of public institutions or through the activities of private institutions. To the extent that private institutions influence the exercise of rights or the availability of opportunities, the state party must ensure that the result has neither the purpose nor the effect of creating or perpetuating racial discrimination.

- **Article 5(a)**—The rule laid down in article 5(a) to equal treatment before tribunals, without distinction as to race, colour or national or ethnic origin, applies to all types of judicial proceedings, including trial by jury. If members of a jury are suspected of displaying or voicing racial bias against the accused, it is incumbent upon the national judicial authorities to investigate, and to disqualify the juror if there is a suspicion that the juror might be biassed.

  Nevertheless, on a complaint of juror bias, the Committee will be reluctant to interfere with a decision by a competent judicial body as to the interpretation and application of domestic rules concerning disqualification of jurors. As long as the competent judicial body has duly and diligently investigated any claim of racial bias on the part of a juror, the Committee is unlikely to second-guess its decision.

- **Article 5(c)**—Article 5(c) requires that governments represent the whole population, without distinction as to race, colour, descent or national or ethnic origin. The Committee considers this protection to be an aspect of the right to self-determination of peoples, which is protected in other international instruments.

- **Article 5(d)**—Article 5(d) concerns the right to equality in the enjoyment of other "civil" rights.

  Article 5(d)(i), which protects the right to freedom of movement and residence within the border of the state, protects against forced resettlement of groups of people.

  The right to nationality under article 5(d)(iii) is denied if, for example, citizenship requires that persons prove they have several generations of ancestry in the country of residence.

- **Article 5(e)**—Article 5(e) protects against discrimination in the provision of economic, social and cultural rights. The Committee's task is to monitor the implementation of these rights, once they have been granted, on equal terms. In other words, the Committee's role is to ensure that to the extent such rights are available within a state, the availability is not determined on a discriminatory basis.

  The Committee has expressed grave concerns to states parties about socio-economic conditions such as poverty, housing, education, employment, absence of social security, medical care, and lack of access to basic social services such as water and electricity. The Committee has also noted that the withholding of basic supplies of food and medicine from a racial or ethnic group in itself constitutes a grave violation of human rights.

By way of an example of a violation of the right to non-discrimination in the right to work under article 5(i)(e), the Committee considered that there had been such a violation where a Court had upheld a decision by an employer to terminate the author's employment when she became pregnant, on the basis that the employer had dismissed the author because of his view that foreign women workers take their children to a neighbour or family and, at the "slightest setback," take sick leave.

- ***The state's obligation to provide effective protection and remedies (article 6)***

The state's obligations under article 6 are to provide effective protection and remedies against acts of racial discrimination, as well as to provide a right to just and adequate reparation or satisfaction for any damages suffered as a result of discrimination.

  - **Extent of obligation to investigate and prosecute**—States parties are required to initiate a proper investigation into allegations of discrimination. The investigation must be full and comprehensive, and not simply rely on the explanations offered by the alleged perpetrator of the discrimination. Thus, where a Danish bank refused the author a loan, purportedly because he was not a Danish citizen, and the prosecuting authority had accepted the Bank's explanations without investigating further, the Committee considered that the state's obligations under article 6 had been violated. The state should have initiated a proper investigation into the "real reasons" behind the bank's loan policy in order to ascertain whether or not criteria involving racial discrimination were being applied. Because the police had not done so, the author had been denied an effective remedy within the meaning of article 6.

    The Committee recognizes that state authorities have a discretion about whether to prosecute criminal offences, which is governed by considerations of public policy. Nevertheless, that discretion should be applied in each case of alleged racial discrimination in the light of the Convention guarantees. The Committee will not necessarily accept at face value a decision not to prosecute, particularly if the Committee does not consider that a careful investigation has been conducted. Thus, where the perpetrator had called the author and his brother "a bunch of monkeys" and the prosecuting authority had discontinued the investigation because the statements were made in connection with a "tense episode" and might have referred to the nature of the author's conduct rather than his race, the Committee found a violation of article 6. Because the investigation was discontinued, it had never been established whether the author had been insulted on the grounds of his national or ethnic origin, in violation of the Convention. It followed that the author had been denied effective protection and remedies against racial discrimination.

- **Extent of judicial review/appeal rights**—The Committee is likely to look more favourably on state prosecutorial and other decisions if judicial review or a right to an appeal were made available. At the same time, the Committee does not consider that article 6 necessarily imposes upon states parties the duty to institute a mechanism of sequential remedies, up to and including the court of final appeal, in cases of alleged racial discrimination.

- **The state's obligation to provide economic compensation** —The Committee considers that the conviction and punishment of the perpetrator of a criminal act, and the order to pay economic compensation to the victim are legal sanctions with different functions and purposes. Thus, although the victim is not necessarily entitled to compensation in addition to the criminal sanction under all circumstances, in accordance with article 6, the victim's claim for compensation has to at least be considered. This is the case even where no bodily harm has been inflicted and where the damage to the victim is in the nature of humiliation, defamation or other attacks against his or her reputation and self esteem. Thus, where the author was refused access to a place of service intended for the use of the general public solely on the ground of his national or ethnic background, the Committee observed that this was a humiliating experience which may merit economic compensation and cannot always be adequately repaired or satisfied by merely imposing a criminal sanction on the perpetrator.

- **Delay**—The Committee has given states parties a certain amount of leeway in relation to the length of time they take to provide a remedy, and has held in at least one case that the condemnation of a perpetrator and imposition of a penalty satisfied the states party's obligations under article 6, even though there had been a considerable lapse of time following the events giving rise to the communication.

- ***The kind of recommendations that can be expected from the Committee***

If the Committee concludes there has been a violation of the Convention, the Committee usually concludes its Opinions with a recommendation to the state party as to how to redress the violation. The remedies proposed by the Committee are not always personal in nature. In some cases, the Committee does no more than recommend that the state party review its policy and procedures in the relevant area, or otherwise take general measures to counteract racial discrimination in the future.

However, in other cases, the Committee has recommended a personalized remedy to assist the author. For example:

- in a case where the right to work had been breached, the Committee recommended that the state party secure alternative employment for the author and/or provide her with such other relief as may be considered equitable.
- in a case where the author had been refused a bank loan in violation of the Convention, the Committee recommended that the state party provide the author with reparation or satisfaction commensurate with any damage he had suffered.

In some cases the Committee has also made recommendations of a general nature to a state party about how it can improve its practice, even though the Committee has ultimately concluded that the communication did not disclose a violation of the Convention.

The cases or circumstances discussed here are only samples of decisions made by CERD, or suggested from its General Recommendations, or concluding observations on state reports. This list is not exhaustive, and individuals are entitled to make additional kinds of claims on the basis of the rights in the Racial Discrimination Convention.

CHAPTER VI

THE COMMITTEE ON THE ELIMINATION OF DISCRIMINATION AGAINST WOMEN (CEDAW)

1. OVERVIEW OF THE COMMITTEE ON THE ELIMINATION OF DISCRIMINATION AGAINST WOMEN (CEDAW)

The Committee on the Elimination of Discrimination Against Women (CEDAW) is responsible for considering all communications submitted under the Optional Protocol to the Convention. CEDAW is composed of 23 experts, nominated and elected by states parties to the Convention. Members serve in their personal capacity.

The Optional Protocol entered into force on 22 December 2000. Although the Committee has not yet considered a complaint, it has formally adopted Rules of Procedure to govern the consideration of individual communications when they are received.

To help maintain impartiality in the complaint process, the Rules of Procedure of CEDAW provide that members shall not take part in the deliberation of a case in which they have a personal interest, or in which they have participated in the making of any decision in the case before it reached the Committee (Rule 60).

When the Committee considers individual communications, the meetings are closed (Rule 74).

The Committee's Rules of Procedure allow it to make decisions on individual communications by majority. However, the practice of other Committees has been to attempt to reach consensus where possible, and it is likely CEDAW will do the same. In cases where no consensus can be reached, the individual members may express individual Views which are attached to the Committee's decision (Rules 64, 70,72).

a) Working Group

The Committee has established a Working Group, composed of five of its members selected on a geographic basis, to assist with the individual communications process. Under the Rules of Procedure, working groups can undertake the following functions on behalf of the Committee:

- decide to register a case, on the basis of a majority;
- request interim measures from states parties (Rule 63);
- declare a communication admissible, by unanimous decision (Rule 64); and
- make recommendations to the full Committee on the merits of a communication (Rule 72).

b) Rapporteurs

The Committee is also entitled to designate rapporteurs to make recommendations to the Committee in connection with individual cases and to assist in its work under the Optional Protocol.

See Diagram on pp. 130-1.

2. INDIVIDUAL COMPLAINTS PROCEDURE OF CEDAW

a) Registration of the Communication and Preliminary Procedures

i) Submission of the Communication

A communication should be submitted to the Secretariat of the Division for the Advancement of Women in writing, by letter, fax or email. Faxed or electronic communications must be confirmed by signed copies received by the Secretariat. Communications cannot be anonymous. The state that is the subject of the communication must be clearly identified. Although there is no mandatory format for communications, the Committee has created a model communication form for potential complainants. Use of the form can streamline the communication process and is advisable. (See Annex 1)

Where the communication does not provide the necessary information for it to be registered, the Secretariat may request further information from the author. Since the Committee will be relying heavily on the facts in each particular case, it is especially important to set out all the relevant information at the outset.

It is important to include, at minimum, the following information:

- the identity and contact information of the victim;
- the state against which the communication is directed;
- the provisions of the Convention alleged to have been breached;
- all the relevant facts together with any supporting documentation (such as a statement signed by the victim, witness statements, court documents);
- steps taken to exhaust local remedies, or evidence why local remedies are ineffective, unavailable or unreasonably prolonged;
- information regarding whether this matter is or has been before any other procedure of international investigation or settlement; and
- the remedy requested.

Other important points:

• **Languages**

The Committee's working languages are at present all six official UN languages, English, French, Spanish, Chinese, Arabic and Russian.

• **Time Limitations**

There is no stipulated time limit within which to bring a claim, but very long delays in bringing the claim may be considered by CEDAW to lessen the credibility of the claim.

• **Legal Aid**

The UN does not provide legal aid or financial assistance to authors, nor does CEDAW require that states parties provide legal aid where an individual wishes to submit a communication. Authors should determine whether or not their own domestic legal aid system provides for the possibility of legal aid.

However, NGOs and other legal professionals are allowed to represent the victims (with their approval). There is no prohibition on victims seeking assistance from NGOs or appointing them as their representatives.

• **Withdrawal of the Communication**

Complainants may subsequently withdraw their communications.

• **Confidentiality**

Decisions concerning inadmissibility, discontinuation or merits (Views) will be made public. The Committee may decide that the identity of the complainant remain confidential.

However, the communication must not be anonymous. In order for a communication to be considered, the identity of both the victim and the complainant (if different from the victim) must be revealed to the state party.

The author and the state party may make public 'any submissions or information bearing on the proceedings,' provided that the Committee does not expressly ask them to refrain from doing so. At all times, the Committee may decide that certain elements of the case must remain confidential.

ii) Registration of the Communication

Communications will initially be reviewed by the UN secretariat servicing the Committee (the Division for the Advancement of Women) prior to their registration. The secretariat will report to the Working Group of the Committee on the numbers of submissions which on their face do not meet admissibility requirements and whose correspondents which have been so informed by the Secretariat (CEDAW/C/2002/II/CRP.4). The Secretariat will also report to the Working Group on correspondence

The CEDAW Complaints Procedure

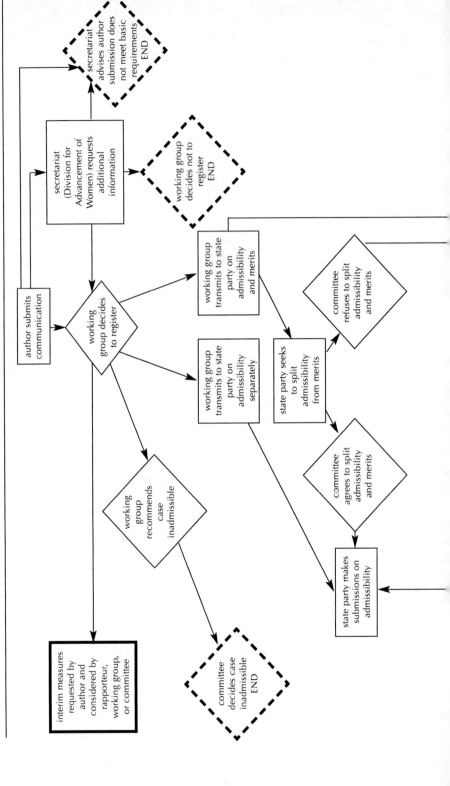

author submits communication

secretariat (Division for Advancement of Women) requests additional information

secretariat advises author submission does not meet basic requirements END

working group decides to register

working group decides not to register END

interim measures requested by author and considered by rapporteur, working group, or committee

working group recommends case inadmissible

working group transmits to state party on admissibility and merits

working group transmits to state party on admissibility separately

committee decides case inadmissible END

state party seeks to split admissibility from merits

committee refuses to split admissibility and merits

committee agrees to split admissibility and merits

state party makes submissions on admissibility

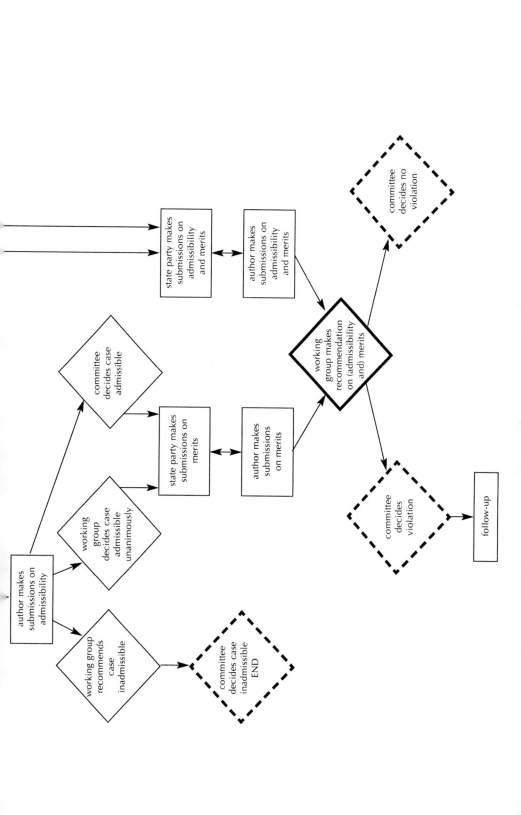

which they have redirected to alternative venues including the Office of the High Commissioner for Human Rights.

The secretariat may ask the complainant for clarification regarding any or all of the following issues (Rule 58):

- name, address, age and occupation of the complainant and verification of identity;
- the state against which the communication is directed;
- the object of the communication;
- the precise CEDAW provision which is being invoked;
- information about which local or domestic remedies have been used;
- information about other international procedures that are being or have been used; and
- clarification of the facts of the claim.

The secretariat will indicate a time limit for replying to such requests (Rule 58). Failure to provide adequate information necessary to register a case, may result in a communication not being registered. The Working Group of the Committee will register decisions on the basis of a majority of its members.

iii) Transmittal to the State Party

Once the secretariat is satisfied the communication contains sufficient information, the communication will be transmitted by the Committee to the state party for a response.

iv) Interim Measures

At any time after receipt of the communication, the Committee may request the state party to take interim measures to avoid possible irreparable damage to the claimant. Any such requests are not prejudicial to the Committee's final Views (Rule 63), nor are they an indication that the Committee has made any final decision as to the merits of the claim.

b) Admissibility and Submissions from the Parties

Once the communication has been transmitted to the state party, the state has six months in which to respond to the communication in writing (Rule 69).

According to its Rules of Procedure, the regular practice of the Committee will be to seek a response from the state party simultaneously on both the issue of the admissibility and the merits of the communication. The state party's response will then be transmitted to the author, who will be given an opportunity to comment, within a time frame fixed by the Committee.

The Committee may request the state party or the author to submit additional written explanations or statements relevant to the issues of the admissibility or merits and, if it does so, will give the other party an opportunity to comment, again within a fixed time frame.

The Committee is also entitled to obtain any documents that may assist in the disposal of the communication (for example, general country information held by NGOs or other United Nations bodies). If it does so, however, the Committee is obliged to offer both parties an opportunity to comment on the information before relying on it (Rule 72).

If the Committee thinks it is warranted, the Committee may chose to depart from its ordinary procedure, and request that the state party's initial written explanation or statement relate only to the admissibility of a communication.

It is also possible for the state party to request that the Committee deal separately with the admissibility question. Within two months of receiving a request from the Committee for its response to a communication, the state party may submit a request in writing that the communication be rejected as inadmissible, together with reasons in support of that request. The Committee will then decide whether to accede to the request to deal separately with the admissibility question. However, unless the Committee grants the state party an extension, the state party is still obligated to respond on the merits within the six month time frame. Having given the author a chance to comment on the state party's submission on admissibility, CEDAW will review all the information submitted by the parties, and adopt an admissibility decision. If the Committee decides that the communication is inadmissible, the case is finished. Where a communication has been found to be inadmissible, the author may subsequently seek review of the decision if the circumstances that gave rise to the inadmissibility of the decision no longer exist (Rule 70).

If the Committee decides that the communication is admissible, then it will move on to the merits stage. After considering the state party's submissions on the merits, the Committee is entitled to revoke its decision that the communication is admissible (Rule 71).

Both parties will be informed of its decision. The Views of the Committee will not necessarily be unanimous. Any member of the Committee may request that his or her individual opinion be attached to the Views of the Committee.

c) Follow-up

The Committee's Rules of Procedure provide for follow-up of states parties' responses to the Committee's Views (Rule 73).

Within six months of the Committee issuing its Views, the state party is directed to submit to the Committee a written response, including information on any action taken in light of the Committee's Views and recommendations. The Committee may subsequently invite the state party to submit further information about measures taken by it, and may request the state party to include relevant information in its subsequent state reports.

Under its Rules of Procedure, the Committee is to designate a rapporteur or working group on follow-up. The individual or working group will ascertain the measures taken by states parties in response to the Committee's Views.

The Committee is also to include information on follow-up in its Annual Reports to the General Assembly.

Important points:

- **Annual Report**

There is no sanction for failure to comply with the Committee's Views. The Committee will follow the practice adopted by other Committees of giving publicity to its Views and follow-up information through the Committee's Annual Reports to the General Assembly.

- **Reservations**

Reservations to CEDAW may substantially limit the ability of an individual to successfully make a case against a particular state party. It is, therefore, necessary to check any reservations made by the state party. At the same time, some reservations may not be compatible with the object and purpose of the treaty. In these cases, it *is possible* that CEDAW will refuse to apply the reservation in a manner which would limit the application of the Convention in the context of a communication. CEDAW has stated that it considers a number of the reservations that have been made by states parties to be incompatible with the object and purpose of the Convention. The concluding observations of CEDAW which are made following their consideration of a state party's report should, therefore, be consulted for any possible comments concerning a state party's reservations.

3. EXAMPLES OF POTENTIAL CASES RELATING TO CEDAW

The Committee has not yet received or considered any individual communications. The Committee's General Recommendations provide some assistance to their approach to the interpretation of Convention rights and freedoms, together with their concluding observations on state reports.

The following information taken from General Recommendations and concluding observations suggests subject matter for potential communications. At the same time, the application of these general principles and statements to specific circumstances will have to be further developed in the context of an individual case.

- ### *Definition of "discrimination against women" (article 1)*

  - **Gender-based violence**—Although the Convention nowhere expressly mentions gender-based violence, the Committee considers that it is a form of discrimination that seriously inhibits women's ability to enjoy rights and freedoms on a basis of equality with men.

    The Committee defines gender-based violence as violence that is directed against a woman because she is a woman, or that affects women disproportionately. It can comprise acts that inflict physical, mental or sexual harm or suffering, threats of such acts, or coercion and other deprivations of liberty.

    Gender-based violence is "discrimination" in terms of article 1 of the Convention. Its effect on the physical and mental integrity of women is to impair or nullify their equal enjoyment of human rights and fundamental freedoms. These rights and freedoms include rights held under international law such as: the right to life; the right not to be subject to torture or to cruel, inhuman or degrading treatment or punishment; the right to equal protection according to humanitarian norms in time of international or internal armed conflict; the right to liberty and security of the person; the right to equal protection under the law; the right to equality in the family; the right to the highest standard attainable of physical and mental health; and the right to just and favourable conditions of work.

    Given that gender-based violence amounts to "discrimination" under the Convention, states parties are required under article 2 to condemn and eliminate it, whether perpetrated by public authorities or by private parties. By way of example, the Committee has criticized one state party for allowing in its penal code less than rigorous sanctions or penalties for "honour killings." Honour killings constitute a grave violation of the right to life and security, and therefore must be appropriately addressed under the law.

    In addition, the Committee considers that numerous other articles in the Convention are involved in gender-based violence, including articles 5, 10(c), 11, 12 and 16. These provisions cumulatively require states parties to act to protect women against violence of any kind occurring within the family, at the workplace or in any other area of social life. *(See General Recommendations 12 and 19)*

- **Guidance with respect to particular vulnerable groups**—The Committee recognizes that, because of the different life experiences of certain groups of women, gender-based discrimination may affect women in different ways. The Committee has emphasized states parties' obligations to eliminate discrimination against particularly vulnerable groups and to ensure their advancement. For example:

- **Prostitutes**—The Committee has stressed the particular vulnerability of prostitutes because of their marginalized, and potentially unlawful, status. Prostitutes need the equal protection of laws, particularly against rape and other forms of violence.

- **Disabled women**—The Committee has expressed particular concern as to the situation of disabled women, and has asked states parties to ensure their equal access to employment, education, health services and social security, and their participation in all areas of social and cultural life.

- **Women at various stages of the life cycle**—The Committee has drawn attention to the varying needs and concerns of women at different stages of the life cycle, for example, girl children, adolescents, and aging women.

- **Other groups**—The Committee has additionally recognized the special vulnerability of migrant women, refugee and internally displaced women, indigenous women and rural women.

- *Condemnation and elimination of discrimination against women (article 2); and measures to ensure advancement (article 3)*

Articles 2 and 3, together, establish a comprehensive obligation to eliminate discrimination in all its forms, which is additional to—and wider than—the specific obligations contained under articles 5–16.

The Committee has stressed on a number of occasions that it is not sufficient for states parties simply to guarantee rights in their laws. States parties must take measures to ensure that such rights are actually available and able to be exercised. This includes the condemnation and elimination of private discrimination.

- *"Temporary Special Measures" (or affirmative action) (article 4)*

As embodied in the Convention, temporary special measures (sometimes referred to as affirmative action) means the establishment of law, policies and programmes that give greater advantage to women over men. Such programmes require undermining formal or legal equality for a certain period of time in order to achieve substantive equality in fact in the long term.

The provision of maternity leave is not a temporary special measure requiring justification under article 4(1) of the Convention, but is guaranteed under article 4(2).

• *Modification of social and cultural patterns (article 5)*

Article 5 has been read together with articles 2(f) and 10(c), which cumulatively condemn gender stereotyping.

The Committee has drawn particular attention to the role of tradition, culture and gender stereotyping in justifying and perpetuating practices of violence and coercion against women (including family violence and abuse, forced marriage, dowry deaths, acid attacks and female circumcision).

• *Suppression of trafficking in women (article 6)*

The Committee has drawn attention to new forms of sexual exploitation, such as:

* sex tourism;
* recruitment of labour under false pretenses; and
* organized marriages between women from developing countries and foreign nationals.

The Committee considers such practices to be incompatible with the equal enjoyment of rights by women, and to put women at special risk of violence and abuse.

The Committee has also observed that situations of war and armed conflict often lead to increased prostitution, trafficking in women and sexual assault of women, and that accordingly, specific protective and punitive measures are required in such circumstances.

• *Participation in political and public life (article 7)*

The obligation of states parties under article 7 extends to all areas of public and political life. The political and public life of a country is a broad concept that refers to:

* the exercise of political power, in particular legislative, judicial, executive and administrative powers;
* all aspects of public administration;
* the formulation and implementation of policy at the international, national, regional and local levels; and
* many aspects of civil society, including public boards and local councils, and the activities of organizations concerned with public and political life, such as political parties, trade unions, professional or industry associations, women's organizations and community-based organizations.

• *Rights to vote and be elected (article 7(a))*

The enjoyment of the right to vote should not be subject to restrictions or conditions that do not apply to men or that have a disproportionate impact on women. For example, a requirement that voters have a specified level of education or are literate, or possess a minimum property qualification, would violate the Convention if it had a disproportionate impact on women.

The rights to vote and to be eligible for election must be enjoyed both in law and in fact. Therefore, states parties must take measures to overcome social or customary impediments to the exercise of these rights. Such impediments might include:

- illiteracy and lack of knowledge of the political system, or of their rights;
- lack of access to information about candidates, parties, and voting procedures;
- cultural and social stereotypes, and influence from male relatives;
- restrictions on freedom of movement.

- **Right to participate in the formulation of government policy (article 7(b))**

State parties have responsibilities:

- where it is within their control, to appoint women to senior decision-making roles and to consult and incorporate the advice of representative women's groups;
- to ensure that barriers to women's full participation in the formulation of government policy are identified and overcome. Such barriers might include complacency after token women are appointed, and traditional and customary attitudes that discourage women's participation;
- to endeavour to ensure that women are appointed to government advisory bodies on an equal basis with men and that these bodies take appropriate account of the views of representative women's groups; and
- to encourage initiatives to change social attitudes that discourage women's involvement in political and public life.

- **The right to hold public office and to perform public functions (article 7(b))**

The Committee has expressed concern over the continued exclusion of women, in many countries, from top-ranking positions in cabinets, the civil service and public administration, and in the judicial and justice systems.

The Committee considers that laws are discriminatory which exclude women from:

- exercising royal powers;
- serving as judges in religious or traditional tribunals, which have been vested with jurisdiction on behalf of the state; or
- full participation in the military.

• *Participation in non-governmental organizations (article 7(c))*

The Committee has expressed particular concern about women's participation in two kinds of organizations that are important vehicles to participation in public life: political parties and trade unions. The Committee considers that states parties are under an obligation to take all appropriate measures, including enactment of legislation, to ensure that such organisations do not discriminate against women. Such organisations should be under an obligation to demonstrate their commitment to the principle of gender equality in their constitutions, in the application of their rules and in the composition of their membership at all levels.

With respect to under-representation of women in political parties, the Committee has said that Governments should encourage political parties to adopt effective measures to overcome obstacles to women's participation, including allowing for temporary special measures. *(See General Recommendation 23)*

• *Representation at international level (article 8)*

The Committee has stressed that governments are obliged to ensure the presence of women at all levels and in all areas of international affairs, including in economic and military matters, in multilateral and bilateral diplomacy, and in official delegations to international and regional conferences.

The Committee has expressed particular concern about the gross under-representation of women in diplomatic and foreign service, particularly at the highest ranks. Restrictions on access to the foreign service pertaining to marital status are discriminatory, as is inequality in the availability of spousal and family benefits. *(See General Recommendation 23)*

• *Nationality (article 9)*

Citizenship or nationality is a fundamental right which men and women must be able to enjoy equally, and which is critical to women's full participation in society. Without status as nationals or citizens, women may be deprived of the right to vote or to stand for pubic office, and may be denied access to public benefits and choice of residence.

The Committee has indicated that nationality should be capable of change by an adult woman and should not be arbitrarily removed because of marriage or dissolution of marriage, or because her husband or father changes his nationality.

• *Education (article 10)*

The Committee has noted, for example, that the expulsion of girls from school because they have become pregnant violates the Convention.

- **Employment (article 11)**

  - **Dismissal on ground of pregnancy**—The Committee has pointed out, for example, that the dismissal of unwed teachers who become pregnant is in violation of the Convention.

  - **Unpaid women working in family enterprises**—The Committee has expressed particular concern about the high percentage of women working without payment, social security or social benefits in rural and urban family enterprises, usually owned by a male member of the family. The Committee considers that unpaid work of this kind constitutes a form of women's exploitation that is contrary to the Convention.

  - **Sexual harassment**—The Committee considers that sexual harassment in the workplace is a form of gender-specific violence that seriously impairs women's equality in employment. Sexual harassment includes such unwelcome, sexually determined behaviour as:
    - physical contact and advances;
    - sexually coloured remarks;
    - showing pornography; and
    - sexual demands whether by words or actions.

    Such conduct can be humiliating and may constitute a health and safety problem. It is discriminatory when a woman has reasonable grounds to believe that her objection would disadvantage her employment opportunities, including recruitment or promotion, or when it creates a hostile work environment.

  - **Equal remuneration for work of equal value**—The Committee has stressed the need to ensure the application of the principle of equal remuneration for work of equal value in practice. This may require, for instance, the development and adoption of job evaluation systems based on gender-neutral criteria. Such criteria would facilitate the comparison of the value of jobs of a different nature in which women presently predominate, with jobs in which men presently predominate.

- **Health care (article 12)**

  States are required to eliminate discrimination against women in their access to health-care services throughout the life cycle, particularly in the areas of family planning, pregnancy and confinement, and during the post-natal period. The Committee has emphasized the interconnection between this provision and other articles in the Convention that have a bearing on women's health. (These include articles 5(b), 10, 10(h), 11, 14(2)(b), 14(2)(h), 16(1)(e) and 16(2).)

  States parties have a responsibility, through legislation, and executive action and policy, to "respect," "protect" and "fulfill" women's rights to health care. They must, in addition, ensure the availability of effective judicial action where rights have been violated.

- **Obligation to "respect" women's rights to health care—** The obligation to "respect" requires states parties to refrain from obstructing women's access to health services. Unacceptable restrictions on access to health services include:
  - restricting access solely on the basis of gender or marital status;
  - requiring authorization of husbands, partners, parents or health authorities (for example, a requirement of prior spousal consent for an abortion contravenes the Convention);
  - refusing to provide for the performance of certain reproductive health services for women;
  - criminalizing medical procedures only needed by women or punishing women who undergo such procedures; and
  - imposing prohibitive fees which have the effect of restricting access to services.

- **Obligation to "protect" women's right to health care—**The obligation to "protect" requires states parties, their agents and officials, to take action to prevent violations of rights by private persons and organizations and to impose sanctions for violations.

  If health service providers refuse to perform certain services based on conscientious objection, the state is obliged to introduce measures to ensure that women are referred to alternative health providers.

  The Committee has particularly stressed the protective obligation in the context of gender-based violence. In that context, the obligation includes:
  - the enactment and enforcement of laws, policies, protocols and procedures to detect and address gender-based violence against women and sexual abuse of girl children, and the provision of appropriate health services;
  - the provision of gender sensitive training to enable health care workers to detect and manage health consequences of gender based violence;
  - the provision of fair and protective procedures for hearing complaints against health care professionals and imposing sanctions for sexual abuse; and
  - the enactment and enforcement of laws that prohibit female genital mutilation and marriage of girl children. *(See General Recommendation 14)*

- **The duty to "fulfill" women's right to health care**—The duty to "fulfill" places an obligation on states parties to take appropriate legislative, judicial, administrative, budgetary, economic and other measures, to the maximum extent of their available resources, to ensure that women realize their rights to health care.

- **Informed consent**—Women have the right to be fully informed, by properly trained personnel, of their options in agreeing to treatment or research, including likely benefits and potential adverse effects of proposed procedures, and available alternatives.

  States parties are required to prohibit forms of coercion, such as non-consensual sterilization, mandatory testing for sexually transmitted diseases, mandatory pregnancy testing as a condition of employment, and forced gynaecological examinations of women in the investigation of allegations of sexual assault.

- **Female-specific health concerns**—Measures undertaken by states parties to eliminate discrimination will be regarded as insufficient if they do not include the provision of services to prevent, detect and treat illnesses specific to women. There are a number of biological, societal and cultural factors that lead to differences between women and men in health status. These include:
  - biological factors relating to reproductive issues and differing impact of sexually transmitted diseases;
  - the impact of gender-based violence on women's health (including sexual abuse of girl children);
  - cultural practices such as female genital mutilation; and
  - psycho-social factors that may vary between women and men (for example, psychological conditions such as post-natal depression; anorexia that might disproportionately or only affect women).

- **Sexual health and HIV/AIDS**—The Committee has stressed the need for adolescent girls and women to be provided with adequate access to information, education and services necessary to ensure sexual health. Such information and services should be provided, without prejudice or discrimination, to all women and girls, including those who have been trafficked, and including women who are not legally resident in the country.

  The Committee has expressed particular concern about discrimination against women in national strategies for the prevention and control of acquired immunodeficiency syndrome (AIDS).

- **Nutrition**—The full realization of women's right to health can be achieved only when states parties fulfill their obligation to respect, protect and promote women's fundamental human right to nutritional well-being throughout their lifespan by means of a food supply that is safe, nutritious and adapted to local conditions. To this end, states parties should take steps to facilitate physical and economic access to productive resources, especially for rural women, and to otherwise ensure that the special nutritional needs of all women within their jurisdiction are met.

- **Vulnerable sub-categories of women**—The Committee recognizes that societal factors that determine health status can vary among women themselves and believes that the Convention requires that special attention should be given to the health needs of women belonging to vulnerable and disadvantaged groups. Such groups include migrant women, refugees and internally displaced women, women in prostitution, indigenous women, women with physical or mental disabilities, rural women and women trapped in situations of armed conflict.

  The Committee has also emphasized that appropriate health services need to be provided for women throughout the life cycle, including girl children, adolescents and older women.

- **Privatization of health services**—The Committee has indicated that states parties cannot absolve themselves of responsibility in these areas by delegating or transferring the state's health functions to private sector agencies.

- **Maternity**—The Committee has pointed out that it is the duty of states parties to ensure women's right to safe motherhood, including emergency obstetric services. States parties should allocate support to these services to the maximum extent of available resources. *(See General Recommendation 24)*

- *Equality before the law (article 15)*

  - **Unequal application of laws**—An example of a breach of this article arising from unequal application of laws is the existence of gender-specific laws on adultery.

  - **Ability to enter contracts**—Impermissible restrictions on this right would include a requirement of the concurrence or guarantee of a male husband or relative before a woman was entitled to enter a contract or have access to financial credit.

  - **Ability to bring litigation**—Impermissible restrictions on this right include restrictions, resulting from either law or custom, on a woman's:
    - ability to bring litigation;
    - access to legal advice; or
    - equality in status as a witness or the weight given to her evidence.

- **Domicile**—This is a concept used in common law countries to refer to the country in which a person intends to reside and to which jurisdiction she will submit. Domicile is originally acquired by a child through its parents but, in adulthood, denotes the country in which a person normally resides and in which she intends to reside permanently.

  Domicile, like nationality, should be capable of change at will by an adult woman, regardless of her marital status.

  Migrant women who live and work temporarily in another country should be permitted the same rights as men to have their spouses, partners and children join them.

- *Marriage and family relations (article 16)*

  - **The various forms of family**—The Committee recognises that the form and concept of the family can vary from state to state and even between regions within a state. Whatever form it takes and whatever the legal system, religion, custom or tradition within the country, the treatment of women in the family, both at law and in private, must accord with the principles of equality and justice for all people.

  - **Polygamous marriage**—Laws that permit polygamous marriage violate the equality rights of women.

- *Rights to enter marriage and choose a spouse (articles 16(1)(a) and (b))*

A woman's right to choose when, if, and whom she will marry must be protected and enforced at law, subject to reasonable restrictions based, for example, on a woman's youth or close familial relationship with her partner.

This right can be violated not only by laws but also by custom, tradition and failure of enforcement. Practices of concern to the Committee include:

- Countries that, on the basis of custom, religious beliefs or the ethnic origins of particular groups of people, permit forced marriages or remarriages;
- Countries that allow a woman's marriage to be arranged for payment or preferment; and
- Countries where poverty forces women to marry foreign nationals for financial security.

- *Equal rights and responsibilities during marriage and at its dissolution (article 16(1)(c))*

Common law principles, religious or customary law that restrict women's rights to equal status and responsibility within marriage (for example, by according the husband the status of head of household and primary decision-maker) will contravene the Convention.

A failure by the state to give legal protection to women living in unions other than marriage contravenes the Convention. Women living in such relationships should have equality of status with men both in family life and in sharing of income and assets protected by law, and should share equal rights and responsibilities with men for the care and raising of dependent children or family members.

- ***Parental responsibilities (article 16(1)(d) and (f))***

States parties should ensure that, by law both parents, regardless of their marital status and whether they live with their children or not, share equal rights and responsibilities for their children.

Of particular concern to the Committee are:

- the status of parents and children when the parents are not married; and
- fathers sharing the responsibility of care, protection and maintenance of children when the parents are divorced or living apart.

- ***Control over reproduction (article 16(1)(e))***

The rationale for this protection is that the bearing and raising of children places inequitable burdens of work on women, affects their right of access to education, employment and other activities relating to their personal development, and their physical and mental health.

Decisions whether to have children or not, while preferably made in consultation with a spouse or partner, must not be limited by spouse, parent, partner or Government. Coercive practices such as forced pregnancies, abortions or sterilization breach this provision.

- ***Equality of personal rights between husband and wife (article 16(1)(g))***

The same rights, on a basis of equality of men and women, to choose a profession or employment that is best suited to one's abilities, qualification and aspiration.

The same rights, on a basis of equality of men and women, to choose one's name, thereby preserving individuality and identity in the community. A woman is denied these rights when, by law or custom, she is obliged to change her name on marriage or at its dissolution.

- ***Equality of property rights between husband and wife (article 16(1)(h))***

The right to own, manage, enjoy and dispose of property is central to a woman's right to enjoy financial independence, and in many countries, will be critical to her ability to earn a livelihood and to provide adequate housing and nutrition for herself and her family. The Committee considers that any law or custom that grants men a right to a greater share of property either during or on dissolution of a marriage or other form of union (*de facto* relationship), or on the death of a relative, is discriminatory.

Property accumulated during a *de facto* relationship or union should be treated on the same basis as property acquired during marriage.

The Committee has expressed the view that on dissolution of marriage, financial and non-financial contributions to property acquired during marriage should be given the same weight. This is because non-financial contributions such as raising children, caring for elderly relatives and discharging household duties may have freed the other partner to earn an income and increase the assets.

Regimes that require property owned by a woman during marriage or on divorce to be managed by a man are discriminatory. Such regimes are particularly of concern to the Committee where there is no legal requirement that a woman be consulted when property owned by the parties during marriage or *de facto* relationship or union is sold or otherwise disposed of.

In countries undergoing a programme of agrarian reform or redistribution of land among groups of different ethnic origins, the Committee has said that the right of women, regardless of marital status, to share such redistributed land on equal terms with men should be carefully observed.

Discrimination against women in the law and practice concerning inheritance contravenes the Convention. Examples are:

- women receiving a smaller share of their husband's or father's property at death than would widowers and sons; and
- limited and controlled rights to receive income from a deceased's property. *(See General Recommendation 20)*

• *Child marriage (article 16(2))*

The Committee considers that the minimum age for marriage should be 18 years for both men and women. Marriage of girls before they have attained full maturity and capacity to act may have adverse affects on health and education and thereby restrict economic autonomy.

The Committee is of the view that stipulations of different ages for marriage for men and women should be abolished.

Betrothal of girls, or undertakings by family members on their behalf, contravene the Convention and a women's right to freely choose her partner.

These substantive examples or illustrations of the substance of possible future cases, which are suggested from CEDAW's General Recommendations and concluding observations on state reports, are not exhaustive. Individuals are entitled to make many more kinds of claims on the basis of the rights in the Women's Discrimination Convention.

CHAPTER VII

THE INVESTIGATIVE MECHANISMS

1. INTRODUCTION

In addition to the individual communication procedures, the Convention Against Torture and the Optional Protocol to the Convention on the Elimination of Discrimination Against Women, authorize the treaty bodies to undertake investigations in response to allegations of rights violations.

The standard for initiating such an inquiry is that there must be "reliable information" which indicates that "torture is being systematically practised" (article 20) in the case of CAT, or "grave or systematic violations," in the case of CEDAW (article 8 of the Optional Protocol). In other words, in contrast to the individual complaints procedure which may address a single violation, the inquiry procedure is available in the case of CAT only where there is significant evidence indicating a pattern of misconduct. In the case of CEDAW, the violations must be grave if not "systematic." Secondly, it is not sufficient that there are grounds to believe that a violation of treaty rights has occurred. CAT authorizes an investigation where "reliable information" has been submitted to the Committee that torture is being systematically practised . The CEDAW Optional Protocol permits an investigation where there is "reliable information indicating grave or systematic violations."

The investigation procedure is most commonly instigated by NGOs which may be in a better position to document a pattern of violations. Nevertheless, individuals are not barred from providing information to CAT or CEDAW and suggesting to the Committee that an investigation is warranted according to the information provided.

Other contrasts between the individual complaints and inquiry procedures:

- there have been very few investigations as compared to individual communications;
- a petition for investigation may be made anonymously, although this may undermine the requirement that the information be reliable before an investigation is commenced. A communication may not be anonymous;

- an investigation may be sought on behalf of others, unlike a communication;
- interim measures are not available under the investigation procedure; and
- domestic remedies need not be exhausted as a prerequisite to an investigation.

2. CONVENTION AGAINST TORTURE

a) Introduction

The investigation mechanism allows the Committee to conduct its own investigation into allegations that "torture is being systematically practised" (article 20 and Rules 69 to 84 of the CAT Rules of Procedure).

In the fifteen years that the CAT has been in force, only a handful of reports on investigations have been published, and only a few others have been, or are being, conducted.

States that are party to CAT have not necessarily permitted the Committee to undertake investigations. Article 28 specifically allows states parties to opt out of article 20. The Committee may not consider information submitted regarding countries which have opted out of the procedure. It is, therefore, necessary to ensure not only that the state against whom information is submitted under article 20 is a party to CAT, but that they have made no declaration opting out of the inquiry mechanism.

b) The Preliminary Stages of Consideration

The procedure for establishing and conducting an inquiry is set out in article 20. There are two distinct stages to the process of determining whether an inquiry is to be initiated. The first hurdle is the "preliminary consideration of information" in which the Committee must receive "reliable information which appears to it to contain well-founded indications that torture is being systematically practised in the territory of the state party." This information may be furnished by individuals and organizations specifically for the purpose of encouraging the Committee to undertake an article 20 investigation. Information arising from the state reporting process may also be sufficient in form and substance to suggest to the Committee that an article 20 investigation is warranted.

Submissions made under article 20 should be as thoroughly documented as possible. As with individual communications, submissions should clearly indicate that the information is submitted for the purpose of initiating an article 20 proceeding. Submissions may be considered by the Committee even if they are made anonymously, in whole or in part. If the information submitted in itself appears insufficient to meet the requisite standard of proof, the Committee is entitled to make its own inquiries to determine whether, at this threshold stage, the information is reliable and accurate (Rule 75).

If the preliminary consideration hurdle is cleared, a more extensive "examination" stage may be initiated. At this stage, the Committee "shall invite the state party to co-operate in the examination of the information and to this end to submit observations with regard to the information concerned" (article 20, paragraph 1). In addition to the views of the state party involved, the Committee may also actively solicit information from anyone it deems appropriate, including NGOs, individuals, governments, or other UN institutions to ascertain whether the information received is reliable. Once this process is complete, the Committee may decide formally to establish an inquiry. In general, an inquiry is warranted where there are "well-founded indications that torture is being systematically practised."

In order for torture to be "systematically practised," the Committee has said that the incidents must not have occurred fortuitously in a particular place or at a particular time, but are seen to be habitual, widespread and deliberate in at least a considerable part of the territory of the country in question. However, there need be no direct intention of a Government to perpetrate torture. According to the Committee, the systematic practice "may be the consequence of factors which the Government has difficulty in controlling, and its existence may indicate a discrepancy between policy as determined by the central Government and its implementation by the local administration. Inadequate legislation, which in practice allows room for the use of torture, may also add to the systematic nature of this practice."

c) The Inquiry Procedure

The Committee may designate one or more of its members to conduct the inquiry. The members designated by the Committee have wide latitude in the methods of inquiry and the sources on which they may rely. Article 20 authorizes the Committee or its delegates, with the consent of the state party involved, to visit the territory of the state party to conduct an on-site investigation. The Committee's rules and practice permit oral hearings to elicit testimony, conduct interviews with individuals, inspect specific sites, and consult with government officials and local non-governmental organizations. Such activities must be approved and supported by the state party involved. In the one investigation to date in which the state party (Egypt) refused permission to visit, adverse inferences were drawn by the Committee in its final report.

Upon completion of the inquiry, the members responsible for the investigation submit their findings to the Committee. The Committee considers their findings and transmits them to the state party with any additional comments or suggestions it deems appropriate. The state party is then invited to inform the Committee of any action it plans to take in response to the findings.

The entire inquiry process is supposed to be confidential. Thus, an individual or organization which submits information to the Committee for the purpose of initiating the procedure may not be aware that the Committee has commenced an inquiry. At the same time, the Committee has wide latitude in the conduct of its investigation and may solicit further information from individuals or organizations as part of its investigation. Should that be the case, the latter are also under an obligation of confidentiality.

Confidentiality may end once the investigation has been completed, the findings transmitted to the state party, and the state party has had the opportunity to indicate what measures it may take in response. The Committee may then decide, after consultation with the state party, to publish a summary account of the results of the inquiry in its annual report. This may mean that the scrutiny and embarrassment occasioned by publication of a report may only emerge years after the incidents have taken place.

3. CONVENTION ON THE ELIMINATION OF ALL FORMS OF DISCRIMINATION AGAINST WOMEN

a) Introduction

The investigation mechanism for violations of the Convention on the Elimination of all Forms of Discrimination Against Women was established by the CEDAW Optional Protocol when it entered into force in December 2000. The Committee has as yet not undertaken any such investigations. The procedure adopted closely follows the model set out in CAT, though there are some potentially significant differences. To be subject to the investigation procedure, a state must have ratified the Optional Protocol, and must not have exercised the right to opt out of the procedure as specifically permitted by article 10 of the Optional Protocol. Thus, before submitting information for the purpose of instigating an inquiry for violations of CEDAW, a petitioner should ascertain the state party has (1) ratified the Optional Protocol, and (2) not declared under article 10 that it is not subject to the investigation procedure. Petitioners should also be aware of any state party reservations to substantive provisions of the Convention which might purport to have a limiting effect.

b) The Preliminary Stages of Consideration

The Committee can initiate an investigation upon receiving "reliable information indicating grave or systematic violations by a state party of rights set forth in the Convention" (article 8). Under the CEDAW Optional Protocol, the use of the disjunctive "grave *or* systematic" indicates that even an isolated but egregious violation of the Convention could satisfy the requisite standard (article 8).

There is a two-stage process for determining whether to initiate an inquiry. The preliminary consideration stage is initiated by the receipt of information. Information submitted to the Committee for the purpose of triggering an inquiry should state explicitly that it is submitted for this purpose. The Committee is authorized to seek out information substantiating the information received, but the information submitted should be as well-documented as possible. Information may be furnished by individuals and organizations. In addition, information arising from the state reporting process may be sufficient in form and substance to suggest to the Committee that an article 20 investigation is warranted. There is no rule against the submission of anonymous information.

Should the Committee decide that the information is reliable and indicative of grave or systematic violations of rights, the Committee shall invite the state party involved to submit its observations on the information. At this "examination" stage, the Committee may also solicit information from governmental organizations, non-governmental organizations, and individuals (Rule 83). Based on that information, the Committee may designate one or more of its members to conduct an inquiry and report to the Committee. The standard for deciding whether an inquiry should be held is that there is "reliable information indicating grave or systematic violations by a state party of rights set forth in the Convention."

c) The Inquiry Procedure

The Rules of Procedure adopted by the Committee as regards the conduct of investigations are nearly identical to the Rules adopted by the Committee Against Torture, and the practice of that Committee will likely be an influential guide.

The Committee and the members designated to conduct an inquiry have wide latitude in determining the methods of their investigation. Article 8 specifically authorizes that "where warranted and with the consent of the state party, the inquiry may include a visit to its territory." Hearings may be conducted as part of the visit and the state party is expressly required to "take all appropriate steps to ensure that individuals under its jurisdiction are not subject to ill treatment or intimidation as a consequence of communicating with the Committee" (article 11). The state party's consent is a prerequisite to any visit and any hearings that occur during the visit.

Upon completion of the inquiry, the members responsible for the investigation submit their findings to the Committee, which then transmits the findings to the state party concerned with any additional comments or recommendations it deems appropriate. The Optional Protocol obligates the state party to submit its observations in response to these findings, comments or recommendations within six months.

As with CAT, investigations are to be "conducted confidentially" and "all documents and proceedings of the Committee relating to the conduct of an inquiry . . . are to be confidential" (article 8, and Rule 80). However, the Committee is required to include a summary of its activities under the Protocol in its annual report, which includes the existence and results of any investigations (article 12). The publication of the results of an inquiry differs from CAT in two significant respects. First, the Committee is required to indicate the existence (though perhaps not the content) of an ongoing inquiry in its annual report. Second, the Committee must publish a summary of its findings and recommendations and need not consult with the state party before doing so (Rule 80).

d) Follow-Up

The Committee is required to maintain pressure on the state party by inviting it to give details of the measures taken in response to an inquiry in its periodic report to the Committee as part of the state reporting obligations (article 9). The Committee may also make this request after the expiration of six months from the date of transmittal of the final report of an inquiry, in order to encourage a more timely response.

4. CONCLUSION

Requests to trigger an inquiry, either under CAT or the CEDAW Optional Protocol, do not preclude the submission of an individual communication related to the same set of facts. The inquiry procedure cannot yield a recommendation for an individual remedy. However, an inquiry which finds a state party in violation of the treaty's provisions would bolster any related claim of individual rights violations. The inquiry procedure also offers the potential for international public scrutiny of widespread or gross human rights violations, with the concomitant hope of attendant international pressure and incentive for reform.

CHAPTER VIII

THE STATE REPORTING SYSTEM

1. INTRODUCTION

One of the principal mechanisms by which the treaty bodies monitor the extent of compliance by states parties with their obligations under the human rights treaties is through a system of state reporting.

Under each of the treaties, states parties undertake to submit reports to the treaty bodies explaining the progress made and problems encountered in implementing treaty obligations. The state reporting system intersects with the system of individual complaints, and may be able to be used to the advantage of authors or prospective authors of individual complaints.

2. HOW DOES THE STATE REPORTING SYSTEM WORK?

There are differences in the procedure adopted by each of the treaty bodies in monitoring state reports. However, there are common elements.

a) Submission of Initial and Periodic Reports by States Parties

Under the treaties, each state party undertakes to submit an initial report within a time frame specified in the treaty (normally one or two years from the entry into force of the treaty for the state concerned). The report is supposed to detail:

- the measures that the state party has adopted to give effect to the provisions of the treaty;
- the progress made in giving effect to the provisions of the treaty; and
- the factors and difficulties the state party has encountered that have affected the degree of fulfilment of its obligations under the treaty.

States parties also undertake to submit subsequent periodic reports, at an interval that is either specified in the treaty itself, or stipulated by the relevant treaty body.

In order to assist states parties in their reporting tasks, the treaty bodies issue general guidelines for the preparation of reports, which detail the preferred format and the information that should be included in the reports.

b) Lists of Issues

On receipt of states parties' initial and periodic reports, the practice of many (but not all) of the treaty bodies is to prepare a list of issues, which notifies the state party of the matters of particular interest to the treaty body.

Some of the treaty bodies ask the state party to submit written answers to the list of issues in advance of the treaty body's formal consideration of the state party's report.

c) Formal Consideration of the State Party's Report

The state report is scheduled for examination at a meeting of the treaty body, and the state party is invited to send representatives to present the report and answer the treaty body's questions.

At the scheduled meeting, the representatives of the state party make an initial presentation, and then the members of the treaty body engage in a dialogue with the representatives, asking questions about the state party's implementation of the treaty and raising any concerns they might have.

d) Concluding Observations or Comments

The treaty body then adopts concluding "observations" or "comments" on the state party's report. In the concluding comments or observations, the treaty body identifies concerns that it has about non-compliance. The treaty body makes recommendations for action by the state party to enable improved implementation.

Important points to note:

- **Country rapporteurs**

In the case of all six treaty bodies, one member of the treaty body (called the "country rapporteur") is appointed by the treaty body to take a leading role in the evaluation of a particular state party's report, the drafting of lists of issues (where applicable), and concluding comments. Some of the treaty bodies refuse to disclose which of their members has been appointed as the country rapporteur.

- **Country information and NGO involvement**

The treaty bodies evaluate states parties' reports in light of whatever information is available to them about the situation in the country at issue, including external sources. This may include, for example, country information prepared by the treaty body's secretariat, information provided by other UN agencies, and information provided by any non-governmental organizations that may have a particular interest in the subject matter or the country at issue.

Practices differ between the respective treaty bodies as to how actively they seek out such information.

• Publicity

States parties' reports are made available to the public, if not by the state party (contrary to their responsibilities), then by the UN secretariat. The treaty bodies' formal consideration of states parties' reports also takes place in public.

Practices differ among treaty bodies as to whether lists of issues are made available to the public and whether the meeting at which concluding observations are adopted is open to the public.

Once adopted, however, the treaty bodies' concluding observations are always released publicly.

Practices differ between treaty bodies as to when and in what circumstances Committee members meet with the press. However, a press statement is released by the media section of the United Nations secretariat at the end of each session. A "summary record," which summarizes the dialogue between the treaty bodies and the states parties' representatives, is sometimes published as a UN document, but practices vary widely as to the timing of the availability of the summary record which may be years after the actual meeting.

• Practical difficulties faced by the treaty bodies in monitoring states parties' reports

The treaty bodies face a number of practical impediments in monitoring states parties' reports. In particular:

- Many states parties have fallen significantly behind in the submission of reports. A significant number of states parties have never submitted their initial reports.
- The treaty bodies do not have adequate resources to keep up with the burden of considering states parties' reports, and consequently there are considerable delays, sometimes of several years, between receipt of a report by a treaty body and the formal consideration of the report. This phenomenon is decreasing, however, as treaty bodies have adopted rules permitting states to expunge their whole record of overdue reports with the submission of a single report. It remains to be seen whether this approach will have the ultimate effect of encouraging or discouraging the submission of state reports at regular intervals (as required by the treaties).
- When states have failed to produce a report for many years, some of the treaty bodies will now examine the country situation in the absence of a report. This process entails additional difficulties, concerning information-gathering and the ability of the process to encourage reform at the domestic level without the engagement of the state party.

3. HOW CAN COMPLAINANTS MAKE USE OF THE STATE REPORTING SYSTEM?

For the complainant or prospective complainant, the state reporting system may be relevant in the following ways.

a) A Source of Information about the Committee's Approach to Convention Obligations

The concluding comments or observations issued by the treaty bodies on the states parties' reports are a potential source of information for gauging the treaty bodies' approach to the interpretation of the treaties. This information can be used to assess the likelihood that an individual complaint will succeed before a particular treaty body and to inform the preparation of the complaint.

In the concluding comments, the treaty bodies identify practices engaged in by the state party that are of "concern." Occasionally, the treaty body will go further and actually state that a particular practice violates the state party's treaty obligations. When faced with an individual complaint based on similar practices, such expressions of "concern" will tend to support a conclusion of a treaty violation.

b) Method of Bringing Attention to an Individual Complaint

If the state party that has violated a person's rights under one of the treaties is due to have a state report examined by that treaty body, the state reporting system can be used as a means of bringing the violation to the treaty body's attention, and putting pressure on the state party to rectify the situation.

Points to note about this potential use of the state reporting system are as follows:

- In practice, this option will generally only be available at selected times, that is, if the state party has provided its written report to the relevant treaty body but the report has not yet been formally considered. That is the time when the treaty body will be interested in receiving information from external sources that bears on the state party's record of implementation of its treaty obligations, including its obligation to comply with the Committee's Views in individual cases.
- In contrast to the individual complaint system, there are no formal restrictions on who can bring information to the Committee's attention. It could be the alleged victim of a violation, a non-governmental organization, or any other third party. However, in the case of previously unexamined individual complaints the more established and authoritative the source of the information, the more weight the treaty body is likely to attach to it.

- The treaty bodies' focus in the context of state reporting is on a state party's overall record of compliance rather than on individual and isolated instances of violation. Accordingly, the treaty bodies are more likely to be interested if the violation was particularly egregious, if it involved a violation of more than one individual's rights, or if the complaint is an ongoing one and involves a policy or practice that has not been addressed by the state party.
- It should be made clear in the information provided to the treaty body why the information is being provided. In other words, it should be clearly stated that it is relevant to the treaty body's assessment of the state party's record of implementing its treaty obligations in the course of its consideration of the state report. Where the information relates to a situation which has not been the subject of a complaint, and the victim wants his or her identity to be protected from disclosure to the state party, that should also be made clear.
- The state reporting system is extremely unlikely to result in the treaty body recommending that the state party provide an individual remedy for violation of the treaty. More likely outcomes are:
  - The treaty body might include questions about the alleged violation in its list of issues.
  - At the formal consideration of the state report, the treaty body might question the state party about the violation.
  - Although unlikely, the treaty body might express concern about the alleged violation in its concluding comments, or recommend that laws or policies be examined to ensure that similar violations do not occur in the future.
  - Media coverage of the state reporting system might pick up on the violation, thereby bringing further pressure to bear on the state party to remedy the violation.

c) Follow-up from Successful Individual Communications

The state reporting system similarly permits complainants to bring situations of non-compliance with prior Views to the treaty bodies' attention and to have the non-compliance directly and publicly raised with the state party. Thus, the state reporting system can be used as a method for putting pressure on the state party to remedy the violation.

Two of the treaty bodies have formally recognized the important role that the state reporting system can play in providing an opportunity for subsequent follow-up from successful individual communications.

- The Human Rights Committee, in its consolidated guidelines for state reports, has asked that state parties include in their state reports information on any steps they have taken to respond to the Committee's recommendations and concerns expressed in "Views" on individual communications.

- The CEDAW Committee has provided in its Rules of Procedure that the Committee may request states parties to include information in their state reports on any action taken in light of the Committee's Views and recommendations on individual communications (Rule 73).

The victim or author and his or her supporters should treat the state reporting system as a valuable vehicle for putting additional pressure on the state party to grant a remedy for the violation. The relevant time period for utilizing the state reporting system is after the state party has provided its written report to the relevant treaty body but before the report has been formally considered. The limitation of the state reporting system as a vehicle for follow-up to individual complaints, however, is that the actual consideration of a state report from the particular state party may be years after the Committee's finding of a violation.

CHAPTER IX

CHOOSING A FORUM

---

1. INTRODUCTION

There are currently four treaties which involve an individual complaints procedure, and in some fact situations more than one treaty may be available to potential complainants. In these cases, a complainant must decide which of the procedures would be the best avenue to advance their case. The process will involve determining whether there is more than one complaints procedure open to the complainant, and deciding which of the available avenues is preferable.

2. IS THERE A CHOICE OF FORUM?

The individual will have an initial choice of forum, if at least:

(a) the state has ratified more than one of the optional protocols and/or given more than one of the required declarations recognizing the competence of the Committees to examine individual complaints, and

(b) the fact situation relates to a right which is found in more than one of these treaties.

If these two conditions are met, admissibility criteria varying among complaint mechanisms may still affect the potential effectiveness of the different treaty complaints procedures in relation to the individual's case.

a) Ratification

An individual can only bring a complaint against a state that has both ratified the treaty, and accepted the associated individual complaint mechanism. Therefore, the first step is to determine the treaties and individual complaint mechanisms to which the state (that is the object of the complaint) is a party. If the state has accepted more than one individual complaint mechanism, it is possible that the individual may have a choice of forum.

Differences as to the date of acceptance of different complaint mechanisms may also limit the choice of forum, since the violation must have occurred after ratification, unless the violation is continuing.

b) Treaty Rights

An individual can only bring a complaint of a violation of rights which are set out in the treaty associated with the complaint mechanism. The next step is, therefore, to determine whether the fact situation relates to a violation of rights in more than one of the treaties (having a complaint mechanism which the state in question has ratified).

c) Reservations

A state party may have made reservations to one or more of the treaties which would affect the viability of the complaint. The complainant should, therefore, review any reservations entered by the state, and any commentary by the treaty body on the reservation.

3. CHOOSING THE BEST FORUM

The following factors should be considered in choosing the most appropriate forum if more than one treaty may apply.

a) Admissibility Considerations

A particular case may or may not be admissible under all or some of the complaint mechanisms. That is, a case may be inadmissible under one treaty but admissible under another.

- **Individuals versus groups**

Claims under CAT and ICCPR are limited to individuals, whereas claims under CERD or CEDAW may be brought by groups of individuals as well as by individuals.

- **Time limits**

CERD requires that a complainant submit his or her case within six months following the exhaustion of domestic remedies.

There is no time limit within which to bring a claim in the case of the ICCPR, but very long delays in bringing the claim may be considered by the Human Rights Committee to be an abuse of the right of submission. The Human Rights Committee will require that a 'convincing' or 'reasonable' explanation be given to justify a significant delay in bringing a complaint.

In the case of CAT, there is no time limit within which to bring a claim.

In the case of CEDAW, there is no time limit within which to bring a claim.

- **Has the case ever been considered by another international forum**

  - **ICCPR**—According to the ICCPR, the same complaint must not be pending before another international forum. In other words, at the time the complaint is lodged, the matter must not be under investigation by another procedure of international investigation or settlement. Once a procedure of international investigation or settlement has fully ended, there is, in theory, nothing to prevent an individual communication being brought about the same matter. However in practice, many states parties have made reservations to the relevant treaties that preclude recourse to the Human Rights Committee once another international procedure, whether regional or universal (UN), has been utilized.

The Human Rights Committee, however, allows the same petitioner to bring the same facts to different bodies if the treaty provisions are different. For instance, a petitioner may bring a freedom of association issue before the European Court of Human Rights and a discrimination claim arising out of the same facts before the Human Rights Committee.

- **CAT**—According to CAT, there must not be a parallel complaint before another international forum, either currently, or in the past. A complaint is inadmissible if the matter is being, or has ever been, examined under another procedure of international investigation or settlement (article 22(5)(a); Rule 107(d)). This limitation applies whenever a procedure of international investigation has been invoked, even if that procedure has been concluded.

  As to what constitutes the "same matter," CAT interprets this to mean the same petitioner who brings the same set of facts to different bodies.

  Some international procedures will not be considered to amount to procedures of "international investigation or settlement." For example, the fact that the matter has been brought to the attention of the United Nations Special Rapporteur on Torture, or is being considered under the UN Economic and Social Council "1503 procedure" by the Working Groups of the United Nations Sub-Commission on the Promotion and Protection of Human Rights (the Working Group on Communications) or the Commission on Human Rights (the Working Group on Situations), will not be considered sufficient to render an individual complaint inadmissible.

- **CERD**—There is no requirement concerning the bringing of a complaint to CERD and bringing the same case before or simultaneously to another procedure of international investigation.

- **CEDAW**—Under the Optional Protocol to CEDAW, a communication is inadmissible where the same matter has already been, or is being, examined under another procedure of international investigation or settlement (article 4(2)(a)). This limitation applies whenever a procedure of international investigation has been invoked, even if that procedure has been concluded.

Some international procedures will likely not be considered by CEDAW to amount to procedures of "international investigation or settlement." For example, the fact that the matter has been brought to the attention of the United Nations Special Rapporteur on Violence against Women, its causes and consequences, or is being considered under the UN Economic and Social Council "1503 procedure" by the Working Group on Communications or the Working Group on Situations will likely not be considered sufficient to render an individual communication inadmissible.

b) Expertise of the Treaty Bodies

CAT, CEDAW and CERD all have a narrower focus with respect to the category of persons or rights that are protected than the ICCPR. This difference may be important in deciding which forum is best suited to a particular case. Thus, if a case involves not only discrimination, but also a denial of a fair hearing or a violation of freedom of expression, it would likely be preferable to raise multiple or interrelated violations simultaneously before the Human Rights Committee. The same would be true if a case is not limited to a claim of torture, but there are also considerations of due process or of arbitrary detention.

c) Substantive Provisions of the Treaties

Although treaty rights do overlap, rights contained in more than one treaty may differ in terms of their specificity, breadth and the categories of people they protect. It is important to read the provisions of each treaty to compare their terms, their limitations, and their past interpretation by the Committees to ensure their applicability in a particular case.

Overlapping rights found in more than one treaty associated with a complaints procedure are the following:

- **Discrimination against women**
The CEDAW Convention covers a broad number of contexts involving discrimination against women. Anti-discrimination provisions are found in general form in the ICCPR, notably in articles 3 and 26. The CEDAW definition of discrimination in the treaty entails elements which should be applied to the concept of discrimination in the ICCPR, but which are subject to the Committee's interpretation. For example, the CEDAW definition makes clear that discrimination entails acts which have the purpose or *effect* of impairing equal rights, and hence clearly covers legislation or policies which appear neutral on their face.

- **Discrimination in matters relating to marriage and family relations**

Measures to eliminate discrimination concerning marriage and family relations are covered in both article 16 of CEDAW, and article 23(4) of ICCPR.

- **Discrimination in matters relating to race, colour, descent, or national or ethnic origin**

The CERD Convention covers a broad number of contexts involving discrimination on the basis of race, colour, descent or national or ethnic origin. Anti-discrimination provisions are found in general form in the ICCPR, notably in article 26. The CERD definition of discrimination in the treaty entails elements which should be applied to the concept of discrimination in the ICCPR, but which are subject to the Committee's interpretation. For example, the CERD definition makes clear that discrimination entails acts which have the purpose or *effect* of impairing equal rights, and hence clearly covers legislation or policies which appear neutral on their face.

- **Propagation of racial hatred**

Both article 4 of CERD and article 20 of ICCPR place obligations on states to prohibit incitement to racial hatred.

- **Prohibition of torture, cruel, inhuman or degrading treatment or punishment**

The CAT Convention covers a range of rights relating to the prohibition of torture, and of cruel, inhuman or degrading treatment or punishment. Torture, or cruel, inhuman or degrading treatment or punishment is also prohibited in article 7 of the ICCPR. The understanding of torture by CAT, and by the Human Rights Committee as indicated in their General Comment Number 19, is similar.

However, the CAT definition contains certain elements which indicate that ICCPR article 7 may be of wider application. In contrast to the CAT Convention, the concept of "torture" is not defined in the ICCPR, and may not therefore be subject to the explicit limitations contained in the CAT Convention.

- The Human Rights Committee has stressed that under article 7, the state has an obligation to protect everyone against acts of torture, or cruel, inhuman or degrading treatment or punishment whether inflicted by persons acting in their official capacity, outside of their official capacity or in a private capacity. This is in contrast to the Torture Convention definitions in articles 1 and 16.
- To amount to torture under the ICCPR, the acts do not need to have been inflicted for any particular purpose. Under the CAT Convention, the pain or suffering must have been inflicted for

one of the purposes stated in article 1 of the Convention, which include obtaining information or a confession, punishment, intimidation or coercion, or discrimination.

In addition, there may be a threshold of severity applied in the context of CAT which is not applied in the context of the ICCPR.

On the other hand, CAT, unlike the ICCPR, contains a specific number of contingent rights and duties (such as to prevent, prosecute, investigate, non-refoulement), which are not express in the ICCPR.

d) The Case Law of the Treaty Bodies

The Human Rights Committee has developed case law on many of the ICCPR rights. CAT has developed much more limited case law, and largely on the issue of return or extradition in circumstances where persons would likely be subjected to torture. CERD has very little case law, as a result of receiving very few complaints. Since CEDAW's Optional Protocol entered into force only on December 22, 2000, it has yet to develop case law.

Where it exists, the case law on the provisions of the treaty which are sought to be invoked should be examined in making a choice of the best forum. A Committee may or may not have made a ruling on a similar case in the past. The Committees attempt to maintain consistency in the interpretation of the treaties. Hence, a previous ruling in a similar case will provide a good indication of the chances of a successful or unsuccessful outcome in each case. Subsequently, when a forum is selected, it is also helpful in an author's submission to point out similarities in his or her case with previously decided cases.

e) The General Comments or Recommendations of the Treaty Bodies

The Committees may have issued a "General Comment" or "General Recommendation" concerning the subject matter or related issues of the potential complaint. A General Comment or Recommendation is a statement that has been formally adopted by the Committee which interprets, clarifies or expands upon a particular treaty right. General Comments and Recommendations are published in the annual reports of the Committees. Even if a Committee has no developed case law on a treaty right, it may have issued a General Comment that indicates its interpretation or position on a specific subject. These General Comments can be used to evaluate the Committee's likely position on an issue in the absence of case law. Subsequently, when a forum is selected, an author should also refer to any language of General Comments or Recommendations which supports his or her case in their submissions to the Committee.

f)   Time Taken to Decide Cases

The four Committees differ in the time taken to consider complaints. For example, the Human Rights Committee has the longest delay. On average, from the time a complaint is registered, inadmissibility decisions may take about two years, and final Views on the merits may take four years from registration to conclusion. Cases are dealt with more expeditiously when both the petitioner and the state party furnish the Committee with all information within the prescribed time limits. Decisions which combine the issues of admissibility and merits sometimes take as little as two years, especially in capital punishment cases.

CAT does not have a significant backlog of complaints: decisions on cases, including both admissibility and merits are usually taken in less than two years. Few cases are submitted to CERD, so delays associated with the volume of cases are not applicable. As CEDAW's complaint process is in its infancy, backlog is currently not an issue.

g)   Interim Measures/Urgent Action

If a case is urgent in nature and the author wants the Committee to ask the state to take interim measures (such as stay of execution or deferral of deportation), the willingness or ability of the Committee to make such requests to states parties is a key factor. The success rate of such requests should also be taken into account.

Interim measures may be ordered to avoid irreparable damage to the victim of the alleged violation. While the Annual Report now states the number of occasions in which the Special Rapporteur has made interim measure requests, it does not state how many of these requests have been honoured. The success rate is reportedly more than 90% in the Human Rights Committee and almost 100% in the case of CAT.

h)   Remedies

There may be different remedies for rights violations available in a particular case. Prior case law may indicate the preferences of a treaty body for particular requests of states parties in terms of remedies. A Committee may be more or less likely than another Committee to request the specific remedy that the complainant is seeking, or to specify a particular remedy at all.

For decades, the Human Rights Committee did not specify a particular remedy, and tended to allow the state party to determine the remedy required. On the other hand, the Committee has specifically requested states parties, for example, to: pay a specific sum of compensation, make restitution in full, reinstate a person in public service at a specific level of seniority, amend legislation, release a prisoner, and commute a death sentence.

CAT will be satisfied that a state party has met its obligations under article 3 not to forcibly return an individual to a state where there are substantial grounds for believing that he or she would be in danger of being subjected to torture, by a variety of means. This includes solutions of a legal nature (such as, by granting the petitioner asylum or a temporary or permanent residence permit) or solutions of a political nature (such as by finding a third state that is willing to admit the applicant to its territory and to undertake not to return or expel him or her). Furthermore, a state may be liable to compensate victims of torture, even in the absence of a criminal conviction of a state official.

CERD will sometimes propose remedies which are not personal in nature, and recommend that legislation be amended, or the state party review its policy and procedures in the relevant area, or otherwise take general measures to counteract racial discrimination in the future. CERD has also recommended that investigations into reports of discrimination be conducted, and that petitioners be given compensation or offered alternative employment.

i) Compliance with the Committee's Views
• Human Rights Committee
Of the final Views adopted over the history of the Optional Protocol, three-quarters have revealed a violation of the Covenant. A significant proportion of registered cases, though, come from a very limited number of countries.

According to the Committee, their insistence that a remedy be forthcoming in response to a finding of a violation has been respected in about one-fifth of the cases.
• Committee Against Torture
Thus far, states parties have generally complied with the Committee's Views, particularly in article 3 cases where they have refrained from expelling individuals to countries in which they risk torture.
• Committee on the Elimination of Racial Discrimination
In the few cases decided, states parties have generally complied with the Committee's Opinions, carried out investigations and issued appropriate directives and regulations.
• Committee on the Elimination of Discrimination Against Women
Not yet applicable.

j) Overlap with Non-treaty Mechanisms
• The Special Procedures and Urgent Appeals
Over the past decade, the Commission on Human Rights has created numerous Special Procedures with ever-widening mandates. There are over a dozen country rapporteurs/representatives/independent

experts, and almost two dozen thematic rapporteurs/representatives/independent experts, and two thematic working groups. In recent years, the Special Procedures have conducted over 50 field missions, and issued about 1000 urgent appeals annually.

Procedures which receive and respond in some form to complaints include:

Working Groups
> The Working Group on Arbitrary Detention
> The Working Group on Enforced or Involuntary Disappearances
> The Working Group on Situations

Thematic Rapporteurs/Representatives
> Special Rapporteur on Extrajudicial, Summary or Arbitrary Executions
> Special Representative of the Secretary-General on Human Rights Defenders
> Special Rapporteur on Promotion and Protection of the Right to Freedom of Opinion and Expression
> Special Rapporteur on Independence of Judges and Lawyers
> Special Rapporteur on Contemporary Forms of Racism, Racial Discrimination, Xenophobia and Related Intolerance
> Special Rapporteur on Religious Intolerance
> Special Rapporteur on Question of Torture
> Special Rapporteur on Violence Against Women, its Causes and Consequences

and some Country Rapporteurs or Representatives which are normally appointed on an annual basis.

The Special Procedures have more flexibility in relation to a number of functions as compared with the treaty bodies.

- The mandates or operation of the rapporteurs is not strictly associated with ratification of the human rights treaty standards. The Special Procedures, therefore, cover states which have so far avoided the treaty system, or avoid some dimension of its operation (a particular treaty, individual communications, inquiries). The range of states targeted by the thematic Special Procedures is broader than those subject to the complaints procedures associated with the treaties.

- The issuing of urgent appeals does not depend on any likelihood of satisfaction of conditions of admissibility, such as the exhaustion of domestic remedies. The Special Procedures' normal method of operation is to visit the relevant state(s) concerned, in contrast to the treaty bodies which essentially engage in written and oral dialogue with states outside the state concerned.

At least as long as universal ratification of the human rights treaties and the accompanying individual complaint mechanisms has not occurred, mechanisms which extend the principles of international human rights protection beyond participation in the treaty system will be necessary.

At the same time, there is overlap. Some states are subject to the attention of both special procedures and the treaty bodies. The standards applied by the special procedures in their work are often the human rights treaties, although they also utilize non-treaty provisions such as the Universal Declaration on Human Rights, and the Standard Minimum Rules for the Treatment of Prisoners. Nevertheless, sometimes this overlap is not strictly-speaking duplication. Treaty bodies have limited capacity to deal with general emergency situations, to focus on systemic human rights violations, or to focus on violators for sustained periods of time.

There are situations where individual cases are first sent to the special procedures and later to the treaty bodies on substantially the same issues. To date, the treaty bodies have tended not to count these initial entreaties as running afoul of the provisions in CAT, the Optional Protocol to the ICCPR, and CEDAW's Optional Protocol, that disallow communications relating to matters which have been examined, or are being examined, under another procedure of international investigation or settlement.

In many ways, the work of the special procedures is more visible. Their work often involves on-the-spot investigations or high profile visits. They have more direct media contact, and they usually report to the Commission on Human Rights, and/or the General Assembly in person. There is also an immediacy associated with their work that is frequently not affiliated with the methodical examination of reports, or the lengthy written examinations of a relatively small number of individual cases by the treaty bodies. The visibility of the Special Procedures has resulted, in practice, in the individual complaints received by the UN being directed to country or thematic rapporteurs. A prior analysis of the ability of the treaty bodies to consider these individual complaints often does not occur. No set of clear, transparent priorities in terms of the most appropriate venue for complaints currently exists within the Office of the UN High Commissioner for Human Rights.

Those responsible for directing complaints to treaty or non-treaty mechanisms within the Office of the High Commissioner tend to distinguish between two kinds of communications: so-called "urgent appeals" which are usually directed to the Special Procedures, and substantive complaints without an urgent dimension that may, or may not, end up in the treaty bodies' complaints procedures. The main focus of attention is on channelling urgent appeals to the relevant country or thematic rapporteurs or working groups, and coordinating joint urgent appeals among these procedures when appropriate. Little attention is given to directing the appeal instead to a treaty body.

The ability of the treaty bodies to act in this urgent context has, however, been underestimated. In about 90% of the cases in which the Human Rights Committee has used its interim measures procedure, states have followed their requests. CAT's record is almost 100%.

The Human Rights Committee normally acts through the Special Rapporteur on New Communications in the case of the Optional Protocol; if the Special Rapporteur cannot be reached, the UN Secretariat will reach a member of the Bureau of the Committee. With respect to CAT, the UN Secretariat can deal directly with the Rapporteur for New Complaints and Interim Measures. Hence, in neither case will requests for interim measures be held up until full meetings of the treaty bodies are held.

In addition, the criterion for the use of the urgent action or interim measures procedures is not a final determination that domestic remedies have been exhausted. The test is irreparable damage. According to the Human Rights Committee rules, "interim measures may be desirable to avoid irreparable damage to the victim." Requesting the application of interim measures "does not imply a determination on the merits of the communication." The rules also indicate that a request for interim measures does not imply a positive or final decision on admissibility (although capricious disregard of the conditions underlying the request would not be consistent with the treaty's intent). According to CAT rules, the criteria for the use of the interim measures procedure similarly is the avoidance of "possible irreparable damage" to the individual claiming to be a victim of a violation. According to CAT, such a request addressed to the state party does not imply that any decision has been reached on the question of the admissibility of the complaint.

At the same time, with few relevant cases or requests, the treaty bodies' application of the "irreparable damage" criteria to date has been limited. The Human Rights Committee may believe that arbitrary detention does not constitute irreparable damage if financial compensation for the time spent in prison is an alternative. If someone has disappeared, to date, the Human Rights Committee has not used the interim measures procedure to order the individual to be produced.

Furthermore, an urgent appeal is only properly before a treaty body where there is an allegation of a violation of a treaty right. For example, since the ICCPR does not prohibit the death penalty itself, allegations must relate to Covenant provisions such as the right to a fair hearing. Or, since the ICCPR does not prohibit extradition or expulsion itself, allegations must relate, for example, to the right not to be subjected to torture, cruel, inhuman or degrading treatment or punishment.

In deciding on the comparative usefulness of the treaty bodies and the Special Procedures in a specific case, the following factors should be borne in mind:

- If the author does not specifically direct his or her case to a treaty body, there is a significant risk that it will not be directed there by the UN Secretariat. Hence, it is crucial for individuals who seek to have their cases decided by a treaty body to specifically address it to the treaty body in their initial correspondence.
- If a case relates to a state which has ratified the applicable treaty and accepted the associated right of complaint, then the individual should make use of the treaty mechanism. Although the process is clearly lengthy, the outcome has considerably more weight than the outcomes of appeals from Special Procedures.
- As an advocacy tool, or as a method of applying pressure to states to change legislation, policies or practices, a decision by a treaty body finding a violation of the state's legal obligations is potentially of much greater force.
- The treaty bodies have not held that the prior or concurrent consideration of a case by one of the Special Procedures would disallow the examination of the case by the treaty body. While the decisions of the quasi-judicial treaty bodies are more authoritative, Special Procedures have been in a position to make country visits. It may, therefore, be strategically beneficial to direct some cases, particularly the case of an urgent appeal, to both the relevant Special Procedure and the treaty body simultaneously.
- The treaty bodies to date have tended to apply their interim measure requests to a limited number of circumstances, specifically those in which irreparable harm would otherwise be done. Urgent appeals therefore relating to imminent extradition or expulsion to a state where the individual faces torture, or cases concerning the imminent execution of the death penalty, are likely to be dealt with quickly and efficiently by the treaty bodies. The action of the treaty body in this context also strengthens the individual's case, as it is grounded in legal obligations on the part of the state. There does not appear, however, to be negative consequences in sending such a case simultaneously to the relevant Special Procedures. In the context of other kinds of matters, assessment of whether or not the treaty bodies are likely to act by way of interim measures in an urgent matter should focus on consideration of whether or not irreparable harm will otherwise occur. Since the treaty bodies have not precluded from consideration cases which have gone to the Special Procedures, it may be beneficial to err on the side of believing the treaty bodies can act and sending the case simultaneously to the treaty body and the Special Procedure.

- **ECOSOC Resolution 1503/the Sub-Commission on the Promotion and Protection of Human Rights, the Commission on the Status of Women Mechanism, and Systemic Human Rights Abuses or Communications Affecting Groups and Minorities**

Most complaints coming to the UN, which allege systemic or group rights violations, or complain of abuses in situations of massive violations of human rights, make no mention of the specific UN mechanism they wish to address. Most often, these complaints or letters are sent to a procedure developed under a resolution of the Economic and Social Council (ECOSOC). Cases relating to a systematic pattern of human rights violations, or to groups of victims, in general are not sent to the treaty bodies.

The ECOSOC 1503 Procedure is not directed at an assessment of the accuracy of an isolated individual violation, or the suggestion of a particular remedy. Overall, it is intended to bring to the attention of the UN Commission of Human Rights situations of massive human rights violations, and subsequently to pressure UN states to take action in relation to the state, by for example, appointing a Special Rapporteur to investigate and monitor the situation. ECOSOC 1503 cases are directed at establishing that there are reasonable grounds to believe that "a consistent pattern of gross and reliably attested violations of human rights and fundamental freedoms exists." Cases may be brought by individuals without the same degree of relationship to the victim or proof of authority to act on the victim's behalf, as is required by the treaty complaint mechanisms.

Individuals seeking an evaluation of individual claims, but who are also victims in a broader context of systemic human rights abuses affecting groups or minorities, can and should make use of the treaty system where state ratification of the relevant instruments, and admissibility requirements, permit. The Optional Protocol to the ICCPR clearly covers complaints from minorities (article 27) or systemic discrimination (under article 26). A number of other Covenant provisions relate to group rights, or rights which are exercised in community with others, such as freedom of religion. The distinguishing feature of what can be brought under the Covenant as distinct from ECOSOC 1503 cases should not be whether they apply to groups or are systemic in nature. The qualifications for using the Optional Protocol are that there is an identifiable victim, and the communication has been submitted by the victim or a person close enough to the victim.

In deciding on the comparative usefulness of the treaty bodies and the ECOSOC 1503 Procedure in a specific case, the following factors should be borne in mind:

- If the complainant does not specifically direct his or her case to a treaty body, and the case is made in the context of a situation of massive, gross or systemic violations of human rights, or violations particularly affecting groups or minorities, it is likely that it will not be directed to a treaty body by the UN Secretariat. Hence, it is crucial for individuals who seek to have their cases decided by a treaty body to specifically address it to the treaty body in their initial correspondence.
- If a case relates to a state which has ratified the applicable treaty and accepted the associated right of complaint, then the individual should make use of the treaty mechanism, notwithstanding the individual's membership in a group or minority, or that the circumstances may be one of systemic violations of human rights. Although the process is clearly lengthy, the individual will have an opportunity to have his or her case directly addressed, rather than being dealt with in a highly politicized and indeterminate context.
- Since cases are not resolved on an individual basis under the ECOSOC Resolution 1503 Procedure, there is nothing to prevent the individual from simultaneously making use of the Procedure and drawing attention to the individual example of violations of human rights which has taken place in a context of broad human rights abuse.

Complaints concerning women are also sent to the Commission on the Status of Women (CSW). Through the communications procedure of the CSW, allegations of violations against women which are directed at a particular state are considered by a CSW Working Group. They also consider government replies to these allegations. The Working Group submits a report to the CSW bringing to its attention those communications which appear to reveal a consistent pattern of reliably attested injustice and discriminatory practices against women. The report identifies the categories of violations which the communications reveal. In turn, the CSW may "take note" of the report and/or make recommendations for action to ECOSOC in relation to the trends and patterns revealed by communications.

Similar considerations to the relative usefulness of the ECOSOC 1503 procedure apply in weighing the usefulness of the CSW procedure as against the CEDAW Optional Protocol, or the other treaty body complaints procedures which relate to women's rights. The CSW does not take decisions on the merits of communications, and the communication procedure, therefore, does not provide an avenue for the redress of individual grievances. There is nothing to prevent an individual from simultaneously drawing the attention of CSW to an individual example of violation of women's rights and, where the state party has ratified the CEDAW Optional Protocol, from submitting a complaint to CEDAW.

k) Regional Mechanisms Versus the Treaty Bodies

A person whose human rights have been violated and who wishes to obtain redress can choose between regional bodies (the European Court of Human Rights, the Inter-American Commission and Court of Human Rights, the African Commission of Human and Peoples Rights) and the UN treaty bodies.

In making this choice, factors to consider include:

- the likelihood of obtaining a favourable decision
  - the substantive reach and content of the treaty
  - the competence of the particular body to deal with the substantive issue
  - the past practice of the body in dealing with similar cases;
- the likelihood that the state party will implement the decision of the particular forum;
- the likelihood of obtaining injunctive relief in the form of requests for interim measures in the context of emergencies;
- the speed of the process;
- the cost of the procedure;
- the availability of legal aid; and
- the availability of oral hearings.

The UN Human Rights Committee offers perhaps the highest percentage of decisions favourable to petitioners. Yet, because its decisions are not legally binding, and a non-cooperative state generally need not fear disapprobation in other contexts (such as may be the case with Council of Europe members seeking to join the European Union), the rate of implementation is relatively low.

Many petitioners prefer the regional procedures of the European Court of Human Rights and the Inter-American Commission/Court of Human Rights. The decisions of the European Court under the European Convention on Human Rights are legally binding and persons who have been successful in the Court have received effective relief in most cases. The decisions of the Inter-American Court under the American Convention on Human Rights (excluding "advisory opinions") are also binding. The decisions of the Inter-American Court in most cases also result in the receipt of reparations and the conduct of investigations, although not trials or punishment of those responsible.

The regional systems have other advantages, including the possibility of having legal counsel appointed at no cost, and the availability of oral hearings. Moreover, the European system in particular has a large Secretariat (over 100 lawyers) with a much broader range of linguistic competence. A case can be filed to the European Court of Human Rights in almost 40 languages. Cases can be filed with the Inter-American petition system in English, Spanish, French and Portuguese, and its complement of staff lawyers is approximately 15.

As is evident from the judgments of the European Court of Human Rights, cases are very carefully argued and remedies are spelled out in greater detail. One of the disadvantages of the recommendations of UN bodies is that, frequently, they are vague, and the state party is merely urged to grant the victim "an appropriate remedy."

The backlog of cases in the European system is greater, and the average time required for a final decision may be longer than for the treaty bodies. CAT and CERD can decide cases within two years, while the Human Rights Committee decides cases, on average, within about four years, although some categories of cases may be decided in half that time.

CHAPTER X

FOLLOW-UP

---

1. THE HUMAN RIGHTS COMMITTEE

The Human Rights Committee is the only Committee that formally follows-up on cases where there has been a violation of a treaty right. CEDAW is expected to do so in the future in light of specific provisions in the CEDAW Optional Protocol relating to follow-up. The Human Rights Committee will keep track of whether or not a state has followed through on the Views of the Committee, and whether or not an appropriate remedy has been given to the victim. None of the Committees can force the state to provide a remedy to the victim, but the practice of follow-up may serve to put some pressure on the state party to comply with the Committee's decision.

For the purpose of Follow-up, the Committee appointed one of its members to serve as a Special Rapporteur on Follow-up to Individual Communications. The purpose was to ensure that the Human Rights Committee properly focussed on the issue of follow-up, particularly in light of the poor record of compliance with the Committee's Views.

After the Committee has made a finding on the merits of a violation of a provision of the Covenant, it asks the state party to take appropriate steps to remedy the violation. The recommended remedy may be more or less specific. But in recommending a remedy, the Committee routinely indicates to states parties:

> Bearing in mind that, by becoming a party to the Optional Protocol, the State party has recognized the competence of the Committee to determine whether there has been a violation of the Covenant or not and that, pursuant to article 2 of the Covenant, the State party has undertaken to ensure to all individuals within its territory and subject to its jurisdiction the rights recognized in the Covenant and to provide an effective and enforceable remedy in case a violation has been established, the Committee wishes to receive from the State party, within 90 days, information about the measures taken to give effect to the Committee's Views.

In other words, article 2 of the Covenant legally binds ratifying states to provide an effective remedy for those whose Covenant rights have been violated, and for over two decades the Committee has exercised its competence and responsibility under the Optional Protocol to determine whether there has been a violation. Therefore, although the Optional Protocol refers to the Committee's decisions as "Views," refusal to implement those Views is clearly incompatible with the ***spirit and purpose*** of the Protocol.

To date, the Committee has performed the task of follow-up with minimal transparency and effort. In theory, the Committee's rules of procedure specifically require that information furnished by the parties within the framework of follow-up, and decisions of the Committee relating to follow-up activities, are "not subject to confidentiality" (unless the Committee takes a special decision to the contrary) (Rule 97). The practice is quite different. Authors of cases in which the Committee has found a violation of the Covenant, therefore, need to press the Committee to undertake greater follow-up efforts, including:

- conduct a follow-up meeting between the Special Rapporteur on Follow-up and the state's representative as soon as possible after the expiry of the 90-day period;
- make the content of that meeting and the state's response available to the author and to the public without delay, and include that information in the Committee's annual report;
- if a satisfactory remedy is not provided after the follow-up meeting, invite the state party to send a representative to discuss follow-up in an open session with the Committee; and
- if a satisfactory remedy is not provided after such an open meeting, request a follow-up mission or visit by a Committee representative to the state party.

2. COMMITTEE AGAINST TORTURE

The Committee has recently adopted a follow-up mechanism, which provides for the designation of one of its members as Rapporteur for Follow-up. The Rapporteur is expected to monitor the responses of states parties to the Committee's request for information on the remedy provided, and to meet with representatives of selected states parties that have not responded positively to the Committee's request. They are also enabled to make visits to states parties in the course of follow-up activities (Rule 115).

3. COMMITTEE ON THE ELIMINATION OF RACIAL DISCRIMINATION

CERD does not have a follow-up procedure on individual communications revealing a violation of the Convention. The Committee includes in its annual report to the General Assembly the text of its final Views.

4. COMMITTEE ON THE ELIMINATION OF DISCRIMINATION AGAINST WOMEN

The CEDAW Optional Protocol specifically refers to follow-up (article 7).

Within six months of the Committee issuing its Views and recommendations, the state party will be directed to submit to the Committee a written response, including information on any action taken. The Committee may invite the state party to submit further information about measures taken, and may request that information be included in subsequent state reports.

Under its Rules of Procedure, the Committee is to designate a rapporteur or working group on follow-up, who will ascertain the measures taken by states parties to give effect to the Committee's Views and recommendations. The Committee is also to include information on follow-up in its annual reports to the General Assembly.

In the absence of decided cases to date, CEDAW has yet to develop specific follow-up practices.

5. CONCLUSION

An individual complaint to a treaty body provides a person who believes his or her rights have been violated with an opportunity to receive a determination from an international expert body that supports the claim of a violation and an entitlement to a remedy. Treaty body Views are generally not enforceable in domestic courts of states parties. The treaty bodies themselves, and the political organs of the UN such as the General Assembly or the Commission on Human Rights, engage in little or no follow-up of these Views. Nevertheless, a decision of an international expert body that an individual's human rights, and a particular state's obligations to protect those rights, have been violated can be a powerful tool for applying pressure for redress.

ANNEX 1

COMPLAINT FORMS

(originals from the Human Rights Committee, CEDAW;
others modelled on the HRC form)

COMPLAINT FORM TO THE HUMAN RIGHTS COMMITTEE

Date:....................................

submitted for consideration under the Optional Protocol to the International Covenant on Civil and Political Rights

I. Information concerning the author of the communication

Name.. First name(s)............................
Nationality..Profession................................
Date and place of birth ....

Present address ....
....
Address for exchange of confidential correspondence (if other than present address)
....
....

Submitting the communication as:
(a) Victim of the violation(s) (set forth below)...or
(b) Appointed representative/legal counsel of the alleged victim(s).................or
(c) Other...

If box (c) is marked, the author should explain:
(i) In what capacity she or he is acting on behalf of the victim(s) (e.g. family relationship or other personal links with the alleged victim): ....
....
(ii) Why the victim(s) is (are) unable to submit the communication her or himself (themselves):..

Note: An unrelated third party having no link to the victim(s) cannot submit a communication on her or his (their) behalf.

II. Information concerning the alleged victim(s) (if other than author)

Name... First name(s)...............................

Nationality... Profession ....

Date and place of birth..

Present address or whereabouts ....

....

III. State concerned/articles violated/domestic remedies

Name of the state party (country) to the International Covenant and the Optional Protocol against which the communication is directed:

....

Articles of the International Covenant on Civil and Political Rights allegedly violated:

....

Steps taken by or on behalf of the alleged victim(s) to exhaust domestic remedies-recourse to the courts or other public authorities, when and with what results (if possible, enclose copies of all relevant judicial or administrative decisions):

....

If domestic remedies have not been exhausted, explain why:

....

IV. Other international procedures

Has the same matter ever been submitted for examination under another procedure of international investigation or settlement (e.g. the Inter-American Commission on Human Rights, the European Commission on Human Rights)? If so, when and with what results?

....

....

....

V. Facts of the claim

Detailed description of the facts of the alleged violation or violations (including relevant dates). *Add as many pages as needed for this description.*

....

....

....

Author's signature:...

COMPLAINT FORM TO THE COMMITTEE AGAINST TORTURE

Date:.......................................

submitted for consideration under article 22 of the Convention Against Torture

I. Information concerning the complainant

Name.. First name(s)..........................

Nationality... Profession................................

Date and place of birth ....

Present address ....

....

Address for exchange of confidential correspondence (if other than present address)

....

....

Submitting the communication as: ....

(a) Victim of the violation(s) (set forth below).......................................or

(b) Appointed representative/legal counsel of the alleged victim(s)................or

(c) Other...

If box (c) is marked, the author should explain:

(i) In what capacity she or he is acting on behalf of the victim(s) (e.g. family relationship or other personal links with the alleged victim): ....

....

(ii) Why the victim(s) is (are) unable to submit the communication her or himself (themselves): ....

....

Note: An unrelated third party having no link to the victim(s) cannot submit a communication on her or his (their) behalf.

II. Information concerning the alleged victim(s) (if other than complainant)

Name.. First name(s)..........................

Nationality... Profession................................

Date and place of birth ....

Present address or whereabouts...

III. State concerned/articles violated/domestic remedies

Name of the state party (country) to the Convention Against Torture against which the complaint is directed:

....

Articles of the Convention Against Torture allegedly violated:

....

Steps taken by or on behalf of the alleged victim(s) to exhaust domestic remedies-recourse to the courts or other public authorities, when and with what results (if possible, enclose copies of all relevant judicial or administrative decisions):

....

If domestic remedies have not been exhausted, explain why:

....

IV. Other international procedures

Has the same matter been submitted for examination (in the past or pending) under another procedure of international investigation or settlement (e.g. the Inter-American Commission on Human Rights, the European Commission on Human Rights)? If so, when and with what results?

....
....
....

V. Facts of the claim

Detailed description of the facts of the alleged violation or violations (including relevant dates). *Add as many pages as needed for this description.*

....
....
....

Complainant's signature:..

COMPLAINT FORM TO THE COMMITTEE ON THE ELIMINATION OF RACIAL DISCRIMINATION

Date:...

submitted for consideration under article 14 of the Convention on the Elimination of All Forms of Racial Discrimination

I. Information concerning the author of the communication

Name.. First name(s) ....
Nationality... Profession...............................
Date and place of birth...

Present address...
....

Address for exchange of confidential correspondence (if other than present address)
....
....

Submitting the communication as:
(a) Victim of the violation(s) (set forth below)...or
(b) Appointed representative/legal counsel of the alleged victim(s)................or
(c) Other ....

If box (c) is marked, the author should explain:
(i) In what capacity she or he is acting on behalf of the victim(s) (e.g. family relationship or other personal links with the alleged victim):.....................................
....
(ii) Why the victim(s) is (are) unable to submit the communication her or himself (themselves): ....
....

Note:An unrelated third party having no link to the victim(s) cannot submit a communication on her or his (their) behalf.

II. Information concerning the alleged victim(s) (if other than author)

Name .... First name(s) ....
Nationality .... Profession ....
Date and place of birth ....
Present address or whereabouts...

III. State concerned/articles violated/domestic remedies

Name of the state party (country) to the Convention on the Elimination of All Forms of Racial Discrimination against which the communication is directed:

....

Articles of the Convention on the Elimination of All Forms of Racial Discrimination allegedly violated:

....

Steps taken by or on behalf of the alleged victim(s) to exhaust domestic remedies-recourse to the courts or other public authorities, when and with what results (if possible, enclose copies of all relevant judicial or administrative decisions):

....

If domestic remedies have not been exhausted, explain why:

....

IV. Other international procedures

Has the same matter been submitted for examination under another procedure of international investigation or settlement (e.g. the Inter-American Commission on Human Rights, the European Commission on Human Rights)? If so, when and with what results?

....

....

....

V. Facts of the claim

Detailed description of the facts of the alleged violation or violations (including relevant dates). *Add as many pages as needed for this description*

....

....

....

Author's signature:..

COMPLAINT FORM TO THE COMMITTEE ON THE ELIMINATION OF DISCRIMINATION AGAINST WOMEN

The following questionnaire provides a guideline for those who wish to submit a communication. Please provide as much information as available in response to the items listed below. Attach additional pages as necessary.

<u>Note:</u>

To be considered by the Committee, a communication:
- must be in writing;
- may not be anonymous;
- must refer to a State which is a party to both the Convention on the Elimination of All Forms of Discrimination against Women and the Optional Protocol; and
- must be submitted by, or on behalf of, an individual or a group of individuals under the jurisdiction of a State which is a party to the Convention and the Optional Protocol. In cases where a communication is submitted on behalf of an individual or a group of individuals, their consent is necessary unless the person submitting the communication can justify acting on their behalf without such consent.

A communication will not normally be considered by the Committee:
- unless all available domestic remedies have been exhausted;
- where the same matter is being or has already been examined by the Committee or another international procedure;
- if it concerns an alleged violation occurring before the entry into force of the Optional Protocol for the State.

In order for a communication to be considered, the victim or victims must agree to disclose her/their identity to the State against which the violation is alleged. The communication, if admissible, will be brought confidentially to the attention of the State party concerned.

If you wish to submit a communication, please follow the guidelines below as much as possible. Also, please submit any relevant information which becomes available after you have submitted this form.

Further information on the Convention on the Elimination of All Forms of Discrimination against Women and its Optional Protocol, as well as the rules of procedure of the Committee can be found at: http://www.un.org/women-watch/daw/cedaw/index.html

1. Information concerning the author of the communication

Family Name...

First name(s)...

Date and place of birth...

Nationality/citizenship...

Passport/identity card number (if available)...

Sex...

Profession ....

Ethnic background, religious affiliation, social group (if relevant)........................

Present address..

Mailing address for exchange of confidential correspondence (if other than present address)...

Fax/telephone/e-mail ....

Indicate whether you are submitting the communication as:

(a) Alleged victim(s). If there is a group of individuals alleged to be victims, provide basic information about each individual ....

(b) On behalf of the alleged victim(s). Provide evidence showing the consent of the victim(s), or reasons that justify submitting the communication without such consent...

2. Information concerning the alleged victim(s) (if other than the author)

Family Name ....

First name(s) ....

Date and place of birth...

Nationality/citizenship..

Passport/identity card number (if available)..

Sex...

Marital status/children ....

Profession..

Ethnic background, religious affiliation, social group (if relevant)

Present address..

Mailing address for confidential correspondence (if other than present address)

....

Fax/telephone/e-mail..

3. Information on the State party concerned

Name of the State party (country)..

4. Nature of the alleged violation(s)

Provide detailed information to substantiate your claim, including:

- Description of alleged violation(s) and alleged perpetrator(s).........................
- Date(s)..
- Place(s)...
- Provisions of the Convention on the Elimination of All Forms of Discrimination against Women that were allegedly violated. If the communication refers to more than one provision, describe each issue separately.

5. Steps taken to exhaust domestic remedies

Describe the action taken to exhaust domestic remedies; for example, attempts to obtain legal, administrative, legislative, policy or programme remedies, including:
- Type(s) of remedy sought...
- Date(s) ....
- Place(s) ....
- Who initiated the action ....
- Which authority or body was addressed ....
- Name of court hearing the case (if any) ....

If domestic remedies have not been exhausted, explain why.

....

....

Please note: Enclose copies of all relevant documentation.

6. Other international procedures

Has the same matter already been examined or is it being examined under another procedure of international investigation or settlement? If yes, explain:
- Type of procedure(s) ....
- Date(s)..
- Place(s) ....
- Results (if any) ....

Please note: Enclose copies of all relevant documentation.

7. Date and signature

Date/place: ....

Signature of author(s) and/or victim(s): ....

8. List of documents attached (do *not* send originals, only copies)

....

CONTACT INFORMATION OF THE HUMAN RIGHTS COMMITTEE, CAT, CERD, CEDAW

1. HUMAN RIGHTS COMMITTEE
Human Rights Committee,
c/o Office of the UN High Commissioner for Human Rights,
Palais Wilson,
52 Rue des Pacquis,
1211 Geneva, Switzerland

fax: (41) (22) 917-9022
e-mail: tb-petitions.hchr@unog.ch

2. COMMITTEE ON THE ELIMINATION OF RACIAL DISCRIMINATION
Committee on the Elimination of Racial Discrimination,
c/o Office of the UN High Commissioner for Human Rights,
Palais Wilson,
52 Rue des Pacquis,
1211 Geneva, Switzerland

fax: (41) (22) 917-9022
e-mail: tb-petitions.hchr@unog.ch

3. COMMITTEE AGAINST TORTURE
Committee Against Torture,
c/o Office of the UN High Commissioner for Human Rights,
Palais Wilson,
52 Rue des Pacquis,
1211 Geneva, Switzerland

fax: (41) (22) 917-9022
e-mail: tb-petitions.hchr@unog.ch

4. COMMITTEE FOR THE ELIMINATION OF DISCRIMINATION AGAINST WOMEN
Committee on the Elimination of Discrimination Against Women
c/o Division for the Advancement of Women, Department of Economic and Social Affairs
United Nations Secretariat
2 United Nations Plaza
DC-2/12th Floor
New York, New York 10017
U.S.A.

fax: (1) (212) 963-3463
[no e-mail address yet]

ANNEX 3

CHECKLIST FOR SUBMITTING COMPLAINTS

Notes:

There is no page limit for a complaint submission.

If the details of the complaint are lengthy, it is useful to submit a short summary (approx. 1500 words) of the contents of the complaint.

The complaint will be handled more quickly if it is submitted in English, French or Spanish.

Complaints submitted in Russian will be initially processed but likely delayed in subsequent translation, as will complaints submitted in the two other official languages of the UN, Arabic and Chinese. Complaints submitted in Arabic and Chinese may also be returned with a request to resubmit in English, French, Spanish or Russian. Complaints submitted in any other language will be returned with a request to resubmit in English, French, Spanish, or Russian.

CHECKLIST

- the name of the treaty body to which the complaint is directed
- the name of the alleged victim(s)
- the name of the complainant or author of the complaint, if different from the victim

Note:

Any person lodging the complaint on behalf of another individual must establish a close personal relationship with the alleged victim, and that the alleged victim is incapable of bringing the complaint on his or her own behalf. An unrelated third party having no link to the victim(s) cannot submit a complaint on his or her behalf). In the case of CERD and CEDAW, a complaint may also be made on behalf of a group of individuals.

- the signature of the author of the complaint
- contact information of the victim
- contact information of the author of the complaint, and any person (such as legal counsel) authorized to act on behalf of the author of the complaint
- the nationality, date and place of birth of the victim
- the nationality, date and place of birth of the author of the complaint, if the author is not the victim
- the name of the state against which the complaint is brought; the state must have ratified the individual complaint provision of the relevant treaty or pro-

tocol, (CERD article 14, ICCPR Optional Protocol, CEDAW Optional Protocol, CAT article 22)

- the rights and the specific articles in the treaty which are alleged to have been violated; keep in mind any relevant state reservations and respond to them if necessary
- in the case of the ICCPR, a statement that no complaint on the same subject-matter is pending before another procedure of international investigation or settlement; in the case of ICCPR, (and CERD for information), if the matter has ever been the subject of another procedure of international investigation or settlement, the date and results of that investigation or procedure should be provided
- in the case of CAT and CEDAW, a statement that no complaint on the same matter has either been decided by another procedure of international investigation or settlement, or is pending before another such procedure
- a description of the steps taken by or on behalf of the alleged victim to exhaust domestic remedies (descriptions of recourse to the courts, or to public authorities, the dates of such steps, and the details of the results; enclose copies of all relevant judicial or administrative decisions, if possible)
- if domestic remedies have not been exhausted, evidence must be provided as to why such remedies are ineffective, unavailable or unreasonably prolonged
- a detailed fact statement, including all available evidence supporting the claim; it is the complainant's responsibility to sufficiently substantiate his or her claim; include such evidence as:
  - all relevant dates
  - a signed statement from the victim, setting out in as much detail as possible the factual basis of the complained violation
  - signed statements, where relevant, from available witnesses
  - in the case of torture, cruel, inhuman or degrading treatment or punishment: medical reports or certificates, including both physical and psychological assessments that might support the allegation that torture has occurred, autopsy reports if applicable, photographs, general information about the country situation that might prove a practice of torture in the country
- a request for interim measures pending a final decision on the merits, where such measures are necessary to ensure that irreparable harm is not done to the victim in the course of the treaty bodies' consideration of the complaint; irreparable harm does not include damage which can be compensated by a financial award
- the remedy requested (as applicable), for example:
  - financial compensation to the victim or his or her family
  - a new trial
  - commutation of a sentence of death
  - release from police custody
  - the amendment of legislation
  - non-refoulement
  - investigation of reported cases of torture
  - punishment of persons responsible for torture and ill-treatment

PITFALLS TO AVOID

Common grounds for failing to satisfy preliminary criteria for the registration and subsequent examination of the petition:

- the state alleged to violate the rights of the petitioner is not a party to the relevant complaints procedure (the Optional Protocol to the ICCPR, article 14 CERD, article 22 CAT, the Optional Protocol to CEDAW)
- the state party has entered a reservation to the relevant treaty as a result of which the petition cannot be examined
- the complaint is being examined (in the case of ICCPR, CAT and CEDAW) by the European Court of Human Rights, the Inter-American Commission or Court of Human Rights, the African Commission on Human and People's Rights
- the complaint has been examined (in the case of CAT and CEDAW) by the European Court of Human Rights, the Inter-American Commission or Court of Human Rights, the African Commission on Human and People's Rights
- the object of the petition, such as the rights violations cited, fall outside the scope of the relevant treaty
- the events complained of occurred prior to the entry into force of the relevant treaty or treaty provision (the Optional Protocol to the ICCPR, article 14 CERD, article 22 CAT, the Optional Protocol to CEDAW) for the state concerned
- domestic judicial/administrative remedies do not appear to have been exhausted, and it has not been substantiated that the application of domestic remedies would be unreasonably prolonged or that the remedies would be otherwise unavailable or ineffective
- the Human Rights Committee will generally not review the evaluation of facts and evidence by the national courts and authorities, nor the interpretation of domestic legislation
- the Human Rights Committee will generally not review a sentence imposed by national courts, nor the question of innocence or guilt
- the treaty bodies will not generally examine disputes between private individuals or alleged violations of human rights that have been committed by non-state actors
- the individual petition has not been presented by the alleged victims themselves or by duly authorized representatives
- the petition is anonymous
- the petition does not provide sufficient details as to the facts of the case, and/or how the alleged victim's rights under the relevant treaty have been violated
- correspondence has been submitted in a language which is not a working language of the Secretariat (the working languages being English, French, Spanish and Russian)

ANNEX 4

LIST OF STATES PARTIES TO THE OPTIONAL PROTOCOL TO THE ICCPR AND HOW TO UPDATE

updated 13 May 2002
to update see: www.unhchr.ch/pdf/report.pdf   see also www.bayefsky.com

State	Signature	Ratification, Accession (a), Succession (d)	Entry into Force
Algeria		12 Sep 1989 a	12 Dec 1989
Angola		10 Jan 1992 a	10 Apr 1992
Argentina		8 Aug 1986 a	8 Nov 1986
Armenia		23 Jun 1993	23 Sep 1993
Australia		25 Sep 1991 a	25 Dec 1991
Austria		10 Dec 1987	10 Mar 1988
Azerbaijan		27 Nov 2001 a	27 Feb 2002
Barbados		5 Jan 1973 a	23 Mar 1976
Belarus		30 Sep 1992 a	30 Dec 1992
Belgium		17 May 1994 a	17 Aug 1994
Benin		12 Mar 1992 a	12 Jun 1992
Bolivia		12 Aug 1982 a	12 Nov 1982
Bosnia and Herzegovina		1 Mar 1995	1 Jun 1995
Bulgaria		26 Mar 1992 a	26 Jun 1992
Burkina Faso		4 Jan 1999 a	4 Apr 1999
Cameroon		27 Jun 1984 a	27 Sep 1984
Canada		19 May 1976 a	19 Aug 1976
Cape Verde		19 May 2000 a	19 Aug 2000
Central African Republic		8 May 1981 a	8 Aug 1981
Chad		9 Jun 1995 a	9 Sep 1995
Chile		28 May 1992 a	28 Aug 1992
Colombia		29 Oct 1969	23 Mar 1976
Congo		5 Oct 1983 a	5 Jan 1984
Costa Rica		29 Nov 1968	23 Mar 1976

State	Signature	Ratification, Accession (a), Succession (d)	Entry into Force
Côte d'Ivoire		5 Mar 1997 a	5 Jun 1997
Croatia		12 Oct 1995 a	12 Jan 1996
Cyprus		15 Apr 1992	15 Jul 1992
Czech Republic		22 Feb 1993 d	1 Jan 1993
Democratic Republic of the Congo		1 Nov 1976 a	1 Feb 1977
Denmark		6 Jan 1972	23 Mar 1976
Dominican Republic		4 Jan 1978 a	4 Apr 1978
Ecuador		6 Mar 1969	23 Mar 1976
El Salvador		6 Jun 1995	6 Sep 1995
Equatorial Guinea		25 Sep 1987 a	25 Dec 1987
Estonia		21 Oct 1991 a	21 Jan 1992
Finland		19 Aug 1975	23 Mar 1976
France		17 Feb 1984 a	17 May 1984
Gambia		9 Jun 1988 a	9 Sep 1988
Georgia		3 May 1994 a	3 Aug 1994
Germany		25 Aug 1993 a	25 Nov 1993
Ghana		8 Sept 2000	7 Dec 2000
Greece		5 May 1997 a	5 Aug 1997
Guatemala		28 Nov 2000 a	28 Feb 2001
Guinea		17 Jun 1993	17 Sep 1993
Guinea-Bissau	12 Sep 2000		
Guyana (see note)		10 May 1993 a	10 Aug 1993
Honduras	19 Dec 1966		
Hungary		7 Sep 1988 a	7 Dec 1988
Iceland		22 Aug 1979 a	22 Nov 1979
Ireland		8 Dec 1989	8 Mar 1990
Italy		15 Sep 1978	15 Dec 1978
Kyrgyzstan		7 Oct 1994 a	7 Jan 1995
Latvia		22 Jun 1994 a	22 Sep 1994
Lesotho		7 Sep 2000 a	6 Dec 2000
Libyan Arab Jamahiriya		16 May 1989 a	16 Aug 1989
Liechtenstein		10 Dec 1998 a	10 Mar 1999
Lithuania		20 Nov 1991 a	20 Feb 1992
Luxembourg		18 Aug 1983 a	18 Nov 1983
Madagascar		21 Jun 1971	23 Mar 1976
Malawi		11 Jun 1996	11 Sep 1996
Mali		24 Oct 2001 a	24 Jan 2002
Malta		13 Sep 1990 a	13 Dec 1990
Mauritius		12 Dec 1973 a	23 Mar 1976

State	Signature	Ratification, Accession (a), Succession (d)	Entry into Force
Mexico		15 Mar 2002	15 Jun 2002
Mongolia		16 Apr 1991 a	16 Jul 1991
Namibia		28 Nov 1994 a	28 Feb 1995
Nauru	12 Nov 2001		
Nepal		14 May 1991 a	14 Aug 1991
Netherlands		11 Dec 1978	11 Mar 1979
New Zealand		26 May 1989 a	26 Aug 1989
Nicaragua		12 Mar 1980 a	12 Jun 1980
Niger		7 Mar 1986 a	7 Jun 1986
Norway		13 Sep 1972	23 Mar 1976
Panama		8 Mar 1977	8 Jun 1977
Paraguay		10 Jan 1995 a	10 Apr 1995
Peru		3 Oct 1980 a	3 Jan 1981
Philippines		22 Aug 1989 a	22 Nov 1989
Poland		7 Nov 1991 a	7 Feb 1992
Portugal		3 May 1983	3 Aug 1983
Republic of Korea		10 Apr 1990 a	10 Jul 1990
Romania		20 Jul 1993 a	20 Oct 1993
Russian Federation		1 Oct 1991 a	1 Jan 1992
Saint Vincent and the Grenadines		9 Nov 1981 a	9 Feb 1982
San Marino		18 Oct 1985 a	18 Jan 1986
Sao Tome and Principe	6 Sep 2000		
Senegal		13 Feb 1978	13 May 1978
Seychelles		5 May 1992 a	5 Aug 1992
Sierra Leone		23 Aug 1996 a	23 Nov 1996
Slovakia		28 May 1993	1 Jan 1993
Slovenia		16 Jul 1993 a	16 Oct 1993
Somalia		24 Jan 1990 a	24 Apr 1990
Spain		25 Jan 1985 a	25 Apr 1985
Sri Lanka		3 Oct 1997 a	3 Jan 1998
Suriname		28 Dec 1976 a	28 Mar 1977
Sweden		6 Dec 1971	23 Mar 1976
Tajikistan		4 Jan 1999 a	4 Apr 1999
The Former Yugoslav Republic of Macedonia		12 Dec 1994 a	12 Mar 1995
Togo		30 Mar 1988 a	30 Jun 1988
Turkmenistan		1 May 1997 a	1 Aug 1997

State	Signature	Ratification, Accession (a), Succession (d)	Entry into Force
Uganda		14 Nov 1995	14 Feb 1996
Ukraine		25 Jul 1991 a	25 Oct 1991
Uruguay		1 Apr 1970	23 Mar 1976
Uzbekistan		28 Sep 1995 a	28 Dec 1995
Venezuela		10 May 1978	10 Aug 1978
Yugoslavia		6 Sep 2001	6 Dec 2001
Zambia		10 Apr 1984 a	10 Jul 1984

Notes:

- Guyana had initially acceded to the Optional Protocol on 10 May 1993. On 5 January 1999, the Government of Guyana denounced the Optional Protocol with effect from 5 April 1999. On that same date, the Government of Guyana re-acceded to the Optional Protocol with a reservation.
- Jamaica had ratified the Optional Protocol on 3 October 1975. Jamaica subsequently denounced the Optional Protocol, effective 23 January 1998.
- Trinidad and Tobago had ratified the Optional Protocol on 14 November 1980. Trinidad and Tobago subsequently denounced the Optional Protocol, effective 27 June 2002.

ANNEX 5

LIST OF STATES PARTIES ACCEPTING ARTICLE 22 CAT AND HOW TO UPDATE

updated 13 May 2002
to update see: www.unhchr.ch/pdf/report.pdf   see also www.bayefsky.com

State	Article 22 Declaration	Entry into Force
Algeria	12 Sep 1989	12 Oct 1989
Argentina	24 Sep 1986	26 Jun 1987
Australia	28 Jan 1993	28 Jan 1993
Austria	29 Jul 1987	29 Aug 1987
Azerbaijan	4 Feb 2002	4 Feb 2002
Belgium	25 Jun 1999	25 Jul 1999
Bulgaria	12 May 1993	12 May 1993
Cameroon	12 Oct 2000	12 Oct 2000
Canada	13 Nov 1989	13 Nov 1989
Costa Rica	27 Feb 2002	27 Feb 2002
Croatia	12 Oct 1992[1]	8 Oct 1991[1]
Cyprus	8 Apr 1993	8 Apr 1993
Czech Republic	3 Sep 1996	3 Sep 1996
Denmark	27 May 1987	26 Jun 1987
Ecuador	6 Sep 1988	6 Sep 1988
Finland	30 Aug 1989	30 Sep 1989
France	26 Jun 1987	26 Jun 1987
Germany	19 Oct 2001	19 Oct 2001
Ghana	7 Sep 2000	7 Oct 2000
Greece	6 Oct 1988	6 Nov 1988
Hungary	13 Sep 1989	13 Sep 1989
Iceland	23 Oct 1996	23 Nov 1996
Italy	10 Oct 1989	10 Oct 1989
Liechtenstein	2 Nov 1990	2 Dec 1990
Luxembourg	29 Sep 1987	29 Oct 1987
Malta	13 Sep 1990	13 Oct 1990
Monaco	6 Dec 1991	6 Jan 1992
Netherlands	21 Dec 1988	21 Jan 1989
New Zealand	10 Dec 1989	10 Jan 1990

State	Article 22 Declaration	Entry into Force
Norway	9 Jul 1986	26 Jun 1987
Poland	12 May 1993	12 May 1993
Portugal	9 Feb 1989	9 Mar 1989
Russian Federation	1 Oct 1991	1 Oct 1991
Senegal	16 Oct 1996	16 Oct 1996
Seychelles	6 Aug 2001	6 Aug 2001
Slovakia	17 Mar 1995	17 Mar 1995
Slovenia	16 Jul 1993	16 Jul 1993
South Africa	10 Dec 1998	10 Dec 1998
Spain	21 Oct 1987	21 Nov 1987
Sweden	8 Jan 1986	26 Jun 1987
Switzerland	2 Dec 1986	26 Jun 1987
Togo	18 Nov 1987	18 Dec 1987
Tunisia	23 Sep 1988	23 Oct 1988
Turkey	2 Aug 1988	2 Sep 1988
Uruguay	27 Jul 1988	27 Jul 1988
Venezuela	26 Apr 1994	26 Apr 1994
Yugoslavia	10 Sep 1991[2]	10 Oct 1991[2]

[1] The former Yugoslavia had previously ratified CAT on 10 September 1991. Subsequent to dissolution, the Government of Croatia deposited with the Secretary-General a notification of succession dated 12 October 1992, which included accepting the article 22 procedure to take effect from 8 October 1991, the date on which Croatia became an independent state.

[2] The former Yugoslavia had previously ratified CAT and made the declaration under article 22 on 10 September 1991. On 12 March 2001, however, the Government of Yugoslavia notified the Secretary-General of its intent to succeed to the Convention, included acceptance of the article 22 procedure, as from 27 April 1992.

LIST OF STATES PARTIES ACCEPTING ARTICLE 14 CERD AND HOW TO UPDATE

updated 13 May 2002
to update see: www.unhchr.ch/pdf/report.pdf   see also www.bayefsky.com

State	Article 14 Declaration	Entry into Force
Algeria	12 Sep 1989	12 Sep 1989
Australia	28 Jan 1993	28 Jan 1993
Austria	20 Feb 2002	20 Feb 2002
Azerbaijan	27 Sep 2001	27 Sep 2001
Belgium	10 Oct 2000	10 Oct 2000
Bulgaria	12 May 1993	12 May 1993
Chile	18 May 1994	18 May 1994
Costa Rica	8 Jan 1974	8 Jan 1974
Cyprus	30 Dec 1993	30 Dec 1993
Czech Republic	11 Oct 2000	11 Oct 2000
Denmark	11 Oct 1985	11 Oct 1985
Ecuador	18 Mar 1977	18 Mar 1977
Finland	16 Nov 1994	16 Nov 1994
France	16 Aug 1982	16 Aug 1982
Germany	30 Aug 2001	30 Aug 2001
Hungary	13 Sep 1989	13 Sep 1989
Iceland	10 Aug 1981	10 Aug 1981
Ireland	29 Dec 2000	29 Jan 2001
Italy	5 May 1978	5 May 1978
Luxembourg	22 Jul 1996	22 Jul 1996
Malta	16 Dec 1998	16 Dec 1998
Mexico	15 Mar 2002	15 Mar 2002
Monaco	6 Nov 2001	6 Nov 2001
Netherlands	10 Dec 1971	10 Jan 1972
Norway	23 Jan 1976	23 Jan 1976
Peru	27 Nov 1984	27 Nov 1984
Poland	1 Dec 1999	1 Dec 1999
Portugal	2 Mar 2000	2 Mar 2000
Republic of Korea	5 Mar 1997	5 Mar 1997
Russian Federation	1 Oct 1991	1 Oct 1991
Senegal	3 Dec 1982	3 Dec 1982
Slovakia	17 Mar 1995	17 Mar 1995
South Africa	10 Dec 1998	10 Jan 1999
Spain	13 Jan 1998	13 Jan 1998
Sweden	6 Dec 1971	6 Jan 1972
The Former Yugoslav Republic of Macedonia	22 Dec 1999	22 Dec 1999
Ukraine	28 Jul 1992	28 Jul 1992
Uruguay	11 Sep 1972	11 Sep 1972
Yugoslavia	27 Jun 2001	27 Jun 2001

ANNEX 7

LIST OF STATES PARTIES TO THE OPTIONAL PROTOCOL TO CEDAW AND HOW TO UPDATE

updated 22 May 2002
to update see: www.unhchr.ch/pdf/report.pdf   see also www.bayefsky.com

State	Signature	Ratification	Entry into Force
Andorra	9 Jul 2001		
Argentina	28 Feb 2000		
Austria		6 Sep 2000	22 Dec 2000
Azerbaijan		1 Jun 2001	1 Sep 2001
Bangladesh		6 Sep 2000	22 Dec 2000
Belarus	29 Apr 2002		
Belgium	10 Dec 1999		
Benin	25 May 2000		
Bolivia		27 Sep 2000	27 Dec 2000
Bosnia and Herzegovina	7 Sep 2000		
Brazil	13 Mar 2001		
Bulgaria	6 Jun 2000		
Burkina Faso	16 Nov 2001		
Burundi	13 Nov 2001		
Cambodia	11 Nov 2001		
Chile	10 Dec 1999		
Colombia	10 Dec 1999		
Costa Rica		20 Sep 2001	20 Dec 2001
Croatia		7 Mar 2001	7 Jun 2001
Cuba	17 Mar 2000		
Cyprus		26 Apr 2002	26 Jul 2002
Czech Republic		26 Feb 2001	26 May 2001
Denmark		31 May 2000	22 Dec 2000
Dominican Republic	10 Aug 2001	10 Nov 2001	
Ecuador		5 Feb 2002	5 May 2002
El Salvador	4 Apr 2001		
Finland		29 Dec 2000	29 Mar 2001
France		9 Jun 2000	22 Dec 2000
Germany		15 Jan 2002	15 Apr 2002
Ghana	24 Feb 2000		

State	Signature	Ratification	Entry into Force
Greece		24 Jan 2002	24 Apr 2002
Guatemala		9 May 2002	9 Aug 2002
Guinea-Bissau	12 Sep 2000		
Hungary		22 Dec 2000	22 Mar 2001
Iceland		6 Mar 2001	6 Jun 2001
Indonesia	28 Feb 2000		
Ireland		7 Sep 2000	22 Dec 2000
Italy		22 Sep 2000	22 Dec 2000
Kazakhstan		24 Aug 2001	24 Nov 2001
Lesotho	6 Sep 2000		
Liechtenstein		24 Oct 2001	24 Jan 2002
Lithuania	8 Sep 2000		
Luxembourg	10 Dec 1999		
Madagascar	7 Sep 2000		
Malawi	7 Sep 2000		
Mali		5 Dec 2000 a	5 Mar 2001
Mauritius	11 Nov 2001		
Mexico		15 Mar 2002	15 Jun 2002
Mongolia		28 Mar 2002	28 Jun 2002
Namibia		26 May 2000	22 Dec 2000
Nepal	18 Dec 2001		
Netherlands		22 May 2002	22 Aug 2002
New Zealand		7 Sep 2000	22 Dec 2000
Nigeria	8 Sep 2000		
Norway		5 Mar 2002	5 Jun 2002
Panama		9 May 2001	9 Aug 2001
Paraguay		14 May 2001	14 Aug 2001
Peru		9 Apr 2001	9 Jul 2001
Philippines	21 Mar 2000		
Portugal		26 Apr 2002	26 Jul 2002
Romania	6 Sep 2000		
Russian Federation	8 May 2001		
Sao Tome and Principe	6 Sep 2000		
Senegal		26 May 2000	22 Dec 2000
Sierra Leone	8 Sep 2000		
Slovakia		17 Nov 2000	17 Feb 2001
Slovenia	10 Dec 1999		
Solomon Islands		6 May 2002	6 Aug 2002
Spain		6 Jul 2001	6 Oct 2001
Sweden	10 Dec 1999		
Tajikistan	7 Sep 2000		
Thailand		14 Jun 2000	22 Dec 2000
The Former Yugoslav Republic of Macedonia	3 Apr 2000		
Turkey	8 Sep 2000		
Ukraine	7 Sep 2000		
Uruguay		26 Jul 2001	26 Oct 2001
Venezuela		13 May 2002	13 Aug 2002

HOW TO FIND A STATE PARTY'S RESERVATIONS

* see www.unhchr.ch/tbs/doc.nsf/Statusfrset?OpenFrameSet
* go to country
* go to treaty

* see also www.bayefsky.com

RULES OF PROCEDURE OF THE HUMAN RIGHTS COMMITTEE CONCERNING COMMUNICATIONS

HRI/GEN/3-6 June 2001

....

Transmission of Communications to the Committee

Rule 78

1. The Secretary-General shall bring to the attention of the Committee, in accordance with the present rules, communications which are or appear to be submitted for consideration by the Committee under article 1 of the Protocol.

2. The Secretary-General, when necessary, may request clarification from the author of a communication as to whether the author wishes to have the communication submitted to the Committee for consideration under the Protocol. In case there is still doubt as to the wish of the author, the Committee shall be seized of the communication.

3. No communication shall be received by the Committee or included in a list under rule 79 if it concerns a State which is not a party to the Protocol.

Rule 79

1. The Secretary-General shall prepare lists of the communications submitted to the Committee in accordance with rule 78 above, with a brief summary of their contents, and shall circulate such lists to the members of the Committee at regular intervals. The Secretary-General shall also maintain a permanent register of all such communications.

2. The full text of any communication brought to the attention of the Committee shall be made available to any member of the Committee upon request by that member.

Rule 80

1. The Secretary-General may request clarification from the author of a communication concerning the applicability of the Protocol to his communication, in particular regarding:

   (a) The name, address, age and occupation of the author and the verification of the author's identity;

(b) The name of the State party against which the communication is directed;

(c) The object of the communication;

(d) The provision or provisions of the Covenant alleged to have been violated;

(e) The facts of the claim;

(f) Steps taken by the author to exhaust domestic remedies;

(g) The extent to which the same matter is being examined under another procedure of international investigation or settlement.

2. When requesting clarification or information, the Secretary-General shall indicate an appropriate time limit to the author of the communication with a view to avoiding undue delays in the procedure under the Protocol.

3. The Committee may approve a questionnaire for the purpose of requesting the above-mentioned information from the author of the communication.

4. The request for clarification referred to in paragraph 1 of the present rule shall not preclude the inclusion of the communication in the list provided for in rule 79, paragraph 1, of these rules.

Rule 81

For each registered communication the Secretary-General shall as soon as possible prepare and circulate to the members of the Committee a summary of the relevant information obtained.

Consideration of Communications by the Committee or Its Subsidiary Bodies

Rule 82

Meetings of the Committee or its subsidiary bodies during which communications under the Protocol will be examined shall be closed. Meetings during which the Committee may consider general issues such as procedures for the application of the Protocol may be public if the Committee so decides.

Rule 83

The Committee may issue communiqués, through the Secretary-General, for the use of the information media and the general public regarding the activities of the Committee at its closed meetings.

Rule 84

1. A member shall not take part in the examination of a communication by the Committee:

(a) If the State party in respect of which he or she was elected to the Committee is a party to the case;

(b) If the member has any personal interest in the case; or

(c) If the member has participated in any capacity in the making of any decision on the case covered by the communication.

2. Any question which may arise under paragraph 1 above shall be decided by the Committee.

Rule 85

If, for any reason, a member considers that he or she should not take part or continue to take part in the examination of a communication, the member shall inform the Chairperson of his or her withdrawal.

Rule 86

The Committee may, prior to forwarding its views on the communication to the State party concerned, inform that State of its views as to whether interim measures may be desirable to avoid irreparable damage to the victim of the alleged violation. In doing so, the Committee shall inform the State party concerned that such expression of its views on interim measures does not imply a determination on the merits of the communication.

Determination of Admissibility

Rule 87

1. The Committee shall decide as soon as possible and in accordance with the following rules whether the communication is admissible or is inadmissible under the Protocol.

2. A working group established under rule 89, paragraph 1, may also declare a communication admissible when it is composed of five members and all the members so decide.

Rule 88

1. Communications shall be dealt with in the order in which they are received by the Secretariat, unless the Committee or a working group established under rule 89, paragraph 1, decides otherwise.

2. Two or more communications may be dealt with jointly if deemed appropriate by the Committee or a working group established under rule 89, paragraph 1.

Rule 89

1. The Committee may establish one or more working groups to make recommendations to the Committee regarding the fulfilment of the conditions of admissibility laid down in articles 1, 2, 3 and 5 (2) of the Protocol.

2. The rules of procedure of the Committee shall apply as far as possible to the meetings of the working group.

3. The Committee may designate special rapporteurs from among its members to assist in the handling of communications.

Rule 90

With a view to reaching a decision on the admissibility of a communication, the Committee, or a working group established under rule 89, paragraph 1, shall ascertain:
  (a) That the communication is not anonymous and that it emanates from an individual, or individuals, subject to the jurisdiction of a State party to the Protocol;
  (b) That the individual claims, in a manner sufficiently substantiated, to be a victim of a violation by that State party of any of the rights set forth in the Covenant. Normally, the communication should be submitted by the

individual personally or by that individual's representative; a communication submitted on behalf of an alleged victim may, however, be accepted when it appears that the individual in question is unable to submit the communication personally;

(c) That the communication does not constitute an abuse of the right of submission;

(d) That the communication is not incompatible with the provisions of the Covenant;

(e) That the same matter is not being examined under another procedure of international investigation or settlement;

(f) That the individual has exhausted all available domestic remedies.

<u>Rule 91</u>

1. As soon as possible after the communication has been received, the Committee, a working group established under rule 89, paragraph 1, or a special rapporteur designated under rule 89, paragraph 3, shall request the State party concerned to submit a written reply to the communication.

2. Within six months the State party concerned shall submit to the Committee written explanations or statements that shall relate both to the communication's admissibility and its merits as well as to any remedy that may have been provided in the matter, unless the Committee, working group or special rapporteur has decided, because of the exceptional nature of the case, to request a written reply that relates only to the question of admissibility. A State party that has been requested to submit a written reply that relates only to the question of admissibility is not precluded thereby from submitting, within six months of the request, a written reply that shall relate both to the communication's admissibility and its merits.

3. A State party that has received a request for a written reply under paragraph 1 both on admissibility and on the merits of the communication, may apply in writing, within two months, for the communication to be rejected as inadmissible, setting out the grounds for such inadmissibility. Submission of such an application shall not extend the period of six months given to the State party to submit its written reply to the communication, unless the Committee, a working group established under rule 89, paragraph 1, or a special rapporteur designated under rule 89, paragraph 3, decides to extend the time for submission of the reply, because of the special circumstances of the case, until the Committee has ruled on the question of admissibility.

4. The Committee, a working group established under rule 89, paragraph 1, or a special rapporteur designated under rule 89, paragraph 3, may request the State party or the author of the communication to submit, within specified time limits, additional written information or observations relevant to the question of admissibility of the communication or its merits.

5. A request addressed to a State party under paragraph 1 of this rule shall include a statement of the fact that such a request does not imply that any decision has been reached on the question of admissibility.

6. Within fixed time limits, each party may be afforded an opportunity to comment on submissions made by the other party pursuant to this rule.

<u>Rule 92</u>

1. Where the Committee decides that a communication is inadmissible under the Protocol it shall as soon as possible communicate its decision, through the Secretary-General, to the author of the communication and, where the communication has been transmitted to a State party concerned, to that State party.

2. If the Committee has declared a communication inadmissible under article 5, paragraph 2, of the Protocol, this decision may be reviewed at a later date by the Committee upon a written request by or on behalf of the individual concerned containing information to the effect that the reasons for inadmissibility referred to in article 5, paragraph 2, no longer apply.

<u>Consideration of Communications on the Merits</u>

<u>Rule 93</u>

1. In those cases in which the issue of admissibility is decided before receiving the State party's reply on the merits, if the Committee or a working group established under rule 89, paragraph 1, rules that the communication is admissible, that decision and all other relevant information shall be submitted, through the Secretary-General, to the State party concerned. The author of the communication shall also be informed, through the Secretary-General, of the decision.

2. Within six months, the State party concerned shall submit to the Committee written explanations or statements clarifying the matter under consideration and the remedy, if any, that may have been taken by that State.

3. Any explanations or statements submitted by a State party pursuant to this rule shall be communicated, through the Secretary-General, to the author of the communication, who may submit any additional written information or observations within fixed time limits.

4. Upon consideration of the merits, the Committee may review a decision that a communication is admissible in the light of any explanations or statements submitted by the State party pursuant to this rule.

<u>Rule 94</u>

1. In those cases in which the parties have submitted information relating both to the questions of admissibility and the merits, or in which a decision on admissibility has already been taken and the parties have submitted information on the merits, the Committee shall consider the communication in the light of all written information made available to it by the individual and the State party concerned and shall formulate its views thereon. Prior thereto the Committee may refer the communication to a working group or to a special rapporteur to make recommendations to the Committee.

2. The Committee shall not decide on the merits of the communication without having considered the applicability of all the admissibility grounds referred to in the Optional Protocol.

3. The views of the Committee shall be communicated to the individual and to the State party concerned.

Rule 95

1. The Committee shall designate a Special Rapporteur for follow-up on views adopted under article 5, paragraph 4, of the Optional Protocol, for the purpose of ascertaining the measures taken by States parties to give effect to the Committee's views.

2. The Special Rapporteur may make such contacts and take such action as appropriate for the due performance of the follow-up mandate. The Special Rapporteur shall make such recommendations for further action by the Committee as may be necessary.

3. The Special Rapporteur shall regularly report to the Committee on follow-up activities.

4. The Committee shall include information on follow-up activities in its annual report.

Confidentiality

Rule 96*

1. Communications under the Optional Protocol shall be examined by the Committee and its Working Group established pursuant to rule 89 in closed session. Oral deliberations and summary records shall remain confidential.

2. All working documents issued for the Committee, the Working Group established pursuant to rule 89 or the Special Rapporteur designated pursuant to rule 89 (3) by the Secretariat, including summaries of communications prepared prior to registration, the list of summaries of communications, and all drafts prepared for the Committee, its Working Group established pursuant to rule 89 or the Special Rapporteur designated pursuant to rule 89 (3) shall remain confidential, unless the Committee decides otherwise.

3. Paragraph 1 shall not affect the right of the author of a communication or the State party concerned to make public any submissions or information bearing on the proceedings. However, the Committee, the Working Group established pursuant to rule 89 or the Special Rapporteur designated pursuant to rule 89 (3) may, as deemed appropriate, request the author of a communication or the State party concerned to keep confidential the whole or part of any such submissions or information.

4. When a decision has been taken on the confidentiality pursuant to paragraph 3 above, the Committee, the Working Group established pursuant to rule 89 or the Special Rapporteur designated pursuant to rule 89 (3) may decide that all or part of the submissions and other information, such as the identity of the author, may remain confidential after the Committee's decision on inadmissibility, merits or discontinuance has been adopted.

5. Subject to paragraph 4, the Committee's decisions on inadmissibility, merits and discontinuance shall be made public. The decisions of the Committee or the

---

* Rule 96, adopted at the 1585th meeting of the Committee on 10 April 1997, replaces old rules 96, 97 and 98.

Special Rapporteur designated pursuant to rule 89 (3) under rule 86 shall be made public. No advance copies of any Committee decision shall be issued.

6. The Secretariat is responsible for the distribution of the Committee's final decisions. It shall not be responsible for the reproduction and the distribution of submissions concerning communications.

Rule 97

Information furnished by the parties within the framework of follow-up to the Committee's views is not subject to confidentiality, unless the Committee decides otherwise. Decisions of the Committee relating to follow-up activities are equally not subject to confidentiality, unless the Committee decides otherwise.

Individual Opinions

Rule 98

Any member of the Committee who has participated in a decision may request that his or her individual opinion be appended to the Committee's views or decision.

ANNEX 10

RULES OF PROCEDURE OF CAT CONCERNING COMPLAINTS

May 2002

...

XIX. PROCEDURE FOR THE CONSIDERATION OF COMPLAINTS RECEIVED UNDER ARTICLE 22 OF THE CONVENTION

A. GENERAL PROVISIONS

Declarations by States Parties

Rule 96

1. The Secretary-General shall transmit to the other States parties copies of the declarations deposited with him by States parties recognizing the competence of the Committee, in accordance with article 22 of the Convention.

2. The withdrawal of a declaration made under article 22 of the Convention shall not prejudice the consideration of any matter, which is the subject of a complaint already transmitted under that article; no further complaint by or on behalf of an individual shall be received under that article after the notification of withdrawal of the declaration has been received by the Secretary-General, unless the State party has made a new declaration.

Transmission of Complaints

Rule 97

1. The Secretary-General shall bring to the attention of the Committee, in accordance with the present rules, complaints, which are or appear to be submitted for consideration by the Committee under paragraph 1 of article 22 of the Convention.

2. The Secretary-General, when necessary, may request clarification from the complainant as to his/ her wish to have his/her complaint submitted to the Committee for consideration under article 22 of the Convention. In case there is still doubt as to the wish of the complainant, the Committee shall be seized of the complaint.

Registration of Complaints; Rapporteur for New Complaints and Interim Measures

Rule 98

1. Complaints may be registered by the Secretary-General or by decision of the Committee or by the Rapporteur on New Complaints and Interim Measures.

2. No complaint shall be registered by the Secretary-General if
    (a) It concerns a State which has not made the declaration provided for in article 22, paragraph 1, of the Convention; or
    (b) It is anonymous; or
    (c) It is not submitted in writing by the alleged victim or by close relatives of the alleged victim on his/her behalf or by a representative with appropriate written authorization.

3. The Secretary-General shall prepare lists of the complaints brought to the attention of the Committee in accordance with rule 97 above, with a brief summary of their contents, and shall circulate such lists to the members of the Committee at regular intervals. The Secretary-General shall also maintain a permanent register of all such complaints.

4. An original case file shall be kept for each summarized complaint. The full text of any complaint brought to the attention of the Committee shall be made available to any member of the Committee upon his/ her request.

Request for Clarification or Additional Information

Rule 99

1. The Secretary-General or the Rapporteur on New Complaints and Interim Measures may request clarification from the complainant concerning the applicability of article 22 of the Convention to his/her complaint, in particular regarding:
    (a) The name, address, age and occupation of the complainant and the verification of his/her identity;
    (b) The name of the State party against which the complaint is directed;
    (c) The object of the complaint;
    (d) The provision or provisions of the Convention alleged to have been violated;
    (e) The facts of the claim;
    (f) Steps taken by the complainant to exhaust domestic remedies;
    (g) Whether the same matter is being or has been examined under another procedure of international investigation or settlement.

2. When requesting clarification or information, the Secretary-General shall indicate an appropriate time limit to the complainant with a view to avoiding undue delays in the procedure under article 22 of the Convention. Such time limit may be extended in appropriate circumstances.

3. The Committee may approve a questionnaire for the purpose of requesting the above-mentioned information from the complainant.

4. The request for clarification referred to in paragraphs 1 (c)–(g) of the present rule shall not preclude the inclusion of the complaint in the list provided for in rule 98, paragraph 3.

5. The Secretary-General shall instruct the complainant on the procedure that will be followed and inform him/her that the text of the complaint shall be transmitted confidentially to the State party concerned in accordance with article 22, paragraph 3, of the Convention.

Summary of the Information

Rule 100

For each registered complaint the Secretary-General shall prepare and circulate to the members of the Committee a summary of the relevant information obtained.

Meetings and Hearings

Rule 101

1. Meetings of the Committee or its subsidiary bodies during which complaints under article 22 of the Convention will be examined shall be closed.

2. Meetings during which the Committee may consider general issues, such as procedures for the application of article 22 of the Convention, may be public if the Committee so decides.

Issue of Communiqués Concerning Closed Meetings

Rule 102

The Committee may issue communiqués, through the Secretary-General, for the use of the information media and the general public regarding the activities of the Committee under article 22 of the Convention.

Inability of A Member to Take Part in the Examination of A Complaint

Rule 103

1. A member shall not take part in the examination of a complaint by the Committee or its subsidiary body:
   - (a) If he/she has any personal interest in the case; or
   - (b) If he/she has participated in any capacity, other than as a member of the Committee, in the making of any decision on the case; or
   - (c) If he/she is a national of the State party concerned or is employed by that country.

2. Any question, which may arise under paragraph 1 above, shall be decided by the Committee without the participation of the member concerned.

Optional Non-Participation of A Member in the Examination of A Complaint

Rule 104

If, for any other reason, a member considers that he/she should not take part or continue to take part in the examination of a complaint, he/she shall inform the Chairman of his/her withdrawal.

B. PROCEDURE FOR DETERMINING ADMISSIBILITY OF COMPLAINTS

Method of Dealing with Complaints

Rule 105

1. In accordance with the following provisions, the Committee shall decide by simple majority as soon as practicable whether or not a complaint is admissible under article 22 of the Convention.

2. The Working Group established under rule 106, paragraph 1, may also declare a complaint admissible by majority vote or inadmissible by unanimity.

3. The Committee, the Working Group established under rule 106, paragraph 1, or the rapporteur(s) designated under rule 106, paragraph 3, shall, unless they decide otherwise, deal with complaints in the order in which they are received by the Secretariat.

4. The Committee may, if it deems it appropriate, decide to consider jointly two or more complaints.

5. The Committee may, if it deems appropriate, decide to sever consideration of complaints of multiple complainants. Severed complaints may receive a separate registry number.

Establishment of A Working Group and Designation of Rapporteurs for Specific Complaints

Rule 106

1. The Committee may, in accordance with rule 61, set up a working group to meet shortly before its sessions, or at any other convenient time to be decided by the Committee in consultation with the Secretary-General, for the purpose of taking decisions on admissibility or inadmissibility, and making recommendations to the Committee regarding the merits of complaints and assisting the Committee in any manner which the Committee may decide.

2. The Working Group shall comprise no less than three, no more than five members of the Committee. The Working Group shall elect its own officers, develop its own working methods, and apply as far as possible the rules of procedure of the Committee to its meetings. The members of the Working Group shall be elected by the Committee every other session.

3. The Working Group may designate rapporteurs from among its members to deal with specific complaints.

Conditions for Admissibility of Complaints

Rule 107

With a view to reaching a decision on the admissibility of a complaint, the Committee, its Working Group, or a rapporteur designated under rules 98 or 106, paragraph 3, shall ascertain:

   (a) That the individual claims to be a victim of a violation by the State party concerned of the provisions of the Convention. The complaint should be submitted by the individual himself/herself or by his/her relatives or designated representatives or by others on behalf of an alleged victim when it appears that the alleged victim is unable personally to submit the complaint and when appropriate authorization is submitted to the Committee;

(b) That the complaint is not an abuse of the Committee's process or manifestly unfounded;

(c) That the complaint is not incompatible with the provisions of the Convention;

(d) That the same matter has not been and is not being examined under another procedure of international investigation or settlement;

(e) That the individual has exhausted all available domestic remedies. However, this shall not be the rule where the application of the remedies is unreasonably prolonged or is unlikely to bring effective relief to the person who is the victim of the violation of this Convention.

(f) That the time elapsed since the exhaustion of domestic remedies is not so unreasonably prolonged as to render consideration of the claims unduly difficult by the Committee or the State party.

Interim Measures

Rule 108

1. At any time after the receipt of a complaint, the Committee, a working group, or the Rapporteur(s) for New Complaints and Interim Measures may transmit to the State party concerned, for its urgent consideration, a request that it take such interim measures, as the Committee considers necessary to avoid irreparable damage to the victim or victims of alleged violations.

2. Where the Committee, the Working Group, or Rapporteur(s) request(s) interim measures under this rule, the request shall not imply a determination of the admissibility or the merits of the communication. The State party shall be so informed upon transmittal.

3. Where a request for interim measures is made by the Working Group or Rapporteur(s) under the present rule, the working group or rapporteur(s) should inform the Committee members of the nature of the request and the complaint to which the request relates at the next regular session of the Committee.

4. The Secretary-General shall maintain a list of such requests for interim measures.

5. The Rapporteur for New Complaints and Interim Measures shall also monitor compliance with the Committee's requests for interim measures.

6. The State party may inform the Committee that the reasons for the interim measures have lapsed or present arguments why the request for interim measures should be lifted.

7. The Rapporteur, the Committee or the Working Group may withdraw the request for interim measures.

Additional Information, Clarifications and Observations

Rule 109

1. As soon as possible after the complaint has been registered, it should be transmitted to the State party requesting it to submit a written reply within six months.

2. The State party concerned shall include in its written reply explanations or statements that shall relate both to the admissibility and the merits of the complaint as well as to any remedy that may have been provided in the matter, unless the Committee, Working Group or rapporteur has decided, because of the exceptional nature of the case, to request a written reply that relates only to the question of admissibility.

3. A State party that has received a request for a written reply under paragraph 1 both on admissibility and on the merits of the complaint, may apply in writing, within two months, for the complaint to be rejected as inadmissible, setting out the grounds for such inadmissibility. The Committee or the Rapporteur on New Complaints and Interim Measures may or may not agree to consider admissibility separately from the merits.

4. Following a separate decision on admissibility, the Committee shall fix the deadline for submissions on a case-by-case basis.

5. The Committee or the Working Group established under rule 106 or rapporteur(s) designated under rule 106, paragraph 3, may request, through the Secretary-General, the State party concerned or the complainant to submit additional written information, clarifications or observations relevant to the question of admissibility or merits.

6. The Committee or the Working Group or rapporteur(s) designated under rule 106, paragraph 3, shall indicate a time-limit for the submission of additional information or clarification with a view to avoiding undue delay.

7. If the time limit provided is not respected by the State party concerned or the complainant, the Committee or the Working Group may decide to consider the admissibility and/or merits of the complaint in the light of available information.

8. A complaint may not be declared admissible unless the State party concerned has received its text and has been given an opportunity to furnish information or observations as provided in paragraph 1 of this rule.

9. If the State party concerned disputes the contention of the complainant that all available domestic remedies have been exhausted, the State party is required to give details of the effective remedies available to the alleged victim in the particular circumstances of the case and in accordance with the provisions of article 22, paragraph 5 (b), of the Convention.

10. Within such time-limit as indicated by the Committee or the Working Group or rapporteur(s) designated under rule 106, paragraph 3, the State party or the complainant may be afforded an opportunity to comment on any submission received from the other party pursuant to a request made under the present rule. Non-receipt of such comments within the established time limit should not generally delay the consideration of the admissibility of the complaint.

Inadmissible Complaints

Rule 110

1. Where the Committee or the Working Group decides that a complaint is inadmissible under article 22 of the Convention, or its consideration is suspended or discontinued, the Committee shall as soon as possible transmit its decision,

through the Secretary-General, to the complainant and, where the complaint has been transmitted to a State party concerned.

2. If the Committee or the Working Group has declared a complaint inadmissible under article 22, paragraph 5, of the Convention, this decision may be reviewed at a later date by the Committee upon a request from a member of the Committee or a written request by or on behalf of the individual concerned. Such written request shall contain evidence to the effect that the reasons for inadmissibility referred to in article 22, paragraph 5, of the Convention no longer apply.

C. CONSIDERATION OF THE MERITS

<u>Method of Dealing with Admissible Complaints; Oral Hearings</u>

<u>Rule 111</u>

1. When the Committee or the Working Group has decided that a complaint is admissible under article 22 of the Convention, before receiving the State party's reply on the merits, the Committee shall transmit to the State party, through the Secretary-General, the text of its decision together with any submission received from the author of the communication not already transmitted to the State party under rule 109, paragraph 1. The Committee shall also inform the complainant, through the Secretary-General, of its decision.

2. Within the period established by the Committee, the State party concerned shall submit to the Committee written explanations or statements clarifying the case under consideration and the measures, if any, that may have been taken by it. The Committee may indicate, if it deems it necessary, the type of information it wishes to receive from the State party concerned.

3. Any explanations or statements submitted by a State party pursuant to this rule shall be transmitted, through the Secretary-General, to the complainant who may submit any additional written information or observations within such time limit as the Committee shall decide.

4. The Committee may invite the complainant or his/her representative and representatives of the State party concerned to be present at specified closed meetings of the Committee in order to provide further clarifications or to answer questions on the merits of the complaint. Whenever one party is so invited, the other party shall be informed and invited to attend and make appropriate submissions. The non-appearance of a party will not prejudice the consideration of the case.

5. The Committee may revoke its decision that a complaint is admissible in the light of any explanations or statements thereafter submitted by the State party pursuant to this rule. However, before the Committee considers revoking that decision, the explanations or statements concerned must be transmitted to the complainant so that he/she may submit additional information or observations within a time limit set by the Committee.

<u>Findings of the Committee; Decisions on the Merits</u>

<u>Rule 112</u>

1. In those cases in which the parties have submitted information relating both to the questions of admissibility and the merits, or in which a decision on admis-

sibility has already been taken and the parties have submitted information on the merits, the Committee shall consider the complaint in the light of all information made available to it by or on behalf of the complainant and by the State party concerned and shall formulate its findings thereon. Prior thereto, the Committee may refer the communication to a Working Group or to case rapporteurs to make recommendations to the Committee.

2. The Committee, the Working Group, or the case rapporteur(s) may at any time, in the course of the examination, obtain any document from United Nations bodies, specialized agencies, or other sources that may assist in the consideration of the complaint.

3. The Committee shall not decide on the merits of a complaint without having considered the applicability of all the admissibility grounds referred to in article 22 of the Convention. The findings of the Committee shall be forwarded, through the Secretary-General, to the complainant and to the State party concerned.

4. The Committee's findings on the merits shall be known as "decisions."

5. The State party concerned shall generally be invited to inform the Committee whithin a specific time period of the action it has taken in conformity with the Committee's decisions.

Individual Opinions

Rule 113

Any member of the Committee who has participated in a decision may request that his/her individual opinion be appended to the Committee's decisions.

Follow-up Procedure

Rule 114

1. The Committee may designate one or more Rapporteur(s) for Follow-up on decisions adopted under article 22 of the Convention, for the purpose of ascertaining the measures taken by States parties to give effect to the Committee's findings.

2. The Rapporteur(s) may make such contacts and take such action as appropriate for the due performance of the follow-up mandate and report accordingly to the Committee. The Rapporteur(s) may make such recommendations for further action by the Committee as may be necessary for follow-up.

3. The Rapporteur(s) shall regularly report to the Committee on follow-up activities.

4. The Rapporteur(s), in discharge of his/her follow-up mandate, may, with the approval of the Committee, engage in necessary visits to the State party concerned.

Summaries in the Committee's Annual Report and Inclusion of Texts of Final Decisions

Rule 115

1. The Committee may decide to include in its annual report a summary of the complaints examined and, where the Committee considers appropriate, a summary of the explanations and statements of the States parties concerned and of the Committee's evaluation thereof.

2. The Committee shall include in its annual report the text of its final decisions, including its views under article 22, paragraph 7, of the Convention, as well as the text of any decision declaring a complaint inadmissible under article 22 of the Convention.

3. The Committee shall include information on follow-up activities in its annual report.

ANNEX 11

RULES OF PROCEDURE OF THE COMMITTEE ON THE ELIMINATION OF RACIAL DISCRIMINATION CONCERNING COMMUNICATIONS

HRI/GEN/3-6 June 2001

...

A. General Provisions

Competence of the Committee

Rule 80

1. The Committee shall be competent to receive and consider communications and exercise the functions provided, for in article 14 of the Convention only when at least 10 States parties are bound by declarations recognizing the competence of the Committee in conformity with paragraph 1 thereof.

2. The Secretary-General shall transmit to the other States parties copies of the declarations deposited with him by States parties recognizing the competence of the Committee.

3. Consideration of communications pending before the Committee shall not be affected by the withdrawal of a declaration made under article 14 of the Convention.

4. The Secretary-General shall inform the other States parties of the name, composition and functions of any national legal body which has been established or indicated by a State party, in conformity with paragraph 3 of article 14.

National Bodies

Rule 81

The Secretary-General shall keep the Committee informed of the name, composition and functions of any national legal body established or indicated under paragraph 2 of article 14 as competent to receive and consider petitions from individuals or groups of individuals claiming to be victims of a violation of any of the rights set forth in the Convention.

Certifies Copies of Registers of Petitions

Rule 82

1. The Secretary-General shall keep the Committee informed of the contents of all certified copies of the register of petitions filed with him in accordance with paragraph 4 of article 14.

2. The Secretary-General may request clarifications from the States parties concerning the certified copies or the registers of petitions emanating from the national legal bodies responsible for such registers.

3. The contents of the certified copies of the registers of petitions transmitted to the Secretary-General shall not be publicly disclosed.

Record of Communications Received by the Secretary-General

Rule 83

1. The Secretary-General shall keep a record of all communications which are or appear to be submitted to the Committee by individuals or groups of individuals claiming to be victims of a violation of any of the rights set forth in the Convention and who are subject to the jurisdiction of a State party bound by a declaration under article 14.

2. The Secretary-General may, if he deems it necessary, request clarification of the author of a communication as to his wish to have his communication submitted to the Committee for consideration under article 14. In case of doubt as to the wish of the author, the Committee shall be seized of the communication.

3. No communication shall be received by the Committee or included in a list under rule 85 below if it concerns a State party which has not made a declaration as provided for in paragraph 1 of article 14.

Information to be Contained in A Communication

Rule 84

1. The Secretary-General may request clarification from the author of a communication concerning the applicability of article 14 to his communication, in particular:
   (a) The name, address, age and occupation of the author and the verification of his identity;
   (b) The name(s) of the State party or States parties against which the communication is directed;
   (c) The object of the communication;
   (d) The provision or provisions of the Convention alleged to have been violated;
   (e) The facts of the claim;
   (f) Steps taken by the author to exhaust domestic remedies, including pertinent documents;
   (g) The extent to which the same matter is being examined under another procedure of international investigation or settlement.

2. When requesting clarification or information, the Secretary-General shall indicate an appropriate time limit to the author of the communication with a view to avoiding undue delays in the procedure.

3. The Committee may approve a questionnaire for the purpose of requesting the above-mentioned information from the author of the communication.

4. The request for clarification referred to in paragraph 1 of the present rule shall not preclude the inclusion of the communication in the list provided for in rule 85, paragraph 1, below.

5. The Secretary-General shall inform the author of a communication of the procedure that will be followed and that the text of his communication shall be transmitted confidentially to the State party concerned in accordance with paragraph 6 (a) of article 14.

Transmission of Communications to the Committee

Rule 85

1. The Secretary-General shall summarize each communication thus received and shall place the summaries, individually or in composite lists of communications, before the Committee at its next regular session, together with the relevant certified copies of the registers of petitions kept by the national legal body of the country concerned and filed with the Secretary-General in compliance with paragraph 4 of article 14.

2. The Secretary-General shall draw the attention of the Committee to those cases for which certified copies of the registers of petitions have not been received.

3. The contents of replies to requests for clarification and relevant subsequent submissions from either the author of the communication or the State party concerned shall be placed before the Committee in a suitable form.

4. An original case file shall be kept for each summarized communication. The full text of any communication brought to the attention of the Committee shall be made available to any member of the Committee upon request.

B. Procedure for Determining Admissibility of Communications

Methods of Dealing with Communications

Rule 86

1. In accordance with the following rules, the Committee shall decide as soon as possible whether or not a communication is admissible in conformity with article 14 of the Convention.

2. The Committee shall, unless it decides otherwise, deal with communications in the order in which they have been placed before it by the Secretariat. The Committee may, if it deems appropriate, decide to consider jointly two or more communications.

Establishment of A Working Group

Rule 87

1. The Committee may, in accordance with rule 61, set up a Working Group to meet shortly before its sessions, or at any other convenient time to be decided by the Committee in consultation with the Secretary-General, for the purpose of making recommendations to the Committee regarding the fulfilment of the con-

ditions of admissibility of communications laid down in article 14 of the Convention and assisting the Committee in any manner which the Committee may decide.

2. The Working Group shall not comprise more than five members of the Committee. The Working Group shall elect its own officers, develop its own working methods, and apply as far as possible the rules of procedure of the Committee to its meetings.

3. The Committee may designate a special rapporteur from among its members to assist it in the handling of new communications.

Meetings

Rule 88

Meetings of the Committee or its Working Group during which communications under article 14 of the Convention will be examined shall be closed. Meetings during which the Committee may consider general issues such as procedures for the application of article 14 may be public if the Committee so decides.

Inability of A Member to Take Part in the Examination of A Communication

Rule 89

1. A member of the Committee shall not take part in the examination of a communication by the Committee or its Working Group:
   (a) If he has any personal interest in the case; or
   (b) If he has participated in any capacity in the making of any decision on the case covered by the communication.

2. Any question which may arise under paragraph 1 above shall be decided by the Committee without the participation of the member concerned.

Withdrawal of A Member

Rule 90

If, for any reason, a member considers that he should not take part or continue to take part in the examination of a communication, he shall inform the Chairman of his withdrawal.

Conditions for Admissibility of Communications

Rule 91

With a view to reaching a decision on the admissibility of a communication, the Committee or its Working Group shall ascertain:
   (a) That the communication is not anonymous and that it emanates from an individual or group of individuals subject to the jurisdiction of a State party recognizing the competence of the Committee under article 14 of the Convention;
   (b) That the individual claims to be a victim of a violation by the State party concerned of any of the rights set forth in the Convention. As a general rule, the communication should be submitted by the individual himself or by his relatives or designated representatives; the Committee may,

however, in exceptional cases accept to consider a communication submitted by others on behalf of an alleged victim when it appears that the victim is unable to submit the communication himself, and the author of the communication justifies his acting on the victim's behalf;

(c) That the communication is compatible with the provisions of the Convention;

(d) That the communication is not an abuse of the right to submit a communication in conformity with article 14;

(e) That the individual has exhausted all available domestic remedies, including, when applicable, those mentioned in paragraph 2 of article 14. However, this shall not be the rule where the application of the remedies is unreasonably prolonged;

(f) That the communication is, except in the case of duly verified exceptional circumstances, submitted within six months after all available domestic remedies have been exhausted, including, when applicable, those indicated in paragraph 2 of article 14.

Additional Information, Clarifications and Observations

Rule 92

1. The Committee or the Working Group established under rule 87 may request, through the Secretary-General, the State party concerned or the author of the communication to submit additional written information or clarifications relevant to the question of admissibility of the communication. A request for information my also emanate from a special rapporteur designated under rule 87, paragraph 3.

2. Such requests shall contain a statement to the effect that the request does not imply that a decision has been reached on the question of admissibility of the communication by the Committee.

3. A communication may not be declared admissible unless the State party concerned has received the text of the communication and has been given an opportunity to furnish information or observations as provided in paragraph 1 of this rule, including information relating to the exhaustion of domestic remedies.

4. The Committee or the Working Group may adopt a questionnaire for requesting such additional information or clarifications.

5. The Committee or the Working Group shall indicate a deadline for the submission of such additional information or clarification.

6. If the deadline is not kept by the State party concerned or the author of a communication, the Committee or the Working Group may decide to consider the admissibility of the communication in the light of available information.

7. If the State party concerned disputes the contention of the author of a communication that all available domestic remedies have been exhausted, the State party is required to give details of the effective remedies available to the alleged victim in the particular circumstances of the case.

Inadmissible Communications

Rule 93

1. When the Committee decides that a communication is inadmissible, or its consideration is suspended or discontinued, the Committee shall transmit its deci-

sions as soon as possible, through the Secretary-General, to the petitioner and to the State party concerned.

2. A decision taken by the Committee, in conformity with paragraph 7 (a) of article 14, that a communication is inadmissible, may be reviewed at a later date by the Committee upon a written request by the petitioner concerned. Such written request shall contain documentary evidence to the effect that the reasons for inadmissibility referred to in paragraph 7 (a) of article 14 are no longer applicable.

C. Consideration of Communications on Their Merits

Methods of Dealing with Admissible Communications

Rule 94

1. After it has been decided that a communication is admissible in conformity with article 14, the Committee shall transmit, confidentially, through the Secretary-General, the text of the communication and other relevant information to the State party concerned without revealing the identity of the individual unless he has given his express consent. The Committee shall also inform, through the Secretary-General, the petitioner of the communication of its decision.

2. The State party concerned shall submit within three months to the Committee written explanations or statements clarifying the case under consideration and the remedy, if any, that may have been taken by that State party. The Committee may indicate, if it deems it necessary, the type of information it wishes to receive from the State party concerned.

3. In the course of its consideration, the Committee may inform the State party of its views on the desirability, because of urgency, of taking interim measures to avoid possible irreparable damage to the person or persons who claim to be victim(s) of the alleged violation. In doing so, the Committee shall inform the State party concerned that such expression of its views on interim measures does not prejudge either its final opinion on the merits of the communication or its eventual suggestions and recommendation.

4. Any explanations or statements submitted by a State party pursuant to this rule may be transmitted, through the Secretary-General, to the petitioner of the communication who may submit any additional written information or observations within such time limit as the Committee shall decide.

5. The Committee may invite the presence of the petitioner or his representative and the presence of representatives of the State party concerned in order to provide additional information or to answer questions on the merits of the communication.

6. The Committee may revoke its decision that a communication is admissible in the light of any explanations or statements submitted by the State party. However, before the Committee considers revoking that decision, the explanations or statements concerned must be transmitted to the petitioner so that he may submit additional information or observations within the time limit set by the Committee.

7. The Committee may, in appropriate cases and with the consent of the parties concerned, decide to deal jointly with the question of admissibility and the merits of a communication.

Opinion of the Committee on Admissible Communications and the Committee's Suggestions and Recommnedations

Rule 95

1. Admissible communications shall be considered by the Committee in the light of all information made available to it by the petitioner and the State party concerned. The Committee may refer the communication to the Working Group in order to be assisted in this task.

2. The Committee or the working group set up by it to consider a communication may at any time, in the course of the examination, obtain through the intermediary or the Secretary-General any documentation that may assist in the disposal of the case from United Nations bodies or the specialized agencies.

3. After consideration of an admissible communication, the Committee shall formulate its opinion thereon. The opinion of the Committee shall be forwarded, through the Secretary-General, to the petitioner and to the State party concerned, together with any suggestions and recommendations the Committee may wish to make.

4. Any member of the Committee may request that a summary of his individual opinion be appended to the opinion of the Committee when it is forwarded to the petitioner and to the State party concerned.

5. The State party concerned shall be invited to inform the Committee in due course of the action it takes in conformity with the Committee's suggestions and recommendations.

Summaries in the Committee's Annual Report

Rule 96

The Committee shall include in its annual report a summary of the communications examined and, where appropriate a summary of the explanations and statements of the States parties concerned and of its own suggestions and recommendations.

Press Communiqués

Rule 97

The Committee may also issue communiqués, through the Secretary-General, for the use of information media and the general public regarding the activities of the Committee under article 14 of the Convention.

ANNEX 12

RULES OF PROCEDURE FOR THE CONVENTION ON THE ELIMINATION OF ALL FORMS OF DISCRIMINATION AGAINST WOMEN CONCERNING COMMUNICATIONS

HRI/GEN/3-6 June 2001

...

Transmission of Communications to the Committee

Rule 56

1. The Secretary-General shall bring to the attention of the Committee, in accordance with the present rules, communications that are, or appear to be, submitted for consideration by the Committee under article 2 of the Optional Protocol.

2. The Secretary-General may request clarification from the author or authors of a communication as to whether they wish to have the communication submitted to the Committee for consideration under the Optional Protocol. Where there is doubt as to the wish of the author or authors, the Secretary-General will bring the communication to the attention of the Committee.

3. No communication shall be received by the Committee if it:
   (a) Concerns a State that is not a party to the Protocol;
   (b) Is not in writing; or
   (c) Is anonymous.

List and Register of Communications

Rule 57

1. The Secretary-General shall maintain a permanent register of all communications submitted for consideration by the Committee under article 2 of the Optional Protocol.

2. The Secretary-General shall prepare lists of the communications submitted to the Committee, together with a brief summary of their contents.

Request for Clarification or Additional Information

Rule 58

1. The Secretary-General may request clarification from the author of a communication, including:
   (a) The name, address, date of birth and occupation of the victim and verification of the victim's identity;
   (b) The name of the State party against which the communication is directed;
   (c) The objective of the communication;
   (d) The facts of the claim;
   (e) Steps taken by the author and/or victim to exhaust domestic remedies;
   (f) The extent to which the same matter is being or has been examined under another procedure of international investigation or settlement;
   (g) The provision or provisions of the Convention alleged to have been violated.

2. When requesting clarification or information, the Secretary-General shall indicate to the author or authors of the communication a time limit within which such information is to be submitted.

3. The Committee may approve a questionnaire to facilitate requests for clarification or information from the victim and/or author of a communication.

4. A request for clarification or information shall not preclude the inclusion of the communication in the list provided for in rule 59 below.

5. The Secretary-General shall inform the author of a communication of the procedure that will be followed and in particular that, provided that the individual or individuals consent to the disclosure of her identity to the State party concerned, the communication will be brought confidentially to the attention of that State party.

Summary of the Information

Rule 59

1. A summary of the relevant information obtained with respect to each registered communication shall be prepared and circulated to the members of the Committee by the Secretary-General at the next regular session of the Committee.

2. The full text of any communication brought to the attention of the Committee shall be made available to any member of the Committee upon that member's request.

Inability of A Member to Take Part in the Examination of A Communication

Rule 60

1. A member of the Committee may not take part in the examination of a communication if:
   (a) The member has any personal interest in the case;
   (b) The member has participated in the making of any decision on the case covered by the communication in any capacity other than under the procedures applicable to this Optional Protocol; or
   (c) The member is a national of the State party concerned.

2. Any question that may arise under paragraph 1 above shall be decided by the Committee without the participation of the member concerned.

Withdrawal of A Member

Rule 61

If, for any reason, a member considers that she or he should not take part or continue to take part in the examination of a communication, the member shall inform the Chairperson of her or his withdrawal.

Establishment of Working Groups and Designation of Rapporteurs

Rule 62

1. The Committee may establish one or more working groups, each comprising no more than five of its members, and may designate one or more rapporteurs to make recommendations to the Committee and to assist it in any manner in which the Committee may decide.

2. In the present part of the rules, reference to a working group or rapporteur is a reference to a working group or rapporteur established under these rules.

3. The rules of procedure of the Committee shall apply as far as possible to the meetings of its working groups.

Interim Measures

Rule 63

1. At any time after the receipt of a communication and before a determination on the merits has been reached, the Committee may transmit to the State party concerned, for its urgent consideration, a request that it take such interim measures as the Committee considers necessary to avoid irreparable damage to the victim or victims of the alleged violation.

2. A working group or rapporteur may also request that the State party concerned take such interim measures as the working group or rapporteur considers necessary to avoid irreparable damage to the victim or victims of the alleged violation.

3. Where a request for interim measures is made by a working group or rapporteur under the present rule, the working group or rapporteur shall forthwith thereafter inform the Committee members of the nature of the request and the communication to which the request relates.

4. Where the Committee, a working group or a rapporteur requests interim measures under this rule, the request shall state that it does not imply a determination of the merits of the communication.

Method of Dealing with Communications

Rule 64

1. The Committee shall, by simple majority and in accordance with the following rules, decide whether the communication is admissible or inadmissible under the Optional Protocol.

2. A working group may also declare that a communication is admissible under the Optional Protocol, provided that it is composed of five members and all the members so decide.

Order of Communications

Rule 65

1. Communications shall be dealt with in the order in which they are received by the Secretariat, unless the Committee or a working group decides otherwise.

2. The Committee may decide to consider two or more communications jointly.

Separate Consideration of Admissibility and Merits

Rule 66

The Committee may decide to consider the question of admissibility of a communication and the merits of a communication separately.

Conditions of Admissibility of Communications

Rule 67

With a view to reaching a decision on the admissibility of a communication, the Committee, or a working group, shall apply the criteria in articles 2, 3 and 4 of the Optional Protocol.

Authors of Communications

Rule 68

1. Communications may be submitted by individuals or groups of individuals who claim to be victims of violations of the rights set forth in the Convention, or by their designated representatives, or by others on behalf of an alleged victim where the alleged victim consents.

2. In cases where the author can justify such action, communications may be submitted on behalf of an alleged victim without her consent.

3. Where an author seeks to submit a communication within paragraph 2 of the present rule, she or he shall provide written reasons justifying such action.

Procedures with Regard to Communications Received

Rule 69

1. As soon as possible after the communication has been received, and provided that the individual or group of individuals consent to the disclosure of their identity to the State party concerned, the Committee, working group or rapporteur shall bring the communication confidentially to the attention of the State party and shall request that State party to submit a written reply to the communication.

2. Any request within paragraph 1 above shall include a statement indicating that such a request does not imply that any decision has been reached on the question of admissibility of the communication.

3. Within six months after receipt of the Committee's request under the present rule, the State party shall submit to the Committee a written explanation or statement that relates to the admissibility of the communication and its merits, as well as to any remedy that may have been provided in the matter.

4. The Committee, working group or rapporteur may request a written explanation or statement that relates only to the admissibility of a communication, but in such cases, the State party may nonetheless submit a written explanation or statement that relates to both the admissibility and the merits of a communication, provided that such written explanation or statement is submitted within six months of the Committee's request.

5. A State party that has received a request for a written reply in accordance with paragraph 1 may submit a request in writing that the communication be rejected as inadmissible, setting out the grounds for such inadmissibility, provided that such a request is submitted to the Committee within two months of the request made under paragraph 1.

6. If the State party concerned disputes the contention of the author or authors in accordance with article 4.1 of the Optional Protocol that all available domestic remedies have been exhausted, the State party shall give details of the remedies available to the alleged victim or victims in the particular circumstances of the case.

7. Submission by the State party of a request in accordance with paragraph 5 above shall not affect the period of six months given to the State party to submit its written explanation or statement unless the Committee, working group or rapporteur decides to extend the time for submission for such a period as the Committee considers appropriate.

8. The Committee, working group or rapporteur may request the State party or the author of the communication to submit, within fixed time limits, additional written explanations or statements relevant to the issues of the admissibility or merits of a communication.

9. The Committee, working group or rapporteur shall transmit to each party the submissions made by the other party pursuant to this rule and shall afford each party an opportunity to comment on those submissions within fixed time limits.

Inadmissible Communications

Rule 70

1. Where the Committee decides that a communication is inadmissible, it shall, as soon as possible, communicate its decision and the reasons for that decision through the Secretary-General to the author of the communication and to the State party concerned.

2. A decision of the Committee declaring a communication inadmissible may be reviewed by the Committee upon receipt of a written request submitted by or on behalf of the author or authors of the communication containing information indicating that the reasons for inadmissibility no longer apply.

3. Any member of the Committee who has participated in the decision regarding admissibility may request that a summary of her or his individual opinion be appended to the Committee's decision declaring a communication inadmissible.

<u>Additional Procedures Whereby Admissibility May Be Considered Separately from the Merits</u>

<u>Rule 71</u>

1. Where the issue of admissibility is decided by the Committee or a working group before the State party's written explanations or statements on the merits of the communication are received, that decision and all other relevant information shall be submitted through the Secretary-General to the State party concerned. The author of the communication shall, through the Secretary-General, be informed of the decision.

2. The Committee may revoke its decision that a communication is admissible in the light of any explanation or statements submitted by the State party.

<u>Views of the Committee on Admissible Communications</u>

<u>Rule 72</u>

1. Where the parties have submitted information relating both to the admissibility and to the merits of a communication, or where a decision on admissibility has already been taken and the parties have submitted information on the merits of that communication, the Committee shall consider and shall formulate its views on the communication in the light of all written information made available to it by the author or authors of the communication and the State party concerned, provided that this information has been transmitted to the other party concerned.

2. The Committee or the working group set up by it to consider a communication may, at any time in the course of the examination, obtain through the Secretary-General any documentation from organizations in the United Nations system or other bodies that may assist in the disposal of the communication, provided that the Committee shall afford each party an opportunity to comment on such documentation or information within fixed time limits.

3. The Committee may refer any communication to a working group to make recommendations to the Committee on the merits of the communication.

4. The Committee shall not decide on the merits of the communication without having considered the applicability of all the admissibility grounds referred to in articles 2, 3 and 4 of the Optional Protocol.

5. The Secretary-General shall transmit the views of the Committee, determined by simple majority, together with any recommendations, to the author or authors of the communication and to the State party concerned.

6. Any member of the Committee who has participated in the decision may request that a summary of her or his individual opinion be appended to the Committee's views.

<u>Follow-up to the Committee's Views</u>

<u>Rule 73</u>

1. Within six months of the Committee's issuing its views on a communication, the State party concerned shall submit to the Committee a written response, includ-

ing any information on any action taken in the light of the views and recommendations of the Committee.

2. Following the six-month period referred to in paragraph 1 above, the Committee may invite the State party concerned to submit further information about any measures the State party has taken in response to its views or recommendations.

3. The Committee may request the State party to include information on any action taken in response to its views or recommendations in its subsequent reports under article 18 of the Convention.

4. The Committee shall designate for follow-up on views adopted under article 7 of the Optional Protocol a rapporteur or working group which shall ascertain the measures taken by States parties to give effect to the Committee's views and recommendations.

5. The rapporteur or working group may make such contacts and take such action as may be appropriate for the due performance of her, his or its functions and shall make such recommendations for further action by the Committee as may be necessary.

6. The rapporteur or working group shall report to the Committee on follow-up activities on a regular basis.

7. The Committee shall include information on any follow-up activities in its annual report under article 21 of the Convention.

Confidentiality of Communications

Rule 74

1. Communications submitted under the Optional Protocol shall be examined by the Committee, working group or rapporteur in closed meetings.

2. All working documents prepared by the Secretariat for the Committee, working group or rapporteur, including summaries of communications prepared prior to registration and the list of summaries of communications, shall be confidential unless the Committee decides otherwise.

3. The Committee, working group or rapporteur shall not make public any communication, submissions or information relating to a communication prior to the date on which its views are issued.

4. The author or authors of a communication or the individuals who are alleged to be the victim or victims of a violation of the rights set forth in the Convention may request that the names and identifying details of the alleged victim or victims (or any of them) not be published.

5. If the Committee, working group or rapporteur so decides, the name or names and identifying details of the author or authors of a communication or the individuals who are alleged to be the victim or victims of a violation of rights set forth in the Convention shall not be made public by the Committee, the author or the State party concerned.

6. The Committee, working group or rapporteur may request the author of a communication or the State party concerned to keep confidential the whole or part of any submissions or information relating to the proceedings.

7. Subject to paragraphs 5 and 6 of the present rule, nothing in this rule shall affect the right of the author or authors or the State party concerned to make public any submissions or information bearing on the proceedings.

8. Subject to paragraphs 5 and 6 above, the Committee's decisions on admissibility, merits and discontinuance shall be made public.

9. The Secretariat shall be responsible for the distribution of the Committee's final decisions to the author or authors and the State party concerned.

10. The Committee shall include in its annual report under article 21 of the Convention a summary of the communications examined and, where appropriate, a summary of the explanations and statements of the States parties concerned, and of its own suggestions and recommendations.

11. Unless the Committee decides otherwise, information furnished by the parties in follow-up to the Committee's views and recommendations within articles 7.4 and 7.5 of the Optional Protocol shall not be confidential. Unless the Committee decides otherwise, decisions of the Committee with regard to follow-up activities shall not be confidential.

Communiqués

Rule 75

The Committee may issue communiqués regarding its activities under articles 1 to 7 of the Optional Protocol, through the Secretary-General, for the use of the information media and the general public.

ANNEX 13

CHART OF OUTCOMES OF HUMAN RIGHTS COMMITTEE COMMUNICATIONS AND HOW TO UPDATE

updated 17 April 2002
to update see: www.unhchr.ch/html/menu2/8/stat2.htm   see also www.bayefsky.com

States Parties		Living Cases		Concluded Cases			
State	Entry into Force	Pre-admis-sible	Admis-sible	Inadmis-sible	Discon-tinued	Views (1)/(2)	Total
Algeria	12 Dec 1989	1	–	–	–	–	1
Angola	10 Apr 1992	–	–	–	1	1/0	2
Argentina	8 Nov 1986	–	–	4	–	1/0	5
Armenia	23 Sep 1993	1	–	–	–	–	1
Australia	25 Dec 1991	22	–	16	4	3/2	47
Austria	10 Mar 1988	11	–	3	–	2/0	16
Azerbaijan	27 Feb 2002	–	–	–	–	–	–
Barbados	23 Mar 1976	1	–	3	–	–	4
Belarus	30 Dec 1992	11	–	–	–	1/0	12
Belgium	17 Aug 1994	3	–	–	–	–	3
Benin	12 Jun 1992	–	–	–	–	–	–
Bolivia	12 Nov 1982	–	–	–	–	2/0	2
Bosnia and Herzegovina	1 Jun 1995	–	–	–	–	–	–
Bulgaria	26 Jun 1992	1	–	2	–	–	3
Burkina Faso	4 Apr 1999	–	–	–	–	–	–
Cameroon	27 Sep 1984	–	–	–	–	2/0	2
Canada	19 Aug 1976	13	2	49	23	9/9	105
Cape Verde	19 Aug 2000	–	–	–	–	–	–

States Parties		Living Cases		Concluded Cases			
State	Entry into Force	Pre-admis-sible	Admis-sible	Inadmis-sible	Discon-tinued	Views (1)/(2)	Total
Central African Republic	8 Aug 1981	–	–	–	–	1/0	1
Chad	9 Sep 1995	–	–	–	–	–	–
Chile	28 Aug 1992	2	–	4	–	–	6
Colombia	23 Mar 1976	2	2	3	5	10/0	22
Congo	5 Jan 1984	–	–	–	–	–	–
Costa Rica	23 Mar 1976	–	–	1	2	–	3
Côte d'Ivoire	5 Jun 1997	1	–	–	–	–	1
Croatia	12 Jan 1996	–	–	1	–	1/0	2
Cyprus	15 Jul 1992	1	–	–	1	–	2
Czech Republic	1 Jan 1993	8	1	5	–	6/0	20
Democratic Republic of the Congo	1 Feb 1977	3	1	4	2	10/0	20
Denmark	23 Mar 1976	–	–	7	1	–	8
Dominican Republic	4 Apr 1978	–	–	–	–	3/0	3
Ecuador	23 Mar 1976	–	–	–	4	5/0	9
El Salvador	6 Sep 1995	–	–	–	–	–	–
Equatorial Guinea	25 Dec 1987	–	–	–	–	2/0	2
Estonia	21 Jan 1992	–	–	–	–	–	–
Finland	23 Mar 1976	1	–	14	2	5/7	29
France	17 May 1984	7	–	25	9	6/8	55
Gambia	9 Sep 1988	–	–	–	–	–	–
Georgia	3 Aug 1994	2	–	–	–	4/0	6
Germany	25 Nov 1993	3	–	4	–	–	7
Ghana	7 Dec 2000	–	–	–	–	–	–
Greece	5 Aug 1997	2	–	–	–	–	2
Guatemala	28 Feb 2001	–	–	–	–	–	–
Guinea	17 Sep 1993	–	–	–	–	–	–
Guyana (d)	10 Aug 1993	7	–	–	1	2/0	10
Hungary	7 Dec 1988	1	–	4	2	2/1	10
Iceland	22 Nov 1979	1	–	1	1	–	3
Ireland	8 Mar 1990	1	–	1	–	1/0	3
Italy	15 Dec 1978	–	–	8	3	1/1	13
Jamaica (a)		8	2	39	14	95/19	177
Kyrgyzstan	7 Jan 1995	–	–	–	–	–	–
Latvia	22 Sep 1994	–	–	–	2	1/1	4
Lesotho	6 Dec 2000	–	–	–	–	–	–

States Parties		Living Cases		Concluded Cases			
State	Entry into Force	Pre-admis-sible	Admis-sible	Inadmis-sible	Discon-tinued	Views (1)/(2)	Total
Libyan Arab Jamahiriya	16 Aug 1989	–	–	1	–	1/0	2
Liechtenstein	10 Mar 1999	–	–	–	–	–	–
Lithuania	20 Feb 1992	3	–	–	–	–	3
Luxembourg	18 Nov 1983	–	–	–	–	–	–
Madagascar	23 Mar 1976	–	–	–	2	4/0	6
Malawi	11 Sep 1996	–	–	–	–	–	–
Mali	24 Jan 2002	–	–	–	–	–	–
Malta	13 Dec 1990	–	–	–	–	–	–
Mauritius	23 Mar 1976	2	–	3	–	1/0	6
Mexico	15 Jun 2002	–	–	–	–	–	–
Mongolia	16 Jul 1991	–	–	–	–	–	–
Namibia	28 Feb 1995	1	–	–	–	1/0	2
Nepal	14 Aug 1991	–	–	–	–	–	–
Netherlands	11 May 1979	5	–	43	–	6/16	70
New Zealand	26 Aug 1989	4	–	6	7	0/4	21
Nicaragua	12 Jun 1980	–	–	1	3	1/0	5
Niger	7 Jun 1986	–	–	–	–	–	–
Norway	23 Mar 1976	1	–	8	–	1/3	13
Panama	8 Jun 1977	–	–	4	7	2/0	13
Paraguay	10 Apr 1995	–	–	–	–	–	–
Peru	3 Jan 1981	5	–	–	4	7/0	16
Philippines	22 Nov 1989	2	–	–	1	1/1	5
Poland	7 Feb 1992	6	–	–	–	0/1	7
Portugal	3 Aug 1983	1	–	1	–	–	2
Republic of Korea	10 Jul 1990	3	1	–	1	3/1	9
Romania	20 Oct 1993	–	–	–	–	–	–
Russian Federation	1 Jan 1992	12	3	1	1	1/1	19
Saint Vincent and the Grenadines	9 Feb 1982	–	–	–	–	1/0	1
San Marino	18 Jan 1986	–	–	–	–	–	–
Senegal	13 May 1978	–	–	–	–	1/0	1
Seychelles	5 Aug 1992	–	–	–	–	–	–
Sierra Leone	23 Nov 1996	–	–	–	–	3/0	3
Slovak Republic	1 Jan 1993	2	1	2	–	–	5
Slovenia	16 Oct 1993	–	–	–	–	–	–
Somalia	24 Apr 1990	–	–	–	–	–	–
Spain	25 Apr 1985	17	1	9	4	3/3	37
Sri Lanka	3 Jan 1998	4	1	–	–	–	5

States Parties		Living Cases		Concluded Cases			
State	Entry into Force	Pre-admissible	Admissible	Inadmissible	Discontinued	Views (1)/(2)	Total
Suriname	28 Mar 1977	–	–	–	–	8/0	8
Sweden	23 Mar 1976	1	–	3	1	0/6	11
Tajikistan	4 Apr 1999	5	–	–	–	–	5
The former Yugoslav Republic of Macedonia	12 Mar 1995	–	–	–	–	–	–
Togo	30 Jun 1988	–	1	–	–	4/0	5
Trinidad and Tobago (c)		5	7 (b)	15	5	14/2	48
Turkmenistan	1 Aug 1997	–	–	–	–	–	–
Uganda	14 Feb 1996	–	–	–	–	–	–
Ukraine	25 Oct 1991	6	2	–	–	–	8
Uruguay	23 Mar 1976	–	–	5	28	45/1	79
Uzbekistan	28 Dec 1995	22	–	–	–	–	22
Venezuela	10 Aug 1978	–	–	1	–	1/0	2
Yugoslavia	6 Dec 2001	–	–	–	–	–	–
Zambia	10 Jul 1984	5	–	–	1	5/0	11
98		**226**	**25**	**301**	**142**	**290/87 (377)**	**1071**

251 living cases
1071 registered communications with respect to 70 countries

(1) Disclose a Violation
(2) Disclose No Violation
(a) Denunciation by Jamaica of the Optional Protocol took effect on 23 January 1998. However, the cases relating to Jamaica, still under consideration at the time the denunciation became effective, are still to be considered by the Human Rights Committee.
(b) The Human Rights Committee decided at its 67th session to make public an admissibility decision concerning Trinidad and Tobago. This decision is reproduced in document CCPR/C/67/D/845/1999 available in the Treaty Body Database of the Office of the UN High Commissioner for Human Rights.
(c) Denunciation by Trinidad and Tobago of the Optional Protocol took effect on 27 June 2000. However, the cases relating to Trinidad and Tobago, still under consideration at the time the denunciation became effective, will still be considered by the Human Rights Committee.
(d) The Government of Guyana had initially acceded to the Optional Protocol on 10 May 1993. On 5 January 1999, the Government of Guyana notified the Secretary-General that it had decided to denounce the said Optional Protocol with effect from 5 April 1999. On that same date, the Government of Guyana re-acceded to the Optional Protocol with a reservation.

ANNEX 14

CHART OF OUTCOMES OF CAT COMPLAINTS AND HOW TO UPDATE

updated 20 February 2002
to update see: www.unhchr.ch/html/menu2/8/stat3.htm   see also www.bayefsky.com

State	Entry into force	Pre-adm.	Admis-sible	Sus-pend	Inadmis-sible	Discon-tinued	Views (1)/(2)	Total
Algeria	12 Oct 1989	–	–	–	–	–	–	–
Argentina	26 Jun 1987	–	–	–	3	–	–	3
Australia	29 Jan 1993	5	–	–	–	9	1/3	18
Austria	28 Aug 1987	–	1	–	1	–	1/0	3
Azerbaijan	4 Feb 2002*	–	–	–	–	–	–	–
Belgium	25 Jul 1999	–	–	–	–	–	–	–
Bulgaria	12 May 1993*	–	–	–	–	–	–	–
Cameroon	12 Oct 2000	–	–	–	–	–	–	–
Canada	13 Nov 1989*	5	1	3	9	10	1/5	34
Costa Rica	27 Feb 2002*	–	–	–	–	–	–	–
Croatia	8 Oct 1991	–	–	–	–	–	–	–
Cyprus	8 Apr 1993	–	–	–	–	–	–	–
Czech Republic	3 Sep 1996	–	–	–	–	–	–	–
Denmark	26 Jun 1987	2	–	–	–	1	0/1	4
Ecuador	6 Sep 1988*	–	–	–	–	1	–	1
Finland	29 Sep 1989	1	–	–	–	–	–	1
France	26 Jun 1987	3	–	1	5	19	1/0	29
Germany	19 Oct 2001	–	–	–	–	–	–	–
Ghana	7 Oct 2000	–	–	–	–	–	–	–
Greece	5 Nov 1988	–	–	–	–	–	0/1	1
Hungary	13 Sep 1989*	–	–	–	1	–	–	1
Iceland	22 Nov 1996	–	–	–	–	–	–	–
Italy	10 Oct 1989*	–	–	–	–	–	–	–
Liechtenstein	2 Dec 1990	–	–	–	–	–	–	–
Luxembourg	29 Oct 1987	–	–	–	–	–	–	–
Malta	13 Oct 1990	–	–	–	–	–	–	–
Monaco	6 Jan 1992	–	–	–	–	–	–	–

State	Entry into force	Pre-adm.	Admis-sible	Sus-pend	Inadmis-sible	Discon-tinued	Views (1)/(2)	Total
Netherlands	20 Jan 1989	4	–	–	1	1	1/5	12
New Zealand	9 Jan 1990	–	–	–	–	–	–	–
Norway	26 Jun 1987	–	–	–	2	–	–	2
Poland	12 May 1993*	–	–	–	–	–	–	–
Portugal	11 Mar 1989	–	–	–	–	–	–	–
Russian Federation	1 Oct 1991	1	–	–	–	–	–	1
Senegal	16 Oct 1996	–	1	–	–	–	–	1
Seychelles	6 Aug 2001	–	–	–	–	–	–	–
Slovakia	17 Mar 1995	–	–	–	–	–	–	–
Slovenia	16 Jul 1993	–	–	–	–	–	–	–
South Africa	10 Dec 1998	–	–	–	–	–	–	–
Spain	21 Nov 1987*	1	–	–	4	–	1/1	7
Sweden	26 Jun 1987	6	–	–	5	4	8/9	32
Switzerland	26 Jun 1987	3	–	–	4	9	3/17	36
Togo	18 Dec 1987	–	–	–	–	–	–	–
Tunisia	23 Oct 1988	3	–	–	1	1	1/0	6
Turkey	2 Sep 1988*	–	–	–	1	–	–	1
Uruguay	27 Jul 1988*	–	–	–	–	–	–	–
Venezuela	26 Apr 1994	–	–	–	–	–	1/0	1
Yugoslavia	10 Oct 1991	4	1	–	–	–	1/0	6
45	–	38	4	4	37	55	20/42	200

46 living cases
200 registered communications with respect to 21 countries

(1) Disclose a Violation
(2) Disclose No Violation
*   Dates are based on article 27, paragraph 1, of the Convention Against Torture and Other Cruel, Inhuman or Degrading Treatment or Punishment, which states that the date of entry into force is 30 days after date of ratification.

ANNEX 15

CHART OF OUTCOMES OF CERD COMMUNICATIONS AND HOW TO UPDATE

updated 25 April 2002
to update see: www.unhchr.ch/html/menu2/8/stat4.htm   see also www.bayefsky.com

State	Date of Entry into Force	Living Cases		Concluded Cases			Total
		Pre-adm.	Admis-sible	Inadmis-sible	Discon-tinued	Views (1)/(2)	
Algeria	12 Sep 1989	–	–	–	–	–	–
Australia	28 Jan 1993	–	–	2	–	0/2	4
Austria	20 Feb 2002	–	–	–	–	–	–
Azerbaijan	27 Sep 2001	–	–	–	–	–	–
Belgium	10 Oct 2000	–	–	–	–	–	–
Bulgaria	12 May 1993	–	–	–	–	–	–
Chile	18 May 1994	–	–	–	–	–	–
Costa Rica	8 Jan 1974	–	–	–	–	–	–
Cyprus	30 Dec 1993	–	–	–	–	–	–
Czech Republic	11 Oct 2000	–	–	–	–	–	–
Denmark	11 Oct 1985	–	–	2	–	2/2	6
Ecuador	18 Mar 1977	–	–	–	–	–	–
Finland	16 Nov 1994	–	–	–	–	–	–
France	16 Aug 1982	–	–	–	–	0/1	1
Germany	30 Aug 2001	–	–	–	–	–	–
Hungary	13 Sep 1989*	–	–	–	–	–	–
Iceland	10 Aug 1981	–	–	–	–	–	–
Ireland	29 Jan 2001*	–	–	–	–	–	–
Italy	5 May 1978	–	–	–	–	–	–
Luxem-bourg	22 Jul 1996	–	–	–	–	–	–
Malta	16 Dec 1998	–	–	–	–	–	–
Mexico	15 Mar 2002	–	–	–	–	–	–
Monaco	6 Nov 2001*	–	–	–	–	–	–

State	Date of Entry into Force	Living Cases		Concluded Cases			Total
		Pre-adm.	Admis-sible	Inadmis-sible	Discon-tinued	Views (1)/(2)	
Nether-lands	10 Jan 1972*	–	–	–	–	2/1	3
Norway	23 Jan 1976	–	–	1	–	1/0	2
Peru	27 Nov 1984	–	–	–	–	–	–
Poland	1 Dec 1998	–	–	–	–	–	–
Portugal	2 Mar 2000*	–	–	–	–	–	–
Republic of Korea	5 Mar 1997	–	–	–	–	–	–
Russian Federation	1 Oct 1991	–	–	–	–	–	–
Senegal	3 Dec 1982	–	–	–	–	–	–
Slovakia	17 Mar 1995	–	–	–	–	1/1	2
South Africa	9 Jan 1999	–	–	–	–	–	–
Spain	13 Jan 1998	–	–	–	–	–	–
Sweden	6 Jan 1972*	–	–	3	–	–	3
The Former Yugoslav Republic of Macedonia	22 Dec 1999*	–	–	–	–	–	–
Ukraine	28 Jul 1992	–	–	–	–	–	–
Uruguay	11 Sep 1972	–	–	–	–	–	–
Yugoslavia	27 Jun 2001	–	–	–	–	–	–
38	–	–	–	**8**	–	**6/7**	**21**

1 living case
21 registered communications with respect to 7 countries

(1) Disclose a Violation
(2) Disclose No Violation
* Dates are based on Article 19, paragraph 1, of the Convention on the Elimination of Discrimination Against Racism, which states that the date of entry into force is 30 days after the date of ratification.

THEMATIC INDEX OF THE PRINCIPAL UN HUMAN RIGHTS TREATIES

Note:

- *This index allows the user to search for the relevant articles of the principal UN human rights treaties by subject matter or theme.*
- *The numerous cross-references are intended to move the user from language which does not necessarily appear in any of the treaties, to the terms utilized by the treaties.*
- *Also included within the thematic index are the related substantive General Comments or Recommendations of the Treaty Bodies. The text of General Comments and Recommendations can be found, and updated, online at http://www.unhchr.ch/tbs/doc.nsf*

Abbreviations:

CAT
Convention Against Torture

CEDAW
Convention on the Elimination of All Forms of Discrimination Against Women

CERD
Convention on the Elimination of All Forms of Racial Discrimination

CRC
Convention on the Rights of the Child

CRC OP (ARMED CONFLICT)
Optional Protocol to the Convention on the Rights of the Child on the involvement of children in armed conflicts

CRC OP (SALE, PROSTITUTION, PORNOGRAPHY)
Optional Protocol to the Convention on the Rights of the Child on the sale of children, child prostitution and child pornography

ICCPR
International Covenant on Civil and Political Rights

ICCPR OP 2
Second Optional Protocol to the International Covenant on Civil and Political Rights

ICESCR
International Covenant on Economic, Social and Cultural Rights

MWC
International Convention on the Protection of the Rights of All Migrant Workers and Members of Their Families

ABORIGINAL PEOPLES
See **INDIGENOUS PEOPLES**

ABORTION
See **HEALTH**—FAMILY PLANNING
See **MATERNITY AND PREGNANCY**

ACCESS TO INFORMATION
See also **EDUCATION**—RIGHT TO EDUCATION
See also **EXPRESSION—FREEDOM OF**—GENERAL
See also **EXPRESSION—FREEDOM OF**—INTERNET

Article 19.2 and 19.3, ICCPR
Article 10(h), CEDAW
Article 9.1–9.4, CRC
Article 13, CRC
Article 17, CRC

General Comment 10, ICCPR, at para. 2
General Comment 16, ICCPR at para. 10
General Recommendation 23, CEDAW at paras. 18, 20 and 32
General Recommendation 24, CEDAW at paras. 13, 18 and 28

ADEQUATE OR DECENT STANDARD OF LIVING
(including: food and nutrition, water, clothing, housing, sanitation, electricity, transport, communications)
See also **HEALTH**—HEALTH CARE AND TREATMENT
See also **HEALTH**—PUBLIC HEALTH AND PREVENTION
See also **SOCIAL SECURITY AND INSURANCE**
See also **WORK**—WORKING CONDITIONS

GENERAL
Article 7(a)(ii), ICESCR
Article 11.1, ICESCR
Article 14.2(h), CEDAW
Article 27, CRC

General Comment 3, ICESCR at para. 10
General Comment 4, ICESCR at paras. 8(b), 8(d) and 11
General Comment 5, ICESCR at paras. 23 and 33

FOOD, CLOTHING, SHELTER
Article 5(e)(iii), CERD
Article 11, ICESCR
Article 12, CEDAW
Article 14.2(h), CEDAW
Article 24.1 and 24.2(c) and (e), CRC
Article 27.1–27.3, CRC

General Comment 4, ICESCR at paras. 1, 3, 4, and 6–19
General Comment 7, ICESCR
General Comment 12, ICESCR
General Recommendation 21, CEDAW at paras. 26 and 27
General Recommendation 24, CEDAW at paras. 7 and 28

General Recommendation XX, CERD
General Comment 5, ICESCR at para. 33
General Comment 6, ICESCR at paras. 32 and 33

ADOPTION
See **CHILDREN'S RIGHTS**—CHILD WELFARE AND INSTITUTIONS

AFFIRMATIVE ACTION
See **EFFECTIVE REMEDIES**—SPECIAL MEASURES
See **EQUALITY AND DISCRIMINATION**—TEMPORARY SPECIAL
MEASURES (AFFIRMATIVE ACTION)

AGE
See **CHILDREN'S RIGHTS**—AGE (OF MAJORITY, OF CONSENT, OF
RESPONSIBILITY)
See **EQUALITY AND DISCRIMINATION**—OLD AGE

AIDS
See **HEALTH**—GENERAL
See **HEALTH**—PUBLIC HEALTH AND PREVENTION

ALIENS
See also **CHILDREN'S RIGHTS**—NAME, IDENTITY AND NATIONALITY
See also **EXTRADITION**
See also **LEAVE OR RETURN—RIGHT TO**
See also **NATIONALITY**
See also **REFUGEES**
See also **WORK**—WORKING CONDITIONS

GENERAL
Article 13, ICCPR
Article 3, CAT
Article 9, CRC

General Comment 13, ICCPR at para. 13
General Comment 15, ICCPR
General Comment 28, ICCPR at para. 17
General Comment 23, ICCPR at paras. 5.1 and 5.2
General Comment 27, ICCPR at paras. 4, 8, 19 and 20
General Comment 1, CAT

MIGRANT WORKERS
Articles 1–71, MWC
Article 82, MWC
Article 83, MWC

General Recommendation 21, CEDAW at para. 10
General Recommendation 24, CEDAW at para. 6

ANTI-SEMITISM
See **ASSOCIATION—FREEDOM OF**—GENERAL
See **EQUALITY AND DISCRIMINATION**—MINORITY RIGHTS
See **EQUALITY AND DISCRIMINATION**—RACIAL DISCRIMINATION
See **EXPRESSION—FREEDOM OF**—HATE SPEECH AND LIMITS ON
PROPAGANDA

See **THOUGHT, CONSCIENCE AND RELIGION—FREEDOM OF**

APARTHEID
See **EQUALITY AND DISCRIMINATION**—APARTHEID

ARMED CONFLICT
See also **CRIMES AGAINST HUMANITY**
See also **DEROGATIONS**
See also **LIFE—RIGHT TO**—GENOCIDE
See also **PUBLIC AND PRIVATE ACTORS**—MILITARY

GENERAL
Article 2.2, CAT

General Recommendation 24, CEDAW at para. 16

CHILDREN
Article 38, CRC
Article 1, CRC OP (ARMED CONFLICT)
Article 2, CRC OP (ARMED CONFLICT)
Article 3, CRC OP (ARMED CONFLICT)
Article 4, CRC OP (ARMED CONFLICT)
Article 5, CRC OP (ARMED CONFLICT)
Article 6, CRC OP (ARMED CONFLICT)
Article 7, CRC OP (ARMED CONFLICT)

ARREST AND DETENTION
See **LEGAL RIGHTS**—CRIMINAL—Conditions of Arrest and Detention
See **LEGAL RIGHTS**—PROPERTY, CIVIL AND CONTRACT RIGHTS
    (PROHIBITION OF IMPRISONMENT)
See **LIBERTY AND SECURITY OF THE PERSON**
See **TORTURE AND OTHER CRUEL, INHUMAN OR DEGRADING
    TREATMENT OR PUNISHMENT**

ASSEMBLY—FREEDOM OF
Article 5(d)(ix), CERD
Article 21, ICCPR
Article 15, CRC

General Recommendation XX, CERD

ASSOCIATION—FREEDOM OF
See also **EXPRESSION—FREEDOM OF**—HATE SPEECH AND LIMITS ON
    PROPAGANDA
See also **EXPRESSION—FREEDOM OF**—INTERNET
See also **WORK**

GENERAL
Article 4(b), CERD
Article 5(d)(ix), CERD
Article 22, ICCPR
Article 14.2(e), CEDAW
Article 15, CRC

General Comment 13, ICESCR at para. 27
General Recommendation VII, CERD

General Recommendation XV, CERD
General Recommendation XX, CERD
General Comment 25, ICCPR at paras. 25 and 26

TRADE UNIONS

Article 5(e)(ii), CERD
Article 22, ICCPR
Article 8, ICESCR

General Comment 5, ICESCR at para. 26
General Comment 6, ICESCR at para. 25
General Recommendation XX, CERD

ASYLUM

See **ALIENS**
See **CHILDREN'S RIGHTS**—REFUGEES
See **REFUGEES**

BAIL

See **LEGAL RIGHTS**—CRIMINAL—Conditions of Arrest and Detention

BIRTH REGISTRATION

See **CHILDREN'S RIGHTS**—NAME, IDENTITY AND NATIONALITY

CENSORSHIP

See **ACCESS TO INFORMATION**
See **EXPRESSION—FREEDOM OF**

CHILDREN'S RIGHTS

See also **ARMED CONFLICT**—CHILDREN
See also **DISABILITY**
See also **EDUCATION**
See also **EQUALITY AND DISCRIMINATION**—CHILDREN
See also **EQUALITY AND**
DISCRIMINATION—GENDER DISCRIMINATION
See also **EXPRESSION—FREEDOM OF**—INTERNET
See also **HEALTH**
See also **LEGAL RIGHTS**—JUVENILE OFFENDERS AND CHILDREN
See also **NATIONALITY**
See also **PERSONHOOD**
See also **PROTECTION OF THE FAMILY**
See also **TRAFFICKING IN PERSONS AND SEXUAL EXPLOITATION**

GENERAL

Article 24, ICCPR
Article 16.2, CEDAW
Article 1, CRC
Article 2, CRC
Article 4, CRC
Article 6, CRC
Article 7, CRC
Article 11, CRC
Article 14, CRC

Article 30, CRC
Article 31, CRC

General Comment 17, ICCPR
General Comment 28, ICCPR at paras. 11 and 28
General Recommendation 21, CEDAW at paras. 21–23 and 41–50

ABUSE

Articles 9.1–9.3, CRC
Article 19, CRC
Article 34, CRC
Article 39, CRC

General Comment 5, ICESCR
General Comment 7, ICESCR
General Recommendation 19, CEDAW
General Recommendation 24, CEDAW

AGE (OF MAJORITY, OF CONSENT, OF RESPONSIBILITY)

Article 6.5, ICCPR
Article 10.3, ICESCR
Article 16.2, CEDAW
Article 1, CRC
Article 12.1, CRC
Article 32.1 and 32.2(a), CRC
Article 37(a), CRC
Article 38.2 and 38.3, CRC
Article 40.3(a), CRC
Article 1, CRC OP (ARMED CONFLICT)
Article 2, CRC OP (ARMED CONFLICT)
Article 3, CRC OP (ARMED CONFLICT)
Article 4, CRC OP (ARMED CONFLICT)
Article 5, CRC OP (ARMED CONFLICT)
Article 6, CRC OP (ARMED CONFLICT)
Article 7, CRC OP (ARMED CONFLICT)

General Comment 13, ICCPR at para. 16
General Comment 17, ICCPR at para. 4
General Comment 19, ICCPR at para. 4
General Comment 21, ICCPR at para. 13
General Comment 25, ICCPR at paras. 4, 10, 15 and 18
General Comment 28, ICCPR
General Recommendation 21, CEDAW at paras. 36–39

BEST INTERESTS

Article 5(b), CEDAW
Article 16.1(d) and (f), CEDAW
Article 3.1 and 3.2, CRC
Article 9, CRC
Article 18.1, CRC
Article 20, CRC
Article 21, CRC

Article 8.3, CRC OP (SALE, PROSTITUTION, PORNOGRAPHY)

General Recommendation 21, CEDAW at paras. 19, 20 and 41–50

CHILD LABOUR AND EXPLOITATION

Article 10.3, ICESCR
Article 32, CRC
Article 33, CRC
Article 34, CRC
Article 35, CRC
Article 36, CRC
Article 1, CRC OP (SALE, PROSTITUTION, PORNOGRAPHY)
Article 2, CRC OP (SALE, PROSTITUTION, PORNOGRAPHY)
Article 3, CRC OP (SALE, PROSTITUTION, PORNOGRAPHY)
Article 4, CRC OP (SALE, PROSTITUTION, PORNOGRAPHY)
Article 5, CRC OP (SALE, PROSTITUTION, PORNOGRAPHY)
Article 6, CRC OP (SALE, PROSTITUTION, PORNOGRAPHY)
Article 7, CRC OP (SALE, PROSTITUTION, PORNOGRAPHY)
Article 8, CRC OP (SALE, PROSTITUTION, PORNOGRAPHY)
Article 9, CRC OP (SALE, PROSTITUTION, PORNOGRAPHY)
Article 10, CRC OP (SALE, PROSTITUTION, PORNOGRAPHY)

General Comment 5, ICESCR at para. 32
General Comment 13, ICESCR at para. 55
General Comment 17, ICCPR at paras. 3 and 4
General Comment 28, ICCPR at paras. 12 and 22

CHILD WELFARE AND INSTITUTIONS

Article 11.2(c), CEDAW
Article 16.1(f), CEDAW
Article 3.3, CRC
Article 11, CRC
Article 19, CRC
Article 20, CRC
Article 21, CRC
Article 22.1, CRC
Article 26, CRC
Article 27, CRC

CIVIL RIGHTS

Article 12, CRC
Article 13, CRC
Article 15, CRC
Article 16, CRC
Article 30, CRC
Article 31, CRC

EDUCATION

Article 17, CRC
Article 23, CRC
Article 28, CRC
Article 29, CRC

Article 3.1 and 3.5, CRC OP (ARMED CONFLICT)
Article 9.2, CRC OP (SALE, PROSTITUTION, PORNOGRAPHY)

General Comment 7, ICCPR at para. 2
General Comment 17, ICCPR at para. 3
General Comment 5, ICESCR at para. 35
General Comment 11, ICESCR
General Comment 13, ICESCR

HEALTH

Article 12.1 and 12.2(a), ICESCR
Article 6.2, CRC
Article 19, CRC
Article 23, CRC
Article 24, CRC
Article 25, CRC
Article 33, CRC
Article 39, CRC
Article 3.1(a)(i), 3.2 and 3.5 CRC OP (SALE, PROSTITUTION, PORNOGRAPHY)
Article 4, CRC OP (SALE, PROSTITUTION, PORNOGRAPHY)
Article 5, CRC OP (SALE, PROSTITUTION, PORNOGRAPHY)
Article 6, CRC OP (SALE, PROSTITUTION, PORNOGRAPHY)

General Comment 6, ICCPR at para. 5
General Recommendation 19, CEDAW at para. 20
General Comment 17, ICCPR at para. 3
General Recommendation 15, CEDAW

LEGAL RIGHTS

Article 12, CRC
Article 37, CRC
Article 40, CRC
Article 8.1(b) and (c) CRC OP (SALE, PROSTITUTION, PORNOGRAPHY)

NAME, IDENTITY AND NATIONALITY

Article 24.2 and 24.3, ICCPR
Article 9.2, CEDAW
Article 7, CRC
Article 8, CRC

General Comment 17, ICCPR at paras. 5, 7 and 8
General Recommendation 21, CEDAW at paras. 6, 9, 43, 48(b), 49 and 50

PARENTS AND FAMILY

Article 23.4, ICCPR
Article 5, CRC
Article 7, CRC
Article 9, CRC
Article 10, CRC
Article 18, CRC
Article 20, CRC

Article 8.1(f), CRC OP (SALE, PROSTITUTION, PORNOGRAPHY)

General Comment 17, ICCPR at para. 6
General Comment 19, ICCPR at para. 6
General Comment 28, ICCPR at paras. 25 and 26

PUNISHMENT

Article 28.2, CRC
Article 37, CRC
Article 40, CRC

General Comment 20, ICCPR at para. 5
General Comment 17, ICCPR at para. 3

REFUGEES

Article 9, CRC
Article 22, CRC

CITIZENSHIP

See **ALIENS**
See **CHILDREN'S RIGHTS**—NAME, IDENTITY, NATIONALITY
See **NATIONALITY**

CIVIL RIGHTS

See **LEGAL RIGHTS**—PROPERTY, CIVIL AND CONTRACT RIGHTS

CIVIL SUIT

See **LEGAL RIGHTS**—PROPERTY, CIVIL AND CONTRACT RIGHTS
See **LEGAL RIGHTS**—RIGHT TO A FAIR AND PUBLIC HEARING

CLOTHING

See **ADEQUATE OR DECENT STANDARD OF LIVING**—FOOD, CLOTHING, SHELTER

COMMUNICATIONS

See **ADEQUATE OR DECENT STANDARD OF LIVING**
See **EXPRESSION—FREEDOM OF**—INTERNET

COMPENSATION

See **EFFECTIVE REMEDIES**—COMPENSATION

CONSCIENCE

See **THOUGHT, CONSCIENCE AND RELIGION—FREEDOM OF**

CONSCIENTIOUS OBJECTION

See **LEGAL RIGHTS**—RIGHT TO A FAIR AND PUBLIC HEARING
See **THOUGHT, CONSCIENCE AND RELIGION—FREEDOM OF**

CONSENT—AGE OF

See **CHILDREN'S RIGHTS**—AGE (OF MAJORITY, OF CONSENT, OF RESPONSIBILITY)

CONTRACT RIGHTS

See **LEGAL RIGHTS**—PROPERTY, CIVIL AND CONTRACT RIGHTS

CORPORAL PUNISHMENT

See **CHILDREN'S RIGHTS**—PUNISHMENT
See **TORTURE AND OTHER CRUEL, INHUMAN OR DEGRADING TREATMENT OR PUNISHMENT**

DEFENCE—PREPARATION OF
   See **LEGAL RIGHTS**—CRIMINAL—Right to Counsel or Consular Assistance
   See **LEGAL RIGHTS**—RIGHT TO A FAIR AND PUBLIC HEARING

DENUNCIATION
   Article 21, CERD
   Article 12, ICCPR OP 1
   Article 19, CEDAW OP
   Article 31, CAT
   Article 52, CRC
   Article 11, CRC OP (ARMED CONFLICT)
   Article 15, CRC OP (SALE, PROSTITUTION, PORNOGRAPHY)

   General Comment 26, ICCPR

DEPORTATION
   See **ALIENS**—GENERAL
   See **EXTRADITION**
   See **REFUGEES**

DEROGATIONS
   See also **ARMED CONFLICT**—GENERAL
   See also **ARMED CONFLICT**—CHILDREN
   See also **CRIMES AGAINST HUMANITY**
   See also **PUBLIC AND PRIVATE ACTORS**—MILITARY

   Article 4, ICCPR
   Article 5, ICCPR
   Article 6, ICCPR OP 2
   Article 5, ICESCR
   Article 2.2 and 2.3, CAT

   General Comment 5, ICCPR
   General Comment 13, ICCPR at para. 4
   General Comment 20, ICCPR at para. 3
   General Comment 5, ICESCR at paras. 1–3
   General Comment 7, ICESCR at para. 6
   General Comment 24, ICCPR at para. 10
   General Comment 28, ICCPR at paras. 7 and 9
   General Comment 13, ICESCR at paras. 42 and 59

DESCENT
   See **EQUALITY AND DISCRIMINATION**—RACIAL DISCRIMINATION

DEVELOPING COUNTRIES
   See also **INTERNATIONAL COOPERATION AND MUTUAL ASSISTANCE**

GENERAL
   Article 2.3, ICESCR
   Article 6, ICESCR
   Article 11.2, ICESCR
   Article 24, CRC
   Article 28.3, CRC

EDUCATION
See also **ACCESS TO INFORMATION**
See also **CHILDREN'S RIGHTS**—EDUCATION
See also **CULTURE**—CULTURAL PARTICIPATION
See also **CULTURE**—MEDIA
See also **EQUALITY AND DISCRIMINATION**—EDUCATION
See also **EXPRESSION—FREEDOM OF**—INTERNET
See also **HEALTH**—FAMILY PLANNING
See also **HEALTH**—PUBLIC HEALTH AND PREVENTION

CURRICULUM
Article 7, CERD
Article 10(b), CEDAW
Article 10.1, CAT
Article 29, CRC
Article 9.2, CRC OP (SALE, PROSTITUTION, PORNOGRAPHY)

General Comment 13, ICESCR at paras. 6(c), 12, 16(b), 18, 24, 49 and 50

DISSEMINATION OF HUMAN RIGHTS INFORMATION
Article 7, CERD
Article 10, CAT
Article 42, CRC

General Recommendation V, CERD, at paras. 1 and 2
General Comment 3, ICCPR at para. 2
General Comment 20, ICCPR at para. 10
General Recommendation 14, CEDAW
General Recommendation 23, CEDAW at para. 50(c)

HEALTH EDUCATION
Article 10(h), CEDAW
Article 19.1, CRC
Article 24.2(e) and (f), CRC
Article 33, CRC

General Recommendation 15, CEDAW
General Recommendation 24, CEDAW at paras. 13, 18, 23, 28, and 31(b) and (c)

LITERACY
Article 14.2(d), CEDAW
Article 17(c), CRC
Article 28.3, CRC

RELIGIOUS, MORAL, CULTURAL EDUCATION
Article 18.1, 18.3 and 18.4, ICCPR
Article 13.3, ICESCR

General Comment 22, ICCPR at paras. 6 and 8
General Comment 6, ICESCR at paras. 36, 38 and 39

RIGHT TO EDUCATION
Article 5(e)(v), CERD
Article 13, ICESCR

Article 14, ICESCR
Article 10, CEDAW
Article 14.2(d), CEDAW
Article 23.2 and 23.3, CRC
Article 28, CRC
Article 29, CRC

General Comment 11, ICESCR
General Comment 13, ICESCR
General Comment 28, ICCPR at paras. 15 and 28
General Comment 5, ICESCR
General Comment 6, ICESCR at paras. 36 and 37

VOCATIONAL TRAINING

Article 5(e)(v), CERD
Article 6, ICESCR
Article 13.1, 13.2(b) and 13.2(c), ICESCR
Article 10(a), (e) and (f), CEDAW
Article 11.1(c), CEDAW
Article 10, CAT
Article 23.4, CRC
Article 28.1(b) and (d), CRC
Article 40.1 and 40.4, CRC

General Recommendation XIII, CERD
General Comment 20, ICCPR at para. 10
General Comment 21, ICCPR at para. 7
General Recommendation 19, CEDAW at paras. 24(b), (f) and (t)(ii)
General Comment 5, ICESCR
General Comment 13, ICESCR at paras. 12 and 15–18

EFFECTIVE REMEDIES

See also **EQUALITY AND DISCRIMINATION**—TEMPORARY SPECIAL
MEASURES (AFFIRMATIVE ACTION)

GENERAL

Article 2.1(c), CERD
Article 6, CERD
Article 2.3, ICCPR
Article 2(f) and (g), CEDAW

General Comment 1, ICESCR at paras. 4 and 6–8
General Comment 3, ICESCR
General Comment 4, ICESCR at para. 17
General Comment 9, ICESCR
General Comment 7, ICCPR at para. 1
General Comment 8, ICCPR at paras. 1 and 4
General Comment 20, ICCPR at paras. 14 and 15
General Comment 24, ICCPR at para. 11
General Comment 7, ICESCR at paras. 10 and 14
General Comment 12, ICESCR at paras. 16, 17, 32 and 33
General Comment 13, ICESCR at paras. 43 and 44

See also **LEGAL RIGHTS**—PROPERTY, CIVIL AND CONTRACT RIGHTS
See also **MATERNITY AND PREGNANCY**
See also **POLITICAL RIGHTS**
See also **PRIVACY—RIGHT TO**
See also **THOUGHT, CONSCIENCE AND RELIGION—FREEDOM OF**
See also **WORK**—EQUALITY IN THE WORKPLACE

GENERAL

Article 2, ICCPR
Article 4.1, ICCPR
Article 25, ICCPR
Article 26, ICCPR
Article 27, ICCPR
Article 2, ICESCR
Article 17(d), CRC
Article 30, CRC

General Comment 3, ICCPR
General Comment 15, ICCPR at para. 2
General Comment 18, ICCPR
General Comment 24, ICCPR at para. 9
General Comment 27, ICCPR at para. 18
General Comment 7, ICESCR at para. 11
General Comment 9, ICESCR at para. 15
General Comment 11, ICESCR at para. 10
General Comment 23, ICCPR
General Comment 25, ICCPR at paras. 3, 4, 6, 10, 11, 15, 16, 23 and 24
General Comment 28, ICCPR at paras. 30 and 31
General Comment 4, ICESCR at paras. 9 and 11
General Comment 6, ICESCR at paras. 11 and 12
General Comment 12, ICESCR
General Comment 13, ICESCR at paras. 16, 26, 28, 30–37, 39, 43 and 59

APARTHEID

Article 3, CERD

General Recommendation XIX, CERD

CHILDREN

Article 24.1, ICCPR
Article 2, CRC

General Comment 17, ICCPR
General Comment 4, ICESCR at para. 8(e)

EDUCATION

Article 5(e)(v), CERD
Article 13.1 and 13.2(c), ICESCR
Article 10, CEDAW

General Comment 22, ICCPR at para. 6
General Recommendation XX, CERD
General Comment 6, ICESCR at paras. 36–38
General Comment 13, ICESCR

EMPLOYMENT

Article 5(e)(i), CERD
Article 7(a)(i) and (c), ICESCR
Article 11, CEDAW

General Recommendation XX, CERD
General Comment 28, ICCPR at para. 31
General Comment 5, ICESCR at paras. 20–22 and 25
General Recommendation 13, CEDAW
General Recommendation 16, CEDAW
General Recommendation 17, CEDAW
General Recommendation 19, CEDAW at paras. 7(h), 17, 18 and 24(j), (p) and (t)(i)

EQUAL PROTECTION OF THE LAW

Article 26, ICCPR
Article 2(c), CEDAW

General Recommendation XIV, CERD at para. 1
General Comment 18, ICCPR at paras. 1, 3, 4 and 12
General Comment 23, ICCPR at paras. 2 and 4
General Comment 28, ICCPR at paras. 15, 20–23 and 32
General Recommendation 19, CEDAW at paras. 7(c) and 15

EQUALITY BEFORE THE LAW

Article 5(a), CERD
Article 4.1 and 4.2, ICCPR
Article 14.1 and 14.3, ICCPR
Article 16, ICCPR
Article 26, ICCPR
Article 15, CEDAW

General Recommendation XIV, CERD at para. 1
General Recommendation 19, CEDAW at para. 7(e)
General Comment 13, ICCPR at paras. 1–4
General Comment 18, ICCPR at paras. 9 and 12
General Comment 23, ICCPR at paras. 2 and 4
General Comment 28, ICCPR at paras. 5 and 18
General Recommendation 21, CEDAW at paras. 6–10, 25–35 and 48–50

FAMILY

Article 23.4, ICCPR
Article 5(b), CEDAW
Article 16, CEDAW

General Comment 4, ICESCR at para. 6
General Comment 12, ICESCR at para. 1
General Recommendation 21, CEDAW at paras. 3 and 6–50
General Comment 19, ICCPR at para. 6
General Comment 28, ICCPR at paras. 20, 25 and 26
General Recommendation 19, CEDAW at paras. 7(f), 11, 22 and 23

GENDER DISCRIMINATION
General

Article 3, ICCPR
Article 3, ICESCR
Article 7(a)(i), ICESCR
Article 1, CEDAW
Article 2, CEDAW
Article 3, CEDAW
Article 4, CEDAW
Article 5, CEDAW
Article 6, CEDAW
Article 7, CEDAW
Article 8, CEDAW
Article 9, CEDAW
Article 10, CEDAW
Article 11, CEDAW
Article 12, CEDAW
Article 13, CEDAW
Article 14, CEDAW
Article 15, CEDAW
Article 16, CEDAW

General Comment 4, ICCPR
General Comment 28, ICCPR
General Comment 4, ICESCR at para. 6
General Comment 5, ICESCR at para. 19
General Comment 7, ICESCR at para. 11
General Comment 11, ICESCR at para. 6
General Comment 12, ICESCR at para. 26
General Recommendation 15, CEDAW
General Recommendation 17, CEDAW
General Comment 27, ICCPR
General Comment 6, ICESCR at paras. 20 and 21
General Comment 13, ICESCR at paras. 5, 24, 32, 50 and 59
General Recommendation 5, CEDAW
General Recommendation 13, CEDAW
General Recommendation 16, CEDAW
General Recommendation 18, CEDAW
General Recommendation 21, CEDAW at paras. 3 and 6–50
General Recommendation 23, CEDAW
General Recommendation 24, CEDAW at paras. 2, 5–7 and 9–31

Genital Mutilation

General Comment 28, ICCPR at para. 11
General Recommendation 14, CEDAW
General Recommendation 19, CEDAW at paras. 11, 20 and 24(l)
General Recommendation 24, CEDAW at paras. 5, 12(b), 15(d) and 18

Stereotypes

Article 5(a), CEDAW
Article 10(c), CEDAW

General Recommendation 19 CEDAW at paras. 11–12
General Recommendation 23, CEDAW at paras. 12, 20(c) and 44

Violence Against Women
General Recommendation 12, CEDAW
General Recommendation 19, CEDAW
General Recommendation 21, CEDAW at para. 40
General Comment 28, ICCPR at paras. 8, 10, 11, 20 and 24
General Recommendation 24, CEDAW at paras. 5, 12(b) and (d), 15(a)–(d), 16, 25, 29 and 31(a) and (f)

MINORITY RIGHTS
Article 27, ICCPR
Article 17(d), CRC
Article 30, CRC

General Comment 23, ICCPR
General Comment 28, ICCPR
General Comment 13, ICESCR at para. 50
General Recommendation XXI, CERD
General Recommendation XXIII, CERD
General Comment 22, ICCPR at paras. 2 and 9
General Comment 24, ICCPR at para. 8

OLD AGE
Article 11.1(e), CEDAW

General Comment 6, ICESCR
General Comment 13, ICESCR at para. 24
General Comment 4, ICESCR at para. 8(e)
General Recommendation 24, CEDAW at paras. 6 and 24

RACIAL DISCRIMINATION
Article 1, CERD
Article 2, CERD
Article 3, CERD
Article 4, CERD
Article 5, CERD
Article 6, CERD
Article 7, CERD

General Recommendation VII, CERD
General Recommendation VIII, CERD
General Recommendation XI, CERD
General Recommendation XIII, CERD
General Recommendation XIV, CERD
General Recommendation XV, CERD
General Recommendation XX, CERD
General Recommendation XXII, CERD
General Recommendation XIX, CERD
General Recommendation XXI, CERD
General Recommendation XXIII, CERD

General Comment 11, ICCPR
General Recommendation VII, CERD
General Recommendation XV, CERD
General Comment 22, ICCPR at paras. 7 and 9
General Comment 24, ICCPR at para. 8

INTERNET

Article 4, CERD
Article 19.2 and 19.3, ICCPR
Article 13, CRC
Article 17, CRC
Preamble, CRC OP (SALE, PROSTITUTION, PORNOGRAPHY)
Article 2, CRC OP (SALE, PROSTITUTION, PORNOGRAPHY)
Article 3, CRC OP (SALE, PROSTITUTION, PORNOGRAPHY)

General Comment 10, ICCPR, at para. 2
General Comment 16, ICCPR, at para. 10
General Comment 13, ICESCR, at para. 6

MEDIA

Article 14.1, ICCPR
Article 19, ICCPR

General Comment 10, ICCPR at para. 2
General Comment 25, ICCPR
General Recommendation 19, CEDAW at para. 24(d)

EXPULSION

See **ALIENS**
See **EXTRADITION**
See **LEAVE OR RETURN—RIGHT TO**
See **REFUGEES**

EXTRADITION

See also **ALIENS**—GENERAL
See also **REFUGEES**

Article 3, CAT
Article 5, CAT
Article 6, CAT
Article 7, CAT
Article 8, CAT
Article 3.1, CRC OP (SALE, PROSTITUTION, PORNOGRAPHY)
Article 5, CRC OP (SALE, PROSTITUTION, PORNOGRAPHY)
Article 6, CRC OP (SALE, PROSTITUTION, PORNOGRAPHY)

General Comment 20, ICCPR, at para. 9
General Comment 1, CAT

FAIR AND PUBLIC HEARING

See **LEGAL RIGHTS**—RIGHT TO A FAIR AND PUBLIC HEARING

FAMILY

See **CHILDREN'S RIGHTS**—PARENTS AND FAMILY

See also **EQUALITY AND DISCRIMINATION**—GENDER DISCRIMINATION
See also **EQUALITY AND DISCRIMINATION**—GENDER DISCRIMINATION
  —Genital Mutilation
See also **MATERNITY AND PREGNANCY**
See also **WORK**—WORKING CONDITIONS

GENERAL

Article 12, ICESCR
Article 6.2, CRC
Article 23, CRC
Article 24, CRC

General Recommendation 24, CEDAW
General Comment 4, ICESCR at paras. 8(b) and 8(d)–(f)
General Comment 5, ICESCR at para. 34
General Comment 6, ICESCR at paras. 34 and 35
General Recommendation 14, CEDAW
General Recommendation 19, CEDAW at paras. 7(g), 19, 20, 22, 23 and
  24(k)–(n)

FAMILY PLANNING

Article 10(h), CEDAW
Article 12.1, CEDAW
Article 14.2(b), CEDAW
Article 16.1(e), CEDAW
Articles 24.1 and 24.2(f), CRC

General Recommendation 19, CEDAW at paras. 22 and 24
General Comment 28, ICCPR at paras. 5, 10, 11 and 20
General Comment 5, ICESCR at para. 31
General Recommendation 21, CEDAW at paras. 21–23 and 41–50
General Recommendation 24, CEDAW at paras. 2, 12(d), 14, 17, 18, 22, 23,
  28 and 31(c)

HEALTH CARE AND TREATMENT

Article 5(e)(iv), CERD
Article 12.1, 12.2(c) and (d), ICESCR
Article 12, CEDAW
Article 14.2(b), CEDAW
Article 23.2–23.4, CRC
Article 24.1 and 24.2(a), (b) and (d), CRC
Article 25, CRC
Article 39, CRC

General Comment 21, ICCPR at para. 2
General Recommendation 19, CEDAW at paras. 19 and 24
General Recommendation XX, CERD
General Comment 7, ICCPR at para. 2
General Comment 9, ICCPR at para. 3
General Comment 28, ICCPR at paras. 15 and 20
General Comment 5, ICESCR at para. 34
General Comment 6, ICESCR at paras. 34 and 35

See also **EQUALITY AND DISCRIMINATION**—MINORITY RIGHTS
See also **LEGAL RIGHTS**—CRIMINAL—Right to an Interpreter

Article 14.3(a) and (f), ICCPR
Article 27, ICCPR
Article 17(d), CRC
Article 29.1(c), CRC
Article 30, CRC
Article 40.1 and 40.2(b)(vi), CRC

General Comment 25, ICCPR at para. 12
General Comment 28, ICCPR at para. 32
General Recommendation XXIII, CERD at paras. 4(a) and (c)
General Comment 13, ICCPR at paras. 8 and 13
General Comment 22, ICCPR at para. 4
General Comment 23, ICCPR at para. 5.3
General Comment 5, ICESCR at para. 35

LEAVE OR RETURN—RIGHT TO

For internal movement see **MOVEMENT—FREEDOM OF**
See also **ALIENS**—GENERAL

Article 5(d)(ii), CERD
Article 12.2–12.4, ICCPR
Article 15.4, CEDAW
Article 10, CRC

General Comment 28, ICCPR at para. 16
General Recommendation XX, CERD
General Recommendation XXII, CERD at Preamble and para. 2
General Comment 15, ICCPR at paras. 7 and 8
General Comment 27, ICCPR at paras. 8–21

LEGAL AID

See **LEGAL RIGHTS**—CRIMINAL—Right to Counsel or Consular Assistance
See **LEGAL RIGHTS**—RIGHT TO A FAIR AND PUBLIC HEARING

LEGAL RIGHTS

See also **CHILDREN'S RIGHTS**—CIVIL RIGHTS
See also **CHILDREN'S RIGHTS**—LEGAL RIGHTS
See also **CHILDREN'S RIGHTS**—PUNISHMENT
See also **EQUALITY AND DISCRIMINATION**—EQUAL PROTECTION OF THE LAW
See also **EQUALITY AND DISCRIMINATION**—EQUALITY BEFORE THE LAW
See also **HUMAN DIGNITY**
See also **LANGUAGE RIGHTS**
See also **LIBERTY AND SECURITY OF THE PERSON**
See also **TORTURE AND OTHER CRUEL, INHUMAN OR DEGRADING TREATMENT OR PUNISHMENT**

CRIMINAL
Conditions of Arrest and Detention Article 9, ICCPR

Article 10, ICCPR
Article 14.3(a), ICCPR
Article 37(b), (c) and (d), CRC
Article 40.4, CRC

General Comment 25, ICCPR at para. 14
General Comment 28, ICCPR at para. 15
General Comment 7, ICCPR at paras. 1 and 2
General Comment 8, ICCPR
General Comment 9, ICCPR
General Comment 20, ICCPR at paras. 6, 10 and 11
General Comment 21, ICCPR at paras. 3, 5 and 7–13

Equal Treatment

Article 5(a), CERD
Article 4.1 and 4.2, ICCPR
Article 14.1 and 14.3, ICCPR
Article 16, ICCPR
Article 15.1, CEDAW

General Comment 21, ICCPR at para. 4
General Recommendation XX, CERD
General Comment 9, ICCPR at para. 3
General Comment 13, ICCPR at paras. 1–4
General Comment 28, ICCPR at para. 31

Presumption of Innocence

Article 14.2, ICCPR
Article 40.1 and 40.2(b)(i), CRC

General Comment 13, ICCPR at para. 7
General Comment 28, ICCPR at para. 18
General Comment 24, ICCPR at para. 8

Protection Against Double Jeopardy

Article 14.7, ICCPR

General Comment 13, ICCPR at para. 19

Protection Against Retroactive Criminalization

Article 4.1 and 4.2, ICCPR
Article 15, ICCPR
Article 40.1 and 40.2(a), CRC

Protection Against Undue Delay

Article 9.2–9.4, ICCPR
Article 14.3(a) and (c), ICCPR
Article 37(d), CRC
Article 40.2(b)(ii) and (iii), CRC

General Comment 8, ICCPR at paras. 2 and 3
General Comment 13, ICCPR at paras. 8 and 10

Right Against Self-Incrimination

Article 14.3(g), ICCPR
Article 40.1 and 40.2(b)(iv), CRC

General Comment 13, ICCPR at para. 14

Right to Appeal
Article 14.5, ICCPR
Article 40.1 and 40.2(b)(v), CRC

General Comment 13, ICCPR at paras. 10 and 17

Right to Counsel or Consular Assistance
Article 14.3(b) and (d), ICCPR
Article 6.1 and 6.3, CAT
Article 37(d), CRC
Article 40.1 and 40.2(b)(ii), CRC

General Comment 13, ICCPR at paras. 9 and 11

Right to Examine and Cross-Examine Witnesses
Article 14.3(e), ICCPR
Article 40.1 and 40.2(b)(iv), CRC

General Comment 13, ICCPR at para. 12

Right to an Interpreter
Article 14.3(a) and (f), ICCPR
Article 40.1 and 40.2(b)(vi), CRC

General Comment 13, ICCPR at paras. 8 and 13
General Comment 23, ICCPR at para. 5.3

INDEPENDENCE OF THE JUDICIARY
Article 14.1, ICCPR
Article 37(d), CRC
Article 40.1 and 40.2(b)(iii) and (v), CRC
Article 8, CRC OP (SALE, PROSTITUTION, PORNOGRAPHY)

General Comment 13, ICCPR at paras. 3 and 4

JUVENILE OFFENDERS AND CHILDREN
Article 4.1 and 4.2, ICCPR
Article 6.5, ICCPR
Article 10.2(b) and 10.3, ICCPR
Article 14.1 and 14.4 ICCPR
Article 12, CRC
Article 37(d), CRC
Article 40, CRC

General Comment 13, ICCPR at para. 16
General Comment 28, ICCPR at para. 15
General Comment 9, ICCPR at paras. 2 and 3
General Comment 17, ICCPR at para. 4
General Comment 21, ICCPR paras. 8 and 13

PROPERTY, CIVIL AND CONTRACT RIGHTS
Article 5(d)(v) and (vi), CERD
Article 4.1 and 4.2, ICCPR
Article 11, ICCPR
Article 14.1, ICCPR
Article 13(b), CEDAW
Article 14.2(g), CEDAW

MUTUAL ASSISTANCE
   See **INTERNATIONAL COOPERATION AND MUTUAL ASSISTANCE**

NATIONALITY
   See also **ALIENS**
   See also **CHILDREN'S RIGHTS**—NAME, IDENTITY AND NATIONALITY
   See also **EQUALITY AND DISCRIMINATION**—RACIAL DISCRIMINATION

   Articles 1.2 and 1.3, CERD
   Article 5(d)(iii), CERD
   Article 24.3, ICCPR
   Article 2.3, ICESCR
   Article 9, CEDAW
   Article 7, CRC
   Article 8.1, CRC

   General Comment 25, ICCPR
   General Recommendation XI, CERD
   General Recommendation XX, CERD
   General Recommendation XXI, CERD at paras. 9 and 10
   General Comment 15, ICCPR at paras. 2 and 8
   General Comment 17, ICCPR at paras. 5 and 8
   General Comment 23, ICCPR at paras. 5.1 and 5.2
   General Comment 27, ICCPR at paras. 4, 9, 10, 17 and 19–21
   General Recommendation 21, CEDAW at paras. 6, 9, 43, 48(b), 49 and 50

NATURAL RESOURCES
   See **SELF-DETERMINATION**

NON-GOVERNMENTAL ORGANIZATIONS
   See **PUBLIC AND PRIVATE ACTORS**—GENERAL

NON-REFOULEMENT
   See **REFUGEES**

NULLA POENA SINE LEGE
   See **LEGAL RIGHTS**—CRIMINAL—Protection Against Retroactive
   Criminalization

NUREMBERG TRIALS
   See **CRIMES AGAINST HUMANITY**

OCCUPATIONAL HEALTH
   See **HEALTH**—OCCUPATIONAL HEALTH
   See **WORK**—WORKING CONDITIONS

OLD AGE
   See **EQUALITY AND DISCRIMINATION**—OLD AGE
   See **SOCIAL SECURITY AND INSURANCE**

OPINION—FREEDOM OF
   See **EXPRESSION—FREEDOM OF**

PARENTS
   See **CHILDREN'S RIGHTS**—PARENTS AND FAMILY
   See **EQUALITY AND DISCRIMINATION**—FAMILY

POVERTY
> See **ADEQUATE OR DECENT STANDARD OF LIVING**

PREGNANCY
> See **HEALTH**—FAMILY PLANNING
> See **MATERNITY AND PREGNANCY**

PRESS—FREEDOM OF
> See **EXPRESSION—FREEDOM OF**—MEDIA

PRISONS
> See **CHILDREN'S RIGHTS**—PUNISHMENT
> See **LEGAL RIGHTS**—CRIMINAL—Conditions of Arrest and Detention
> See **LIBERTY AND SECURITY OF THE PERSON**

PRIVACY—RIGHT TO
> Article 17, ICCPR
> Article 16, CRC
> Article 40.1 and 40.2(b)(vii), CRC
> Article 8.1(e), CRC OP (SALE, PROSTITUTION, PORNOGRAPHY)
>
> General Comment 16, ICCPR
> General Comment 4, ICESCR at para. 9
> General Comment 28, ICCPR at paras. 13 and 20

PROPERTY RIGHTS
> See **LEGAL RIGHTS**—PROPERTY, CIVIL AND CONTRACT RIGHTS

PROSTITUTION
> See **EQUALITY AND DISCRIMINATION**—GENDER DISCRIMINATION
> General
> See **EQUALITY AND DISCRIMINATION**—GENDER DISCRIMINATION
> Violence Against Women
> See **TRAFFICKING IN PERSONS AND SEXUAL EXPLOITATION**

PROTECTION OF THE FAMILY
> See also **CHILDREN'S RIGHTS**—PARENTS AND FAMILY
> See also **EQUALITY AND DISCRIMINATION**—FAMILY
> See also **EQUALITY AND DISCRIMINATION**—GENDER DISCRIMINATION
> —General

GENERAL
> Article 14.1, ICCPR
> Article 17, ICCPR
> Article 23, ICCPR
> Article 10, ICESCR
> Article 11.2(c), CEDAW
> Article 5, CRC
> Article 8.1, CRC
> Article 9.3 and 9.4, CRC
> Article 16, CRC
> Article 22.1 and 22.2, CRC
> Article 37(c), CRC

General Comment 19, ICCPR
General Comment 6, ICESCR at para. 31
General Comment 16, ICCPR at paras. 1–6
General Comment 28, ICCPR at paras. 15 and 27
General Comment 5, ICESCR at paras. 30–32

MARRIAGE

Article 5(d)(iv), CERD
Article 23.2–23.4, ICCPR
Article 10.1, ICESCR
Article 9.1, CEDAW
Article 16, CEDAW

General Recommendation XX, CERD
General Comment 19, ICCPR at paras. 4 and 6
General Comment 24, ICCPR at para. 8
General Comment 28, ICCPR at paras. 23 and 24
General Comment 5, ICESCR
General Recommendation 19, CEDAW at paras. 11 and 14
General Recommendation 21, CEDAW at paras. 6, 10, 14–20, 24–35, 36, 38,
    39 and 41–50

PARENTAL RIGHTS AND RESPONSIBILITIES

Article 18.4, ICCPR
Article 13.3, ICESCR
Article 16.1(d), CEDAW
Article 3.2, CRC
Article 5, CRC
Article 9.1 and 9.2, CRC
Article 10, CRC
Article 14, CRC
Article 18, CRC
Article 27.2 and 27.4, CRC

General Comment 28, ICCPR at para. 26
General Comment 17, ICCPR at para. 6
General Comment 22, ICCPR at paras. 6 and 8.
General Comment 13, ICESCR at paras. 28 and 29
General Recommendation 21, CEDAW at paras. 19, 20 and 41–50

PUBLIC AND PRIVATE ACTORS

GENERAL

Article 2.1(a), (b) and (d), CERD
Article 4, CERD
Article 5(b) and (f), CERD
Article 2.3, ICCPR
Article 5, ICESCR
Article 2(d) and (e), CEDAW
Article 1.1, CAT
Article 2.3, CAT
Article 16.1, CAT
Article 3.1, CRC

Article 7, CRC OP (ARMED CONFLICT)

General Comment 18, ICCPR at para. 9
General Comment 27, ICCPR at para. 6
General Comment 1, CAT at paras. 3 and 8(b), (f) and (g)
General Recommendation XV, CERD
General Recommendation XIX, CERD
General Recommendation XX, CERD
General Comment 7, ICCPR at para. 2
General Comment 16, ICCPR at paras. 1–6
General Comment 20, ICCPR at paras. 2, 3, 10, 13 and 14
General Comment 28, ICCPR at paras. 4, 20 and 31
General Comment 5, ICESCR at paras. 11 and 12
General Comment 12, ICESCR at paras. 19, 20 and 27
General Recommendation 19, CEDAW at paras. 8, 9 and 24(a)
General Recommendation 24, CEDAW at paras. 15 and 17

PUBLIC HEALTH
See **HEALTH**—PUBLIC HEALTH AND PREVENTION

PUBLIC SERVICE
See **POLITICAL RIGHTS**

PUNISHMENT
See **CHILDREN'S RIGHTS**—PUNISHMENT
See **LEGAL RIGHTS**—CRIMINAL—Conditions of Arrest and Detention
See **TORTURE AND OTHER CRUEL, INHUMAN OR DEGRADING TREATMENT OR PUNISHMENT**

RACIAL DISCRIMINATION
See **ASSOCIATION—FREEDOM OF**
See **EFFECTIVE REMEDIES**—SPECIAL MEASURES
See **EQUALITY AND DISCRIMINATION**
See **EQUALITY AND DISCRIMINATION**—RACIAL DISCRIMINATION
See **EXPRESSION—FREEDOM OF**—HATE SPEECH AND LIMITS ON PROPAGANDA
See **EXPRESSION—FREEDOM OF**—INTERNET
See **LEGAL RIGHTS**—PROPERTY, CIVIL AND CONTRACT RIGHTS
See **LEGAL RIGHTS**—CRIMINAL—Equal Treatment
See **WORK**—EQUALITY IN THE WORKPLACE

RAPE
See **EQUALITY AND DISCRIMINATION**—GENDER DISCRIMINATION
Violence Against Women
See **LIBERTY AND SECURITY OF THE PERSON**
See **TRAFFICKING IN PERSONS AND SEXUAL EXPLOITATION**—SEXUAL EXPLOITATION

REFOULEMENT
See **REFUGEES**

REFUGEES
See also **ALIENS**
See also **CHILDREN'S RIGHTS**—REFUGEES

See **PROTECTION OF THE FAMILY**—PARENTAL RIGHTS AND
RESPONSIBILITIES

RIGHT TO PRIVACY
See **PRIVACY—RIGHT TO**

RIGHT TO STRIKE
See **FREEDOM OF ASSOCIATION**—TRADE UNIONS

RURAL AREAS
See **DEVELOPING COUNTRIES**—RURAL AND URBAN AREAS

SANITATION
See **ADEQUATE OR DECENT STANDARD OF LIVING**

SCIENCE
See also **CULTURE**

Article 15, ICESCR
Article 28.3, CRC

General Comment 6, ICESCR at para. 42.

SCIENTIFIC OR MEDICAL EXPERIMENTATION
See **TORTURE AND OTHER CRUEL, INHUMAN, OR DEGRADING
TREATMENT OR PUNISHMENT**

SEARCH AND SEIZURE
See **LEGAL RIGHTS**—RIGHT TO A FAIR AND PUBLIC HEARING
See **LIBERTY AND SECURITY OF THE PERSON**
See **PRIVACY—RIGHT TO**

SECESSION
See **EQUALITY AND DISCRIMINATION**—MINORITY RIGHTS
See **SELF-DETERMINATION**

SECURITY FORCES
See **DEROGATIONS**
See **PUBLIC AND PRIVATE ACTORS**—MILITARY

SECURITY OF THE PERSON
See **LIBERTY AND SECURITY OF THE PERSON**

SELF-DETERMINATION
See also **EQUALITY AND DISCRIMINATION**—MINORITY RIGHTS
See also **INDIGENOUS PEOPLES**

Article 1, ICCPR
Article 47, ICCPR
Article 1, ICESCR
Article 25, ICESCR

General Recommendation XXI, CERD at paras. 6–11
General Comment 11, ICCPR at para. 2
General Comment 12, ICCPR
General Comment 24, ICCPR at para. 9
General Comment 25, ICCPR at para. 2
General Comment 23, ICCPR at paras. 2 and 3.1

SERVITUDE
See **SLAVERY, SERVITUDE AND FORCED LABOUR**

SEXUAL ASSAULT
See **EQUALITY AND DISCRIMINATION**—GENDER DISCRIMINATION—
Violence Against Women
See **LIBERTY AND SECURITY OF THE PERSON**
See **TRAFFICKING IN PERSONS AND SEXUAL EXPLOITATION**—SEXUAL
EXPLOITATION

SEXUAL EXPLOITATION
See **TRAFFICKING IN PERSONS AND SEXUAL EXPLOITATION**

SEXUAL ORIENTATION
See **EQUALITY AND DISCRIMINATION**—SEXUAL ORIENTATION
See **PRIVACY—RIGHT TO**

SLAVERY, SERVITUDE AND FORCED LABOUR
See also **CHILDREN'S RIGHTS**—CHILD LABOUR AND EXPLOITATION
See also **TRAFFICKING IN PERSONS AND SEXUAL EXPLOITATION**
See also **WORK**—WORKING CONDITIONS

Article 4.1 and 4.2, ICCPR
Article 8, ICCPR

General Comment 28, ICCPR at para. 12
General Comment 24, ICCPR at para. 8
General Comment 5, ICESCR at para. 21

SOCIAL SECURITY AND INSURANCE
See also **ADEQUATE OR DECENT STANDARD OF LIVING**—GENERAL

Article 5(e)(iv), CERD
Article 9, ICESCR
Article 10.2, ICESCR
Article 11.1(e), CEDAW
Article 13(a), CEDAW
Article 14.2(c), CEDAW
Article 26, CRC

General Recommendation, CEDAW 21 at para. 6
General Recommendation XX, CERD
General Comment 5, ICESCR at paras. 28 and 29
General Comment 6, ICESCR at paras. 10, 20, 21 and 26–30
General Recommendation 16, CEDAW

SPECIAL MEASURES
See **EFFECTIVE REMEDIES**—SPECIAL MEASURES
See **EQUALITY AND DISCRIMINATION**—TEMPORARY SPECIAL
MEASURES (AFFIRMATIVE ACTION)

SPORTS AND RECREATION
See also **CULTURE**

Article 10(g), CEDAW
Article 13(c), CEDAW

Article 23.2 and 23.3, CRC
Article 31, CRC

General Comment 5, ICESCR at paras. 36 and 37

STANDARD OF LIVING
See **ADEQUATE OR DECENT STANDARD OF LIVING**

STATELESSNESS
See **NATIONALITY**

STATES OF EMERGENCY
See **DEROGATIONS**

STRIKE—RIGHT TO
See **ASSOCIATION—FREEDOM OF**—TRADE UNIONS

STRUCTURAL ADJUSTMENT POLICIES
See **ADEQUATE OR DECENT STANDARD OF LIVING**—GENERAL

SUBSTANCE ABUSE
See **EDUCATION**—HEALTH EDUCATION
See **HEALTH**—PUBLIC HEALTH AND PREVENTION

SUIT AT LAW
See **LEGAL RIGHTS**—PROPERTY, CIVIL AND CONTRACT RIGHTS
See **LEGAL RIGHTS**—RIGHT TO A FAIR AND PUBLIC HEARING

TERRORISM
See **ARMED CONFLICT**
See **LIBERTY AND SECURITY OF THE PERSON**
See **PUBLIC AND PRIVATE ACTORS**—GENERAL

THOUGHT, CONSCIENCE AND RELIGION—FREEDOM OF
See also **EDUCATION**—RELIGIOUS, MORAL, CULTURAL EDUCATION
See also **EQUALITY AND DISCRIMINATION**—MINORITY RIGHTS
See also **EXPRESSION—FREEDOM OF**

Article 5(d)(vii), CERD
Article 4.1 and 4.2, ICCPR
Article 8.3, ICCPR
Article 18, ICCPR
Article 19.1, ICCPR
Article 27, ICCPR
Article 13.3, ICESCR
Article 14, CRC
Article 30, CRC

General Comment 22, ICCPR
General Comment 13, ICESCR at para. 28
General Recommendation XX, CERD
General Comment 23, ICCPR
General Comment 24, ICCPR at para. 8
General Comment 28, ICCPR at paras. 13 and 21

TORTURE AND OTHER CRUEL, INHUMAN OR DEGRADING TREATMENT OR PUNISHMENT
See also **CHILDREN'S RIGHTS**—PUNISHMENT

See **EQUALITY AND DISCRIMINATION**—MINORITY RIGHTS
See **EQUALITY AND DISCRIMINATION**—RACIAL DISCRIMINATION
See **EQUALITY AND DISCRIMINATION**—TEMPORARY SPECIAL
MEASURES (AFFIRMATIVE ACTION)

VOTE—RIGHT TO
See **POLITICAL RIGHTS**

WAR CRIMES
See **ARMED CONFLICT**—GENERAL
See **CRIMES AGAINST HUMANITY**
See **EFFECTIVE REMEDIES**—IMPUNITY
See **PUBLIC AND PRIVATE ACTORS**—MILITARY

WATER
See **ADEQUATE OF DECENT STANDARD OF LIVING**—FOOD, CLOTHING,
SHELTER

WIRETAPPING
See **LEGAL RIGHTS**—RIGHT TO A FAIR AND PUBLIC HEARING
See **LIBERTY AND SECURITY OF THE PERSON**
See **PRIVACY—RIGHT TO**

WOMEN
See **ADEQUATE OR DECENT STANDARD OF LIVING**—GENERAL
See **EDUCATION**
See **EFFECTIVE REMEDIES**—SPECIAL MEASURES
See **EQUALITY AND DISCRIMINATION**—EQUAL PROTECTION OF THE
LAW
See **EQUALITY AND DISCRIMINATION**—EQUALITY BEFORE THE LAW
See **EQUALITY AND DISCRIMINATION**—GENDER DISCRIMINATION
See **EQUALITY AND DISCRIMINATION**—TEMPORARY SPECIAL
MEASURES (AFFIRMATIVE ACTION)
See **EXPRESSION—FREEDOM OF**—INTERNET
See **HEALTH**—FAMILY PLANNING
See **LEGAL RIGHTS**—PROPERTY, CIVIL AND CONTRACT RIGHTS
See **MATERNITY AND PREGNANCY**
See **PROTECTION OF THE FAMILY**
See **TRAFFICKING IN PERSONS AND SEXUAL EXPLOITATION**
See **WORK**—EQUALITY IN THE WORKPLACE

WORK
See also **ADEQUATE OR DECENT STANDARD OF LIVING**—GENERAL
See also **ALIENS**—MIGRANT WORKERS
See also **ASSOCIATION—FREEDOM OF**—TRADE UNIONS
See also **CHILDREN'S RIGHTS**—CHILD LABOUR AND EXPLOITATION
See also **EDUCATION**—VOCATIONAL TRAINING
See also **EQUALITY AND DISCRIMINATION**—EMPLOYMENT
See also **HEALTH**—OCCUPATIONAL HEALTH
See also **SLAVERY, SERVITUDE AND FORCED LABOUR**

EQUALITY IN THE WORKPLACE
Article 5(e)(i), CERD
Article 7(a)(i) and (c), ICESCR

Article 11.1(b)–(d), CEDAW

General Comment 5, ICESCR at para. 22
General Recommendation 13, CEDAW
General Recommendation 16, CEDAW
General Comment 28, ICCPR at para. 31
General Recommendation 19, CEDAW at paras. 7(h), 17, 18 and 24(j), (p) and (t)(i)

RIGHT TO WORK

Article 5(e)(i), CERD
Article 6, ICESCR
Article 11.1(a), CEDAW
Article 14.2(e), CEDAW
Article 16.1(g), CEDAW

General Recommendation XX, CERD
General Comment 5, ICESCR at paras. 20–22 and 27
General Comment 6, ICESCR at paras. 22–24
General Recommendation 21, CEDAW at paras. 24 and 41–50

WORKING CONDITIONS

Article 5(e)(i), CERD
Article 6, ICESCR
Article 7, ICESCR
Article 10.2 and 10.3, ICESCR
Article 12.1 and 12.2(b), ICESCR
Article 11.1(c) and (f) and 11.2, CEDAW
Article 32, CRC

General Comment 5, ICESCR at para. 25
General Recommendation 24, CEDAW at para. 28
General Recommendation XX, CERD
General Recommendation 12, CEDAW
General Recommendation 16, CEDAW
General Recommendation 19, CEDAW at paras. 7(h), 18, 24(j), (p), and (t)(i)

XENOPHOBIA

See **ASSOCIATION—FREEDOM OF**—GENERAL
See **EQUALITY AND DISCRIMINATION**—GENERAL
See **EQUALITY AND DISCRIMINATION**—MINORITY RIGHTS
See **EQUALITY AND DISCRIMINATION**—RACIAL DISCRIMINATION
See **EXPRESSION—FREEDOM OF**—HATE SPEECH AND LIMITS ON PROPAGANDA
See **THOUGHT, CONSCIENCE AND RELIGION—FREEDOM OF**

ANNEX 17

INDEX OF CASES OF THE HUMAN RIGHTS COMMITTEE BY ARTICLE

to update generally see jurisprudence at: www.unhchr.ch/tbs/doc.nsf
see also www.bayefsky.com

A = admissibility decision
DC = discontinued cases
DJ = decision to deal with cases jointly
I = interim measures
V = views

ARTICLE 1

Name of case	Comm. No.	Date of Decision	Outcome
A.D. v. Canada (A)	78/1980	29 July 1984	Inadmissible
G. F. Croes v. The Netherlands (A)	164/1984	7 November 1988	Inadmissible
Lubicon Lake Band v. Canada (V)	167/1984	26 March 1990	Violation
E.P. et al. v. Colombia (A)	318/1988	25 July 1990	Inadmissible
A.B. et al. v. Italy (A)	413/1990	2 November 1990	Inadmissible
Diergaardt et al. v. Namibia (V)	760/1997	25 July 2000	Violation

ARTICLE 2

Name of case	Comm. No.	Date of Decision	Outcome
Lovelace v. Canada (V)	24/1977 (R.6/24)	30 July 1981	Violation
S.H.B. v. Canada (A)	192/1985	24 March 1987	Inadmissible
H. D. P. v. The Netherlands (A)	217/1986	8 April 1987	Inadmissible
Danning v. The Netherlands (V)	180/1984	9 April 1987	No violation
Stalla Costa v. Uruguay (V)	198/1985	9 July 1987	No violation

Name of case	Comm. No.	Date of Decision	Outcome
S.R. v. France (A)	243/1987	5 November 1987	Inadmissible
S.E. v. Argentina (A)	275/1988	26 March 1988	Inadmissible
C.L.D. v. France (A)	228/1987	18 July 1988	Inadmissible
V.M.R.B. v. Canada (A)	236/1987	18 July 1988	Inadmissible
Avellanal v. Peru (V)	202/1986	28 October 1988	Violation
J.R.C. v. Costa Rica (A)	296/1988	30 March 1989	Inadmissible
Gueye et al. v. France (V)	196/1983	3 April 1989	Violation
Nahlik v. Austria (A)	608/1995	22 July 1996	Inadmissible
Drobek v. Slovakia (A)	643/1995	14 July 1997	Inadmissible
Lestourneaud v. France (A)	861/1999	3 November 1999	Inadmissible
Ignatane v. Latvia (V)	884/1999	25 July 2001	Violation
Mazou v. Cameroon (V)	630/1995	26 July 2001	Violation
Äärelä v. Finland (V)	779/1997	24 October 2001	Violation
Des Fours v. Czech Republic (V)	747/1997	30 October 2001	Violation

ARTICLE 2(1)

Name of case	Comm. No.	Date of Decision	Outcome
Mauritian Women v. Mauritius (V)	35/1978	9 April 1981	Violation
Burgos v. Uruguay (V)	52/1979	29 July 1981	Violation
Casariego v. Uruguay (V)	56/1979	29 July 1981	Violation
J.H. v. Canada (A)	187/1985	12 April 1985	Inadmissible
H.S. v. France (A)	184/1984	10 April 1986	Inadmissible
R.T. v. France (A)	262/1987	30 March 1989	Inadmissible
Vuolanne v. Finland (V)	265/1987	7 April 1989	Violation
Toonen v. Australia (V)	488/1992	30 March 1994	Violation
Celis Laureano v. Peru (V)	540/1993	25 March 1996	Violation
A. v. Australia (V)	560/1993	3 April 1997	Violation
G.T. v. Australia (V)	706/1996	4 November 1997	No violation

ARTICLE 2(2)

Name of case	Comm. No.	Date of Decision	Outcome
H. C. M. A. v The Netherlands (A)	213/1986	30 March 1989	Inadmissible
R.T. v. France (A)	262/1987	30 March 1989	Inadmissible
Vuolanne v. Finland (V)	265/1987	7 April 1989	Violation

ARTICLE 2(3)

Name of case	Comm. No.	Date of Decision	Outcome
Mbenge v. Zaire (V)	16/1977	25 March 1983	Violation
Luyeye v. Zaire (V)	90/1981	21 July 1983	Violation
Estradet v. Uruguay (V)	105/1981	21 July 1983	Violation
Acosta v. Uruguay (V)	162/1983	25 October 1988	Violation
Muñoz v. Peru (V)	203/1986	4 November 1988	Violation
H. C. M. A. v. The Netherlands (A)	213/1986	30 March 1989	Inadmissible
R.T. v. France (A)	262/1987	30 March 1989	Inadmissible
Vuolanne v. Finland (V)	265/1987	7 April 1989	Violation
Rodríguez Veiga v. Uruguay (A)	487/1992	18 July 1994	Inadmissible
Rodríguez v. Uruguay (V)	322/1988	19 July 1994	Violation
Bautista v. Colombia (V)	563/1993	27 October 1995	Violation
Kelly v. Jamaica (V)	537/1993	17 July 1996	Violation
A. v. Australia (V)	560/1993	3 April 1997	Violation
Arhuaco v. Colombia (V)	612/1995	29 July 1997	Violation
Thomas v. Jamaica (V)	532/1993	3 November 1997	Violation

ARTICLE 2(4)

Name of case	Comm. No.	Date of Decision	Outcome
Estradet v. Uruguay (V)	105/1981	21 July 1983	Violation

ARTICLE 3

Name of case	Comm. No.	Date of Decision	Outcome
Mauritian Women v. Mauritius (V)	35/1978	9 April 1981	Violation
Lovelace v. Canada (V)	24/1977 (R.6/24)	30 July 1981	Violation
V.M.R.B. v. Canada (A)	236/1987	18 July 1988	Inadmissible
Avellanal v. Peru (V)	202/1986	28 October 1988	Violation
J.R.C. v. Costa Rica (A)	296/1988	30 March 1989	Inadmissible
Bolaños v. Ecuador (V)	238/1987	26 July 1989	Violation

ARTICLE 5

Name of case	Comm. No.	Date of Decision	Outcome
Kelly v. Jamaica (V)	253/1987	8 April 1991	Violation

ARTICLE 5(2)

Name of case	Comm. No.	Date of Decision	Outcome
J.R.C. v. Costa Rica (A)	296/1988	30 March 1989	Inadmissible

ARTICLE 6

Name of case	Comm. No.	Date of Decision	Outcome
Bleier v. Uruguay (V)	30/1978 (R.7/30)	29 March 1982	Violation
Miango v. Zaire (V)	194/1985	27 October 1987	Violation
Herrera v. Colombia (V)	161/1983	2 November 1987	Violation
V.M.R.B. v. Canada (A)	236/1987	18 July 1988	Inadmissible
G. F. Croes v. The Netherlands (A)	164/1984	7 November 1988	Inadmissible
Pratt and Morgan v. Jamaica (V)	225/1987	6 April 1989	Violation
Arévalo v. Colombia (V)	181/1984	3 November 1989	Violation
Pinto v. Trinidad and Tobago (V)	232/1987	20 July 1990	Violation
Reid v. Jamaica (V)	250/1987	20 July 1990	Violation
Kelly v. Jamaica (V)	253/1987	8 April 1991	Violation
Henry v. Jamaica (V)	230/1987	1 November 1991	Violation
Little v. Jamaica (V)	283/1988	1 November 1991	Violation
Campbell v. Jamaica (V)	248/1987	30 March 1992	Violation
Wright v. Jamaica (V)	349/1989	27 July 1992	Violation
Campbell v. Jamaica (V)	307/1988	24 March 1993	Violation
Francis v. Jamaica (V)	320/1988	24 March 1993	Violation
Collins v. Jamaica (V)	356/1989	25 March 1993	Violation
Smith v. Jamaica (V)	282/1988	31 March 1993	Violation
Hamilton v. Jamaica (V)	333/1988	23 March 1994	Violation
Currie v. Jamaica (V)	377/1989	29 March 1994	Violation
Grant v. Jamaica (V)	353/1988	31 March 1994	No violation
Berry v. Jamaica (V)	330/1988	7 April 1994	Violation
Champagnie et al. v. Jamaica (V)	445/1991	18 July 1994	Violation
Cox v. Canada (V)	539/1993	31 October 1994	No violation
Peart and Peart v. Jamaica (DJ), (V)	464 & 482/1991	19 July 1995	Violation
Wright and Harvey v. Jamaica (V)	459/1991	27 October 1995	Violation

Name of case	Comm. No.	Date of Decision	Outcome
E. Johnson v. Jamaica (V)	588/1994	22 March 1996	Violation
Kelly v. Jamaica (V)	537/1993	17 July 1996	Violation
Price v. Jamaica (V)	572/1994	6 November 1996	Violation
McLawrence v. Jamaica (V)	702/1996	18 July 1997	Violation
Taylor v. Jamaica (V)	707/1996	18 July 1997	Violation
Young v. Jamaica (V)	615/1995	4 November 1997	Violation
G.T. v. Australia (V)	706/1996	4 November 1997	No violation
McLeod v. Jamaica (V)	734/1997	31 March 1998	Violation
Shaw v. Jamaica (V)	704/1996	2 April 1998	Violation
Taylor v. Jamaica (V)	705/1996	2 April 1998	Violation
Domukovsky et al. v. Georgia (V)	623, 624, 626 & 627/1995	6 April 1998	Violation
Chadee et al. v. Trinidad and Tobago (V)	813/1998	29 July 1998	No violation
Perkins v. Jamaica (V)	733/1997	30 July 1998	Violation
Daley v. Jamaica (V)	750/1997	31 July 1998	Violation
Phillip v. Trinidad and Tobago (V)	594/1992	20 October 1998	Violation
Brown v. Jamaica (V)	775/1997	23 March 1999	Violation
Piandiong et al. v. Philippines (V)	869/1999	19 October 2000	No violation
Mansaraj et al. v. Sierra Leone (V)	839, 840 & 841/1998	16 July 2001	Violation

ARTICLE 6(1)

Name of case	Comm. No.	Date of Decision	Outcome
de Guerrero v. Colombia (V)	45/1979 (R.11/45)	31 March 1982	Violation
Barbato v. Uruguay (V)	84/1981	21 October 1982	Violation
Baboeram et al. v. Suriname (V)	146 & 148 −154/1983	4 April 1985	Violation
Kindler v. Canada (V)	470/1991	30 July 1993	No violation
Ng v. Canada (V)	469/1991	5 November 1993	Violation
Mojica v. Dominican Republic (V)	449/1991	15 July 1994	Violation
Celis Laureano v. Peru (V)	540/1993	25 March 1996	Violation
Burrell v. Jamaica (V)	546/1993	18 July 1996	Violation
A.R.J. v. Australia (V)	692/1996	28 July 1997	No violation
Arhuaco v. Colombia (V)	612/1995	29 July 1997	Violation

Name of case	Comm. No.	Date of Decision	Outcome
Yasseen and Thomas v. Republic of Guyana (V)	676/1996	30 March 1998	Violation
Thompson v. Saint Vincent and the Grenadines (V)	806/1998	18 October 2000	Violation
Chongwe v. Zambia (V)	821/1998	25 October 2000	Violation

ARTICLE 6(2)

Name of case	Comm. No.	Date of Decision	Outcome
Mbenge v. Zaire (V)	16/1977	25 March 1983	Violation
Kindler v. Canada (V)	470/1991	30 July 1993	No violation
Ng v. Canada (V)	469/1991	5 November 1993	Violation
Lubuto v. Zambia (V)	390/1990	31 October 1995	Violation
Graham and Morrison v. Jamaica (V)	461/1991	25 March 1996	Violation
Burrell v. Jamaica (V)	546/1993	18 July 1996	Violation
Richards v. Jamaica (V)	535/1993	31 March 1997	Violation
Steadman v. Jamaica (V)	528/1993	2 April 1997	Violation
Morrison v. Jamaica (V)	663/1995	3 November 1998	Violation
Levy v. Jamaica (V)	719/1996	3 November 1998	Violation
Marshall v. Jamaica (V)	730/1996	3 November 1998	Violation
Brown and Parish v. Jamaica (V)	665/1995	29 July 1999	Violation

ARTICLE 6(4)

Name of case	Comm. No.	Date of Decision	Outcome
Yasseen and Thomas v. Republic of Guyana (V)	676/1996	30 March 1998	Violation

ARTICLE 6(5)

Name of case	Comm. No.	Date of Decision	Outcome
Allen v. Jamaica (V)	332/1988	31 March 1994	No violation
C. Johnson v. Jamaica (V)	592/1994	20 October 1998	Violation

ARTICLE 7

Name of case	Comm. No.	Date of Decision	Outcome
Bleier v. Uruguay (V)	30/1978 (R.7/30)	29 March 1982	Violation
Izquierdo v. Uruguay (V)	73/1981 (R.18/73)	1 April 1982	Violation
A.M. v. Denmark (A)	121/1982 (R.26/121)	23 July 1982	Inadmissible
Masslotti and Baritussio v. Uruguay (V)	25/1978 (R.6/25)	26 July 1982	Violation
Marais v. Madagascar (V)	49/1979	24 March 1983	Violation
Estrella v. Uruguay (V)	74/1980	29 March 1983	Violation
Larrosa v. Uruguay (V)	88/1981	29 March 1983	Violation
Vasilskis v. Uruguay (V)	80/1980	31 March 1983	Violation
Quinteros v. Uruguay (V)	107/1981	21 July 1983	Violation
Viana v. Uruguay (V)	110/1981	29 March 1984	Violation
Muteba v. Zaire (V)	124/1982	24 July 1984	Violation
M. F. v. The Netherlands (A)	173/1984	2 November 1984	Inadmissible
Wight v. Madagascar (V)	115/1982	1 April 1985	Violation
Conteris v. Uruguay (V)	139/1983	17 July 1985	Violation
Arzuada v. Uruguay (V)	147/1983	1 November 1985	Violation
Cariboni v. Uruguay (V)	159/1983	27 October 1987	Violation
Miango v. Zaire (V)	194/1985	27 October 1987	Violation
Herrera v. Colombia (V)	161/1983	2 November 1987	Violation
Penarrieta et al. v. Bolivia (V)	176/1984	2 November 1987	Violation
Portorreal v. Dominican Republic (V)	188/1984	5 November 1987	Violation
Acosta v. Uruguay (V)	162/1983	25 October 1988	Violation
J.H. v. Finland (A)	300/1988	23 March 1989	Inadmissible
R.M. v. Finland (A)	301/1988	23 March 1989	Inadmissible
H. C. M. A. v. The Netherlands (A)	213/1986	30 March 1989	Inadmissible
Pratt and Morgan v. Jamaica (V)	225/1987	6 April 1989	Violation
Vuolanne v. Finland (V)	265/1987	7 April 1989	Violation
Birindwa and Tshisekedi v. Zaire (V)	241 & 242/1987	2 November 1989	Violation
Torres v. Finland (V)	291/1988	2 April 1990	Violation
Reid v. Jamaica (V)	250/1987	20 July 1990	Violation

Name of case	Comm. No.	Date of Decision	Outcome
Collins v. Jamaica (V)	240/1987	1 November 1991	Violation
García v. Ecuador (V)	319/1988	5 November 1991	Violation
Jijón v. Ecuador (V)	277/1988	26 March 1992	Violation
Prince v. Jamaica (V)	269/1987	30 March 1992	No violation
Barrett and Sutcliffe v. Jamaica (V)	270 & 271/1988	30 March 1992	Violation
Ellis v. Jamaica (V)	276/1988	28 July 1992	No violation
Linton v. Jamaica (V)	255/1987	22 October 1992	Violation
Griffiths v. Jamaica (V)	274/1988	24 March 1993	No violation
Martin v. Jamaica (V)	317/1988	24 March 1993	No violation
Francis v. Jamaica (V)	320/1988	24 March 1993	Violation
Bailey v. Jamaica (V)	334/1988	31 March 1993	Violation
Soogrim v. Trinidad and Tobago (V)	362/1989	8 April 1993	Violation
Kindler v. Canada (V)	470/1991	30 July 1993	No violation
Thomas v. Jamaica (V)	321/1988	19 October 1993	Violation
Kanana v. Zaire (V)	366/1989	2 November 1993	Violation
Ng v. Canada (V)	469/1991	5 November 1993	Violation
El-Megreisi v. Libyan Arab Jamahiriya (V)	440/1990	23 March 1994	Violation
Grant v. Jamaica (V)	353/1988	31 March 1994	No violation
Berry v. Jamaica (V)	330/1988	7 April 1994	Violation
Bozize v. Central African Republic (V)	428/1990	7 April 1994	Violation
Hylton v. Jamaica (V)	407/1990	8 July 1994	Violation
Mika Miha v. Equatorial Guinea (V)	414/1990	8 July 1994	Violation
Mojica v. Dominican Republic (V)	449/1991	15 July 1994	Violation
Rodríguez v. Uruguay (V)	322/1988	19 July 1994	Violation
Blanco v. Nicaragua (V)	328/1988	20 July 1994	Violation
Mukong v. Cameroon (V)	458/1991	21 July 1994	Violation
Cox v. Canada (V)	539/1993	31 October 1994	No violation
Simms v. Jamaica (A)	541/1993	3 April 1995	Inadmissible
Rogers v. Jamaica (A)	494/1992	4 April 1995	Inadmissible
Peart and Peart v. Jamaica (DJ), (V)	464 & 482/1991	19 July 1995	Violation
Francis v. Jamaica (V)	606/1994	25 July 1995	Violation
Stephens v. Jamaica (V)	373/1989	18 October 1995	Violation
Lubuto v. Zambia (V)	390/1990	31 October 1995	Violation
Chaplin v. Jamaica (V)	596/1994	2 November 1995	Violation
E. Johnson v. Jamaica (V)	588/1994	22 March 1996	Violation

Name of case	Comm. No.	Date of Decision	Outcome
Graham and Morrison v. Jamaica (V)	461/1991	25 March 1996	Violation
Celis Laureano v. Peru (V)	540/1993	25 March 1996	Violation
Tshishimbi v. Zaire (V)	542/1993	25 March 1996	Violation
Fuenzalida v. Ecuador (V)	480/1991	12 July 1996	Violation
Pinto v. Trinidad and Tobago (V)	512/1992	16 July 1996	Violation
Hylton v. Jamaica (V)	600/1994	16 July 1996	No violation
Lewis v. Jamaica (V)	527/1993	18 July 1996	Violation
Spence v. Jamaica (V)	599/1994	18 July 1996	Violation
Sterling v. Jamaica (V)	598/1994	22 July 1996	Violation
Henry and Douglas v. Jamaica (V)	571/1994	25 July 1996	Violation
Adams v. Jamaica (V)	607/1994	30 October 1996	Violation
Canepa v. Canada (V)	558/1993	3 April 1997	No violation
Reynolds v. Jamaica (V)	587/1994	3 April 1997	Violation
Ortega v. Ecuador (V)	481/1991	8 April 1997	Violation
Blaine v. Jamaica (V)	696/1996	17 July 1997	Violation
McLawrence v. Jamaica (V)	702/1996	18 July 1997	Violation
Edwards v. Jamaica (V)	529/1993	28 July 1997	Violation
A.R.J. v. Australia (V)	692/1996	28 July 1997	No violation
Arhuaco v. Colombia (V)	612/1995	29 July 1997	Violation
Singh v. Canada (A)	761/1997	29 July 1997	Inadmissible
LaVende v. Trinidad and Tobago (V)	554/1993	29 October 1997	Violation
Bickaroo v. Trinidad and Tobago (V)	555/1993	29 October 1997	No violation
Williams v. Jamaica (V)	609/1995	4 November 1997	Violation
Young v. Jamaica (V)	615/1995	4 November 1997	Violation
G.T. v. Australia (V)	706/1996	4 November 1997	No violation
Yasseen and Thomas v. Republic of Guyana (V)	676/1996	30 March 1998	Violation
McTaggart v. Jamaica (V)	749/1997	31 March 1998	Violation
Shaw v. Jamaica (V)	704/1996	2 April 1998	Violation
Taylor v. Jamaica (V)	705/1996	2 April 1998	Violation
Domukovsky et al. v. Georgia (V)	623, 624, 626 & 627/1995	6 April 1998	Violation
Chung v. Jamaica (V)	591/1994	9 April 1998	Violation
Deidrick v. Jamaica (V)	619/1995	9 April 1998	Violation

Name of case	Comm. No.	Date of Decision	Outcome
Morrison v. Jamaica (V)	635/1995	27 July 1998	Violation
Whyte v. Jamaica (V)	732/1997	27 July 1998	Violation
Chadee et al. v. Trinidad and Tobago (V)	813/1998	29 July 1998	No violation
Perkins v. Jamaica (V)	733/1997	30 July 1998	Violation
Leslie v. Jamaica (V)	564/1993	31 July 1998	Violation
Finn v. Jamaica (V)	617/1995	31 July 1998	Violation
Daley v. Jamaica (V)	750/1997	31 July 1998	Violation
C. Johnson v. Jamaica (V)	592/1994	20 October 1998	Violation
Henry v. Jamaica (V)	610/1995	20 October 1998	Violation
Pennant v. Jamaica (V)	647/1995	20 October 1998	Violation
Colin Johnson v. Jamaica (V)	653/1995	20 October 1998	Violation
Morrison v. Jamaica (V)	663/1995	3 November 1998	Violation
Henry v. Trinidad and Tobago (V)	752/1997	3 November 1998	Violation
Brown v. Jamaica (V)	775/1997	23 March 1999	Violation
Fraser and Fisher v. Jamaica (V)	722/1996	31 March 1999	No violation
Smith and Stewart v. Jamaica (V)	668/1995	8 April 1999	Violation
Leehong v. Jamaica (V)	613/1995	13 July 1999	Violation
Ajaz and Jamil v. Republic of Korea (V)	644/1995	13 July 1999	No violation
Bailey v. Jamaica (V)	709/1996	21 July 1999	Violation
Gallimore v. Jamaica (V)	680/1996	23 July 1999	Violation
Rawle Kennedy v. Trinidad and Tobago (A)	845/1999	2 November 1999	Admissible
Osbourne v. Jamaica (V)	759/1997	15 March 2000	Violation
Freemantle v. Jamaica (V)	625/1995	24 March 2000	Violation
Robinson v. Jamaica (V)	731/1996	29 March 2000	Violation
Thompson v. Saint Vincent and the Grenadines (V)	806/1998	18 October 2000	Violation
Jensen v. Australia (A)	762/1997	22 March 2001	Inadmissible
Rojas García v. Colombia (V)	687/1996	3 April 2001	Violation
Sookal v. Trinidad and Tobago (V)	928/2000	25 October 2001	Violation

ARTICLE 8

Name of case	Comm. No.	Date of Decision	Outcome
Maille v. France (V)	689/1996	10 July 2000	Violation
Venier and Nicolas v. France (V)	690 & 691/1996	10 July 2000	Violation

ARTICLE 9

Name of case	Comm. No.	Date of Decision	Outcome
Bleier v. Uruguay (V)	30/1978 (R.7/30)	29 March 1982	Violation
Quinteros v. Uruguay (V)	107/1981	21 July 1983	Violation
V.M.R.B. v. Canada (A)	236/1987	18 July 1988	Inadmissible
H. C. M. A. v. The Netherlands (A)	213/1986	30 March 1989	Inadmissible
J.R.C. v. Costa Rica (A)	296/1988	30 March 1989	Inadmissible
Arévalo v. Colombia (V)	181/1984	3 November 1989	Violation
van Alphen v. The Netherlands (V)	305/1988	23 July 1990	Violation
Kelly v. Jamaica (V)	253/1987	8 April 1991	Violation
García v. Ecuador (V)	319/1988	5 November 1991	Violation
Jijón v. Ecuador (V)	277/1988	26 March 1992	Violation
El-Megreisi v. Libyan Arab Jamahiriya (V)	440/1990	23 March 1994	Violation
Bozize v. Central African Republic (V)	428/1990	7 April 1994	Violation
Mika Miha v. Equatorial Guinea (V)	414/1990	8 July 1994	Violation
Mukong v. Cameroon (V)	458/1991	21 July 1994	Violation
Peart and Peart v. Jamaica (DJ), (V)	464 & 482/1991	19 July 1995	Violation
Bautista v. Colombia (V)	563/1993	27 October 1995	Violation
Fuenzalida v. Ecuador (V)	480/1991	12 July 1996	Violation
Arhuaco v. Colombia (V)	612/1995	29 July 1997	Violation
G.T. v. Australia (V)	706/1996	4 November 1997	No violation
McTaggart v. Jamaica (V)	749/1997	31 March 1998	Violation
Whyte v. Jamaica (V)	732/1997	27 July 1998	Violation
Perkins v. Jamaica (V)	733/1997	30 July 1998	Violation
Daley v. Jamaica (V)	750/1997	31 July 1998	Violation

ARTICLE 9(1)

Name of case	Comm. No.	Date of Decision	Outcome
Massera et al. v. Uruguay (V)	5/1977 (R.1/5)	15 August 1979	Violation
Weismann and Perdomo v. Uruguay (V)	8/1977	3 April 1980	Violation
Ramirez v. Uruguay (V)	4/1977 (R.1/4)	23 July 1980	Violation
Carballal v. Uruguay (V)	33/1978	27 March 1981	Violation
Burgos v. Uruguay (V)	52/1979	29 July 1981	Violation
Casariego v. Uruguay (V)	56/1979	29 July 1981	Violation
Masslotti and Baritussio v. Uruguay (V)	25/1978 (R.6/25)	26 July 1982	Violation
Schweizer v. Uruguay (V)	66/1980	12 October 1982	Violation
Luyeye v. Zaire (V)	90/1981	21 July 1983	Violation
Jaona v. Madagascar (V)	132/1982	1 April 1985	Violation
Conteris v. Uruguay (V)	139/1983	17 July 1985	Violation
Mpandanjila et al. v. Zaire (V)	138/1983	26 March 1986	Violation
Mpaka-Nsusu v. Zaire (V)	157/1983	26 March 1986	Violation
Portorreal v. Dominican Republic (V)	188/1984	5 November 1987	Violation
G. F. Croes v. The Netherlands (A)	164/1984	7 November 1988	Inadmissible
Delgado Páez v. Colombia (V)	195/1985	12 July 1990	Violation
Campbell v. Jamaica (V)	248/1987	30 March 1992	Violation
González del Rio v. Peru (V)	263/1987	28 October 1992	Violation
Bwalya v. Zambia (V)	314/1988	14 July 1993	Violation
Bahamonde v. Equatorial Guinea (V)	468/1991	20 October 1993	Violation
Kanana v. Zaire (V)	366/1989	2 November 1993	Violation
Mojica v. Dominican Republic (V)	449/1991	15 July 1994	Violation
Blanco v. Nicaragua (V)	328/1988	20 July 1994	Violation
Colamarco v. Panama (A)	437/1990	21 October 1994	Inadmissible

Name of case	Comm. No.	Date of Decision	Outcome
Thompson v. Panama (A)	438/1990	21 October 1994	Inadmissible
Celis Laureano v. Peru (V)	540/1993	25 March 1996	Violation
Tshishimbi v. Zaire (V)	542/1993	25 March 1996	Violation
Aduayom et al. v. Togo (V)	422, 423, & 424/1990	12 July 1996	Violation
A. v. Australia (V)	560/1993	3 April 1997	Violation
Domukovsky et al. v. Georgia (V)	623, 624, 626 & 627/1995	6 April 1998	Violation
Forbes v. Jamaica (V)	649/1995	20 October 1998	Violation
Leehong v. Jamaica (V)	613/1995	13 July 1999	Violation
A v. New Zealand (V)	754/1997	15 July 1999	No violation
Spakmo v. Norway (V)	631/1995	5 November 1999	Violation
Dias v. Angola (V)	711/1996	20 March 2000	Violation
Gridin v. Russian Federation (V)	770/1997	20 July 2000	Violation
Arredondo v. Peru (V)	688/1996	27 July 2000	Violation
Chongwe v. Zambia (V)	821/1998	25 October 2000	Violation

ARTICLE 9(2)

Name of case	Comm. No.	Date of Decision	Outcome
Carballal v. Uruguay (V)	33/1978	27 March 1981	Violation
Pietraroia v. Uruguay (V)	44/1979	27 March 1981	Violation
Caldas v. Uruguay (V)	43/1979	21 July 1983	Violation
Luyeye v. Zaire (V)	90/1981	21 July 1983	Violation
Jaona v. Madagascar (V)	132/1982	1 April 1985	Violation
Conteris v. Uruguay (V)	139/1983	17 July 1985	Violation
Portorreal v. Dominican Republic (V)	188/1984	5 November 1987	Violation
Birindwa and Tshisekedi v. Zaire (V)	241 & 242/1987	2 November 1989	Violation
Fillastre and Bizouarn v. Bolivia (V)	336/1988	5 November 1991	Violation
Kalenga v. Zambia (V)	326/1988	27 July 1993	Violation
Thompson v. Panama (A)	438/1990	21 October 1994	Inadmissible
Griffin v. Spain (V)	493/1992	4 April 1995	Violation
Stephens v. Jamaica (V)	373/1989	18 October 1995	Violation
Grant v. Jamaica (V)	597/1994	22 March 1996	Violation
Hill v. Spain (V)	526/1993	2 April 1997	Violation
Blaine v. Jamaica (V)	696/1996	17 July 1997	Violation

Name of case	Comm. No.	Date of Decision	Outcome
McLawrence v. Jamaica (V)	702/1996	18 July 1997	Violation
Taylor v. Jamaica (V)	707/1996	18 July 1997	Violation
Shaw v. Jamaica (V)	704/1996	2 April 1998	Violation
Taylor v. Jamaica (V)	705/1996	2 April 1998	Violation
Jones v. Jamaica (V)	585/1994	6 April 1998	Violation
Domukovsky et al. v. Georgia (V)	623, 624, 626 & 627/1995	6 April 1998	Violation
Morrison v. Jamaica (V)	635/1995	27 July 1998	Violation
Morrison v. Jamaica (V)	663/1995	3 November 1998	Violation
Freemantle v. Jamaica (V)	625/1995	24 March 2000	Violation

ARTICLE 9(3)

Name of case	Comm. No.	Date of Decision	Outcome
Massera et al. v. Uruguay (V)	5/1977 (R.1/5)	15 August 1979	Violation
Weismann and Perdomo v. Uruguay (V)	8/1977	3 April 1980	Violation
Sequeira v. Uruguay (V)	6/1977	29 July 1980	Violation
Motta et al. v. Uruguay (V)	11/1977	29 July 1980	Violation
Weinberger v. Uruguay (V)	28/1978	29 October 1980	Violation
Carballal v. Uruguay (V)	33/1978	27 March 1981	Violation
de Bouton v. Uruguay (V)	37/1978	27 March 1981	Violation
Pietraroia v. Uruguay (V)	44/1979	27 March 1981	Violation
Touron v. Uruguay (V)	32/1978	31 March 1981	Violation
Burgos v. Uruguay (V)	52/1979	29 July 1981	Violation
Sendic v. Uruguay (V)	63/1979 (R.14/63)	28 October 1981	Violation
Altesor v. Uruguay (V)	10/1977 (R.2/10)	29 March 1982	Violation
Borda et al. v. Colombia (V)	46/1979 (R.11/46)	27 July 1982	Violation
Schweizer v. Uruguay (V)	66/1980	12 October 1982	Violation
Barbato v. Uruguay (V)	84/1981	21 October 1982	Violation
Luyeye v. Zaire (V)	90/1981	21 July 1983	Violation
Muteba v. Zaire (V)	124/1982	24 July 1984	Violation
Conteris v. Uruguay (V)	139/1983	17 July 1985	Violation

Name of case	Comm. No.	Date of Decision	Outcome
Solorzano v. Venezuela (V)	156/1983	26 March 1986	Violation
Penarrieta et al. v. Bolivia (V)	176/1984	2 November 1987	Violation
Bolaños v. Ecuador (V)	238/1987	26 July 1989	Violation
Birindwa and Tshisekedi v. Zaire (V)	241 & 242/1987	2 November 1989	Violation
Fillastre and Bizouarn v. Bolivia (V)	336/1988	5 November 1991	Violation
Wolf v. Panama (V)	289/1988	26 March 1992	Violation
Campbell v. Jamaica (V)	248/1987	30 March 1992	Violation
W. B. E. v. The Netherlands (A)	432/1990	23 October 1992	Inadmissible
Bwalya v. Zambia (V)	314/1988	14 July 1993	Violation
Kalenga v. Zambia (V)	326/1988	27 July 1993	Violation
Bahamonde v. Equatorial Guinea (V)	468/1991	20 October 1993	Violation
Berry v. Jamaica (V)	330/1988	7 April 1994	Violation
Koné v. Senegal (V)	386/1989	21 October 1994	Violation
Shalto v. Trinidad and Tobago (V)	447/1991	4 April 1995	Violation
del Cid v. Panama (V)	473/1991	19 July 1995	Violation
Stephens v. Jamaica (V)	373/1989	18 October 1995	Violation
Kulomin v. Hungary (V)	521/1992	22 March 1996	Violation
Grant v. Jamaica (V)	597/1994	22 March 1996	Violation
Neptune v. Trinidad and Tobago (V)	523/1992	16 July 1996	Violation
Henry and Douglas v. Jamaica (V)	571/1994	25 July 1996	Violation
Hill v. Spain (V)	526/1993	2 April 1997	Violation
Steadman v.Jamaica (V)	528/1993	2 April 1997	Violation
Lewis v. Jamaica (V)	708/1996	17 July 1997	Violation
McLawrence v. Jamaica (V)	702/1996	18 July 1997	Violation
Taylor v. Jamaica (V)	707/1996	18 July 1997	Violation
Elahie v. Trinidad and Tobago (V)	533/1993	28 July 1997	Violation
Walker and Richards v. Jamaica (V)	639/1995	28 July 1997	Violation
Shaw v. Jamaica (V)	704/1996	2 April 1998	Violation
Taylor v. Jamaica (V)	705/1996	2 April 1998	Violation
Jones v. Jamaica (V)	585/1994	6 April 1998	Violation
Morrison v. Jamaica (V)	635/1995	27 July 1998	Violation
Smart v. Trinidad and Tobago (V)	672/1995	29 July 1998	Violation
Finn v. Jamaica (V)	617/1995	31 July 1998	Violation

Name of case	Comm. No.	Date of Decision	Outcome
Pennant v. Jamaica (V)	647/1995	20 October 1998	Violation
Morrison v. Jamaica (V)	663/1995	3 November 1998	Violation
Marshall v. Jamaica (V)	730/1996	3 November 1998	Violation
Brown v. Jamaica (V)	775/1997	23 March 1999	Violation
Bennett v. Jamaica (V)	590/1994	25 March 1999	Violation
Leehong v. Jamaica (V)	613/1995	13 July 1999	Violation
Hamilton v. Jamaica (V)	616/1995	23 July 1999	Violation
Brown and Parish v. Jamaica (V)	665/1995	29 July 1999	Violation
Freemantle v. Jamaica (V)	625/1995	24 March 2000	Violation
Arredondo v. Peru (V)	688/1996	27 July 2000	Violation
Sextus v. Trinidad and Tobago (V)	818/1998	16 July 2001	Violation
Sookal v. Trinidad and Tobago (V)	928/2000	25 October 2001	Violation

ARTICLE 9(4)

Name of case	Comm. No.	Date of Decision	Outcome
Massera et al. v. Uruguay (V)	5/1977 (R.1/5)	15 August 1979	Violation
Valcada v. Uruguay (V)	9/1977	26 October 1979	Violation
Weismann and Perdomo v. Uruguay (V)	8/1977	3 April 1980	Violation
Ramirez v. Uruguay (V)	4/1977 (R.1/4)	23 July 1980	Violation
Sequeira v. Uruguay (V)	6/1977	29 July 1980	Violation
Motta et al. v. Uruguay (V)	11/1977	29 July 1980	Violation
Weinberger v. Uruguay (V)	28/1978	29 October 1980	Violation
Carballal v. Uruguay (V)	33/1978	27 March 1981	Violation
de Bouton v. Uruguay (V)	37/1978	27 March 1981	Violation
Pietraroia v. Uruguay (V)	44/1979	27 March 1981	Violation
Touron v. Uruguay (V)	32/1978	31 March 1981	Violation
Altesor v. Uruguay (V)	10/1977 (R.2/10)	29 March 1982	Violation
Masslotti and Baritussio v. Uruguay (V)	25/1978 (R.6/25)	26 July 1982	Violation
Borda et al. v. Colombia (V)	46/1979 (R.11/46)	27 July 1982	Violation

Name of case	Comm. No.	Date of Decision	Outcome
Schweizer v. Uruguay (V)	66/1980	12 October 1982	Violation
Barbato v. Uruguay (V)	84/1981	21 October 1982	Violation
Caldas v. Uruguay (V)	43/1979	21 July 1983	Violation
Luyeye v. Zaire (V)	90/1981	21 July 1983	Violation
Muteba v. Zaire (V)	124/1982	24 July 1984	Violation
Conteris v. Uruguay (V)	139/1983	17 July 1985	Violation
Solorzano v. Venezuela (V)	156/1983	26 March 1986	Violation
Hammel v. Madagascar (V)	155/1983	3 April 1987	Violation
Vuolanne v. Finland (V)	265/1987	7 April 1989	Violation
Torres v. Finland (V)	291/1988	2 April 1990	Violation
Campbell v. Jamaica (V)	248/1987	30 March 1992	Violation
González del Rio v. Peru (V)	263/1987	28 October 1992	Violation
Kalenga v. Zambia (V)	326/1988	27 July 1993	Violation
Berry v. Jamaica (V)	330/1988	7 April 1994	Violation
del Cid v. Panama (V)	473/1991	19 July 1995	Violation
Stephens v. Jamaica (V)	373/1989	18 October 1995	Violation
Grant v. Jamaica (V)	597/1994	22 March 1996	Violation
A. v. Australia (V)	560/1993	3 April 1997	Violation
Pennant v. Jamaica (V)	647/1995	20 October 1998	Violation
A. v. New Zealand (V)	754/1997	15 July 1999	No violation
Freemantle v. Jamaica (V)	625/1995	24 March 2000	Violation

ARTICLE 9(5)

Name of case	Comm. No.	Date of Decision	Outcome
Bolaños v. Ecuador (V)	238/1987	26 July 1989	Violation
W. B. E. v. The Netherlands (A)	432/1990	23 October 1992	Inadmissible
A. v. Australia (V)	560/1993	3 April 1997	Violation

ARTICLE 10

Name of case	Comm. No.	Date of Decision	Outcome
Manera v. Uruguay (V)	123/1982	6 April 1984	Violation
Kelly v. Jamaica (V)	253/1987	8 April 1991	Violation
Fillastre and Bizouarn v. Bolivia (V)	336/1988	5 November 1991	Violation
Jijón v. Ecuador (V)	277/1988	26 March 1992	Violation
Wolf v. Panama (V)	289/1988	26 March 1992	Violation
Barrett and Sutcliffe v. Jamaica (V)	270 & 271/1988	30 March 1992	Violation

Name of case	Comm. No.	Date of Decision	Outcome
Wright v. Jamaica (V)	349/1989	27 July 1992	Violation
Párkányi v. Hungary (V)	410/1990	27 July 1992	Violation
Ng v. Canada (V)	469/1991	5 November 1993	Violation
Grant v. Jamaica (V)	353/1988	31 March 1994	No violation
Bozize v. Central African Republic (V)	428/1990	7 April 1994	Violation
Rogers v. Jamaica (A)	494/1992	4 April 1995	Inadmissible
Kulomin v. Hungary (V)	521/1992	22 March 1996	Violation
Fuenzalida v. Ecuador (V)	480/1991	12 July 1996	Violation
Hill v. Spain (V)	526/1993	2 April 1997	Violation
McLawrence v. Jamaica (V)	702/1996	18 July 1997	Violation
Whyte v. Jamaica (V)	732/1997	27 July 1998	Violation
Perkins v. Jamaica (V)	733/1997	30 July 1998	Violation
Daley v. Jamaica (V)	750/1997	31 July 1998	Violation
D. Thomas v. Jamaica (V)	800/1998	8 April 1999	Violation
Bailey v. Jamaica (V)	709/1996	21 July 1999	Violation
Gallimore v. Jamaica (V)	680/1996	23 July 1999	Violation
Wuyts v. The Netherlands (A)	785/1997	17 July 2000	Inadmissible

ARTICLE 10(1)

Name of case	Comm. No.	Date of Decision	Outcome
Massera et al. v. Uruguay (V)	5/1977 (R.1/5)	15 August 1979	Violation
Weismann and Perdomo v. Uruguay (V)	8/1977	3 April 1980	Violation
Ramirez v. Uruguay (V)	4/1977 (R.1/4)	23 July 1980	Violation
Motta et al. v. Uruguay (V)	11/1977	29 July 1980	Violation
Weinberger v. Uruguay (V)	28/1978	29 October 1980	Violation
Carballal v. Uruguay (V)	33/1978	27 March 1981	Violation
de Bouton v. Uruguay (V)	37/1978	27 March 1981	Violation
Pietraroia v. Uruguay (V)	44/1979	27 March 1981	Violation
Casariego v. Uruguay (V)	56/1979	29 July 1981	Violation
Sendic v. Uruguay (V)	63/1979 (R.14/63)	28 October 1981	Violation

Name of case	Comm. No.	Date of Decision	Outcome
Pinkney v. Canada (V)	27/1977 (R.7/27)	29 October 1981	Violation
Altesor v. Uruguay (V)	10/1977 (R.2/10)	29 March 1982	Violation
Bleier v. Uruguay (V)	30/1978 (R.7/30)	29 March 1982	Violation
Simones v. Uruguay (V)	70/1981 (R.17/70)	1 April 1982	Violation
Izquierdo v. Uruguay (V)	73/1981 (R.18/73)	1 April 1982	Violation
Masslotti and Baritussio v. Uruguay (V)	25/1978 (R.6/25)	26 July 1982	Violation
Schweizer v. Uruguay (V)	66/1980	12 October 1982	Violation
Marais v. Madagascar (V)	49/1979	24 March 1983	Violation
Estrella v. Uruguay (V)	74/1980	29 March 1983	Violation
Larrosa v. Uruguay (V)	88/1981	29 March 1983	Violation
Vasilskis v. Uruguay (V)	80/1980	31 March 1983	Violation
Caldas v. Uruguay (V)	43/1979	21 July 1983	Violation
Luyeye v. Zaire (V)	90/1981	21 July 1983	Violation
Estradet v. Uruguay (V)	105/1981	21 July 1983	Violation
Quinteros v. Uruguay (V)	107/1981	21 July 1983	Violation
Nieto v. Uruguay (V)	92/1981	25 July 1983	Violation
Machado v. Uruguay (V)	83/1981	4 November 1983	Violation
Romero v. Uruguay (V)	85/1981	29 March 1984	Violation
Viana v. Uruguay (V)	110/1981	29 March 1984	Violation
de Voituret v. Uruguay (V)	109/1981	10 April 1984	Violation
Muteba v. Zaire (V)	124/1982	24 July 1984	Violation
Wight v. Madagascar (V)	115/1982	1 April 1985	Violation
Conteris v. Uruguay (V)	139/1983	17 July 1985	Violation
Arzuada v. Uruguay (V)	147/1983	1 November 1985	Violation
Mpandanjila et al. v. Zaire (V)	138/1983	26 March 1986	Violation
Solorzano v. Venezuela (V)	156/1983	26 March 1986	Violation
Cariboni v. Uruguay (V)	159/1983	27 October 1987	Violation
Herrera v. Colombia (V)	161/1983	2 November 1987	Violation
Penarrieta et al. v. Bolivia (V)	176/1984	2 November 1987	Violation
Portorreal v. Dominican Republic (V)	188/1984	5 November 1987	Violation
Acosta v. Uruguay (V)	162/1983	25 October 1988	Violation
H. C. M. A. v. The Netherlands (A)	213/1986	30 March 1989	Inadmissible

Name of case	Comm. No.	Date of Decision	Outcome
Vuolanne v. Finland (V)	265/1987	7 April 1989	Violation
Birindwa and Tshisekedi v. Zaire (V)	241 & 242/1987	2 November 1989	Violation
Collins v. Jamaica (V)	240/1987	1 November 1991	Violation
Linton v. Jamaica (V)	255/1987	22 October 1992	Violation
Francis v. Jamaica (V)	320/1988	24 March 1993	Violation
Bailey v. Jamaica (V)	334/1988	31 March 1993	Violation
Soogrim v. Trinidad and Tobago (V)	362/1989	8 April 1993	Violation
Orihuela v. Peru (V)	309/1988	14 July 1993	Violation
Kalenga v. Zambia (V)	326/1988	27 July 1993	Violation
Thomas v. Jamaica (V)	321/1988	19 October 1993	Violation
Kanana v. Zaire (V)	366/1989	2 November 1993	Violation
El-Megreisi v. Libyan Arab Jamahiriya (V)	440/1990	23 March 1994	Violation
Berry v. Jamaica (V)	330/1988	7 April 1994	Violation
Hylton v. Jamaica (V)	407/1990	8 July 1994	Violation
Mika Miha v. Equatorial Guinea (V)	414/1990	8 July 1994	Violation
Blanco v. Nicaragua (V)	328/1988	20 July 1994	Violation
Griffin v. Spain (V)	493/1992	4 April 1995	Violation
Peart and Peart v. Jamaica (DJ), (V)	464 & 482/1991	19 July 1995	Violation
Francis v. Jamaica (V)	606/1994	25 July 1995	Violation
Stephens v. Jamaica (V)	373/1989	18 October 1995	Violation
Chaplin v. Jamaica (V)	596/1994	2 November 1995	Violation
E. Johnson v. Jamaica (V)	588/1994	22 March 1996	Violation
Pinto v. Trinidad and Tobago (V)	512/1992	16 July 1996	Violation
Neptune v. Trinidad and Tobago (V)	523/1992	16 July 1996	Violation
Hylton v. Jamaica (V)	600/1994	16 July 1996	No violation
Lewis v. Jamaica (V)	527/1993	18 July 1996	Violation
Spence v. Jamaica (V)	599/1994	18 July 1996	Violation
Sterling v. Jamaica (V)	598/1994	22 July 1996	Violation
Henry and Douglas v. Jamaica (V)	571/1994	25 July 1996	Violation
Adams v. Jamaica (V)	607/1994	30 October 1996	Violation
Reynolds v. Jamaica (V)	587/1994	3 April 1997	Violation
Ortega v. Ecuador (V)	481/1991	8 April 1997	Violation
Blaine v. Jamaica (V)	696/1996	17 July 1997	Violation
Lewis v. Jamaica (V)	708/1996	17 July 1997	Violation
Taylor v. Jamaica (V)	707/1996	18 July 1997	Violation
Edwards v. Jamaica (V)	529/1993	28 July 1997	Violation
Elahie v. Trinidad and Tobago (V)	533/1993	28 July 1997	Violation

Name of case	Comm. No.	Date of Decision	Outcome
Walker and Richards v. Jamaica (V)	639/1995	28 July 1997	Violation
LaVende v. Trinidad and Tobago (V)	554/1993	29 October 1997	Violation
Bickaroo v. Trinidad and Tobago (V)	555/1993	29 October 1997	No violation
Williams v. Jamaica (V)	609/1995	4 November 1997	Violation
Yasseen and Thomas v. Republic of Guyana (V)	676/1996	30 March 1998	Violation
Matthews v. Trinidad and Tobago (V)	569/1993	31 March 1998	Violation
McLeod v. Jamaica (V)	734/1997	31 March 1998	Violation
Shaw v. Jamaica (V)	704/1996	2 April 1998	Violation
Taylor v. Jamaica (V)	705/1996	2 April 1998	Violation
Jones v. Jamaica (V)	585/1994	6 April 1998	Violation
Domukovsky et al. v. Georgia (V)	623, 624, 626 & 627/1995	6 April 1998	Violation
Chung v. Jamaica (V)	591/1994	9 April 1998	Violation
Deidrick v. Jamaica (V)	619/1995	9 April 1998	Violation
Morrison v. Jamaica (V)	635/1995	27 July 1998	Violation
Leslie v. Jamaica (V)	564/1993	31 July 1998	Violation
Finn v. Jamaica (V)	617/1995	31 July 1998	Violation
Phillip v. Trinidad and Tobago (V)	594/1992	20 October 1998	Violation
Henry v. Jamaica (V)	610/1995	20 October 1998	Violation
Campbell v. Jamaica (V)	618/1995	20 October 1998	Violation
Pennant v. Jamaica (V)	647/1995	20 October 1998	Violation
Forbes v. Jamaica (V)	649/1995	20 October 1998	Violation
Colin Johnson v. Jamaica (V)	653/1995	20 October 1998	Violation
Morrison v. Jamaica (V)	663/1995	3 November 1998	Violation
Levy v. Jamaica (V)	719/1996	3 November 1998	Violation
Morgan and Williams v. Jamaica (V)	720/1996	3 November 1998	Violation
Marshall v. Jamaica (V)	730/1996	3 November 1998	Violation
Henry v. Trinidad and Tobago (V)	752/1997	3 November 1998	Violation
Brown v. Jamaica (V)	775/1997	23 March 1999	Violation
Bennett v. Jamaica (V)	590/1994	25 March 1999	Violation
Fraser and Fisher v. Jamaica (V)	722/1996	31 March 1999	No violation
Smith and Stewart v. Jamaica (V)	668/1995	8 April 1999	Violation
Leehong v. Jamaica (V)	613/1995	13 July 1999	Violation
Hamilton v. Jamaica (V)	616/1995	23 July 1999	Violation
Freemantle v. Jamaica (V)	625/1995	24 March 2000	Violation

Name of case	Comm. No.	Date of Decision	Outcome
Robinson v. Jamaica (V)	731/1996	29 March 2000	Violation
Arredondo v. Peru (V)	688/1996	27 July 2000	Violation
Thompson v. Saint Vincent and the Grenadines (V)	806/1998	18 October 2000	Violation
Jensen v. Australia (A)	762/1997	22 March 2001	Inadmissible
Sextus v. Trinidad and Tobago (V)	818/1998	16 July 2001	Violation
Simpson v. Jamaica (V)	695/1996	31 October 2001	Violation

ARTICLE 10(2)

Name of case	Comm. No.	Date of Decision	Outcome
Pinkney v. Canada (V)	27/1977 (R.7/27)	29 October 1981	Violation
Berry v. Jamaica (V)	330/1988	7 April 1994	Violation
Lewis v. Jamaica (V)	708/1996	17 July 1997	Violation
Yasseen and Thomas v. Republic of Guyana (V)	676/1996	30 March 1998	Violation
Morrison v. Jamaica (V)	663/1995	3 November 1998	Violation

ARTICLE 10(3)

Name of case	Comm. No.	Date of Decision	Outcome
McTaggart v. Jamaica (V)	749/1997	31 March 1998	Violation
Jensen v. Australia (A)	762/1997	22 March 2001	Inadmissible

ARTICLE 12

Name of case	Comm. No.	Date of Decision	Outcome
Lovelace v. Canada (V)	24/1977 (R.6/24)	30 July 1981	Violation
J. M. v. Jamaica (A)	165/1984	26 March 1986	Inadmissible

ARTICLE 12(1)

Name of case	Comm. No.	Date of Decision	Outcome
Mpandanjila et al. v. Zaire (V)	138/1983	26 March 1986	Violation
Mpaka-Nsusu v. Zaire (V)	157/1983	26 March 1986	Violation
Birindwa and Tshisekedi v. Zaire (V)	241 & 242/1987	2 November 1989	Violation

Name of case	Comm. No.	Date of Decision	Outcome
Bwalya v. Zambia (V)	314/1988	14 July 1993	Violation
Kalenga v. Zambia (V)	326/1988	27 July 1993	Violation
Bahamonde v. Equatorial Guinea (V)	468/1991	20 October 1993	Violation
Mika Miha v. Equatorial Guinea (V)	414/1990	8 July 1994	Violation
Celepli v. Sweden (V)	456/1991	18 July 1994	No violation
Peltonen v. Finland (V)	492/1992	21 July 1994	No violation

ARTICLE 12(2)

Name of case	Comm. No.	Date of Decision	Outcome
Martins v. Uruguay (V)	57/1979 (R.13/57)	23 March 1982	Violation
Lichtensztejn v. Uruguay (V)	77/1980	31 March 1983	Violation
Montero v. Uruguay (V)	106/1981	31 March 1983	Violation
Nunez v. Uruguay (V)	108/1981	22 July 1983	Violation
González del Rio v. Peru (V)	263/1987	28 October 1992	Violation
Bahamonde v. Equatorial Guinea (V)	468/1991	20 October 1993	Violation
Mika Miha v. Equatorial Guinea (V)	414/1990	8 July 1994	Violation

ARTICLE 12(3)

Name of case	Comm. No.	Date of Decision	Outcome
Celepli v. Sweden (V)	456/1991	18 July 1994	No violation
Peltonen v. Finland (V)	492/1992	21 July 1994	No violation
Karker v. France (V)	833/1998	26 October 2000	No violation

ARTICLE 12(4)

Name of case	Comm. No.	Date of Decision	Outcome
Stewart v. Canada (V)	538/1993	1 November 1996	No violation
Canepa v. Canada (V)	558/1993	3 April 1997	No violation
Toala et al. v. New Zealand (V)	675/1995	2 November 2000	No violation

ARTICLE 13

Name of case	Comm. No.	Date of Decision	Outcome
Hammel v. Madagascar (V)	155/1983	3 April 1987	Violation
V.M.R. B. v. Canada (A)	236/1987	18 July 1988	Inadmissible
Giry v. Dominican Republic (V)	193/1985	20 July 1990	Violation
García v. Ecuador (V)	319/1988	5 November 1991	Violation
Karker v. France (V)	833/1998	26 October 2000	No violation

ARTICLE 13(2)

Name of case	Comm. No.	Date of Decision	Outcome
Sohn v. Republic of Korea (V)	518/1992	19 July 1995	Violation

ARTICLE 14

Name of case	Comm. No.	Date of Decision	Outcome
Burgos v. Uruguay (V)	52/1979	29 July 1981	Violation
A.M. v. Denmark (A)	121/1982 (R.26/121)	23 July 1982	Inadmissible
Borda et al. v. Colombia (V)	46/1979 (R.11/46)	27 July 1982	Violation
V.M.R.B. v. Canada (A)	236/1987	18 July 1988	Inadmissible
Muñoz v. Peru (V)	203/1986	4 November 1988	Violation
J.R.C. v. Costa Rica (A)	296/1988	30 March 1989	Inadmissible
Pratt and Morgan v. Jamaica (V)	225/1987	6 April 1989	Violation
Reid v. Jamaica (V)	250/1987	20 July 1990	Violation
Little v. Jamaica (V)	283/1988	1 November 1991	Violation
Jijón v. Ecuador (V)	277/1988	26 March 1992	Violation
Wolf v. Panama (V)	289/1988	26 March 1992	Violation
Barrett and Sutcliffe v. Jamaica (V)	270 & 271/1988	30 March 1992	Violation
Ellis v. Jamaica (V)	276/1988	28 July 1992	No violation
Cox v. Canada (V)	539/1993	31 October 1994	No violation
de Groot v. The Netherlands (A)	578/1994	14 July 1995	Inadmissible
Simunek et al. v. Czech Republic (V)	516/1992	19 July 1995	Violation
Kulomin v. Hungary (V)	521/1992	22 March 1996	Violation
Adu v. Canada (A)	654/1995	18 July 1997	Inadmissible
Hopu and Bessert v. France (V)	549/1993	29 July 1997	Violation

Name of case	Comm. No.	Date of Decision	Outcome
Arhuaco v. Colombia (V)	612/1995	29 July 1997	Violation
Ajaz and Jamil v. Republic of Korea (V)	644/1995	13 July 1999	No violation
Hankle v. Jamaica (V)	710/1996	28 July 1999	No violation
G. v. Canada (A)	934/2000	17 July 2000	Inadmissible
Piandiong et al. v. Philippines (V)	869/1999	19 October 2000	No violation
Rogl v. Germany (A)	808/1998	25 October 2000	Inadmissible

ARTICLE 14(1)

Name of case	Comm. No.	Date of Decision	Outcome
Massera et al. v. Uruguay (V)	5/1977 (R.1/5)	15 August 1979	Violation
Weismann and Perdomo v. Uruguay (V)	8/1977	3 April 1980	Violation
Sequeira v. Uruguay (V)	6/1977	29 July 1980	Violation
Weinberger v. Uruguay (V)	28/1978	29 October 1980	Violation
Pietraroia v. Uruguay (V)	44/1979	27 March 1981	Violation
Touron v. Uruguay (V)	32/1978	31 March 1981	Violation
Altesor v. Uruguay (V)	10/1977 (R.2/10)	29 March 1982	Violation
Simones v. Uruguay (V)	70/1981 (R.17/70)	1 April 1982	Violation
Estrella v. Uruguay (V)	74/1980	29 March 1983	Violation
Vasilskis v. Uruguay (V)	80/1980	31 March 1983	Violation
C.A. v. Italy (A)	127/1982	31 March 1983	Inadmissible
J.K. v. Canada (A)	174/1984	26 October 1984	Inadmissible
Conteris v. Uruguay (V)	139/1983	17 July 1985	Violation
Mpandanjila et al. v. Zaire (V)	138/1983	26 March 1986	Violation
Y.L. v. Canada (A)	112/1981	8 April 1986	Inadmissible
F. G. G. v The Netherlands (A)	209/1986	25 March 1987	Inadmissible
Cariboni v. Uruguay (V)	159/1983	27 October 1987	Violation
Avellanal v. Peru (V)	202/1986	28 October 1988	Violation
J.H. v. Finland (A)	300/1988	23 March 1989	Inadmissible
R.M. v. Finland (A)	301/1988	23 March 1989	Inadmissible
H. C. M. A. v. The Netherlands (A)	213/1986	30 March 1989	Inadmissible
Robinson v. Jamaica (V)	223/1987	30 March 1989	Violation
B. d. B. et al. v. The Netherlands (A)	273/1989	30 March 1989	Inadmissible

Name of case	Comm. No.	Date of Decision	Outcome
Morael v. France (V)	207/1986	28 July 1989	No violation
van Meurs v. The Netherlands (V)	215/1986	13 July 1990	Violation
Guesdon v. France (V)	219/1986	25 July 1990	No violation
Sawyers and McLean v. Jamaica (V)	226 & 256/1987	11 April 1991	No violation
Barzhig v. France (V)	327/1988	11 April 1991	No violation
Z.P. v. Canada (A)	341/1988	11 April 1991	Inadmissible
Collins v. Jamaica (V)	240/1987	1 November 1991	Violation
Wolf v. Panama (V)	289/1988	26 March 1992	Violation
Campbell v. Jamaica (V)	248/1987	30 March 1992	Violation
Thomas v. Jamaica (V)	272/1988	31 March 1992	Violation
Hibbert v. Jamaica (V)	293/1988	27 July 1992	No violation
Wright v. Jamaica (V)	349/1989	27 July 1992	Violation
Párkányi v. Hungary (V)	410/1990	27 July 1992	Violation
Linton v. Jamaica (V)	255/1987	22 October 1992	Violation
Karttunen v. Finland (V)	387/1989	23 October 1992	Violation
González del Rio v. Peru (V)	263/1987	28 October 1992	Violation
Gordon v. Jamaica (V)	237/1987	5 November 1992	No violation
Griffiths v. Jamaica (V)	274/1988	24 March 1993	No violation
Campbell v. Jamaica (V)	307/1988	24 March 1993	Violation
Bahamonde v. Equatorial Guinea (V)	468/1991	20 October 1993	Violation
Allen v. Jamaica (V)	332/1988	31 March 1994	No violation
Grant v. Jamaica (V)	353/1988	31 March 1994	No violation
Berry v. Jamaica (V)	330/1988	7 April 1994	Violation
Casanovas v. France (V)	441/1990	19 July 1994	No violation
Poongavanam v. Mauritius (A)	567/1993	26 July 1994	Inadmissible
Fei v. Colombia (V)	514/1992	4 April 1995	Violation
Bullock v. Trinidad and Tobago (A)	553/1993	19 July 1995	Inadmissible
Pons v. Spain (V)	454/1991	30 October 1995	No violation
Kelly v. Jamaica (V)	537/1993	17 July 1996	Violation
Adams v. Jamaica (V)	607/1994	30 October 1996	Violation
Richards v. Jamaica (V)	535/1993	31 March 1997	Violation
Hill v. Spain (V)	526/1993	2 April 1997	Violation
A. v. Australia (V)	560/1993	3 April 1997	Violation
Williams v. Jamaica (V)	561/1993	8 April 1997	Violation
Blaine v. Jamaica (V)	696/1996	17 July 1997	Violation
McLawrence v. Jamaica (V)	702/1996	18 July 1997	Violation
Taylor v. Jamaica (V)	707/1996	18 July 1997	Violation
A.R.J. v. Australia (V)	692/1996	28 July 1997	No violation
Young v. Jamaica (V)	615/1995	4 November 1997	Violation

Name of case	Comm. No.	Date of Decision	Outcome
Polay Campos v. Peru (V)	577/1994	6 November 1997	Violation
Perel v. Latvia (V)	650/1995	30 March 1998	No violation
Yasseen and Thomas v. Republic of Guyana (V)	676/1996	30 March 1998	Violation
Shaw v. Jamaica (V)	704/1996	2 April 1998	Violation
Taylor v. Jamaica (V)	705/1996	2 April 1998	Violation
Jones v. Jamaica (V)	585/1994	6 April 1998	Violation
Chung v. Jamaica (V)	591/1994	9 April 1998	Violation
Deidrick v. Jamaica (V)	619/1995	9 April 1998	Violation
Finn v. Jamaica (V)	617/1995	31 July 1998	Violation
Henry v. Trinidad and Tobago (V)	752/1997	3 November 1998	Violation
Fraser and Fisher v. Jamaica (V)	722/1996	31 March 1999	No violation
Maleki v. Italy (V)	699/1996	15 July 1999	Violation
Bailey v. Jamaica (V)	709/1996	21 July 1999	Violation
Gallimore v. Jamaica (V)	680/1996	23 July 1999	Violation
Mukunto v. Zambia (V)	768/1997	23 July 1999	Violation
Tamihere v. New Zealand (A)	891/1999	15 March 2000	Inadmissible
Ben Said v. Norway (V)	767/1997	29 March 2000	No violation
Gridin v. Russian Federation (V)	770/1997	20 July 2000	Violation
Diergaardt et al. v. Namibia (V)	760/1997	25 July 2000	Violation
Arredondo v. Peru (V)	688/1996	27 July 2000	Violation
Mahuika et al. v. New Zealand (V)	547/1993	27 October 2000	No violation
Jansen-Gielen v. The Netherlands (V)	846/1999	3 April 2001	Violation
Kavanagh v. Ireland (V)	819/1998	4 April 2001	Violation
Torregrosa Lafuente et al. v. Spain (A)	866/1999	16 July 2001	Inadmissible
Äärelä v. Finland (V)	779/1997	24 October 2001	Violation
Des Fours v. Czech Republic (V)	747/1997	30 October 2001	Violation

ARTICLE 14(2)

Name of case	Comm. No.	Date of Decision	Outcome
Massera et al. v. Uruguay (V)	5/1977 (R.1/5)	15 August 1979	Violation
Weismann and Perdomo v. Uruguay (V)	8/1977	3 April 1980	Violation
Bolaños v. Ecuador (V)	238/1987	26 July 1989	Violation

Name of case	Comm. No.	Date of Decision	Outcome
Morael v. France (V)	207/1986	28 July 1989	No violation
Collins v. Jamaica (V)	240/1987	1 November 1991	Violation
W. J. H. v. The Netherlands (A)	408/1990	22 July 1992	Inadmissible
W. B. E. v. The Netherlands (A)	432/1990	23 October 1992	Inadmissible
del Cid v. Panama (V)	473/1991	19 July 1995	Violation
Adams v. Jamaica (V)	607/1994	30 October 1996	Violation
Hill v. Spain (V)	526/1993	2 April 1997	Violation
Blaine v. Jamaica (V)	696/1996	17 July 1997	Violation
Lewis v. Jamaica (V)	708/1996	17 July 1997	Violation
Singh v. Canada (A)	761/1997	29 July 1997	Inadmissible
Polay Campos v. Peru (V)	577/1994	6 November 1997	Violation
Perel v. Latvia (V)	650/1995	30 March 1998	No violation
Jones v. Jamaica (V)	585/1994	6 April 1998	Violation
Chung v. Jamaica (V)	591/1994	9 April 1998	Violation
Deidrick v. Jamaica (V)	619/1995	9 April 1998	Violation
Finn v. Jamaica (V)	617/1995	31 July 1998	Violation
Henry v. Trinidad and Tobago (V)	752/1997	3 November 1998	Violation
Sánchez López v. Spain (A)	777/1997	18 October 1999	Inadmissible
Gridin v. Russian Federation (V)	770/1997	20 July 2000	Violation

ARTICLE 14(3)

Name of case	Comm. No.	Date of Decision	Outcome
Massera et al. v. Uruguay (V)	5/1977 (R.1/5)	15 August 1979	Violation
Weismann and Perdomo v. Uruguay (V)	8/1977	3 April 1980	Violation
Ramirez v. Uruguay (V)	4/1977 (R.1/4)	23 July 1980	Violation
Sequeira v. Uruguay (V)	6/1977	29 July 1980	Violation
Weinberger v. Uruguay (V)	28/1978	29 October 1980	Violation
Carballal v. Uruguay (V)	33/1978	27 March 1981	Violation
Pietraroia v. Uruguay (V)	44/1979	27 March 1981	Violation
Touron v. Uruguay (V)	32/1978	31 March 1981	Violation
Sendic v. Uruguay (V)	63/1979 (R.14/63)	28 October 1981	Violation
Altesor v. Uruguay (V)	10/1977 (R.2/10)	29 March 1982	Violation
Mbenge v. Zaire (V)	16/1977	25 March 1983	Violation

Name of case	Comm. No.	Date of Decision	Outcome
Estrella v. Uruguay (V)	74/1980	29 March 1983	Violation
Vasilskis v. Uruguay (V)	80/1980	31 March 1983	Violation
Manera v. Uruguay (V)	123/1982	6 April 1984	Violation
Muteba v. Zaire (V)	124/1982	24 July 1984	Violation
Conteris v. Uruguay (V)	139/1983	17 July 1985	Violation
Cariboni v. Uruguay (V)	159/1983	27 October 1987	Violation
G. F. Croes v. The Netherlands (A)	164/1984	7 November 1988	Inadmissible
R.M. v. Finland (A)	301/1988	23 March 1989	Inadmissible
Robinson v. Jamaica (V)	223/1987	30 March 1989	Violation
Pinto v. Trinidad and Tobago (V)	232/1987	20 July 1990	Violation
van Alphen v. The Netherlands (V)	305/1988	23 July 1990	Violation
Berry v. Jamaica (V)	330/1988	7 April 1994	Violation
del Cid v. Panama (V)	473/1991	19 July 1995	Violation
A.R.J. v. Australia (V)	692/1996	28 July 1997	No violation

ARTICLE 14(3)(a)

Name of case	Comm. No.	Date of Decision	Outcome
N. B. v. Sweden (A)	175/1984	11 July 1985	Inadmissible
Kelly v. Jamaica (V)	253/1987	8 April 1991	Violation
Mukong v. Cameroon (V)	458/1991	21 July 1994	Violation
Williams v. Jamaica (V)	561/1993	8 April 1997	Violation
Blaine v. Jamaica (V)	696/1996	17 July 1997	Violation
Singh v. Canada (A)	761/1997	29 July 1997	Inadmissible
Yasseen and Thomas v. Republic of Guyana (V)	676/1996	30 March 1998	Violation
McLeod v. Jamaica (V)	734/1997	31 March 1998	Violation
McTaggart v. Jamaica (V)	749/1997	31 March 1998	Violation
Jones v. Jamaica (V)	585/1994	6 April 1998	Violation

ARTICLE 14(3)(b)

Name of case	Comm. No.	Date of Decision	Outcome
Casariego v. Uruguay (V)	56/1979	29 July 1981	Violation
Simones v. Uruguay (V)	70/1981 (R.17/70)	1 April 1982	Violation
Izquierdo v. Uruguay (V)	73/1981 (R.18/73)	1 April 1982	Violation

Name of case	Comm. No.	Date of Decision	Outcome
Marais v. Madagascar (V)	49/1979	24 March 1983	Violation
Caldas v. Uruguay (V)	43/1979	21 July 1983	Violation
Nieto v. Uruguay (V)	92/1981	25 July 1983	Violation
Machado v. Uruguay (V)	83/1981	4 November 1983	Violation
Oxandabarat v. Uruguay (V)	103/1981	4 November 1983	Violation
Viana v. Uruguay (V)	110/1981	29 March 1984	Violation
J.K. v. Canada (A)	174/1984	26 October 1984	Inadmissible
Wight v. Madagascar (V)	115/1982	1 April 1985	Violation
Penarrieta et al. v. Bolivia (V)	176/1984	2 November 1987	Violation
Kelly v. Jamaica (V)	253/1987	8 April 1991	Violation
Z.P. v. Canada (A)	341/1988	11 April 1991	Inadmissible
Henry v. Jamaica (V)	230/1987	1 November 1991	Violation
Fillastre and Bizouarn v. Bolivia (V)	336/1988	5 November 1991	Violation
Wolf v. Panama (V)	289/1988	26 March 1992	Violation
Campbell v. Jamaica (V)	248/1987	30 March 1992	Violation
Thomas v. Jamaica (V)	272/1988	31 March 1992	Violation
Hibbert v. Jamaica (V)	293/1988	27 July 1992	No violation
Wright v. Jamaica (V)	349/1989	27 July 1992	Violation
Linton v. Jamaica (V)	255/1987	22 October 1992	Violation
Quelch v. Jamaica (V)	292/1988	23 October 1992	No violation
Simmonds v. Jamaica (V)	338/1988	23 October 1992	Violation
Collins v. Jamaica (V)	356/1989	25 March 1993	Violation
Smith v. Jamaica (V)	282/1988	31 March 1993	Violation
Gentles et al. v. Jamaica (V)	352/ 1989	19 October 1993	No violation
Reid v. Jamaica (V)	335/1989	8 July 1994	Violation
Harward v. Norway (V)	451/1991	15 July 1994	No violation
Mukong v. Cameroon (V)	458/1991	21 July 1994	Violation
Simms v. Jamaica (A)	541/1993	3 April 1995	Inadmissible
Wright and Harvey v. Jamaica (V)	459/1991	27 October 1995	Violation
Marriot v. Jamaica (V)	519/1992	27 October 1995	Violation
Graham and Morrison v. Jamaica (V)	461/1991	25 March 1996	Violation
Tomlin v. Jamaica (V)	589/1994	16 July 1996	No violation
Kelly v. Jamaica (V)	537/1993	17 July 1996	Violation
Lewis v. Jamaica (V)	527/1993	18 July 1996	Violation
Burrell v. Jamaica (V)	546/1993	18 July 1996	Violation
Sterling v. Jamaica (V)	598/1994	22 July 1996	Violation
Adams v. Jamaica (V)	607/1994	30 October 1996	Violation
Richards v. Jamaica (V)	535/1993	31 March 1997	Violation

Name of case	Comm. No.	Date of Decision	Outcome
Hill v. Spain (V)	526/1993	2 April 1997	Violation
Steadman v. Jamaica (V)	528/1993	2 April 1997	Violation
A. v. Australia (V)	560/1993	3 April 1997	Violation
Blaine v. Jamaica (V)	696/1996	17 July 1997	Violation
Lewis v. Jamaica (V)	708/1996	17 July 1997	Violation
Taylor v. Jamaica (V)	707/1996	18 July 1997	Violation
Thomas v. Jamaica (V)	532/1993	3 November 1997	Violation
Young v. Jamaica (V)	615/1995	4 November 1997	Violation
Polay Campos v. Peru (V)	577/1994	6 November 1997	Violation
Yasseen and Thomas v. Republic of Guyana (V)	676/1996	30 March 1998	Violation
McLeod v. Jamaica (V)	734/1997	31 March 1998	Violation
McTaggart v. Jamaica (V)	749/1997	31 March 1998	Violation
Shaw v. Jamaica (V)	704/1996	2 April 1998	Violation
Taylor v. Jamaica (V)	705/1996	2 April 1998	Violation
Jones v. Jamaica (V)	585/1994	6 April 1998	Violation
Whyte v. Jamaica (V)	732/1997	27 July 1998	Violation
Smart v. Trinidad and Tobago (V)	672/1995	29 July 1998	Violation
Perkins v. Jamaica (V)	733/1997	30 July 1998	Violation
Leslie v. Jamaica (V)	564/1993	31 July 1998	Violation
Phillip v. Trinidad and Tobago (V)	594/1992	20 October 1998	Violation
Brown and Parish v. Jamaica (V)	665/1995	29 July 1999	Violation
Gridin v. Russian Federation (V)	770/1997	20 July 2000	Violation

ARTICLE 14(3)(c)

Name of case	Comm. No.	Date of Decision	Outcome
Casariego v. Uruguay (V)	56/1979	29 July 1981	Violation
Pinkney v. Canada (V)	27/1977 (R.7/27)	29 October 1981	Violation
Izquierdo v. Uruguay (V)	73/1981 (R.18/73)	1 April 1982	Violation
Schweizer v. Uruguay (V)	66/1980	12 October 1982	Violation
Barbato v. Uruguay (V)	84/1981	21 October 1982	Violation
Caldas v. Uruguay (V)	43/1979	21 July 1983	Violation
Nieto v. Uruguay (V)	92/1981	25 July 1983	Violation
Machado v. Uruguay (V)	83/1981	4 November 1983	Violation

Name of case	Comm. No.	Date of Decision	Outcome
Oxandabarat v. Uruguay (V)	103/1981	4 November 1983	Violation
Viana v. Uruguay (V)	110/1981	29 March 1984	Violation
O. F. v. Norway (A)	158/1983	26 October 1984	Inadmissible
J.K. v. Canada (A)	174/1984	26 October 1984	Inadmissible
N. B. v. Sweden (A)	175/1984	11 July 1985	Inadmissible
Martin v. Jamaica (A)	317/1988	15 March 1990	Admissible
Kelly v. Jamaica (V)	253/1987	8 April 1991	Violation
Fillastre and Bizouarn v. Bolivia (V)	336/1988	5 November 1991	Violation
Wolf v. Panama (V)	289/1988	26 March 1992	Violation
Campbell v. Jamaica (V)	248/1987	30 March 1992	Violation
Martin v. Jamaica (V)	317/1988	24 March 1993	No violation
Francis v. Jamaica (V)	320/1988	24 March 1993	Violation
Collins v. Jamaica (V)	356/1989	25 March 1993	Violation
Smith v. Jamaica (V)	282/1988	31 March 1993	Violation
Hamilton v. Jamaica (V)	333/1988	23 March 1994	Violation
Currie v. Jamaica (V)	377/1989	29 March 1994	Violation
Allen v. Jamaica (V)	332/1988	31 March 1994	No violation
Grant v. Jamaica (V)	353/1988	31 March 1994	No violation
Bozize v. Central African Republic (V)	428/1990	7 April 1994	Violation
Reid v. Jamaica (V)	335/1989	8 July 1994	Violation
Champagnie et al v. Jamaica (V)	445/1991	18 July 1994	Violation
Shalto v. Trinidad and Tobago (V)	447/1991	4 April 1995	Violation
Francis v. Jamaica (V)	606/1994	25 July 1995	Violation
Stephens v. Jamaica (V)	373/1989	18 October 1995	Violation
Wright and Harvey v. Jamaica (V)	459/1991	27 October 1995	Violation
Bautista v. Colombia (V)	563/1993	27 October 1995	Violation
Lubuto v. Zambia (V)	390/1990	31 October 1995	Violation
E. Johnson v. Jamaica (V)	588/1994	22 March 1996	Violation
Fuenzalida v. Ecuador (V)	480/1991	12 July 1996	Violation
Neptune v. Trinidad and Tobago (V)	523/1992	16 July 1996	Violation
Burrell v. Jamaica (V)	546/1993	18 July 1996	Violation
Henry and Douglas v. Jamaica (V)	571/1994	25 July 1996	Violation
Price v. Jamaica (V)	572/1994	6 November 1996	Violation
Steadman v. Jamaica (V)	528/1993	2 April 1997	Violation
A. v. Australia (V)	560/1993	3 April 1997	Violation
Williams v. Jamaica (V)	561/1993	8 April 1997	Violation
Lewis v. Jamaica (V)	708/1996	17 July 1997	Violation

Name of case	Comm. No.	Date of Decision	Outcome
McLawrence v. Jamaica (V)	702/1996	18 July 1997	Violation
Taylor v. Jamaica (V)	707/1996	18 July 1997	Violation
Elahie v. Trinidad and Tobago (V)	533/1993	28 July 1997	Violation
Walker and Richards v. Jamaica (V)	639/1995	28 July 1997	Violation
Thomas v. Jamaica (V)	532/1993	3 November 1997	Violation
Yasseen and Thomas v. Republic of Guyana (V)	676/1996	30 March 1998	Violation
Taylor v. Jamaica (V)	705/1996	2 April 1998	Violation
Jones v. Jamaica (V)	585/1994	6 April 1998	Violation
Morrison v. Jamaica (V)	635/1995	27 July 1998	Violation
Whyte v. Jamaica (V)	732/1997	27 July 1998	Violation
Smart v. Trinidad and Tobago (V)	672/1995	29 July 1998	Violation
Chadee et al. v. Trinidad and Tobago (V)	813/1998	29 July 1998	No violation
Perkins v. Jamaica (V)	733/1997	30 July 1998	Violation
Leslie v. Jamaica (V)	564/1993	31 July 1998	Violation
Finn v. Jamaica (V)	617/1995	31 July 1998	Violation
Daley v. Jamaica (V)	750/1997	31 July 1998	Violation
Morrison v. Jamaica (V)	663/1995	3 November 1998	Violation
Brown v. Jamaica (V)	775/1997	23 March 1999	Violation
Bennett v. Jamaica (V)	590/1994	25 March 1999	Violation
Thomas v. Jamaica (V)	614/1995	31 March 1999	Violation
Smith and Stewart v. Jamaica (V)	668/1995	8 April 1999	Violation
Hamilton v. Jamaica (V)	616/1995	23 July 1999	Violation
Brown and Parish v. Jamaica (V)	665/1995	29 July 1999	Violation
Arredondo v. Peru (V)	688/1996	27 July 2000	Violation
Paraga v. Croatia (V)	727/1996	4 April 2001	Violation
Sextus v. Trinidad and Tobago (V)	818/1998	16 July 2001	Violation
Sookal v. Trinidad and Tobago (V)	928/2000	25 October 2001	Violation

ARTICLE 14(3)(d)

Name of case	Comm. No.	Date of Decision	Outcome
Simones v. Uruguay (V)	70/1981 (R.17/70)	1 April 1982	Violation
Marais v. Madagascar (V)	49/1979	24 March 1983	Violation
J.S. v. Canada (A)	130/1982	6 April 1983	Inadmissible

Name of case	Comm. No.	Date of Decision	Outcome
Nieto v. Uruguay (V)	92/1981	25 July 1983	Violation
Viana v. Uruguay (V)	110/1981	29 March 1984	Violation
O. F. v. Norway (A)	158/1983	26 October 1984	Inadmissible
Reynolds v. Jamaica (V)	229/1987	8 April 1991	No violation
Kelly v. Jamaica (V)	253/1987	8 April 1991	Violation
Sawyers and McLean v. Jamaica (V)	226 & 256/1987	11 April 1991	No violation
Henry v. Jamaica (V)	230/1987	1 November 1991	Violation
Fillastre and Bizouarn v. Bolivia (V)	336/1988	5 November 1991	Violation
Wolf v. Panama (V)	289/1988	26 March 1992	Violation
Campbell v. Jamaica (V)	248/1987	30 March 1992	Violation
Linton v. Jamaica (V)	255/1987	22 October 1992	Violation
Quelch v. Jamaica (V)	292/1988	23 October 1992	No violation
Simmonds v. Jamaica (V)	338/1988	23 October 1992	Violation
Gordon v. Jamaica (V)	237/1987	5 November 1992	No violation
Campbell v. Jamaica (V)	307/1988	24 March 1993	Violation
Collins v. Jamaica (V)	356/1989	25 March 1993	Violation
Gentles et. al. v. Jamaica (V)	352/ 1989	19 October 1993	No violation
Wright and Harvey v. Jamaica (V)	459/1991	27 October 1995	Violation
Chaplin v. Jamaica (V)	596/1994	2 November 1995	Violation
Graham and Morrison v. Jamaica (V)	461/1991	25 March 1996	Violation
Kelly v. Jamaica (V)	537/1993	17 July 1996	Violation
Lewis v. Jamaica (V)	527/1993	18 July 1996	Violation
Sterling v. Jamaica (V)	598/1994	22 July 1996	Violation
Price v. Jamaica (V)	572/1994	6 November 1996	Violation
Richards v. Jamaica (V)	535/1993	31 March 1997	Violation
Hill v. Spain (V)	526/1993	2 April 1997	Violation
Steadman v. Jamaica (V)	528/1993	2 April 1997	Violation
A. v. Australia (V)	560/1993	3 April 1997	Violation
Lewis v. Jamaica (V)	708/1996	17 July 1997	Violation
Taylor v. Jamaica (V)	707/1996	18 July 1997	Violation
LaVende v. Trinidad and Tobago (V)	554/1993	29 October 1997	Violation
Thomas v. Jamaica (V)	532/1993	3 November 1997	Violation
Polay Campos v. Peru (V)	577/1994	6 November 1997	Violation
Yasseen and Thomas v. Republic of Guyana (V)	676/1996	30 March 1998	Violation
Taylor v. Jamaica (V)	705/1996	2 April 1998	Violation
Jones v. Jamaica (V)	585/1994	6 April 1998	Violation

Name of case	Comm. No.	Date of Decision	Outcome
Domukovsky et al. v. Georgia (V)	623, 624, 626 & 627/1995	6 April 1998	Violation
Whyte v. Jamaica (V)	732/1997	27 July 1998	Violation
Perkins v. Jamaica (V)	733/1997	30 July 1998	Violation
Leslie v. Jamaica (V)	564/1993	31 July 1998	Violation
Finn v. Jamaica (V)	617/1995	31 July 1998	Violation
Daley v. Jamaica (V)	750/1997	31 July 1998	Violation
C. Johnson v. Jamaica (V)	592/1994	20 October 1998	Violation
Phillip v. Trinidad and Tobago (V)	594/1992	20 October 1998	Violation
Morrison v. Jamaica (V)	663/1995	3 November 1998	Violation
Levy v. Jamaica (V)	719/1996	3 November 1998	Violation
Marshall v. Jamaica (V)	730/1996	3 November 1998	Violation
Brown v. Jamaica (V)	775/1997	23 March 1999	Violation
Lumley v. Jamaica (V)	662/1995	31 March 1999	Violation
Smith and Stewart v. Jamaica (V)	668/1995	8 April 1999	Violation
Maleki v. Italy (V)	699/1996	15 July 1999	Violation
Bailey v. Jamaica (V)	709/1996	21 July 1999	Violation
Gallimore v. Jamaica (V)	680/1996	23 July 1999	Violation
Brown and Parish v. Jamaica (V)	665/1995	29 July 1999	Violation
Tamihere v. New Zealand (A)	891/1999	15 March 2000	Inadmissible
Robinson v. Jamaica (V)	731/1996	29 March 2000	Violation
Sookal v. Trinidad and Tobago (V)	928/2000	25 October 2001	Violation
Simpson v. Jamaica (V)	695/1996	31 October 2001	Violation

ARTICLE 14(3)(e)

Name of case	Comm. No.	Date of Decision	Outcome
O. F. v. Norway (A)	158/1983	26 October 1984	Inadmissible
N. B. v. Sweden (A)	175/1984	11 July 1985	Inadmissible
Guesdon v. France (V)	219/1986	25 July 1990	No violation
Reynolds v. Jamaica (V)	229/1987	8 April 1991	No violation
Kelly v. Jamaica (V)	253/1987	8 April 1991	Violation
Cadoret and Bihan v. France (V)	221 & 323/1988	11 April 1991	No violation
Sawyers and McLean v. Jamaica (V)	226 & 256/1987	11 April 1991	No violation
Henry v. Jamaica (V)	230/1987	1 November 1991	Violation
Collins v. Jamaica (V)	240/1987	1 November 1991	Violation
Campbell v. Jamaica (V)	248/1987	30 March 1992	Violation
Prince v. Jamaica (V)	269/1987	30 March 1992	No violation

Name of case	Comm. No.	Date of Decision	Outcome
Hibbert v. Jamaica (V)	293/1988	27 July 1992	No violation
Wright v. Jamaica (V)	349/1989	27 July 1992	Violation
Párkányi v. Hungary (V)	410/1990	27 July 1992	Violation
Gordon v. Jamaica (V)	237/1987	5 November 1992	No violation
Collins v. Jamaica (V)	356/1989	25 March 1993	Violation
Compass v. Jamaica (V)	375/1989	19 October 1993	No violation
Allen v. Jamaica (V)	332/1988	31 March 1994	No violation
Grant v. Jamaica (V)	353/1988	31 March 1994	No violation
Peart and Peart v. Jamaica (DJ), (V)	464 & 482/1991	19 July 1995	Violation
Bullock v. Trinidad and Tobago (A)	553/1993	19 July 1995	Inadmissible
Seerattan v. Trinidad and Tobago (V)	434/1990	26 October 1995	Violation
Marriot v. Jamaica (V)	519/1992	27 October 1995	Violation
Fuenzalida v. Ecuador (V)	480/1991	12 July 1996	Violation
Tomlin v. Jamaica (V)	589/1994	16 July 1996	No violation
Lewis v. Jamaica (V)	527/1993	18 July 1996	Violation
Adams v. Jamaica (V)	607/1994	30 October 1996	Violation
Richards v. Jamaica (V)	535/1993	31 March 1997	Violation
Hill v. Spain (V)	526/1993	2 April 1997	Violation
Williams v. Jamaica (V)	561/1993	8 April 1997	Violation
Blaine v. Jamaica (V)	696/1996	17 July 1997	Violation
Yasseen and Thomas v. Republic of Guyana (V)	676/1996	30 March 1998	Violation
McLeod v. Jamaica (V)	734/1997	31 March 1998	Violation
McTaggart v. Jamaica (V)	749/1997	31 March 1998	Violation
Jones v. Jamaica (V)	585/1994	6 April 1998	Violation
Whyte v. Jamaica (V)	732/1997	27 July 1998	Violation
Leslie v. Jamaica (V)	564/1993	31 July 1998	Violation
Bailey v. Jamaica (V)	709/1996	21 July 1999	Violation

ARTICLE 14(3)(f)

Name of case	Comm. No.	Date of Decision	Outcome
Guesdon v. France (V)	219/1986	25 July 1990	No violation
Cadoret and Bihan v. France (V)	221 & 323/1988	11 April 1991	No violation
Barzhig v. France (V)	327/1988	11 April 1991	No violation
Griffin v. Spain (V)	493/1992	4 April 1995	Violation
Domukovsky et al. v. Georgia (V)	623, 624, 626 & 627/1995	6 April 1998	Violation

ARTICLE 14(3)(g)

Name of case	Comm. No.	Date of Decision	Outcome
Izquierdo v. Uruguay (V)	73/1981 (R.18/73)	1 April 1982	Violation
J.H. v. Finland (A)	300/1988	23 March 1989	Inadmissible
Kelly v. Jamaica (V)	253/1987	8 April 1991	Violation
Campbell v. Jamaica (V)	248/1987	30 March 1992	Violation
Blanco v. Nicaragua (V)	328/1988	20 July 1994	Violation
E. Johnson v. Jamaica (V)	588/1994	22 March 1996	Violation
Lewis v. Jamaica (V)	527/1993	18 July 1996	Violation
Yasseen and Thomas v. Republic of Guyana (V)	676/1996	30 March 1998	Violation
Chung v. Jamaica (V)	591/1994	9 April 1998	Violation
Sánchez López v. Spain (A)	777/1997	18 October 1999	Inadmissible

ARTICLE 14(5)

Name of case	Comm. No.	Date of Decision	Outcome
Pinkney v. Canada (V)	27/1977 (R.7/27)	29 October 1981	Violation
de Montejo v. Colombia (V)	64/1979 (R.15/64)	24 March 1982	Violation
Fanali v. Italy (V)	75/1980	31 March 1983	No violation
Martin v. Jamaica (A)	317/1988	15 March 1990	Admissible
Henry v. Jamaica (V)	230/1987	1 November 1991	Violation
Martin v. Jamaica (V)	317/1988	24 March 1993	No violation
Francis v. Jamaica (V)	320/1988	24 March 1993	Violation
Collins v. Jamaica (V)	356/1989	25 March 1993	Violation
Gentles et al. v. Jamaica (V)	352/ 1989	19 October 1993	No violation
Hamilton v. Jamaica (V)	333/1988	23 March 1994	Violation
Currie v. Jamaica (V)	377/1989	29 March 1994	Violation
Berry v. Jamaica (V)	330/1988	7 April 1994	Violation
Reid v. Jamaica (V)	335/1989	8 July 1994	Violation
Champagnie et al v. Jamaica (V)	445/1991	18 July 1994	Violation
Perera v. Australia (A)	536/1993	28 March 1995	Inadmissible
Francis v. Jamaica (V)	606/1994	25 July 1995	Violation
Stephens v. Jamaica (V)	373/1989	18 October 1995	Violation
Lubuto v. Zambia (V)	390/1990	31 October 1995	Violation

Name of case	Comm. No.	Date of Decision	Outcome
E. Johnson v. Jamaica (V)	588/1994	22 March 1996	Violation
Fuenzalida v. Ecuador (V)	480/1991	12 July 1996	Violation
Neptune v. Trinidad and Tobago (V)	523/1992	16 July 1996	Violation
Tomlin v. Jamaica (V)	589/1994	16 July 1996	No violation
Burrell v. Jamaica (V)	546/1993	18 July 1996	Violation
Henry and Douglas v. Jamaica (V)	571/1994	25 July 1996	Violation
Price v. Jamaica (V)	572/1994	6 November 1996	Violation
Richards v. Jamaica (V)	535/1993	31 March 1997	Violation
Hill v. Spain (V)	526/1993	2 April 1997	Violation
Blaine v. Jamaica (V)	696/1996	17 July 1997	Violation
McLawrence v. Jamaica (V)	702/1996	18 July 1997	Violation
Walker and Richards v. Jamaica (V)	639/1995	28 July 1997	Violation
LaVende v. Trinidad and Tobago (V)	554/1993	29 October 1997	Violation
Domukovsky et al. v. Georgia (V)	623, 624, 626 & 627/1995	6 April 1998	Violation
Chadee et al. v. Trinidad and Tobago (V)	813/1998	29 July 1998	No violation
Finn v. Jamaica (V)	617/1995	31 July 1998	Violation
Daley v. Jamaica (V)	750/1997	31 July 1998	Violation
Morrison v. Jamaica (V)	663/1995	3 November 1998	Violation
Bennett v. Jamaica (V)	590/1994	25 March 1999	Violation
Thomas v. Jamaica (V)	614/1995	31 March 1999	Violation
Lumley v. Jamaica (V)	662/1995	31 March 1999	Violation
Smith and Stewart v. Jamaica (V)	668/1995	8 April 1999	Violation
Bailey v. Jamaica (V)	709/1996	21 July 1999	Violation
Gallimore v. Jamaica (V)	680/1996	23 July 1999	Violation
Brown and Parish v. Jamaica (V)	665/1995	29 July 1999	Violation
Bryhn v. Norway (V)	789/1997	29 October 1999	No violation
Robinson v. Jamaica (V)	731/1996	29 March 2000	Violation
Gómez v. Spain (V)	701/1996	20 July 2000	Violation
Sextus v. Trinidad and Tobago (V)	818/1998	16 July 2001	Violation
Mansaraj et al. v. Sierra Leone (V)	839, 840 & 841/1998	16 July 2001	Violation

ARTICLE 14(6)

Name of case	Comm. No.	Date of Decision	Outcome
Muhonen v. Finland (V)	89/1981	8 April 1985	No violation
W. J. H. v. The Netherlands (A)	408/1990	22 July 1992	Inadmissible
del Cid v. Panama (V)	473/1991	19 July 1995	Violation
Uebergang v. Australia (A)	963/2001	22 March 2001	Inadmissible

ARTICLE 14(7)

Name of case	Comm. No.	Date of Decision	Outcome
Schweizer v. Uruguay (V)	66/1980	12 October 1982	Violation
A.P. v. Italy (A)	204/1986	2 November 1987	Inadmissible
del Cid v. Panama (V)	473/1991	19 July 1995	Violation
McLawrence v. Jamaica (V)	702/1996	18 July 1997	Violation

ARTICLE 15

Name of case	Comm. No.	Date of Decision	Outcome
Weinberger v. Uruguay (V)	28/1978	29 October 1980	Violation
Kivenmaa v. Finland (V)	412/1990	31 March 1994	Violation
de Groot v. The Netherlands (A)	578/1994	14 July 1995	Inadmissible
Singh v. Canada (A)	761/1997	29 July 1997	Inadmissible
Westerman v. The Netherlands (V)	682/1996	3 November 1999	No violation

ARTICLE 15(1)

Name of case	Comm. No.	Date of Decision	Outcome
Pietraroia v. Uruguay (V)	44/1979	27 March 1981	Violation
Van Duzen v. Canada (V)	50/1979 (R.12/50)	7 April 1982	No violation
MacIsaac v. Canada (V)	55/1979	14 October 1982	No violation

ARTICLE 17

Name of case	Comm. No.	Date of Decision	Outcome
Estrella v. Uruguay (V)	74/1980	29 March 1983	Violation
R.M. v. Finland (A)	301/1988	23 March 1989	Inadmissible
Martin v. Jamaica (A)	317/1988	15 March 1990	Admissible
van Alphen v. The Netherlands (V)	305/1988	23 July 1990	Violation
Orihuela v. Peru (V)	309/1988	14 July 1993	Violation
Coeriel and Aurik v. The Netherlands (V)	453/1991	31 October 1994	Violation
Mónaco v. Argentina (V)	400/1990	3 April 1995	Violation
Fei v. Colombia (V)	514/1992	4 April 1995	Violation
Stewart v. Canada (V)	538/1993	1 November 1996	No violation
Canepa v. Canada (V)	558/1993	3 April 1997	No violation
Hopu and Bessert v. France (V)	549/1993	29 July 1997	Violation
Rogl v. Germany (A)	808/1998	25 October 2000	Inadmissible
Buckle v. New Zealand (V)	858/1999	25 October 2000	No violation
Rojas García v. Colombia (V)	687/1996	3 April 2001	Violation
Winata v. Australia (V)	930/2000	26 July 2001	Violation

ARTICLE 17(1)

Name of case	Comm. No.	Date of Decision	Outcome
Mauritian women v. Mauritius (V)	35/1978	9 April 1981	Violation
Pinkney v. Canada (V)	27/1977 (R.7/27)	29 October 1981	Violation
Morael v. France (V)	207/1986	28 July 1989	No violation
Birindwa and Tshisekedi v. Zaire (V)	241 & 242/1987	2 November 1989	Violation
Toonen v. Australia (V)	488/1992	30 March 1994	Violation
Pinto v. Trinidad and Tobago (V)	512/1992	16 July 1996	Violation
Tomlin v. Jamaica (V)	589/1994	16 July 1996	No violation

ARTICLE 18

Name of case	Comm. No.	Date of Decision	Outcome
L.T.K. v. Finland (A)	185/1984	9 July 1985	Inadmissible
A. and S. N. v. Norway (A)	224/1987	11 July 1988	Inadmissible
V.M.R.B. v. Canada (A)	236/1987	18 July 1988	Inadmissible

Name of case	Comm. No.	Date of Decision	Outcome
Bhinder v. Canada (V)	208/1986	9 November 1989	Violation
Delgado Páez v. Colombia (V)	195/1985	12 July 1990	Violation
Westerman v. The Netherlands (V)	682/1996	3 November 1999	No violation
Ross v. Canada (V)	736/1997	18 October 2000	No violation

ARTICLE 18(4)

Name of case	Comm. No.	Date of Decision	Outcome
Hartikainen v. Finland (V)	40/1978	9 April 1981	No violation

ARTICLE 19

Name of case	Comm. No.	Date of Decision	Outcome
Weinberger v. Uruguay (V)	28/1978	29 October 1980	Violation
Burgos v. Uruguay (V)	52/1979	29 July 1981	Violation
Mbenge v. Zaire (V)	16/1977	25 March 1983	Violation
J.R.T. and the W .G. Party v. Canada (A)	104/1981	6 April 1983	Inadmissible
M.A. v. Italy (A)	117/1981	10 April 1984	Inadmissible
Muteba v. Zaire (V)	124/1982	24 July 1984	Violation
Mpandanjila et al. v. Zaire (V)	138/1983	26 March 1986	Violation
Mpaka-Nsusu v. Zaire (V)	157/1983	26 March 1986	Violation
V.M.R.B. v. Canada (A)	236/1987	18 July 1988	Inadmissible
G. F. Croes v. The Netherlands (A)	164/1984	7 November 1988	Inadmissible
Delgado Páez v. Colombia (V)	195/1985	12 July 1990	Violation
Bwalya v. Zambia (V)	314/1988	14 July 1993	Violation
Koné v. Senegal (V)	386/1989	21 October 1994	Violation
Aduayom et al. v. Togo (V)	422, 423, & 424/1990	12 July 1996	Violation
Park v. Republic of Korea (V)	628/1995	20 October 1998	Violation
Kim v. Republic of Korea (V)	574/1994	3 November 1998	Violation
Ross v. Canada (V)	736/1997	18 October 2000	No violation
Paraga v. Croatia (V)	727/1996	4 April 2001	Violation

ARTICLE 19(1)

Name of case	Comm. No.	Date of Decision	Outcome
Mika Miha v. Equatorial Guinea (V)	414/1990	8 July 1994	Violation

ARTICLE 19(2)

Name of case	Comm. No.	Date of Decision	Outcome
Pietraroia v. Uruguay (V)	44/1979	27 March 1981	Violation
Hertzberg et al. v. Finland (V)	61/1979 (R.14/61)	2 April 1982	No violation
Jaona v. Madagascar (V)	132/1982	1 April 1985	Violation
R.T. v. France (A)	262/1987	30 March 1989	Inadmissible
Ballantyne, Davidson and McIntyre v. Canada (V)	359 & 385/1989	31 March 1993	Violation
Mika Miha v. Equatorial Guinea (V)	414/1990	8 July 1994	Violation
Singer v. Canada (V)	455/1991	26 July 1994	Violation
Sohn v. Republic of Korea (V)	518/1992	19 July 1995	Violation
Gauthier v. Canada (V)	633/1995	7 April 1999	Violation
Laptsevich v. Belarus (V)	780/1997	20 March 2000	Violation

ARTICLE 19(2)(a)

Name of case	Comm. No.	Date of Decision	Outcome
Kivenmaa v. Finland (V)	412/1990	31 March 1994	Violation

ARTICLE 19(2)(b)

Name of case	Comm. No.	Date of Decision	Outcome
Kivenmaa v. Finland (V)	412/1990	31 March 1994	Violation

ARTICLE 19(3)

Name of case	Comm. No.	Date of Decision	Outcome
Izquierdo v. Uruguay (V)	73/1981 (R.18/73)	1 April 1982	Violation
Hertzberg et al. v. Finland (V)	61/1979 (R.14/61)	2 April 1982	No violation

Name of case	Comm. No.	Date of Decision	Outcome
Ballantyne, Davidson and McIntyre v. Canada (V)	359 & 385/1989	31 March 1993	Violation
Koné v. Senegal (V)	386/1989	21 October 1994	Violation
Sohn v. Republic of Korea (V)	518/1992	19 July 1995	Violation
Laptsevich v. Belarus (V)	780/1997	20 March 2000	Violation

ARTICLE 19(3)(a)

Name of case	Comm. No.	Date of Decision	Outcome
Mukong v. Cameroon (V)	458/1991	21 July 1994	Violation
Faurisson v. France (V)	550/1993	8 November 1996	No violation

ARTICLE 19(3)(b)

Name of case	Comm. No.	Date of Decision	Outcome
Mukong v. Cameroon (V)	458/1991	21 July 1994	Violation
Faurisson v. France (V)	550/1993	8 November 1996	No violation

ARTICLE 21

Name of case	Comm. No.	Date of Decision	Outcome
G. F. Croes v. The Netherlands (A)	164/1984	7 November 1988	Inadmissible
Kivenmaa v. Finland (V)	412/1990	31 March 1994	Violation

ARTICLE 22

Name of case	Comm. No.	Date of Decision	Outcome
Burgos v. Uruguay (V)	52/1979	29 July 1981	Violation

ARTICLE 22(3)

Name of case	Comm. No.	Date of Decision	Outcome
J.B. et al. v. Canada (A)	118/1982	18 July 1986	Inadmissible

ARTICLE 23

Name of case	Comm. No.	Date of Decision	Outcome
Mauritian women v. Mauritius (V)	35/1978	9 April 1981	Violation
Stewart v. Canada (V)	538/1993	1 November 1996	No violation
Canepa v. Canada (V)	558/1993	3 April 1997	No violation
Hopu and Bessert v. France (V)	549/1993	29 July 1997	Violation
Rogl v. Germany (A)	808/1998	25 October 2000	Inadmissible
Buckle v. New Zealand (V)	858/1999	25 October 2000	No violation

ARTICLE 23(1)

Name of case	Comm. No.	Date of Decision	Outcome
Santacana v. Spain (V)	417/1990	15 July 1994	No violation
Mónaco v. Argentina (V)	400/1990	3 April 1995	Violation
Winata v. Australia (V)	930/2000	26 July 2001	Violation

ARTICLE 23(4)

Name of case	Comm. No.	Date of Decision	Outcome
Hendricks v. The Netherlands (V)	201/1985	27 July 1988	Violation
Santacana v. Spain (V)	417/1990	15 July 1994	No violation
Fei v. Colombia (V)	514/1992	4 April 1995	Violation
J.P.L. v. France (A)	472/1991	26 October 1995	Inadmissible

ARTICLE 24

Name of case	Comm. No.	Date of Decision	Outcome
Santacana v. Spain (V)	417/1990	15 July 1994	No violation
Rogl v. Germany (A)	808/1998	25 October 2000	Inadmissible

ARTICLE 24(1)

Name of case	Comm. No.	Date of Decision	Outcome
Mónaco v. Argentina (V)	400/1990	3 April 1995	Violation
Celis Laureano v. Peru (V)	540/1993	25 March 1996	Violation
Winata v. Australia (V)	930/2000	26 July 2001	Violation

ARTICLE 24(2)

Name of case	Comm. No.	Date of Decision	Outcome
Mónaco v. Argentina (V)	400/1990	3 April 1995	Violation

ARTICLE 25

Name of case	Comm. No.	Date of Decision	Outcome
Massera et al. v. Uruguay (V)	5/1977 (R.1/5)	15 August 1979	Violation
Pietraroia v. Uruguay (V)	44/1979	27 March 1981	Violation
Silva et al. v. Uruguay (V)	34/1978	8 April 1981	Violation
Mauritian women v. Mauritius (V)	35/1978	9 April 1981	Violation
Altesor v. Uruguay (V)	10/1977 (R.2/10)	29 March 1982	Violation
M.A. v. Italy (A)	117/1981	10 April 1984	Inadmissible
Mpandanjila et al. v. Zaire (V)	138/1983	26 March 1986	Violation
Mpaka-Nsusu v. Zaire (V)	157/1983	26 March 1986	Violation
Stalla Costa v. Uruguay (V)	198/1985	9 July 1987	No violation
G. F. Croes v. The Netherlands (A)	164/1984	7 November 1988	Inadmissible
Bwalya v. Zambia (V)	314/1988	14 July 1993	Violation
Rodríguez Veiga v. Uruguay (A)	487/1992	18 July 1994	Inadmissible
Mónaco v. Argentina (V)	400/1990	3 April 1995	Violation
Aduayom et al. v. Togo (V)	422, 423, & 424/1990	12 July 1996	Violation
Domukovsky et al. v. Georgia (V)	623, 624, 626 & 627/1995	6 April 1998	Violation
Ignatane v. Latvia (V)	884/1999	25 July 2001	Violation
Mazou v. Cameroon (V)	630/1995	26 July 2001	Violation

ARTICLE 25(a)

Name of case	Comm. No.	Date of Decision	Outcome
Marshall et al. v. Canada (V)	205/1986	4 November 1991	No violation
Diergaardt et al. v. Namibia (V)	760/1997	25 July 2000	Violation

ARTICLE 25(b)

Name of case	Comm. No.	Date of Decision	Outcome
C.F. et al. v. Canada (A)	113/1981	12 April 1985	Inadmissible
Debreczeny v. The Netherlands (V)	500/1992	3 April 1995	No violation

ARTICLE 25(c)

Name of case	Comm. No.	Date of Decision	Outcome
Muñoz v. Peru (V)	203/1986	4 November 1988	Violation
Delgado Páez v. Colombia (V)	195/1985	12 July 1990	Violation
Kall v. Poland (V)	522/1993	14 July 1997	No violation
Diergaardt et al. v. Namibia (V)	760/1997	25 July 2000	Violation
Alejandro Marín Gómez v. Spain (V)	865/1999	22 October 2001	No violation

ARTICLE 26

Name of case	Comm. No.	Date of Decision	Outcome
Mauritian women v. Mauritius (V)	35/1978	9 April 1981	Violation
A.M. v. Denmark (A)	121/1982 (R.26/121)	23 July 1982	Inadmissible
Disabled and handicapped persons in Italy v. Italy (A)	163/1984	10 April 1984	Inadmissible
J. D. B. v. The Netherlands (A)	178/1984	26 March 1985	Inadmissible
E.H. v. Finland (A)	170/1984	25 October 1985	Inadmissible
S.W.M. Brooks v. The Netherlands (V)	172/1984	9 April 1987	Violation
Danning v. The Netherlands (V)	180/1984	9 April 1987	No violation
Zwaan-de Vries v. The Netherlands (V)	182/1984	9 April 1987	Violation
Stalla Costa v. Uruguay (V)	198/1985	9 July 1987	No violation
P. P. C. v The Netherlands (A)	212/1986	24 March 1988	Inadmissible
M. J. G. v The Netherlands (A)	267/1987	24 March 1988	Inadmissible
Blom v. Sweden (V)	191/1985	4 April 1988	No violation
V.M.R.B. v. Canada (A)	236/1987	18 July 1988	Inadmissible

Name of case	Comm. No.	Date of Decision	Outcome
Avellanal v. Peru (V)	202/1986	28 October 1988	Violation
Muñoz v. Peru (V)	203/1986	4 November 1988	Violation
G. F. Croes v. The Netherlands (A)	164/1984	7 November 1988	Inadmissible
Vos v. The Netherlands (V)	218/1986	29 March 1989	No violation
R.T. v. France (A)	262/1987	30 March 1989	Inadmissible
B. d. B. et al. v. The Netherlands (A)	273/1989	30 March 1989	Inadmissible
Gueye et al. v. France (V)	196/1983	3 April 1989	Violation
Morael v. France (V)	207/1986	28 July 1989	No violation
Bhinder v. Canada (V)	208/1986	9 November 1989	Violation
Delgado Páez v. Colombia (V)	195/1985	12 July 1990	Violation
Guesdon v. France (V)	219/1986	25 July 1990	No violation
Järvinen v. Finland (V)	295/1988	25 July 1990	No violation
Lindgren et al. and Lundquist et al. v. Sweden (DJ), (V)	298 & 299/1988	9 November 1990	No violation
Cadoret and Bihan v. France (V)	221 & 323/1988	11 April 1991	No violation
Pauger v. Austria (V)	415/1990	26 March 1992	Violation
Sprenger v. The Netherlands (V)	395/1990	31 March 1992	No violation
Oulajin & Kaiss v. The Netherlands (V)	406 & 426/1990	23 October 1992	No violation
Ballantyne, Davidson and McIntyre v. Canada (V)	359 & 385/1989	31 March 1993	Violation
Orihuela v. Peru (V)	309/1988	14 July 1993	Violation
Bwalya v. Zambia (V)	314/1988	14 July 1993	Violation
Brinkhof v. The Netherlands (V)	402/1990	27 July 1993	No violation
Bahamonde v. Equatorial Guinea (V)	468/1991	20 October 1993	Violation
Araujo-Jongen v. The Netherlands (V)	418/1990	22 October 1993	No violation
Sara et al. v. Finland (A)	431/1990	23 March 1994	Inadmissible
Toonen v. Australia (V)	488/1992	30 March 1994	Violation
J. A. M. B. R. v. The Netherlands (A)	477/1991	7 April 1994	Inadmissible
Neefs v. The Netherlands (V)	425/1990	15 July 1994	No violation
Pepels v. The Netherlands (V)	484/1991	15 July 1994	No violation
Cox v. Canada (V)	539/1993	31 October 1994	No violation

Name of case	Comm. No.	Date of Decision	Outcome
Mónaco v. Argentina (V)	400/1990	3 April 1995	Violation
Debreczeny v. The Netherlands (V)	500/1992	3 April 1995	No violation
de Groot v. The Netherlands (A)	578/1994	14 July 1995	Inadmissible
Simunek et al. v. Czech Republic (V)	516/1992	19 July 1995	Violation
Pons v. Spain (V)	454/1991	30 October 1995	No violation
Nahlik v. Austria (A)	608/1995	22 July 1996	Inadmissible
Somers v. Hungary (V)	566/1993	23 July 1996	No violation
Adam v. Czech Republic (V)	586/1994	23 July 1996	Violation
Drake et al. v. New Zealand (A)	601/1994	3 April 1997	Inadmissible
Drobek v. Slovakia (A)	643/1995	14 July 1997	Inadmissible
Oord v. The Netherlands (A)	658/1995	23 July 1997	Inadmissible
Hopu and Bessert v. France (V)	549/1993	29 July 1997	Violation
Singh v. Canada (A)	761/1997	29 July 1997	Inadmissible
Snijders et al. v. The Netherlands (V)	651/1995	27 July 1998	No violation
Hoofdman v. The Netherlands (V)	602/1994	3 November 1998	No violation
Pauger v. Austria (V)	716/1996	25 March 1999	Violation
Byrne and Lazarescu v. Canada (A)	742/1997	25 March 1999	Inadmissible
Vos. v. The Netherlands (V)	786/1997	26 July 1999	Violation
Foin v. France (V)	666/1995	3 November 1999	Violation
Waldman v. Canada (V)	694/1996	3 November 1999	Violation
Hoelen v. The Netherlands (A)	873/1999	3 November 1999	Inadmissible
Maille v. France (V)	689/1996	10 July 2000	Violation
Venier and Nicolas v. France (V)	690 & 691/1996	10 July 2000	Violation
Gómez v. Spain (V)	701/1996	20 July 2000	Violation
Diergaardt et al. v. Namibia (V)	760/1997	25 July 2000	Violation
Toala et al. v. New Zealand (V)	675/1995	2 November 2000	No violation
Kavanagh v. Ireland (V)	819/1998	4 April 2001	Violation
Blazek et al. v. Czech Republic (V)	857/1999	12 July 2001	Violation
Schmitz-de-Jong v. The Netherlands (V)	855/1999	16 July 2001	No violation

Name of case	Comm. No.	Date of Decision	Outcome
Torregrosa Lafuente et al. v. Spain (A)	866/1999	16 July 2001	Inadmissible
Cheban v. Russian Federation (V)	790/1997	24 July 2001	No violation
Alejandro Marín Gómez v. Spain (V)	865/1999	22 October 2001	No violation
Äärelä v. Finland (V)	779/1997	24 October 2001	Violation
Des Fours v. Czech Republic (V)	747/1997	30 October 2001	Violation

ARTICLE 27

Name of case	Comm. No.	Date of Decision	Outcome
Lovelace v. Canada (V)	24/1977 (R.6/24)	30 July 1981	Violation
Kitok v. Sweden (V)	197/1985	27 July 1988	No violation
R.T. v. France (A)	262/1987	30 March 1989	Inadmissible
T.K. v. France (A)	220/1987	8 November 1989	Inadmissible
Lubicon Lake Band v. Canada (V)	167/1984	26 March 1990	Violation
Ballantyne, Davidson and McIntyre v. Canada (V)	359 & 385/1989	31 March 1993	Violation
Sara et al. v. Finland (A)	431/1990	23 March 1994	Inadmissible
Länsman et al. v. Finland (V)	511/1992	26 October 1994	No violation
Länsman et al. v. Finland (V)	671/1995	30 October 1996	No violation
Diergaardt et al. v. Namibia (V)	760/1997	25 July 2000	Violation
Mahuika et al. v. New Zealand (V)	547/1993	27 October 2000	No violation
Äärelä v. Finland (V)	779/1997	24 October 2001	Violation

ANNEX 18

INDEX OF CASES OF THE HUMAN RIGHTS COMMITTEE BY STATE PARTY

to update generally see country at: www.unhchr.ch/tbs/doc.nsf
see also www.bayefsky.com

A = admissibility decision
DC = discontinued
DJ = decision to deal with cases jointly
I = interim measures
V = views

Angola

Name of case	Comm. No.	Date of Decision	Treaty Articles	Outcome
Dias v. Angola (A)	711/1996	20 March 1998		Admissible
Dias v. Angola (V)	711/1996	20 March 2000	9(1)	Violation

Argentina

Name of case	Comm. No.	Date of Decision	Treaty Articles	Outcome
S.E. v. Argentina (A)	275/1988	26 March 1988	2	Inadmissible
R.A.V.N. et al. v. Argentina (DJ),(A)	343, 344 & 345/1988	26 March 1990		Inadmissible
Mónaco v. Argentina (V)	400/1990	3 April 1995	17, 23(1), 24(1, 2), 25, 26	Violation

Australia

Name of case	Comm. No.	Date of Decision	Treaty Articles	Outcome
J.L. v. Australia (A)	491/1992	28 July 1992		Inadmissible
A.S. and L.S. v. Australia (A)	490/1992	30 March 1993		Inadmissible

Name of case	Comm. No.	Date of Decision	Treaty Articles	Outcome
K.L.B.-W. v. Australia (A)	499/1992	30 March 1993		Inadmissible
Toonen v. Australia (V)	488/1992	30 March 1994	2(1), 17(1), 26	Violation
Perera v. Australia (A)	536/1993	28 March 1995	14(5)	Inadmissible
X. v. Australia (A)	557/1993	16 July 1996		Inadmissible
B.L. v. Australia (A)	659/1995	8 November 1996		Inadmissible
Jarman v. Australia (A)	700/1996	8 November 1996		Inadmissible
Werenbeck v. Australia (A)	579/1994	27 March 1997		Inadmissible
A. v. Australia (V)	560/1993	3 April 1997	2(1, 3), 9(1, 4, 5), 14(1, 3b, c, d)	Violation
A.R.J. v. Australia (V)	692/1996	28 July 1997	6(1), 7, 14(1, 3)	No violation
G.T. v. Australia (V)	706/1996	4 November 1997	2(1), 6, 7, 9	No violation
Lindon v. Australia (A)	646/1995	20 October 1998		Inadmissible
Lamagna v. Australia (A)	737/1997	7 April 1999		Inadmissible
Pasla v. Australia (A)	751/1997	7 April 1999		Inadmissible
Y. v. Australia (A)	772/1997	17 July 2000		Inadmissible
Hart v. Australia (A)	947/2000	25 October 2000		Inadmissible
Jensen v. Australia (A)	762/1997	22 March 2001	7, 10(1, 3)	Inadmissible
Uebergang v. Australia (A)	963/2001	22 March 2001	14(6)	Inadmissible
C. v. Australia (A)	832/1998	25 July 2001		Inadmissible
Winata v. Australia (V)	930/2000	26 July 2001	17, 23(1), 24(1)	Violation

Austria

Name of case	Comm. No.	Date of Decision	Treaty Articles	Outcome
Pauger v. Austria (A)	415/1990	22 March 1991		Admissible
Pauger v. Austria (V)	415/1990	26 March 1992	26	Violation
H.H. v. Austria (A)	427/1990	22 October 1992		Inadmissible
Nahlik v. Austria (A)	608/1995	22 July 1996	2, 26	Inadmissible
Pauger v. Austria (A)	716/1996	9 July 1997		Admissible
Darwish v. Austria (A)	679/1996	28 July 1997		Inadmissible
Pauger v. Austria (V)	716/1996	25 March 1999	26	Violation

Barbados

Name of case	Comm. No.	Date of Decision	Treaty Articles	Outcome
S.M. v. Barbados (A)	502/1992	31 March 1994		Inadmissible
Bradshaw v. Barbados (A)	489/1992	19 July 1994		Inadmissible
Roberts v. Barbados (A)	504/1992	19 July 1994		Inadmissible

Belarus

Name of case	Comm. No.	Date of Decision	Treaty Articles	Outcome
Laptsevich v. Belarus (V)	780/1997	20 March 2000	19(2, 3)	Violation

Bolivia

Name of case	Comm. No.	Date of Decision	Treaty Articles	Outcome
Penarrieta et al. v. Bolivia (V)	176/1984	2 November 1987	7, 9(3), 10(1), 14(3b)	Violation
Fillastre and Bizouarn v. Bolivia (A)	336/1988	6 November 1990		Admissible
Fillastre and Bizouarn v. Bolivia (V)	336/1988	5 November 1991	9(2, 3), 10, 14(3b–d)	Violation

Bulgaria

Name of case	Comm. No.	Date of Decision	Treaty Articles	Outcome
Petkov v. Bulgaria (A)	844/1998	25 March 1999		Inadmissible
Nicolov v. Bulgaria (A)	824/1998	24 March 2000		Inadmissible

Cameroon

Name of case	Comm. No.	Date of Decision	Treaty Articles	Outcome
Mukong v. Cameroon (V)	458/1991	21 July 1994	7, 9, 14(3a, b), 19(3a, b)	Violation

Name of case	Comm. No.	Date of Decision	Treaty Articles	Outcome
Mazou v. Cameroon (A)	630/1995	6 July 1998		Admissible
Mazou v. Cameroon (V)	630/1995	26 July 2001	2, 25	Violation

Canada

Name of case	Comm. No.	Date of Decision	Treaty Articles	Outcome
C.E. v. Canada (A)	13/1977	25 August 1977		Inadmissible
Z.Z. v. Canada (A)	17/1977	18 July 1978		Inadmissible
N.S. v. Canada (A)	26/1978	28 July 1978		Inadmissible
D.B. v. Canada (A)	15/1977	24 April 1979		Inadmissible
C.J. v. Canada (A)	19/1977	13 August 1979		Inadmissible
L.P. v. Canada (A)	2/1976	14 August 1979		Inadmissible
Lovelace v. Canada (A)	24/1977	14 August 1979		Admissible
Pinkney v. Canada (A)	27/1978	2 April 1980		Admissible
A.S. v. Canada (A)	68/1980	31 March 1981		Inadmissible
Lovelace v. Canada (V)	24/1977 (R.6/24)	30 July 1981	2, 3, 12, 27	Violation
A.R.S. v. Canada (A)	91/1981	28 October 1981		Inadmissible
Pinkney v. Canada (V)	27/1977 (R.7/27)	29 October 1981	10(1, 2), 14(3c, 5), 17(1)	Violation
Van Duzen v. Canada (V)	50/1979 (R.12/50)	7 April 1982	15(1)	No violation
MacIsaac v. Canada (V)	55/1979	14 October 1982	15(1)	No violation
E.H.P. v. Canada (A)	67/1980	27 October 1982		Inadmissible
J.R.T. and the W.G. Party v. Canada (A)	104/1981	6 April 1983	19	Inadmissible
J.S. v. Canada (A)	130/1982	6 April 1983	14(3d)	Inadmissible
L.S.N. v. Canada (A)	94/1981	30 March 1984		Admissible (discontinued)
A.D. v. Canada (A)	78/1980	29 July 1984	1	Inadmissible
J.K. v. Canada (A)	174/1984	26 October 1984	14(1, 3b, c)	Inadmissible
C.F. et al. v. Canada (A)	113/1981	12 April 1985	25(b)	Inadmissible
J.H. v. Canada (A)	187/1985	12 April 1985	2(1)	Inadmissible
Y.L. v. Canada (A)	112/1981	8 April 1986	14(1)	Inadmissible
J.B. et al. v. Canada (A)	118/1982	18 July 1986	22(3)	Inadmissible
S.H.B. v. Canada (A)	192/1985	24 March 1987	2	Inadmissible
V.M.R.B. v. Canada (A)	236/1987	18 July 1988	2, 3, 6, 9, 13, 14, 18, 19, 26	Inadmissible
R.L. v. Canada (A)	342/1989	7 April 1989		Inadmissible

Name of case	Comm. No.	Date of Decision	Treaty Articles	Outcome
Bhinder v. Canada (V)	208/1986	9 November 1989	18, 26	Violation
Lubicon Lake Band v. Canada (V)	167/1984	26 March 1990	27, 1	Violation
Ballantyne, Davidson and McIntyre v. Canada (DJ)	359 & 385/1989	18 October 1990		
Z.P. v. Canada (A)	341/1988	11 April 1991	14(1, 3b)	Inadmissible
Ballantyne, Davidson and McIntyre v. Canada (A)	359 & 385/1989	11 April 1991		Admissible
Marshall et al. v. Canada (V)	205/1986	4 November 1991	25(a)	No violation
R.L. et al. v. Canada (A)	358/1989	5 November 1991		Inadmissible
J.J.C. v. Canada (A)	367/1989	5 November 1991		Inadmissible
J.P. v. Canada (A)	446/1991	7 November 1991		Inadmissible
K.C. v. Canada (A)	486/1992	29 July 1992		Inadmissible
G.T. v. Canada (A)	420/1990	23 October 1992		Inadmissible
Ballantyne, Davidson and McIntyre v. Canada (V)	359 & 385/1989	31 March 1993	19(2, 3), 26, 27	Violation
Singer v. Canada (A)	455/1991	8 April 1993		Admissible
Kindler v. Canada (V)	470/1991	30 July 1993	6(1, 2), 7	No violation
H.T.B. v. Canada (A)	534/1993	19 October 1993		Inadmissible
Cox v. Canada (A)	539/1993	3 November 1993		Admissible
Ng v. Canada (V)	469/1991	5 November 1993	6(1, 2), 7, 10	Violation
Stewart v. Canada (A)	538/1993	18 March 1994		Admissible
J.M. v. Canada (A)	559/1993	8 April 1994		Inadmissible
M.A.B., W.A.T. and J.-A.Y.T. v. Canada (A)	570/1993	8 April 1994		Inadmissible
Singer v. Canada (V)	455/1991	26 July 1994	19(2)	Violation
Canepa v. Canada (A)	558/1993	13 October 1994		Admissible
Cox v. Canada (V)	539/1993	31 October 1994	6, 7,14, 26	No violation
Atkinson et al. v. Canada (A)	573/1994	31 October 1995		Inadmissible
Lacika v. Canada (A)	638/1995	3 November 1995		Inadmissible
Stewart v. Canada (V)	538/1993	1 November 1996	12(4), 17, 23	No violation
Canepa v. Canada (V)	558/1993	3 April 1997	7, 12(4), 17, 23	No violation
Badu v. Canada (A)	603/1994	18 July 1997		Inadmissible
Nartey v. Canada (A)	604/1994	18 July 1997		Inadmissible
Adu v. Canada (A)	654/1995	18 July 1997	14	Inadmissible

Name of case	Comm. No.	Date of Decision	Treaty Articles	Outcome
Singh v. Canada (A)	761/1997	29 July 1997	7, 14(2, 3a), 15, 26	Inadmissible
Byrne and Lazarescu v. Canada (A)	742/1997	25 March 1999	26	Inadmissible
Gauthier v. Canada (V)	633/1995	7 April 1999	19(2)	Violation
Cziklin v. Canada (A)	741/1997	27 July 1999		Inadmissible
Tadman et al. v. Canada (A)	816/1998	29 October 1999		Inadmissible
Waldman v. Canada (V)	694/1996	3 November 1999	26	Violation
G. v. Canada (A)	934/2000	17 July 2000	14	Inadmissible
Gillan v. Canada (A)	936/2000	17 July 2000		Inadmissible
Ross v. Canada (V)	736/1997	18 October 2000	18, 19	No violation
Devgan v. Canada (A)	948/2000	30 October 2000		Inadmissible
Keshavjee v. Canada (A)	949/2000	2 November 2000		Inadmissible

Central African Republic

Name of case	Comm. No.	Date of Decision	Treaty Articles	Outcome
Bozize v. Central African Republic (A)	428/1990	8 July 1992		Admissible
Bozize v. Central African Republic (V)	428/1990	7 April 1994	7, 9, 10, 14(3c)	Violation

Chile

Name of case	Comm. No.	Date of Decision	Treaty Articles	Outcome
Barzana v. Chile (A)	740/1998	23 July 1998		Inadmissible
Acuña Inostroza et al. v. Chile (A)	717/1996	23 July 1999		Inadmissible
Vargas v. Chile (A)	718/1996	26 July 1999		Inadmissible
Menanteau v. Carrasco v. Chile (A)	746/1997	26 July 1999		Inadmissible

Colombia

Name of case	Comm. No.	Date of Decision	Treaty Articles	Outcome
de Montejo v. Colombia (V)	64/1979 (R.15/64)	24 March 1982	14(5)	Violation
de Guerrero v. Colombia (V)	45/1979 (R.11/45)	31 March 1982	6(1)	Violation

Name of case	Comm. No.	Date of Decision	Treaty Articles	Outcome
Borda et al. v. Colombia (V)	46/1979 (R.11/46)	27 July 1982	9 (3, 4), 14	Violation
Herrera v. Colombia (V)	161/1983	2 November 1987	6, 7, 10(1)	Violation
Arévalo v. Colombia (V)	181/1984	3 November 1989	6, 9	Violation
A.Z. v. Colombia (A)	244/1987	3 November 1989		Inadmissible
Delgado Páez v. Colombia (V)	195/1985	12 July 1990	9(1), 18, 19, 25(c), 26	Violation
E.P. et al. v. Colombia (A)	318/1988	25 July 1990	1	Inadmissible
E.M. v. Colombia (A)	214/1986	21 March 1991		Admissible
O.H.C. v. Colombia (A)	287/1988	1 November 1991		Inadmissible
Fei v. Colombia (A)	514/1992	18 March 1994		Admissible
Fei v. Colombia (V)	514/1992	4 April 1995	14(1), 17, 23(4)	Violation
Bautista v. Colombia (V)	563/1993	27 October 1995	2(3), 6(1), 7, 9, 14(3c)	Violation
Arhuaco v. Colombia (A)	612/1995	14 March 1996		Admissible
Arhuaco v. Colombia (V)	612/1995	29 July 1997	2(3), 6(1), 7, 9, 14	Violation
A.A.G. v. Colombia (A)	697/1996	18 March 1998		Admissible
Rojas García v. Colombia (V)	687/1996	3 April 2001	7, 17	Violation

Costa Rica

Name of case	Comm. No.	Date of Decision	Treaty Articles	Outcome
J.R.C. v. Costa Rica (A)	296/1988	30 March 1989	2, 3, 5(2), 9, 14	Inadmissible

Croatia

Name of case	Comm. No.	Date of Decision	Treaty Articles	Outcome
Paraga v. Croatia (A)	727/1996	24 July 1998		Admissible
Linderholm v. Croatia (A)	744/1997	23 July 1999		Inadmissible
Paraga v. Croatia (V)	727/1996	4 April 2001	14(3c), 19	Violation

Czech Republic

Name of case	Comm. No.	Date of Decision	Treaty Articles	Outcome
Drbal v. Czech Republic (A)	498/1992	22 July 1994		Inadmissible
Simunek et al. v. Czech Republic (V)	516/1992	19 July 1995	14, 26	Violation
Adam v. Czech Republic (V)	586/1994	23 July 1996	26	Violation
Malik v. Czech Republic (A)	669/1995	21 October 1998		Inadmissible
Schlosser v. Czech Republic (A)	670/1995	21 October 1998		Inadmissible
Jakes and Mazurkiewiczova v. Czech Republic (A)	724/1996	26 July 1999		Inadmissible
Koutny v. Czech Republic (A)	807/1998	20 March 2000		Inadmissible
Blazek et al. v. Czech Republic (V)	857/1999	12 July 2001	26	Violation
Des Fours v. Czech Republic (V)	747/1997	30 October 2001	2, 14(1), 26	Violation

Democratic Republic of the Congo

Name of case	Comm. No.	Date of Decision	Treaty Articles	Outcome
Mbenge v. Zaire (V)	16/1977	25 March 1983	2(3), 6(2), 12(2), 14(3), 19	Violation
Luyeye v. Zaire (V)	90/1981	21 July 1983	2(3), 9(1, 2, 3, 4), 10(1)	Violation
Muteba v. Zaire (V)	124/1982	24 July 1984	7, 9(3, 4), 10(1), 14(3), 19	Violation
Mpandanjila et al. v. Zaire (V)	138/1983	26 March 1986	9(1), 10(1), 12(1),14(1), 19, 25	Violation
Mpaka-Nsusu v. Zaire (V)	157/1983	26 March 1986	9(1), 12(1), 19, 25	Violation
Miango v. Zaire (V)	194/1985	27 October 1987	6, 7	Violation
Birindwa and Tshisekedi v. Zaire (V)	241 & 242/1987	2 November 1989	7, 9(2, 3), 10(1), 12(1), 17(1)	Violation

Name of case	Comm. No.	Date of Decision	Treaty Articles	Outcome
D.B.-B. v. Zaire (A)	463/1991	8 November 1991		Inadmissible
Kanana v. Zaire (V)	366/1989	2 November 1993	7, 9(1), 10(1)	Violation
Amisi v. Zaire (A)	497/1992	19 July 1994		Inadmissible
Tshishimbi v. Zaire (V)	542/1993	25 March 1996	7, 9(1)	Violation
N.K.T.G. v. Democratic Republic of the Congo (A)	641/1995	10 July 1997		Admissible

Denmark

Name of case	Comm. No.	Date of Decision	Treaty Articles	Outcome
K.L. v. Denmark (A)	59/1979	26 March 1980		Inadmissible
J.J. v. Denmark (A)	60/1979	26 March 1980		Inadmissible
K.L. v. Denmark (A)	72/1980	31 July 1980		Inadmissible
K.L. v. Denmark (A)	81/1980	27 March 1981		Inadmissible
A.M. v. Denmark (A)	121/1982 (R.26/121)	23 July 1982	7, 14, 26	Inadmissible
P.S. v. Denmark (A)	397/1990	22 July 1992		Inadmissible

Dominican Republic

Name of case	Comm. No.	Date of Decision	Treaty Articles	Outcome
Portorreal v. Dominican Republic (V)	188/1984	5 November 1987	7, 9(1, 2), 10(1)	Violation
Giry v. Dominican Republic (V)	193/1985	20 July 1990	13	Violation
Mojica v. Dominican Republic (A)	449/1991	18 March 1993		Admissible
Mojica v. Dominican Republic (V)	449/1991	15 July 1994	6(1), 7, 9(1)	Violation

Ecuador

Name of case	Comm. No.	Date of Decision	Treaty Articles	Outcome
Bolaños v. Ecuador (V)	238/1987	26 July 1989	3, 9 (3, 5), 14(2)	Violation
García v. Ecuador (A)	319/1988	18 October 1990		Admissible
García v. Ecuador (V)	319/1988	5 November 1991	7, 9, 13	Violation
Jijón v. Ecuador (V)	277/1988	26 March 1992	7, 9, 10, 14	Violation

Name of case	Comm. No.	Date of Decision	Treaty Articles	Outcome
Fuenzalida v. Ecuador (V)	480/1991	12 July 1996	7, 9, 10, 14(3c, e), (5)	Violation
Ortega v. Ecuador (V)	481/1991	8 April 1997	7, 10(1)	Violation

Equatorial Guinea

Name of case	Comm. No.	Date of Decision	Treaty Articles	Outcome
Bahamonde v. Equatorial Guinea (V)	468/1991	20 October 1993	9(1, 3), 12(1, 2), 14(1), 26	Violation
Mika Miha v. Equatorial Guinea (V)	414/1990	8 July 1994	7, 9, 10(1), 12(1, 2), 19(1, 2)	Violation

Finland

Name of case	Comm. No.	Date of Decision	Treaty Articles	Outcome
Hartikainen v. Finland (V)	40/1978	9 April 1981	18(4)	No violation
Hertzberg et al. v. Finland (V)	61/1979 (R.14/61)	2 April 1982	19(2, 3)	No violation
Muhonen v. Finland (V)	89/1981	8 April 1985	14(6)	No violation
L.T.K. v. Finland (A)	185/1984	9 July 1985	18	Inadmissible
E.H. v. Finland (A)	170/1984	25 October 1985	26	Inadmissible
J.H. v. Finland (A)	300/1988	23 March 1989	7, 14(1, 3g)	Inadmissible
R.M. v. Finland (A)	301/1988	23 March 1989	7, 14(1, 3), 17	Inadmissible
Vuolanne v. Finland (V)	265/1987	7 April 1989	2(1, 2, 3), 7, 9(4), 10(1)	Violation
C.W. v. Finland (A)	379/1989	30 March 1990		Inadmissible
Torres v. Finland (V)	291/1988	2 April 1990	7, 9(4)	Violation
Järvinen v. Finland (V)	295/1988	25 July 1990	26	No violation
O.J. v. Finland (A)	419/1990	6 November 1990		Inadmissible
C.E.A. v. Finland (A)	316/1988	10 July 1991		Inadmissible
A.M. v. Finland (A)	398/1990	23 July 1992		Inadmissible
Karttunen v. Finland (V)	387/1989	23 October 1992	14(1)	Violation
I.P. v. Finland (A)	450/1991	26 July 1993		Inadmissible
Länsman et al. v. Finland (A)	511/1992	14 October 1993		Admissible

Name of case	Comm. No.	Date of Decision	Treaty Articles	Outcome
K.J.L. v. Finland (A)	544/1993	3 November 1993		Inadmissible
Sara et al. v. Finland (A)	431/1990	23 March 1994	27	Inadmissible
Kivenmaa v. Finland (V)	412/1990	31 March 1994	15, 19(2a, b), 21	Violation
Peltonen v. Finland (V)	92/1992 4	21 July 1994	12(2, 3)	No violation
Länsman et al. v. Finland (V)	511/1992	26 October 1994	27	No violation
Länsman et al. v. Finland (V)	671/1995	30 October 1996	27	No violation
Hankala v. Finland (A)	850/1999	25 March 1999		Inadmissible
Äärelä v. Finland (V)	779/1997	24 October 2001	2, 14(1), 27	Violation

France

Name of case	Comm. No.	Date of Decision	Treaty Articles	Outcome
H.S. v. France (A)	184/1984	10 April 1986	2(1)	Inadmissible
S.R. v. France (A)	243/1987	5 November 1987	2	Inadmissible
C.L.D. v. France (A)	228/1987	18 July 1988	2	Inadmissible
J.B. and H.K. v. France (DJ), (A)	324 & 325/1988	25 October 1988		Inadmissible
R.T. v. France (A)	262/1987	30 March 1989	2(1, 2, 3), 19(2), 26, 27	Inadmissible
Gueye et al. v. France (V)	196/1983	3 April 1989	2, 26	Violation
Morael v. France (V)	207/1986	28 July 1989	14(1, 2), 17(1), 26	No violation
T.K. v. France (A)	220/1987	8 November 1989	27	Inadmissible
M.K. v. France (A)	222/1987	8 November 1989		Inadmissible
Hervé Le Bihan v. France (DJ), (A)	323/1988	1989		Admissible
Guesdon v. France (V)	219/1986	25 July 1990	14(1, 3e, f), 26	No violation
E.M.E.H. v. France (A)	409/1990	2 November 1990		Inadmissible
Cadoret and Bihan v. France (V)	221 & 323/1988	11 April 1991	14(3e, f), 26	No violation
Barzhig v. France (V)	327/1988	11 April 1991	14(1, 3f)	No violation
S.G. v. France (A)	347/1988	1 November 1991		Inadmissible
G.B. v. France (A)	348/1989	1 November 1991		Inadmissible
C.L.D. v. France (A)	439/1990	8 November 1991		Inadmissible
R.L.M. v. France (A)	363/1989	6 April 1992		Inadmissible
A.C. v. France (A)	393/1990	21 July 1992		Inadmissible

Name of case	Comm. No.	Date of Decision	Treaty Articles	Outcome
Casanovas v. France (A)	441/1990	7 July 1993		Admissible
Hopu and Bessert v. France (A)	549/1993	30 June 1994		Admissible
Trébutien v. France (A)	421/1990	18 July 1994		Inadmissible
Glaziou v. France (A)	452/1991	18 July 1994		Inadmissible
Casanovas v. France (V)	441/1990	19 July 1994	14(1)	No violation
Gire v. France (A)	525/1992	28 March 1995		Inadmissible
J.P.L. v. France (A)	472/1991	26 October 1995	3(4)	Inadmissible
Hopu and Bessert v. France (A)	549/1993	30 October 1995		Admissible
Valentijn v. France (A)	584/1994	22 July 1996		Inadmissible
Bordes and Temeharo v. France (A)	645/1995	22 July 1996		Inadmissible
Faurisson v. France (V)	550/1993	8 November 1996	19(3a, b)	No violation
Foin v. France (A)	666/1995	11 July 1997		Admissible
Maille v. France (A)	689/1996	11 July 1997		Admissible
Venier and Nicholas v. France (DJ), (A)	690 & 691/1996	11 July 1997		Admissible
Hopu and Bessert v. France (V)	549/1993	29 July 1997	14, 17, 23, 26	Violation
Triboulet v. France (A)	661/1995	29 July 1997		Inadmissible
Foin v. France (V)	666/1995	3 November 1999	26	Violation
Lestourneaud v. France (A)	861/1999	3 November 1999	2	Inadmissible
Doukoure v. France (A)	756/1997	29 March 2000		Inadmissible
Maille v. France (V)	689/1996	10 July 2000	8, 26	Violation
Venier and Nicolas v. France (V)	690 & 691/1996	10 July 2000	8, 26	Violation
Karker v. France (V)	833/1998	26 October 2000	12(3), 13	No violation
Vakoumé v. France(A)	822/1998	31 October 2000		Inadmissible
Meiers v. France(A)	831/1998	16 July 2001		Inadmissible

Georgia

Name of case	Comm. No.	Date of Decision	Treaty Articles	Outcome
Domukovsky et al. v. Georgia (V)	623, 624, 626 & 627/1995	6 April 1998	6, 7, 9(1, 2), 10(1), 14(3d, f, 5), 25	Violation

Germany

Name of case	Comm. No.	Date of Decision	Treaty Articles	Outcome
K.V. and C.V. v. Germany (A)	568/1993	8 April 1994		Inadmissible
Maloney v. Germany (A)	755/1997	29 July 1997		Inadmissible
Rogl v. Germany (A)	808/1998	25 October 2000	14, 17, 23, 24	Inadmissible
Kehler v. Germany (A)	834/1998	22 March 2001		Inadmissible
Neremberg v. Germany (A)	991/2001	27 July 2001		Inadmissible

Guyana

Name of case	Comm. No.	Date of Decision	Treaty Articles	Outcome
Yasseen and Thomas v. Republic of Guyana (A)	676/1996	11 July 1997		Admissible
Yasseen and Thomas v. Republic of Guyana (V)	676/1996	30 March 1998	6(1, 4), 7, 10(1, 2), 14(1, 3a–e, g)	Violation

Hungary

Name of case	Comm. No.	Date of Decision	Treaty Articles	Outcome
I.S. v. Hungary (A)	389/1989	9 November 1990		Inadmissible
Párkányi v. Hungary (A)	410/1990	22 March 1991		Admissible
Párkányi v. Hungary (V)	410/1990	27 July 1992	10, 14(1, 3e)	Violation
T.P. v. Hungary (A)	496/1992	30 March 1993		Inadmissible
Kulomin v. Hungary (A)	521/1992	16 March 1994		Admissible
E. and A.K. v. Hungary (A)	520/1992	7 April 1994		Inadmissible
Kulomin v. Hungary (V)	521/1992	22 March 1996	9(3), 10, 14	Violation
Somers v. Hungary (V)	566/1993	23 July 1996	26	No violation
Kalaba v. Hungary (A)	735/1997	7 November 1997		Inadmissible

Iceland

Name of case	Comm. No.	Date of Decision	Treaty Articles	Outcome
Kaaber v. Iceland (A)	674/1995	5 November 1996		Inadmissible

Ireland

Name of case	Comm. No.	Date of Decision	Treaty Articles	Outcome
Holland v. Ireland (A)	593/1994	25 October 1995		Inadmissible
Kavanagh v. Ireland (V)	819/1998	4 April 2001	14(1), 26	Violation

Italy

Name of case	Comm. No.	Date of Decision	Treaty Articles	Outcome
Fanali v. Italy (V)	75/1980	31 March 1983	14(5)	No violation
C.A. v. Italy (A)	127/1982	31 March 1983	14(1)	Inadmissible
M.A. v. Italy (A)	117/1981	10 April 1984	19, 25	Inadmissible
Disabled and handicapped persons in Italy v. Italy (A)	163/1984	10 April 1984	26	Inadmissible
A.P. v. Italy (A)	204/1986	2 November 1987	14(7)	Inadmissible
I.M. v. Italy (A)	266/1987	23 March 1989		Inadmissible
E.E. v. Italy (A)	378/1989	26 March 1990		Inadmissible
A.B. et al. v. Italy (A)	413/1990	2 November 1990	1	Inadmissible
H. v. Italy (A)	565/1993	8 April 1994		Inadmissible
Maleki v. Italy (A)	699/1996	11 July 1997		Admissible
Maleki v. Italy (V)	699/1996	15 July 1999	14(1, 3d)	Violation

Jamaica

Name of case	Comm. No.	Date of Decision	Treaty Articles	Outcome
J. M. v. Jamaica (A)	165/1984	26 March 1986	12	Inadmissible
O. W. v. Jamaica (A)	227/1987	26 July 1988		Inadmissible
C.J. v. Jamaica (A)	252/ 1987	26 July 1988		Inadmissible
L. C. et al. v. Jamaica (A)	257/1987	26 July 1988		Inadmissible
L. G. v. Jamaica (A)	285/1988	26 July 1988		Inadmissible
L. S. v. Jamaica (A)	286/1988	26 July 1988		Inadmissible
Robinson v. Jamaica (V)	223/1987	30 March 1989	14 (1, 3)	Violation

Name of case	Comm. No.	Date of Decision	Treaty Articles	Outcome
Pratt and Morgan v. Jamaica (V)	225/1987	6 April 1989	6, 7, 14 (3,5)	Violation
A. S. v. Jamaica (A)	231/1987	21 July 1989		Inadmissible
A. A. v. Jamaica (A)	251/1987	30 October 1989		Inadmissible
C. G. v. Jamaica (A)	281/1988	30 October 1989		Inadmissible
A. W. v. Jamaica (A)	290/1988	8 November 1989		Inadmissible
G. S. v. Jamaica (A)	369/1989	8 November 1989		Inadmissible
Quelch v. Jamaica (A)	292/1988	15 March 1990		Admissible
Martin v. Jamaica (A)	317/1988	15 March 1990	14(3c, 5), 17	Admissible
Gentles et al. v. Jamaica (A)	352/1989	15 March 1990		Admissible
D. F. v. Jamaica (A)	329/1988	26 March 1990		Inadmissible
L. R. and T. W. v. Jamaica (A)	258/1987	13 July 1990		Inadmissible
D. B. v. Jamaica (A)	259/1987	13 July 1990		Inadmissible
C. B. v. Jamaica (A)	260/1987	13 July 1990		Inadmissible
N. C. v. Jamaica (A)	278/1988	13 July 1990		Inadmissible
Reid v. Jamaica (V)	250/1987	20 July 1990	6, 7, 14	Violation
N. A. J. v. Jamaica (A)	246/1987	26 July 1990		Inadmissible
Wright v. Jamaica (A)	349/1989	17 October 1990		Admissible
Compass v. Jamaica (A)	375/1989	18 October 1990		Admissible
W.W. v. Jamaica (A)	254/1987	26 October 1990		Inadmissible
E. B. v. Jamaica (A)	303/1988	26 October 1990		Inadmissible
R. M. v. Jamaica (A)	315/1988	26 October 1990		Inadmissible
D. S. v. Jamaica (A)	234/1987	8 April 1991		Inadmissible
Reynolds v. Jamaica (V)	229/1987	8 April 1991	14 (3d, e)	No violation
Kelly v. Jamaica (V)	253/1987	8 April 1991	5, 6, 9, 10, 14(3a–e, g)	Violation
Sawyers and McLean v. Jamaica (V)	226 & 256/1987	11 April 1991	14 (1, 3d, e)	No violation
D. S. v. Jamaica (A)	304/1988	11 April 1991		Inadmissible
D. D. v. Jamaica (A)	313/1988	11 April 1991		Inadmissible
J. S. v. Jamaica (A)	312/1988	21 April 1991		Admissible
M. F. v. Jamaica (A)	233/1987	21 October 1991		Admissible
Henry v. Jamaica (V)	230/1987	1 November 1991	6, 14(3b, d, e, 5)	Violation
Collins v. Jamaica (V)	240/1987	1 November 1991	7, 10(1), 14(1, 2, 3e)	Violation
Little v. Jamaica (V)	283/1988	1 November 1991	6, 14	Violation
Campbell v. Jamaica (V)	248/1987	30 March 1992	6, 9 (1–4), 14(1, 3b–e, g)	Violation
Prince v. Jamaica (V)	269/1987	30 March 1992	7, 14(3e)	No violation

Name of case	Comm. No.	Date of Decision	Treaty Articles	Outcome
Barrett and Sutcliffe v. Jamaica (V)	270 & 271/1988	30 March 1992	7, 10, 14	Violation
Thomas v. Jamaica (V)	272/1988	31 March 1992	14(1, 3b)	Violation
N. A. J. v. Jamaica (A)	351/1989	6 April 1992		Inadmissible
M. F. v. Jamaica (A)	335/1988	17 July 1992		Inadmissible
R. W. v. Jamaica (A)	340/1988	21 July 1992		Inadmissible
Hibbert v. Jamaica (V)	293/1988	27 July 1992	14 (1, 3b, e)	No violation
Wright v. Jamaica (V)	349/1989	27 July 1992	6, 10, 14 (1,3b,e)	Violation
Ellis v. Jamaica (V)	276/1988	28 July 1992	7, 14	No violation
C.F. v. Jamaica (A)	382/1989	28 July 1992		Inadmissible
H. C. v. Jamaica (A)	383/1989	28 July 1992		Inadmissible
M. R. v. Jamaica (A)	405/1990	28 July 1992		Inadmissible
Linton v. Jamaica (V)	255/1987	22 October 1992	7, 10(1), 14(1, 3b, d)	Violation
Quelch v. Jamaica (V)	292/1988	23 October 1992	14 (3d)	No violation
Simmonds v. Jamaica (V)	338/1988	23 October 1992	14 (3b,d)	Violation
E. E. v. Jamaica (A)	337/1988	23 October 1992		Inadmissible
G. H. v. Jamaica (A)	370/1989	23 October 1992		Inadmissible
Gordon v. Jamaica (V)	237/1987	5 November 1992	14 (1, 3d, e)	No violation
Champagnie et al. v. Jamaica (A)	445/1991	18 March 1993		Admissible
Peart v. Jamaica (A)	482/1991	19 March 1993		Admissible
Griffiths v. Jamaica (V)	274/1988	24 March 1993	7, 14(1)	No violation
Campbell v. Jamaica (V)	307/1988	24 March 1993	6, 14 (1, 3d)	Violation
Martin v. Jamaica (V)	317/1988	24 March 1993	7, 14 (3c, 5)	No violation
Francis v. Jamaica (V)	320/1988	24 March 1993	6, 7, 10(1), 14 (3c, 5)	Violation
Collins v. Jamaica (V)	356/1989	25 March 1993	6, 14(3b–e, 5)	Violation
Smith v. Jamaica (V)	282/1988	31 March 1993	6, 14(3b, c)	Violation
Bailey v. Jamaica (V)	334/1988	31 March 1993	7, 10(1)	Violation
N. P. v. Jamaica (A)	404/1990	5 April 1993		Inadmissible
Thomas v. Jamaica (V)	321/1988	19 October 1993	7, 10(1)	Violation
Gentles et al. v. Jamaica (V)	352/ 1989	19 October 1993	14(3b, d, 5)	No violation
Compass v. Jamaica (V)	375/1989	19 October 1993	14(3e)	No violation
Wright and Harvey v. Jamaica (A)	459/1991	17 March 1994		Admissible
Peart v. Jamaica (A)	464/1991	17 March 1994		Admissible
Hamilton v. Jamaica (V)	333/1988	23 March 1994	6, 14 (3c, 5)	Violation

Name of case	Comm. No.	Date of Decision	Treaty Articles	Outcome
Currie v. Jamaica (V)	377/1989	29 March 1994	6, 14(3c, 5)	Violation
Allen v. Jamaica (V)	332/1988	31 March 1994	6(5), 14 (1, 3c, e)	No violation
Grant v. Jamaica (V)	353/1988	31 March 1994	6, 7, 10, 14(1, 3c, e)	No violation
Berry v. Jamaica (V)	330/1988	7 April 1994	6, 7, 9 (3, 4), 10 (1, 2), 14 (1, 3, 5)	Violation
Marriott v. Jamaica (A)	519/1992	30 June 1994		Admissible
Reid v. Jamaica (V)	335/1989	8 July 1994	14(3b, c, 5)	Violation
Hylton v. Jamaica (V)	407/1990	8 July 1994	7, 10(1)	Violation
Champagnie et al. v. Jamaica (V)	445/1991	18 July 1994	6, 14 (3c, 5)	Violation
Lambert v. Jamaica (A)	517/1992	21 July 1994		Inadmissible
Simms v. Jamaica (A)	541/1993	3 April 1995	7, 14(3b)	Inadmissible
Rogers v. Jamaica (A)	494/1992	4 April 1995	7, 10	Inadmissible
Peart and Peart v. Jamaica (DJ)	464 & 482/1991	19 July 1995		
Peart and Peart v. Jamaica (V)	464 & 482/1991	19 July 1995	6, 7, 9, 10(1), 14(3e)	Violation
Francis v. Jamaica (V)	606/1994	25 July 1995	7, 10 (1), 14 (3c, 5)	Violation
Leslie v. Jamaica (A)	564/1993	12 October 1995		Admissible
Jones v. Jamaica (A)	585/1994	13 October 1995		Admissible
Chung v. Jamaica (A)	591/1994	13 October 1995		Admissible
Stephens v. Jamaica (V)	373/1989	18 October 1995	7, 9(2–4), 10 (1), 14 (3c, 5)	Violation
Wright and Harvey v. Jamaica (V)	459/1991	27 October 1995	6, 14 (3b, c, d)	Violation
Marriot v. Jamaica (V)	519/1992	27 October 1995	14 (3b, e)	Violation
Edwards v. Jamaica (A)	529/1993	31 October 1995		Inadmissible
Chaplin v. Jamaica (V)	596/1994	2 November 1995	7, 10 (1), 14, (3d)	Violation
C. Johnson v. Jamaica (A)	592/1994	14 March 1996		Admissible
E. Johnson v. Jamaica (V)	588/1994	22 March 1996	6, 7, 10(1), 14 (3c, g, 5)	Violation
Grant v. Jamaica (V)	597/1994	22 March 1996	9 (2, 3, 4)	Violation
Graham and Morrison v. Jamaica (V)	461/1991	25 March 1996	6(2), 7, 14(3b, d)	Violation
Deidrick v. Jamaica (A)	619/1995	4 July 1996		Admissible
Tomlin v. Jamaica (V)	589/1994	16 July 1996	14(3b, e, 5), 17(1)	No violation
Hylton v. Jamaica (V)	600/1994	16 July 1996	7, 10, (1)	No violation

Name of case	Comm. No.	Date of Decision	Treaty Articles	Outcome
Kelly v. Jamaica (V)	537/1993	17 July 1996	2(3), 6, 14(1), (3b, d)	Violation
Lewis v. Jamaica (V)	527/1993	18 July 1996	7, 10(1), 14(3b, d, e, g)	Violation
Burrell v. Jamaica (V)	546/1993	18 July 1996	6(1), (2), 14(3b, c), (5)	Violation
Spence v. Jamaica (V)	599/1994	18 July 1996	7, 10(1)	Violation
Sterling v. Jamaica (V)	598/1994	22 July 1996	7, 10(1), 14 (3b, d)	Violation
Henry and Douglas v. Jamaica (V)	571/1994	25 July 1996	7, 9(3), 10(1), 14 (3c), (5)	Violation
Leehong v. Jamaica (A)	613/1995	16 October 1996		Admissible
Samuel Thomas v. Jamaica (A)	614/1995	17 October 1996		Admissible
Finn v. Jamaica (A)	617/1995	17 October 1996		Admissible
Adams v. Jamaica (V)	607/1994	30 October 1996	7, 10(1), 14(1, 2, 3b, e)	Violation
Price v. Jamaica (V)	572/1994	6 November 1996	6, 14 (3c, d, 5)	Violation
Richards v. Jamaica (V)	535/1993	31 March 1997	6(2), 14 (1,2, 3b, d, e, 5)	Violation
Steadman v. Jamaica (V)	528/1993	2 April 1997	6(2), 9(3), 14(3b–d)	Violation
Reynolds v. Jamaica (V)	587/1994	3 April 1997	7, 10(1)	Violation
Williams v. Jamaica (V)	561/1993	8 April 1997	14(1, 3a–c, e)	Violation
Hamilton v. Jamaica (A)	616/1995	7 July 1997		Admissible
F. M. v. Jamaica (A)	729/1996	9 July 1997		Admissible
Blaine v. Jamaica (V)	696/1996	17 July 1997	7, 9(2), 10(1), 14 (1, 2, 3a, b, e, 5)	Violation
Lewis v. Jamaica (V)	708/1996	17 July 1997	9(3), 10(1, 2), 14(2, 3b –d)	Violation
McLawrence v. Jamaica (V)	702/1996	18 July 1997	6, 7, 9(2, 3) 10, 14(1, 3c, 5, 7)	Violation

Name of case	Comm. No.	Date of Decision	Treaty Articles	Outcome
Taylor v. Jamaica (V)	707/1996	18 July 1997	6, 9(2, 3), 10(1), 14 (1, 3b–d)	Violation
Edwards v. Jamaica (V)	529/1993	28 July 1997	7, 10(1)	Violation
Walker and Richards v. Jamaica (V)	639/1995	28 July 1997	9(3), 10(1), 14(3c, 5)	Violation
Thomas v. Jamaica (V)	532/1993	3 November 1997	2(3), 14 (3b–d)	Violation
Williams v. Jamaica (V)	609/1995	4 November 1997	7, 10(1)	Violation
Young v. Jamaica (V)	615/1995	4 November 1997	6, 7, 14 (1, 3b)	Violation
McIntosh v. Jamaica (A)	640/1995	7 November 1997		Inadmissible
Freemantle v. Jamaica (A)	625/1995	30 March 1998		Inadmissible
McLeod v. Jamaica (V)	734/1997	31 March 1998	6, 10(1), 14(3a, b, e)	Violation
McTaggart v. Jamaica (V)	749/1997	31 March 1998	7, 9, 10(3), 14(3a, b, e)	Violation
Shaw v. Jamaica (V)	704/1996	2 April 1998	6, 7, 9(2,3), 10 (1), 14 (1, 3b)	Violation
Taylor v. Jamaica (V)	705/1996	2 April 1998	6, 7, 9(2, 3), 10(1), 14(1, 3b–d)	Violation
Jones v. Jamaica (V)	585/1994	6 April 1998	9(2, 3), 10(1), 14 (1, 2, 3a–e)	Violation
Chung v. Jamaica (V)	591/1994	9 April 1998	7, 10(1), 14(1, 2, 3g)	Violation
Deidrick v. Jamaica (V)	619/1995	9 April 1998	7, 10(1), 14 (1, 2)	Violation
Morrison v. Jamaica (V)	635/1995	27 July 1998	7, 9(2, 3), 10(1), 14(3c)	Violation
Whyte v. Jamaica (V)	732/1997	27 July 1998	7, 9, 10, 14(3b–e)	Violation
Perkins v. Jamaica (V)	733/1997	30 July 1998	6, 7, 9, 10, 14(3b–d)	Violation
Leslie v. Jamaica (V)	564/1993	31 July 1998	7, 10(1), 14(3b–e)	Violation
Finn v. Jamaica (V)	617/1995	31 July 1998	7, 9(3), 10 (1), 14 (1, 2, 3c, d, 5)	Violation
Daley v. Jamaica (V)	750/1997	31 July 1998	6, 7, 9, 10, 14(3c, d, 5)	Violation
Morrisson v. Jamaica (A)	611/1995	31 July 1998		Inadmissible

Name of case	Comm. No.	Date of Decision	Treaty Articles	Outcome
C. Johnson v. Jamaica (V)	592/1994	20 October 1998	6(5), 7, 14(3d)	Violation
Henry v. Jamaica (V)	610/1995	20 October 1998	7, 10(1)	Violation
Campbell v. Jamaica (V)	618/1995	20 October 1998	10(1)	Violation
Pennant v. Jamaica (V)	647/1995	20 October 1998	7, 9(3, 4), 10(1)	Violation
Forbes v. Jamaica (V)	649/1995	20 October 1998	9(1), 10(1)	Violation
Colin Johnson v. Jamaica (V)	653/1995	20 October 1998	7, 10(1)	Violation
Morrison v. Jamaica (V)	663/1995	3 November 1998	6(2), 7, 9 (2, 3), 10 (1, 2), 14 (3c, d, 5)	Violation
Levy v. Jamaica (V)	719/1996	3 November 1998	6(2), 10 (1), 14(3d)	Violation
Morgan and Williams v. Jamaica (V)	720/1996	3 November 1998	10(1)	Violation
Marshall v. Jamaica (V)	730/1996	3 November 1998	6(2), 9(3), 10(1), 14(3d)	Violation
Brown v. Jamaica (V)	775/1997	23 March 1999	6, 7, 9(3), 10(1), 14(3c, d)	Violation
Amore v. Jamaica (A)	634/1995	23 March 1999		Inadmissible
Bennett v. Jamaica (V)	590/1994	25 March 1999	9(3), 10 (1), 14 (3c, 5)	Violation
Thomas v. Jamaica (V)	614/1995	31 March 1999	14(3c, 5)	Violation
Lumley v. Jamaica (V)	662/1995	31 March 1999	14(3d, 5)	Violation
Fraser and Fisher v. Jamaica (V)	722/1996	31 March 1999	7, 10(1), 14(1)	No violation
Smith and Stewart v. Jamaica (V)	668/1995	8 April 1999	7, 10(1),14 (3c, d, 5)	Violation
D. Thomas v. Jamaica (V)	800/1998	8 April 1999	10, 24	Violation
Leehong v. Jamaica (V)	613/1995	13 July 1999	7, 9(1, 3), 10(1)	Violation
Bailey v. Jamaica (V)	709/1996	21 July 1999	7, 10, 14(1, 3 d, e, 5)	Violation
Hamilton v. Jamaica (V)	616/1995	23 July 1999	9(3), 10 (1), 14(3c)	Violation
Gallimore v. Jamaica (V)	680/1996	23 July 1999	7, 10, 14 (1, 3d, 5)	Violation

Name of case	Comm. No.	Date of Decision	Treaty Articles	Outcome
Hankle v. Jamaica (V)	710/1996	28 July 1999	14	No violation
Brown and Parish v. Jamaica (V)	665/1995	29 July 1999	6(2), 9(3), 14(3b–d, 5)	Violation
Osbourne v. Jamaica (V)	759/1997	15 March 2000	7	Violation
Freemantle v. Jamaica (V)	625/1995	24 March 2000	7, 9(2, 3, 4), 10(1)	Violation
Robinson v. Jamaica (V)	731/1996	29 March 2000	7, 10(1), 14(3d, 5)	Violation
Simpson v. Jamaica (V)	695/1996	31 October 2001	10(1), 14(3d)	Violation

Latvia

Name of case	Comm. No.	Date of Decision	Treaty Articles	Outcome
Perel v. Latvia (A)	650/1995	3 July 1996		Admissible
Perel v. Latvia (A)	650/1995	30 March 1998	14(1, 2)	No violation
Ignatane v. Latvia (V)	884/1999	25 July 2001	2, 25	Violation

Libyan Arab Jamahiriya

Name of case	Comm. No.	Date of Decision	Treaty Articles	Outcome
A.I.E.v. Libyan Arab Jamahiriya (A)	457/1991	7 November 1991		Inadmissible
El-Megreisi v. Libyan Arab Jamahiriya (V)	440/1990	23 March 1994	7, 9, 10(1)	Violation

Madagascar

Name of case	Comm. No.	Date of Decision	Treaty Articles	Outcome
Marais v. Madagascar (V)	49/1979	24 March 1983	7, 10(1), 14(3b, d)	Violation
Wight v. Madagascar (V)	115/1982	1 April 1985	7, 10(1), 14(3b)	Violation
Jaona v. Madagascar (V)	132/1982	1 April 1985	9(1, 2), 19(2)	Violation
Hammel v. Madagascar (V)	155/1983	3 April 1987	9(4), 13	Violation

Mauritius

Name of case	Comm. No.	Date of Decision	Treaty Articles	Outcome
Mauritian women v. Mauritius (V)	35/1978	9 April 1981	2(1), 3, 17 (1), 23, 25, 26	Violation
L. G. v. Mauritius (A)	354/1989	31 October 1990		Inadmissible
Poongavanam v. Mauritius (A)	567/1993	26 July 1994	14(1)	Inadmissible
Gobin v. Mauritius (A)	787/1997	16 July 2001		Inadmissible

Namibia

Name of case	Comm. No.	Date of Decision	Treaty Articles	Outcome
Diergaardt et al v. Namibia (A)	760/1997	7 July 1998		Admissible
Diergaardt et al. v. Namibia (V)	760/1997	25 July 2000	1, 14(1), 25(a, c), 26, 27	Violation

Netherlands

Name of case	Comm. No.	Date of Decision	Treaty Articles	Outcome
M. F. v. The Netherlands (A)	173/1984	2 November 1984	7	Inadmissible
J. D. B. v. The Netherlands (A)	178/1984	26 March 1985	26	Inadmissible
F. G. G. v. The Netherlands (A)	209/1986	25 March 1987	14(1)	Inadmissible
H. D. P. v. The Netherlands (A)	217/1986	8 April 1987	2	Inadmissible
S.W.M. Brooks v. The Netherlands (V)	172/1984	9 April 1987	26	Violation
Danning v. The Netherlands (V)	180/1984	9 April 1987	2, 26	No violation
Zwaan-de Vries v. The Netherlands (V)	182/1984	9 April 1987	26	Violation
R. T. Z. v. The Netherlands (A)	245/1987	5 November 1987		Inadmissible
P. P. C. v. The Netherlands (A)	212/1986	24 March 1988	26	Inadmissible

Name of case	Comm. No.	Date of Decision	Treaty Articles	Outcome
M. J. G. v The Netherlands (A)	267/1987	24 March 1988	26	Inadmissible
Hendricks v. The Netherlands (V)	201/1985	27 July 1988	23(4)	Violation
G. F. Croes v. The Netherlands (A)	164/1984	7 November 1988	1, 6, 9(1), 14(3), 19, 21, 25, 26	Inadmissible
Vos v. The Netherlands (V)	218/1986	29 March 1989	26	No violation
H. C. M. A. v. The Netherlands (A)	213/1986	30 March 1989	2(2, 3), 7, 9, 10(1), 14(1)	Inadmissible
B. d. B. et al. v. The Netherlands (A)	273/1989	30 March 1989	14(1), 26	Inadmissible
H.A.E.D.J. v. The Netherlands (A)	297/1988	30 October 1989		Inadmissible
van Meurs v. The Netherlands (V)	215/1986	13 July 1990	14(1)	Violation
van Alphen v. The Netherlands (V)	305/1988	23 July 1990	9, 14(3), 17	Violation
J. G. v. The Netherlands (A)	306/1988	25 July 1990		Inadmissible
R.L.A.W. v. The Netherlands (A)	372/1989	2 November 1990		Inadmissible
Sprenger v. The Netherlands (A)	395/1990	22 March 1991		Admissible
J. P. K. v. The Netherlands (A)	401/1990	7 November 1991		Inadmissible
T. W. M. B. v. The Netherlands (A)	403/1990	7 November 1991		Inadmissible
H. J. H. v The Netherlands (A)	448/1991	7 November 1991		Inadmissible
Sprenger v. The Netherlands (V)	395/1990	31 March 1992	26	No violation
L. E. S. K. v The Netherlands (A)	381/1989	21 July 1992		Inadmissible
C. B. D. v. The Netherlands (A)	394/1990	22 July 1992		Inadmissible
M. S. v. The Netherlands (A)	396/1990	22 July 1992		Inadmissible
W. J. H. v. The Netherlands (A)	408/1990	22 July 1992	14(2, 6)	Inadmissible
K. et al. v. The Netherlands (A)	483/1991	23 July 1992		Inadmissible
Oulajin & Kaiss v. The Netherlands (V)	406 & 426/1990	23 October 1992	26	No violation

Name of case	Comm. No.	Date of Decision	Treaty Articles	Outcome
W. B. E. v. The Netherlands (A)	432/1990	23 October 1992	9(3, 5), 14(2)	Inadmissible
Pepels v. The Netherlands (A)	484/1991	19 March 1993		Admissible
E. W. et al. v. The Netherlands (A)	429/1990	8 April 1993		Inadmissible
Coriel and Aurik v. The Netherlands (A)	453/1991	8 July 1993		Admissible
J. H. W. v. The Netherlands (A)	501/1992	16 July 1993		Inadmissible
Neefs v. The Netherlands (A)	425/1990	26 July 1993		Admissible
v. d. M. v The Netherlands (A)	478/1991	26 July 1993		Inadmissible
Brinkhof v. The Netherlands (V)	402/1990	27 July 1993	26	No violation
A. R. U. v. The Netherlands (A)	509/1992	19 October 1993		Inadmissible
P. J. N. v. The Netherlands (A)	510/1992	19 October 1993		Inadmissible
Araujo-Jongen v. The Netherlands (V)	418/1990	22 October 1993	26	No violation
J. S. v. The Netherlands (A)	522/1992	3 November 1993		Inadmissible
E. C. W. v. The Netherlands (A)	524/1992	3 November 1993		Inadmissible
R. E. d. B. v. The Netherlands (A)	548/1993	3 November 1993		Inadmissible
J. A. M. B. R. v. The Netherlands (A)	477/1991	7 April 1994	26	Inadmissible
Neefs v. The Netherlands (V)	425/1990	15 July 1994	26	No violation
Pepels v. The Netherlands (V)	484/1991	15 July 1994	26	No violation
Coeriel and Aurik v. The Netherlands (V)	453/1991	31 October 1994	17	Violation
Debreczeny v. The Netherlands (V)	500/1992	3 April 1995	25(b), 26	No violation
de Groot v. The Netherlands (A)	578/1994	14 July 1995	14, 15, 26	Inadmissible
Houwen v. The Netherlands (A)	583/1994	14 July 1995		Inadmissible
van der Ent v. The Netherlands (A)	657/1995	3 November 1995		Inadmissible
Koning v. The Netherlands (A)	660/1995	3 November 1995		Inadmissible

Name of case	Comm. No.	Date of Decision	Treaty Articles	Outcome
Snijders et al. v. The Netherlands (A)	651/1995	14 March 1996		Admissible
Kruyt-Amesz et al. v. The Netherlands (A)	664/1995	25 March 1996		Inadmissible
Hoofdman v. The Netherlands (A)	602/1994	3 July 1996		Admissible
Oord v. The Netherlands (A)	658/1995	23 July 1997	26	Inadmissible
Westerman v. The Netherlands (A)	682/1996	16 October 1997		Admissible
Snijders et al. v. The Netherlands (V)	651/1995	27 July 1998	26	No violation
Hoofdman v. The Netherlands (V)	602/1994	3 November 1998	26	No violation
Gerritsen v. The Netherlands (A)	714/1996	25 March 1999		Inadmissible
Berg. v. The Netherlands (A)	835/1998	25 March 1999		Inadmissible
Vos. v. The Netherlands (V)	786/1997	26 July 1999	26	Violation
Timmerman v. The Netherlands (A)	871/1999	29 October 1999		Inadmissible
Westerman v. The Netherlands (V)	682/1996	3 November 1999	15, 18	No violation
Hoelen v. The Netherlands (A)	873/1999	3 November 1999	26	Inadmissible
Mansur v. The Netherlands (A)	883/1999	5 November 1999		Inadmissible
Wuyts v. The Netherlands (A)	785/1997	17 July 2000	10	Inadmissible
Jansen-Gielen v. The Netherlands (V)	846/1999	3 April 2001	14(1)	Violation
Schmitz-de-Jong v. The Netherlands (V)	855/1999	16 July 2001	26	No violation

New Zealand

Name of case	Comm. No.	Date of Decision	Treaty Articles	Outcome
S. B. v. New Zealand (A)	475/1991	31 March 1994		Inadmissible
Maori tribes v. New Zealand (A)	547/1993	13 October 1995		Admissible
Drake et al. v. New Zealand (A)	601/1994	3 April 1997	26	Inadmissible
Potter v. New Zealand (A)	632/1995	28 July 1997		Inadmissible

Name of case	Comm. No.	Date of Decision	Treaty Articles	Outcome
Toala et al. v. New Zealand (A)	675/1995	10 July 1998		Admissible
A. v. New Zealand (V)	754/1997	15 July 1999	9(1, 4)	No violation
Tamihere v. New Zealand (A)	891/1999	15 March 2000	14(1, 3d)	Inadmissible
Buckle v. New Zealand (V)	858/1999	25 October 2000	17, 23	No violation
Mahuika et al. v. New Zealand (V)	547/1993	27 October 2000	14(1), 27	No violation
Toala et al. v. New Zealand (V)	675/1995	2 November 2000	12(4), 26	No violation
Parun and Bulmer v. New Zealand (A)	952/2000	22 March 2001		Inadmissible
Singh v. New Zealand (A)	791/1997	12 July 2001		Inadmissible

Nicaragua

Name of case	Comm. No.	Date of Decision	Treaty Articles	Outcome
Blanco v. Nicaragua (V)	328/1988	20 July 1994	7, 9(1), 10 (1), 14(3g)	Violation

Norway

Name of case	Comm. No.	Date of Decision	Treaty Articles	Outcome
K. B. v. Norway (A)	53/1979	14 August 1979		Inadmissible
S. S. v. Norway (A)	79/1980	2 April 1982		Inadmissible
I. M. v. Norway (A)	129/1982	6 April 1983		Inadmissible
O. F. v. Norway (A)	158/1983	26 October 1984	14(3 c, d, e)	Inadmissible
V. O. v. Norway (A)	168/1984	17 July 1985		Inadmissible
A. and S. N. v. Norway (A)	224/1987	11 July 1988	18	Inadmissible
Harward v. Norway (A)	451/1991	26 July 1993		Admissible
Harward v. Norway (V)	451/1991	15 July 1994	14(3b)	No violation
Spakmo v. Norway (A)	631/1995	20 March 1997		Admissible
Ben Said v. Norway (A)	767/1997	21 July 1998		Admissible
Bryhn v. Norway (V)	789/1997	29 October 1999	14(5)	No violation
Spakmo v. Norway (V)	631/1995	5 November 1999	9(1)	Violation
Bech v. Norway (A)	882/1999	15 March 2000		Inadmissible
Ben Said v. Norway (V)	767/1997	29 March 2000	14(1)	No violation

Panama

Name of case	Comm. No.	Date of Decision	Treaty Articles	Outcome
Wolf v. Panama (V)	289/1988	26 March 1992	9(3), 10, 14 (1, 3b–d)	Violation
del Cid v. Panama (A)	473/1991	11 October 1993		Inadmissible
J. E. S. B. v. Panama (A)	443/1991	17 March 1994		Admissible
G. W. G. v. Panama (A)	446/1991	17 March 1994		Admissible
Solis v. Panama (A)	436/1990	18 July 1994		Inadmissible
Colamarco v. Panama (A)	437/1990	21 October 1994	9(1)	Inadmissible
Thompson v. Panama (A)	438/1990	21 October 1994	9(1, 2)	Inadmissible
Omar Simons v. Panama (A)	460/1991	25 October 1994		Inadmissible
del Cid v. Panama (V)	473/1991	19 July 1995	9(3, 4), 14(2, 3, 6, 7)	Violation

Peru

Name of case	Comm. No.	Date of Decision	Treaty Articles	Outcome
Avellanal v. Peru (V)	202/1986	28 October 1988	2, 3, 14 (1), 26	Violation
Muñoz v. Peru (V)	203/1986	4 November 1988	2(3), 14 (1, 2), 25(c), 26	Violation
González del Rio v. Peru (A)	263/1987	6 November 1990		Admissible
Orihuela v. Peru (A)	309/1988	22 March 1991		Admissible
González del Rio v. Peru (V)	263/1987	28 October 1992	9(1, 4), 12 (2), 14(1)	Violation
Orihuela v. Peru (V)	309/1988	14 July 1993	10(1), 17, 26	Violation
Celis Laureano v. Peru (A)	540/1993	4 July 1994		Admissible
Celis Laureano v. Peru (V)	540/1993	25 March 1996	2(1), 6(1), 7, 9(1), 24(1)	Violation
Polay Campos v. Peru (V)	577/1994	6 November 1997	14(1, 2, 3b, d)	Violation
Arredondo v. Peru (V)	688/1996	27 July 2000	9(1, 3), 10(1), 14 (1, 3c)	Violation

Philippines

Name of case	Comm. No.	Date of Decision	Treaty Articles	Outcome
E. A. et al. v. Philippines (A)	503/1992	14 October 1993		Admissible
Piandiong et al. v. Philippines (V)	869/1999	19 October 2000	6, 14	No violation

Poland

Name of case	Comm. No.	Date of Decision	Treaty Articles	Outcome
Kall v. Poland (V)	522/1993	14 July 1997	25(c)	No violation

Republic of Korea

Name of case	Comm. No.	Date of Decision	Treaty Articles	Outcome
Sohn v. Republic of Korea (A)	518/1992	18 March 1994		Admissible
Sohn v. Republic of Korea (V)	518/1992	19 July 1995	13(2), 19(2, 3)	Violation
Kim v. Republic of Korea (A)	574/1994	14 March 1996		Admissible
Park v. Republic of Korea (A)	628/1995	5 July 1996		Admissible
Ajaz and Jamil v. Republic of Korea (A)	644/1995	19 March 1997		Admissible
Park v. Republic of Korea (V)	628/1995	20 October 1998	19	Violation
Kim v. Republic of Korea (V)	574/1994	3 November 1998	19	Violation
Ajaz and Jamil v. Republic of Korea (V)	644/1995	13 July 1999	7, 14	No violation

Russian Federation

Name of case	Comm. No.	Date of Decision	Treaty Articles	Outcome
G.C. and O.B v. Russian Federation (A)	637/1995	14 October 1996		Admissible
E. P. S. v. Russian Federation (A)	712/1996	20 March 1998		Admissible

Name of case	Comm. No.	Date of Decision	Treaty Articles	Outcome
V.A.L. v. Russian Federation (A)	763/1997	7 July 1998		Admissible
Plotnikov v. Russian Federation (A)	784/1997	25 March 1999		Inadmissible
Gridin v. Russian Federation (V)	770/1997	20 July 2000	9(1), 14(1, 2, 3b)	Violation
Cheban v. Russian Federation (V)	790/1997	24 July 2001	26	No violation

Saint Vincent and the Grenadines

Name of case	Comm. No.	Date of Decision	Treaty Articles	Outcome
Thompson v. Saint Vincent and the Grenadines (V)	806/1998	18 October 2000	6(1), 7, 10(1)	Violation

Senegal

Name of case	Comm. No.	Date of Decision	Treaty Articles	Outcome
Koné v. Senegal (V)	386/1989	21 October 1994	9(3), 19	Violation

Sierra Leone

Name of case	Comm. No.	Date of Decision	Treaty Articles	Outcome
Mansaraj et al. v. Sierra Leone (V)	839, 840 & 841/1998	16 July 2001	6, 14(5)	Violation

Slovakia

Name of case	Comm. No.	Date of Decision	Treaty Articles	Outcome
Drobek v. Slovakia (A)	643/1995	14 July 1997	2, 26	Inadmissible
Mahmoud v. Slovakia (A)	935/2000	23 July 2001		Inadmissible

Spain

Name of case	Comm. No.	Date of Decision	Treaty Articles	Outcome
M. I. T. v. Spain (A)	310/1988	11 April 1991		Inadmissible
V. E. M. v. Spain (A)	467/1991	16 July 1993		Inadmissible

Name of case	Comm. No.	Date of Decision	Treaty Articles	Outcome
Griffin v. Spain (A)	493/1992	11 October 1993		Admissible
A. P. A. v. Spain (A)	433/1990	25 March 1994		Inadmissible
Pons v. Spain (A)	454/1991	30 June 1994		Admissible
Santacana v. Spain (V)	417/1990	15 July 1994	23(1, 4), 24	No violation
Griffin v. Spain (V)	493/1992	4 April 1995	9(2), 10(1), 14(3f)	Violation
Pons v. Spain (V)	454/1991	30 October 1995	14(1), 26	No violation
V. E. M. v. Spain (A)	656/1995	30 October 1995		Inadmissible
Hill v. Spain (V)	526/1993	2 April 1997	9(2, 3), 10, 14(1, 2, 3b, d, e, 5)	Violation
Bonelo v. Spain (A)	698/1996	29 July 1997		Inadmissible
Navarro v. Spain (A)	758/1997	29 July 1997		Inadmissible
Sánchez López v. Spain (A)	777/1997	18 October 1999	14(2, 3g)	Inadmissible
Gómez v. Spain (V)	701/1996	20 July 2000	14(5), 26	Violation
Torregrosa Lafuente et al. v. Spain (A)	866/1999	16 July 2001	14(1), 26	Inadmissible
Asensio López v. Spain (A)	905/2000	23 July 2001		Inadmissible
Alejandro Marín Gómez v. Spain (V)	865/1999	22 October 2001	25(c), 26	No violation

Suriname

Name of case	Comm. No.	Date of Decision	Treaty Articles	Outcome
Baboeram et al. v. Suriname (DJ)	146 & 148–154/1983	10 April 1984		
Baboeram et al. v. Suriname (V)	146 & 148–154/1983	4 April 1985	6(1)	Violation

Sweden

Name of case	Comm. No.	Date of Decision	Treaty Articles	Outcome
Maroufidou v. Sweden (V)	58/1979 (R.13/58)	9 April 1981	13	No violation
D. F. et al. v. Sweden (A)	183/1984	26 March 1985		Inadmissible
N. B. v. Sweden (A)	175/1984	11 July 1985	14(3a, c, e)	Inadmissible
Blom v. Sweden (V)	191/1985	4 April 1988	26	No violation
Kitok v. Sweden (V)	197/1985	27 July 1988	27	No violation
Lindgren et al. and Lundquist et al. v. Sweden (DJ),(V)	298 & 299/1988	9 November 1990	26	No violation

Name of case	Comm. No.	Date of Decision	Treaty Articles	Outcome
Celepli v. Sweden (A)	456/1991	19 March 1993		Admissible
Celepli v. Sweden (V)	456/1991	18 July 1994	12(1, 3)	No violation
Silva v. Sweden (A)	748/1997	18 October 1999		Inadmissible

Togo

Name of case	Comm. No.	Date of Decision	Treaty Articles	Outcome
Aduayom et al. v. Togo (DJ), (A)	422, 423, & 424/1990	30 June 1994		Admissible
Ackla v. Togo (V)	505/1992	25 March 1996	12(1), (3)	Violation
Aduayom et al. v. Togo (V)	422, 423, & 424/1990	12 July 1996	9(1), (5), 19, 25	Violation

Trinidad and Tobago

Name of case	Comm. No.	Date of Decision	Treaty Articles	Outcome
A newspaper publishing company v. Trinidad and Tobago (A)	360/1989	14 July 1989		Inadmissible
A publication and a printing v. Trinidad and Tobago (A)	361/1989	14 July 1989		Inadmissible
H. G. B. and S. P. v. Trinidad and Tobago (A)	268/1987	3 November 1989		Inadmissible
Pinto v. Trinidad and Tobago (V)	232/1987	20 July 1990	6, 14(3)	Violation
A. H. v. Trinidad and Tobago (A)	302/1988	31 October 1990		Inadmissible
G. J. v. Trinidad and Tobago (A)	331/1988	5 November 1991		Inadmissible
R. M. v. Trinidad and Tobago (I)	476/1991	23 July 1992		
Soogrim v. Trinidad and Tobago (V)	362/1989	8 April 1993	7, 10(1)	Violation
R. L. M. v. Trinidad and Tobago (A)	380/1989	16 July 1993		Inadmissible
V. B. v. Trinidad and Tobago (A)	485/1991	26 July 1993		Inadmissible
R. M. v. Trinidad and Tobago (A)	384/1989	29 October 1993		Inadmissible
Seerattan v. Trinidad and Tobago (A)	434/1990	17 March 1994		Admissible

Name of case	Comm. No.	Date of Decision	Treaty Articles	Outcome
Shalto v. Trinidad and Tobago (A)	447/1991	17 March 1994		Admissible
R. M. v.Trinidad and Tobago (A)	476/1991	31 March 1994		Inadmissible
Barry v. Trinidad and Tobago (A)	471/1992	18 July 1994		Inadmissible
Shalto v. Trinidad and Tobago (V)	447/1991	4 April 1995	9(3), 14(3c)	Violation
Guerra and Wallen v. Trinidad and Tobago (A)	575 & 576/1994	4 April 1995		Inadmissible
Holder v. Trinidad and Tobago (A)	515/1992	19 July 1995		Inadmissible
Bullock v. Trinidad and Tobago (A)	553/1993	19 July 1995	14(1, 3e)	Inadmissible
Elahie v. Trinidad and Tobago (A)	533/1993	12 October 1995		Admissible
LaVende v. Trinidad and Tobago (A)	554/1993	12 October 1995		Admissible
Bickaroo v. Trinidad and Tobago (A)	555/1993	12 October 1995		Admissible
Matthews v. Trinidad and Tobago (A)	569/1993	13 October 1995		Admissible
Seerattan v. Trinidad and Tobago (V)	434/1990	26 October 1995	14(3e)	Violation
Phillip v. Trinidad and Tobago (A)	594/1992	15 March 1996		Admissible
Smart v. Trinidad and Tobago (A)	672/1995	5 July 1996		Admissible
Pinto v. Trinidad and Tobago (V)	512/1992	16 July 1996	7, 10(1), 17(1)	Violation
Neptune v. Trinidad and Tobago (V)	523/1992	16 July 1996	9(3), 10(1), 14(3c, 5)	Violation
E. P. v. Trinidad and Tobago (A)	636/1995	15 October 1996		Admissible
Elahie v. Trinidad and Tobago (V)	533/1993	28 July 1997	9(3), 10(1), 14(3c)	Violation
M. W. v. Trinidad and Tobago (A)	683/1996	14 October 1997		Admissible
R. S. v. Trinidad and Tobago (A)	684/1996	14 October 1997		Admissible
LaVende v. Trinidad and Tobago (V)	554/1993	29 October 1997	7, 10(1), 14(3d, 5)	Violation
Bickaroo v. Trinidad and Tobago (V)	555/1993	29 October 1997	7, 10(1)	No violation

Name of case	Comm. No.	Date of Decision	Treaty Articles	Outcome
Gonzales v. Trinidad and Tobago (A)	673/1995	23 March 1998		Inadmissible
Matthews v. Trinidad and Tobago (V)	569/1993	31 March 1998	10(1)	Violation
Smart v. Trinidad and Tobago (V)	672/1995	29 July 1998	9(3), 14(3b, c)	Violation
Chadee et al. v. Trinidad and Tobago (V)	813/1998	29 July 1998	6, 7, 14 (3c, 5)	No violation
Phillip v. Trinidad and Tobago (V)	594/1992	20 October 1998	6, 10(1), 14(3b, d)	Violation
Henry v. Trinidad and Tobago (V)	752/1997	3 November 1998	7, 10(1), 14(1)	Violation
Bethel v. Trinidad and Tobago (A)	830/1998	31 March 1999		Inadmissible
Rawle Kennedy v. Trinidad and Tobago (A)	845/1999	2 November 1999	7	Admissible
Sextus v. Trinidad and Tobago (V)	818/1998	16 July 2001	9(3), 10(1), 14(3c, 5)	Violation
Sookal v. Trinidad and Tobago (V)	928/2000	25 October 2001	7, 9(3), 14(3c, d)	Violation

Ukraine

Name of case	Comm. No.	Date of Decision	Treaty Articles	Outcome
Y.G. v. Ukraine (A)	648/1995	19 March 1997		Admissible

Uruguay

Name of case	Comm. No.	Date of Decision	Treaty Articles	Outcome
Waksman v. Uruguay (A)	31/1978	24 April 1979		Admissible
Massera et al. v. Uruguay (V)	5/1977 (R.1/5)	15 August 1979	7, 9(1, 3, 4), 10(1), 14(1, 2, 3), 25	Violation
Valcada v. Uruguay (V)	9/1977	26 October 1979	9(4)	Violation
Waksman v. Uruguay (DC)	31/1978	28 March 1980		
Weismann and Perdomo v. Uruguay (V)	8/1977	3 April 1980	7, 9(1, 3, 4), 10(1), 14(1–3)	Violation

Name of case	Comm. No.	Date of Decision	Treaty Articles	Outcome
Ramirez v. Uruguay (V)	4/1977 (R.1/4)	23 July 1980	7, 9(1, 4), 10(1), 14(3)	Violation
Sequeira v. Uruguay (V)	6/1977	29 July 1980	9(3, 4), 14(1, 3)	Violation
Motta et al. v. Uruguay (V)	11/1977	29 July 1980	7, 9(3, 4), 10(1)	Violation
Weinberger v. Uruguay (V)	28/1978	29 October 1980	7, 9(3, 4), 10(1), 14(1, 3), 15, 19	Violation
Carballal v. Uruguay (V)	33/1978	27 March 1981	7, 9(1–4), 10(1), 14(3)	Violation
de Bouton v. Uruguay (V)	37/1978	27 March 1981	7, 9(3, 4), 10(1)	Violation
Pietraroia v. Uruguay (V)	44/1979	27 March 1981	9(2, 3, 4), 10(1), 14 (1, 3), 15 (1), 19(2), 25	Violation
Touron v. Uruguay (V)	32/1978	31 March 1981	9(3, 4), 14(1, 3)	Violation
Silva et al. v. Uruguay (V)	34/1978	8 April 1981	25	Violation
Burgos v. Uruguay (V)	52/1979	29 July 1981	2(1), 7, 9 (1, 3), 14, 19, 22	Violation
Casariego v. Uruguay (V)	56/1979	29 July 1981	2(1), 9(1), 10(1), 14 (3b, c)	Violation
Sendic v. Uruguay (V)	63/1979 (R.14/63)	28 October 1981	7, 9(3), 10 (1), 14(3)	Violation
Martins v. Uruguay (V)	57/1979 (R.13/57)	23 March 1982	12(2)	Violation
Altesor v. Uruguay (V)	10/1977 (R.2/10)	29 March 1982	9(3, 4), 10(1), 14 (1, 3), 25	Violation
Bleier v. Uruguay (V)	30/1978 (R.7/30)	29 March 1982	6, 7, 9, 10(1)	Violation
Simones v. Uruguay (V)	70/1981 (R.17/70)	1 April 1982	14(1, 3b, d), 10(1)	Violation
Izquierdo v. Uruguay (V)	73/1981 (R.18/73)	1 April 1982	14(3b, c, g), 7, 10(1), 19(3)	Violation
Masslotti and Baritussio v. Uruguay (V)	25/1978 (R.6/25)	26 July 1982	7, 9(1, 4), 10(1)	Violation

Name of case	Comm. No.	Date of Decision	Treaty Articles	Outcome
Schweizer v. Uruguay (V)	66/1980	12 October 1982	9(1, 3, 4), 10(1), 14 (3c, 7)	Violation
Barbato v. Uruguay (V)	84/1981	21 October 1982	6(1), 9 (3, 4), 14(3c)	Violation
Estrella v. Uruguay (V)	74/1980	29 March 1983	7, 10(1), 17, 14 (1, 3)	Violation
Larrosa v. Uruguay (V)	88/1981	29 March 1983	7, 10(1)	Violation
Lichtensztejn v. Uruguay (V)	77/1980	31 March 1983	12(2)	Violation
Vasilskis v. Uruguay (V)	80/1980	31 March 1983	7, 10(1), 14(1, 3)	Violation
Montero v. Uruguay (V)	106/1981	31 March 1983	12(2)	Violation
U.R. v. Uruguay (A)	128/1982	6 April 1983		Inadmissible
Caldas v. Uruguay (V)	43/1979	21 July 1983	9(2, 4), 10(1), 14(3b, c)	Violation
Estradet v. Uruguay (V)	105/1981	21 July 1983	2(3, 4), 10(1)	Violation
Quinteros v. Uruguay (V)	107/1981	21 July 1983	7, 9, 10(1)	Violation
Nunez v. Uruguay (V)	108/1981	22 July 1983	12(2)	Violation
Nieto v. Uruguay (V)	92/1981	25 July 1983	10(1), 14 (3b–d)	Violation
S.G.F. v. Uruguay (A)	136/1983	25 July 1983		Inadmissible
J.F. v. Uruguay (A)	137/1983	25 July 1983		Inadmissible
Machado v. Uruguay (V)	83/1981	4 November 1983	10(1), 14(3b, c)	Violation
Oxandabarat v. Uruguay (V)	103/1981	4 November 1983	14(3b, c)	Violation
Romero v. Uruguay (V)	85/1981	29 March 1984	10(1)	Violation
Viana v. Uruguay (V)	110/1981	29 March 1984	7, 10(1), 14(3b–d)	Violation
Manera v. Uruguay (V)	123/1982	6 April 1984	10, 14(3)	Violation
M.M. Q. v. Uruguay (A)	125/1982	6 April 1984		Admissible
de Voituret v. Uruguay (V)	109/1981	10 April 1984	10(1)	Violation
D.C.B. v. Uruguay (A)	131/1982	17 January 1985		Admissible
Conteris v. Uruguay (V)	139/1983	17 July 1985	7, 9(1–4), 10(1), 14(1, 3)	Violation

Name of case	Comm. No.	Date of Decision	Treaty Articles	Outcome
Arzuada v. Uruguay (V)	147/1983	1 November 1985	7, 10(1)	Violation
D.C.B. v. Uruguay (DC)	131/1982	1985		
M.M.Q. v. Uruguay (DC)	125/1982	1986		
Stalla Costa v. Uruguay (V)	198/1985	9 July 1987	2, 25, 26	No violation
Cariboni v. Uruguay (V)	159/1983	27 October 1987	7, 10(1), 14(1, 3)	Violation
Acosta v. Uruguay (V)	162/1983	25 October 1988	2(3), 7, 10(1)	Violation
Rodríguez Veiga v. Uruguay (A)	487/1992	18 July 1994	2(3), 25	Inadmissible
Rodríguez v. Uruguay (V)	322/1988	19 July 1994	2(3), 7	Violation

Venezuela

Name of case	Comm. No.	Date of Decision	Treaty Articles	Outcome
Solorzano v. Venezuela (V)	156/1983	26 March 1986	9(3, 4), 10(1)	Violation
Tovar v. Venezuela (A)	739/1997	25 March 1999		Inadmissible

Zambia

Name of case	Comm. No.	Date of Decision	Treaty Articles	Outcome
Bwalya v. Zambia (A)	314/1988	21 March 1991		Admissible
Bwalya v. Zambia (V)	314/1988	14 July 1993	9(1, 3), 12(1), 19, 25, 26	Violation
Kalenga v. Zambia (V)	326/1988	27 July 1993	9(2–4), 12(1), 10(1), 19	Violation
Lubuto v. Zambia (V)	390/1990	31 October 1995	6(2), 7, 14(3c, 5)	Violation
Mukunto v. Zambia (V)	768/1997	23 July 1999	14(1)	Violation
Chongwe v. Zambia (V)	821/1998	25 October 2000	6(1), 9(1)	Violation

INDEX OF CASES OF CAT BY ARTICLE

to update generally see jurisprudence at: www.unhchr.ch/tbs/doc.nsf
see also www.bayefsky.com

A = admissibility decision
V = views
DJ = decision to deal with cases jointly
I = interim measures

ARTICLE 2

Name of case	Comm. No.	Date of Decision	Outcome
O.R., M.M., and M.S. v. Argentina (DJ)	1, 2 & 3/1988	November 1989	
O. R., M. M., and M.S. v. Argentina (A)	1, 2 & 3/1998	November 1989	Inadmissible
Barakat v. Tunisia (V)	60/1996	10 November 1999	Violation

ARTICLE 3

Name of case	Comm. No.	Date of Decision	Outcome
Mutombo v. Switzerland (V)	13/1993	27 April 1994	Violation
Khan v. Canada (V)	15/1994	15 November 1994	Violation
A. E. v. Switzerland (A)	24/1995	2 May 1995	Inadmissible
M. A. v. Canada (A)	22/1995	3 May 1995	Inadmissible
X. v. Spain (A)	23/1995	15 November 1995	Inadmissible
Alan v. Switzerland (V)	21/1995	8 May 1996	Violation
X. v. The Netherlands (V)	36/1995	8 May 1996	No violation
Muzonzo v. Sweden (V)	41/1996	8 May 1996	Violation
Tala v. Sweden (V)	43/1996	15 November 1996	Violation
X. v. Switzerland (V)	27/1995	28 April 1997	No violation
Mohamed v. Greece (V)	40/1996	28 April 1997	No violation
Tapia Paez v. Sweden (V)	39/1996	28 April 1997	No violation
Aemei v. Switzerland (V)	34/1995	9 May 1997	Violation
X. v. Switzerland (V)	38/1995	9 May 1997	No violation
E.A. v. Switzerland (V)	28/1995	10 November 1997	No violation

Name of case	Comm. No.	Date of Decision	Outcome
P. Q. L. v. Canada (V)	57/1996	17 November 1997	No violation
X., Y. and Z. v. Sweden (V)	61/1996	6 May 1998	No violation
I. A. O v. Sweden (V)	65/1997	6 May 1998	No violation
A. F. v. Sweden (V)	89/1998	8 May 1998	Violation
G. R. B. v. Sweden (V)	83/1997	15 May 1998	No violation
A. L. N. v. Switzerland (V)	90/1997	19 May 1998	No violation
K.N. v. Switzerland (V)	94/1997	19 May 1998	No violation
H. W. A. v. Switzerland (A)	48/1996	20 May 1998	Inadmissible
J. U. A. v. Switzerland (V)	100/1997	10 November 1998	No violation
Núñez Chipana v. Venezuela (V)	110/1998	10 November 1998	Violation
Ayas v. Sweden (V)	97/1997	12 November 1998	Violation
A. v. The Netherlands (V)	91/1997	13 November 1998	Violation
Korban v. Sweden (V)	88/1997	16 November 1998	Violation
Haydin v. Sweden (V)	101/1997	20 November 1998	Violation
H. D. v. Switzerland (V)	112/1998	30 April 1999	No violation
S. M. R. and M. M. R. v. Sweden (V)	103/1998	5 May 1999	No violation
M. B. B. v. Sweden (V)	104/1998	5 May 1999	No violation
N. P. v. Australia (V)	106/1998	6 May 1999	No violation
Elmi v. Australia (V)	120/1998	14 May 1999	Violation
Arkauz v. France (V)	63/1997	9 November 1999	Violation
A. D. v. The Netherlands (V)	96/1997	12 November 1999	No violation
K. M. v. Switzerland (V)	107/1998	16 November 1999	No violation
G. T. v. Switzerland (V)	137/1999	16 November 1999	No violation
K. T. v. Switzerland (V)	118/1998	19 November 1999	No violation
N. M. v. Switzerland (V)	116/1998	9 May 2000	No violation
H. A. D. v. Switzerland (V)	126/1999	10 May 2000	No violation
S. C. v. Denmark (V)	143/1999	10 May 2000	No violation
V. X. N. and H. N. v. Sweden (V)	130 & 131/1999	15 May 2000	No violation
T. P. S. v. Canada (V)	99/1997	16 May 2000	No violation
A. M. v. Switzerland (V)	144/1999	14 November 2000	No violation
Y. S. v. Switzerland (V)	147/1999	14 November 2000	No violation
M. R. P. v. Switzerland (V)	122/1998	24 November 2000	No violation
A. S. v. Sweden (V)	149/1999	24 November 2000	Violation
M. K. O. v. The Netherlands (V)	134/1999	9 May 2001	No violation
S. S. and S. A. v. The Netherlands (V)	142/1999	11 May 2001	No violation

Name of case	Comm. No.	Date of Decision	Outcome
S. L. v. Sweden (V)	150/1999	11 May 2001	No violation
S. V. v. Canada (V)	49/1996	15 May 2001	No violation
Z. Z. v. Canada (V)	123/1998	15 May 2001	No violation
X. Y. v. Switzerland (V)	128/1999	15 May 2001	No violation

ARTICLE 11

Name of case	Comm. No.	Date of Decision	Outcome
Barakat v. Tunisia (V)	60/1996	10 November 1999	Violation

ARTICLE 12

Name of case	Comm. No.	Date of Decision	Outcome
Halimi-Nedzibi v. Austria (A)	8/1991	5 May 1992	Admissible
Halimi-Nedzibi v. Austria (I)	8/1991	26 April 1993	
Halimi-Nedzibi v. Austria (V)	8/1991	18 November 1993	Violation
Blanco Abad v. Spain (V)	59/1996	14 May 1998	Violation
Barakat v. Tunisia (V)	60/1996	10 November 1999	Violation
Ristic v. Yugoslavia (V)	113/1998	11 May 2001	Violation

ARTICLE 13

Name of case	Comm. No.	Date of Decision	Outcome
O.R., M.M., and M.S. v. Argentina (DJ)	1, 2, & 3/1988	November 1989	
O. R., M. M., and M.S. v. Argentina (A)	1, 2 & 3/1998	November 1989	Inadmissible
Parot v. Spain (V)	6/1990	2 May 1995	No violation
Blanco Abad v. Spain (V)	59/1996	14 May 1998	Violation
Barakat v. Tunisia (V)	60/1996	10 November 1999	Violation
Ristic v. Yugoslavia (V)	113/1998	11 May 2001	Violation

ARTICLE 14

Name of case	Comm. No.	Date of Decision	Outcome
O.R., M.M., and M.S. v. Argentina (DJ)	1, 2 & 3/1988	November 1989	
O. R., M. M., and M.S. v. Argentina (A)	1, 2 & 3/1998	November 1989	Inadmissible
Barakat v. Tunisia (V)	60/1996	10 November 1999	Violation
Ristic v. Yugoslavia (V)	113/1998	11 May 2001	Violation

ARTICLE 15

Name of case	Comm. No.	Date of Decision	Outcome
Halimi-Nedzibi v. Austria (A)	8/1991	5 May 1992	Admissible
Halimi-Nedzibi v. Austria (I)	8/1991	26 April 1993	
Halimi-Nedzibi v. Austria (V)	8/1991	18 November 1993	Violation
Blanco Abad v. Spain (V)	59/1996	14 May 1998	Violation

ARTICLE 16

Name of case	Comm. No.	Date of Decision	Outcome
G. R. B. v. Sweden (V)	83/1997	15 May 1998	No violation

INDEX OF CASES OF CAT BY STATE PARTY

to update generally see country at: www.unhchr.ch/tbs/doc.nsf
see also www.bayefsky.com

A = admissibility
V = views
DJ = decision to deal with cases jointly
I = interim measures

Argentina

Name of case	Comm. No.	Date of Decision	Treaty Articles	Outcome
O.R., M.M., and M.S. v. Argentina (DJ)	1, 2 & 3/1988	November 1989	2, 13, 14	
O. R., M. M., and M.S. v. Argentina (A)	1, 2 & 3/1998	November 1989	2, 13, 14	Inadmissible

Australia

Name of case	Comm. No.	Date of Decision	Treaty Articles	Outcome
N. P. v. Australia (V)	106/1998	6 May 1999	3	No violation
Elmi v. Australia (V)	120/1998	14 May 1999	1, 3	Violation

Austria

Name of case	Comm. No.	Date of Decision	Treaty Articles	Outcome
W. J. v. Austria (A)	5/1990	22 November 1990		Inadmissible
Halimi-Nedzibi v. Austria (A)	8/1991	5 May 1992	12, 15	Admissible
Halimi-Nedzibi v. Austria (I)	8/1991	26 April 1993	12, 15	
Halimi-Nedzibi v. Austria (V)	8/1991	18 November 1993	12, 15	Violation

Canada

Name of case	Comm. No.	Date of Decision	Treaty Articles	Outcome
Khan v. Canada (V)	15/1994	15 November 1994	3	Violation
M. A. v. Canada (A)	22/1995	3 May 1995	3	Inadmissible
X. v. Canada (A)	26/1995	20 November 1995		Inadmissible
K. K. H. v. Canada (A)	35/1995	22 November 1995		Inadmissible
P. Q. L. v. Canada (V)	57/1996	17 November 1997	3	No violation
R. K. v. Canada (A)	42/1996	20 November 1997		Inadmissible
V. V. v. Canada (A)	47/1996	19 May 1998		Inadmissible
P. S. S. v Canada	66/1997	13 November 1998		Inadmissible
Akhimien v. Canada (A)	67/1997	17 November 1998		Inadmissible
P. S. v. Canada (A)	86/1997	18 November 1999		Inadmissible
T. P. S. v. Canada (V)	99/1997	16 May 2000	3	No violation
L. O. v. Canada (A)	95/1997	19 May 2000		Inadmissible
S. V. v. Canada (V)	49/1996	15 May 2001	3	No violation
Z. Z. v. Canada (V)	123/1998	15 May 2001	3	No violation

Denmark

Name of case	Comm. No.	Date of Decision	Treaty Articles	Outcome
S. C. v. Denmark (V)	143/1999	10 May 2000	3	No violation

France

Name of case	Comm. No.	Date of Decision	Treaty Articles	Outcome
N. D. v. France (A)	32/1995	20 November 1995		Inadmissible
Le Gayic et al. v. France (A)	46/1996	9 May 1997		Inadmissible
D. v. France (A)	45/1996	10 November 1997		Inadmissible
R. v. France (A)	52/1996	10 November 1997		Inadmissible
Arkauz v. France (V)	63/1997	9 November 1999	3	Violation
K. N. v. France (A)	93/1997	18 November 1999		Inadmissible

Greece

Name of case	Comm. No.	Date of Decision	Treaty Articles	Outcome
Mohamed v. Greece (V)	40/1996	28 April 1997	3	No violation

Hungary

Name of case	Comm. No.	Date of Decision	Treaty Articles	Outcome
E. H. v. Hungary (A)	62/1996	10 May 1999		Inadmissible

Netherlands

Name of case	Comm. No.	Date of Decision	Treaty Articles	Outcome
X. and Y. v. The Netherlands (A)	31/1995	20 November 1995		Inadmissible
X. v. The Netherlands (V)	36/1995	8 May 1996	3	No violation
A. v. The Netherlands (V)	91/1997	13 November 1998	3	Violation
A. D. v. The Netherlands (V)	96/1997	12 November 1999	3	No violation
M. K. O. v. The Netherlands (V)	134/1999	9 May 2001	3	No violation
S. S. and S. A. v. The Netherlands (V)	142/1999	11 May 2001	3	No violation

Norway

Name of case	Comm. No.	Date of Decision	Treaty Articles	Outcome
S. H. v. Norway (A)	121/1998	19 November 1999		Inadmissible
Z. T. v. Norway (A)	127/1999	19 November 1999		Inadmissible

Spain

Name of case	Comm. No.	Date of Decision	Treaty Articles	Outcome
H. U. P. v. Spain (A)	6/1990	12 November 1991		Inadmissible
L. B. v. Spain (A)	9/1991	18 November 1991		Inadmissible
J. E. and E. B. v. Spain (A)	10/1993	14 November 1994		Inadmissible
Parot v. Spain (V)	6/1990	2 May 1995	13	No violation
X. v. Spain (A)	23/1995	15 November 1995	3	Inadmissible
Blanco Abad v. Spain (V)	59/1996	14 May 1998	12, 13, 15	Violation
P. R. v. Spain (A)	160/2000	23 November 2000		Inadmissible

Sweden

Name of case	Comm. No.	Date of Decision	Treaty Articles	Outcome
P. M. P. K v. Sweden (A)	30/1995	20 November 1995		Inadmissible
Muzonzo v. Sweden (V)	41/1996	8 May 1996	3	Violation
Tala v. Sweden (V)	43/1996	15 November 1996	3	Violation
Tapia Paez v. Sweden (V)	39/ 1996	28 April 1997	3	No violation
L. M. V. R. G. and M. A B. C. v. Sweden (A)	64/1991	19 November 1997		Inadmissible
X., Y. and Z. v. Sweden (V)	61/1996	6 May 1998	3	No violation
I. A. O v. Sweden (V)	65/1997	6 May 1998	3	No violation
A. F. v. Sweden (V)	89/1998	8 May 1998	3	Violation
J. M. U. M. v. Sweden (A)	58/1996	15 May 1998		Inadmissible
G. R. B. v. Sweden (V)	83/1997	15 May 1998	3, 16	No violation
Ayas v. Sweden (V)	97/1997	12 November 1998	3	Violation
Korban v. Sweden (V)	88/1997	16 November 1998	3	Violation
Haydin v. Sweden (V)	101/1997	20 November 1998	3	Violation
S. M. R. and M. M. R. v. Sweden (V)	103/1998	5 May 1999	3	No violation
M. B. B. v. Sweden (V)	104/1998	5 May 1999	3	No violation
A. G. v. Sweden (A)	140/1999	2 May 2000		Inadmissible
V. X. N. and H. N. v. Sweden (V)	130 & 131/1999	15 May 2000	3	No violation
A. S. v. Sweden (V)	149/1999	24 November 2000	3	Violation
S. L. v. Sweden (V)	150/1999	11 May 2001	3	No violation

Switzerland

Name of case	Comm. No.	Date of Decision	Treaty Articles	Outcome
Mutombo v. Switzerland (V)	13/1993	27 April 1994	3	Violation
X. v. Switzerland (A)	17/1994	17 November 1994		Inadmissible
Y. v. Switzerland (A)	18/1994	17 November 1994		Inadmissible
A. E. v. Switzerland (A)	24/1995	2 May 1995	3	Inadmissible
Alan v. Switzerland (V)	21/1995	8 May 1996	3	Violation
X. v. Switzerland (V)	27/1995	28 April 1997	3	No violation
Aemei v. Switzerland (V)	34/1995	9 May 1997	3	Violation
X. v. Switzerland (V)	38/1995	9 May 1997	3	No violation
E.A. v. Switzerland (V)	28/1995	10 November 1997	3	No violation

Name of case	Comm. No.	Date of Decision	Treaty Articles	Outcome
A. L. N. v. Switzerland (V)	90/1997	19 May 1998	3	No violation
K.N. v. Switzerland (V)	94/1997	19 May 1998	3	No violation
H. W. A. v. Switzerland (A)	48/1996	20 May 1998	3	Inadmissible
J. U. A. v. Switzerland (V)	100/1997	10 November 1998	3	No violation
H. D. v. Switzerland (V)	112/1998	30 April 1999	3	No violation
K. M. v. Switzerland (V)	107/1998	16 November 1999	3	No violation
G. T. v. Switzerland (V)	137/1999	16 November 1999	3	No violation
K. T. v. Switzerland (V)	118/1998	19 November 1999	3	No violation
N. M. v. Switzerland (V)	116/1998	9 May 2000	3	No violation
H. A. D. v. Switzerland (V)	126/1999	10 May 2000	3	No violation
A. M. v. Switzerland (V)	144/1999	14 November 2000	3	No violation
Y. S. v. Switzerland (V)	147/1999	14 November 2000	3	No violation
M. R. P. v. Switzerland (V)	122/1998	24 November 2000	3	No violation
X. Y. v. Switzerland (V)	128/1999	15 May 2001	3	No violation

Tunisia

Name of case	Comm. No.	Date of Decision	Treaty Articles	Outcome
Barakat v. Tunisia (A)	14/1994	5 May 1994		Inadmissible
Barakat v. Tunisia (V)	60/1996	10 November 1999	2, 11, 12, 13, 14	Violation

Turkey

Name of case	Comm. No.	Date of Decision	Treaty Articles	Outcome
R. E. G. v. Turkey (A)	4/1990	29 April 1991		Inadmissible

Venezuela

Name of case	Comm. No.	Date of Decision	Treaty Articles	Outcome
Núñez Chipana v. Venezuela (V)	110/1998	10 November 1998	3	Violation

Yugoslavia

Name of case	Comm. No.	Date of Decision	Treaty Articles	Outcome
Ristic v. Yugoslavia (V)	113/1998	11 May 2001	12, 13, 14	Violation

INDEX OF CASES OF CERD BY ARTICLE

to update generally see jurisprudence at: www.unhchr.ch/tbs/doc.nsf
see also www.bayefsky.com

A = admissibility decision
V = views

ARTICLE 1

Name of case	Comm. No.	Date of Decision	Outcome
Barbaro v. Australia (A)	7/1995	14 August 1997	Inadmissible

ARTICLE 1(1)

Name of case	Comm. No.	Date of Decision	Outcome
Diop v. France (V)	2/1989	18 March 1991	No violation

ARTICLE 1(2)

Name of case	Comm. No.	Date of Decision	Outcome
Diop v. France (V)	2/1989	18 March 1991	No violation

ARTICLE 2

Name of case	Comm. No.	Date of Decision	Outcome
Z. U. B. S. v. Australia (A)	6/1995	19 August 1997	Admissible
Koptova v. Slovak Republic (V)	13/1998	8 August 2000	Violation
E. I. F. v. The Netherlands (V)	15/1999	21 March 2001	No violation
Lacko v. Slovakia (V)	11/1998	9 August 2001	No violation

ARTICLE 2(1)(a)

Name of case	Comm. No.	Date of Decision	Outcome
B. J. v. Denmark (V)	17/1999	17 March 2000	No violation

ARTICLE 2(1)(b)

Name of case	Comm. No.	Date of Decision	Outcome
B. J. v. Denmark (V)	17/1999	17 March 2000	No violation

ARTICLE 2(1)(d)

Name of case	Comm. No.	Date of Decision	Outcome
Habassi v. Denmark (V)	10/1997	17 March 1999	Violation
Ahmad v. Denmark (V)	16/1999	13 March 2000	Violation
B. J. v. Denmark (V)	17/1999	17 March 2000	No violation

ARTICLE 3

Name of case	Comm. No.	Date of Decision	Outcome
Z. U. B. S. v. Australia (A)	6/1995	19 August 1997	Admissible
Z. U. B. S. v. Australia (V)	6/1995	26 August 1999	No violation
Koptova v. Slovak Republic (V)	13/1998	8 August 2000	Violation
Lacko v. Slovakia (V)	11/1998	9 August 2001	No violation

ARTICLE 4

Name of case	Comm. No.	Date of Decision	Outcome
Yilmaz-Dogan v. The Netherlands (V)	1/1984	10 August 1988	Violation
Koptova v. Slovak Republic (V)	13/1998	8 August 2000	Violation
Lacko v. Slovakia (V)	11/1998	9 August 2001	No violation

ARTICLE 4(a)

Name of case	Comm. No.	Date of Decision	Outcome
L. K. v. The Netherlands (V)	4/1991	16 March 1993	Violation

ARTICLE 5

Name of case	Comm. No.	Date of Decision	Outcome
Barbaro v. Australia (A)	7/1995	14 August 1997	Inadmissible
Z. U. B. S. v. Australia (A)	6/1995	19 August 1997	Admissible
B. M. S. v. Australia (A)	8/1995	19 August 1997	Admissible
Koptova v. Slovak Republic (V)	13/1998	8 August 2000	Violation
E. I. F. v. The Netherlands (V)	15/1999	21 March 2001	No violation
Lacko v. Slovakia (V)	11/1998	9 August 2001	No violation

ARTICLE 5(a)

Name of case	Comm. No.	Date of Decision	Outcome
Narrainen v. Norway (V)	3/1991	15 March 1994	No violation
Z. U. B. S. v. Australia (V)	6/1995	26 August 1999	No violation

ARTICLE 5(e)

Name of case	Comm. No.	Date of Decision	Outcome
Yilmaz-Dogan v. The Netherlands (V)	1/1984	10 August 1988	Violation
Diop v. France (V)	2/1989	18 March 1991	No violation
B. M. S. v. Australia (V)	8/1996	12 March 1999	No violation
Z. U. B. S. v. Australia (V)	6/1995	26 August 1999	No violation

ARTICLE 5(f)

Name of case	Comm. No.	Date of Decision	Outcome
B. J. v. Denmark (V)	17/1999	17 March 2000	No violation

ARTICLE 5(i)

Name of case	Comm. No.	Date of Decision	Outcome
Yilmaz-Dogan v. The Netherlands (V)	1/1984	10 August 1988	Violation
B. M. S. v. Australia (V)	8/1996	12 March 1999	No violation
Z. U. B. S. v. Australia (V)	6/1995	26 August 1999	No violation

ARTICLE 6

Name of case	Comm. No.	Date of Decision	Outcome
Yilmaz-Dogan v. The Netherlands (V)	1/1984	10 August 1988	Violation
L. K. v. The Netherlands (V)	4/1991	16 March 1993	Violation
C. P. and M. P. v. Denmark (A)	5/1994	15 March 1995	Inadmissible
Z. U. B. S. v. Australia (A)	6/1995	19 August 1997	Admissible
Habassi v. Denmark (V)	10/1997	17 March 1999	Violation
Z. U. B. S. v. Australia (V)	6/1995	26 August 1999	No violation
Ahmad v. Denmark (V)	16/1999	13 March 2000	Violation
B. J. v. Denmark (V)	17/1999	17 March 2000	No violation
Koptova v. Slovak Republic (V)	13/1998	8 August 2000	Violation
E. I. F. v. The Netherlands (V)	15/1999	21 March 2001	No violation
Lacko v. Slovakia (V)	11/1998	9 August 2001	No violation

ARTICLE 7

Name of case	Comm. No.	Date of Decision	Outcome
E. I. F. v. The Netherlands (V)	15/1999	21 March 2001	No violation

ANNEX 22

INDEX OF CASES OF CERD BY STATE PARTY

---

to update generally see state party at: www.unhchr.ch/tbs/doc.nsf
see also www.bayefsky.com

A = admissibility decision
V = views

Australia

Name of case	Comm. No.	Date of Decision	Treaty Articles	Outcome
Barbaro v. Australia (A)	7/1995	14 August 1997	1, 5	Inadmissible
Z.U.B.S. v. Australia (A)	6/1995	19 August 1997	2, 3, 5, 6	Admissible
B.M.S. v. Australia (A)	8/1995	19 August 1997	5	Admissible
B.M.S. v. Australia (V)	8/1996	12 March 1999	5 (e, i)	No violation
Z.U.B.S. v. Australia (V)	6/1995	26 August 1999	3, 5(a, e, i), 6	No violation
Barbaro v. Australia (A)	12/1998	8 August 2000		Inadmissible

Denmark

Name of case	Comm. No.	Date of Decision	Treaty Articles	Outcome
C.P. and M.P. v. Denmark (A)	5/1994	15 March 1995	6	Inadmissible
Habassi v. Denmark (V)	10/1997	17 March 1999	2(1d), 6	Violation
Ahmad v. Denmark (V)	16/1999	13 March 2000	2(1d), 6	Violation
B.J. v. Denmark (V)	17/1999	17 March 2000	2(1a, b, d), 5(f), 6	No violation
Mostafa v. Denmark (A)	19/2000	10 August 2001		Inadmissible

France

Name of case	Comm. No.	Date of Decision	Treaty Articles	Outcome
Diop v. France	2/1989	22 August 1990		Admissible
Diop v. France	2/1989	18 March 1991	1(1, 2), 5(e)	No violation

Netherlands

Name of case	Comm. No.	Date of Decision	Treaty Articles	Outcome
Yilmaz-Dogan v. The Netherlands	1/1984	10 August 1988	4, 5 (e, i), 6	Violation
L. K. v. The Netherlands	4/1991	16 March 1993	4(a), 6	Violation
E.I.F. v. The Netherlands	15/1999	21 March 2001	2, 5, 6, 7	No violation

Norway

Name of case	Comm. No.	Date of Decision	Treaty Articles	Outcome
Narrainen v. Norway (A)	3/1991	16 March 1993		Admissible
Narrainen v. Norway (V)	3/1991	15 March 1994	5(a)	No violation
F. A. v. Norway (A)	18/2000	21 March 2001		Inadmissible

Slovakia

Name of case	Comm. No.	Date of Decision	Treaty Articles	Outcome
Koptova v. Slovak Republic (V)	13/1998	8 August 2000	2, 3, 4, 5, 6	Violation
Lacko v. Slovakia (V)	11/1998	9 August 2001	2, 3, 4, 5, 6	No violation

Sweden

Name of case	Comm. No.	Date of Decision	Treaty Articles	Outcome
D. S. v. Sweden	9/1997	17 August 1998		Inadmissible
D. S. v. Sweden	14/1998	10 August 2001		Inadmissible
D. S. v. Sweden	21/2001	10 August 2001		Inadmissible

INDEX